EBURY PRESS

THE JOURNEY TO ADI KAILASH

M.K. Ramachandran is a bestselling writer from Kerala, known for his unique travelogues. He has dedicated his life to travelling in the Himalayas and is perhaps the only pilgrim to have visited all five Kailash, called the 'Panch Kailash'. These are Kailash Manasarovar, Adi Kailash, Kinnaur Kailash, Shrikhand Mahadev Kailash and Manimahesh Kailash.

Ramachandran won the Kerala Sahitya Akademi Award in 2005 for his first work, *Uttarkhandiloode: Kailash Manasa Sarass Yatra*. In 2006, *Malayala Manorama* selected his book, *Thapobhoomi Uttarakhand*, as the best book in the Malayalam language written in the last fifty years. In 2009, he was presented with the Prof. M.P. Manmadhan Memorial Akshaya National Award. In 2013, the king of Travancore, Uthradam Thirunal Marthanda Varma, honoured him with a Raja Mudra (king's knight) and bestowed on him the title 'Himalaya Njana Satma' (the good soul with knowledge of the Himalayas).

Sheela S. Menon is the author of *The 14th G Collision*. In 2019, she translated into Malayalam the book, *The Myth of Arab Piracy in the Gulf*, written by the king of Sharjah, His Highness Sheikh Sultan bin Mohammed bin Sultan Al Qasimi. The book was officially released by His Highness the Sultan at the Sharjah Book Fair in 2019.

T0124134

Celebrating 35 Years of
Penguin Random House India

The

JOURNEY

— to —

ADI
KAILASH

M.K. RAMACHANDRAN

Translated from the Malayalam by
SHEELA S. MENON

EBURY
PRESS

An imprint of Penguin Random House

EBURY PRESS

USA | Canada | UK | Ireland | Australia
New Zealand | India | South Africa | China | Singapore

Ebury Press is part of the Penguin Random House group of companies
whose addresses can be found at global.penguinrandomhouse.com

Published by Penguin Random House India Pvt. Ltd
4th Floor, Capital Tower 1, MG Road,
Gurugram 122 002, Haryana, India

First published in the Malayalam as *Aadhi Kailasa Yathra* by Current Books, Thrissur, 2008.
This paperback edition published in Ebury Press by Penguin Random House India 2023

Copyright © M.K. Ramachandran 2023
Translation © Sheela S. Menon 2023

ISBN 9780143461340

Typeset in Requiem Text by MAP Systems, Bengaluru, India

www.penguin.co.in

Contents

Preface

The Journey in Search of the Ultimate

When the Nobel Prize for Literature was awarded to V.S. Naipaul, the Swedish Academy specially considered his travelogues than his novels. Some years back, a group of researchers conducted a study on the reading habits of the people of Kerala and found that the first place went to travelogues and second to autobiographies. Novel, short story, drama and criticism all came only after that. Maybe because travelogues enjoyed ample marketing potential, travellers going out of Kerala wrote as a routine about the places they went to and published them. Some wrote such books without going anywhere. They simply sat in their reading rooms and wrote 'travelogues' going through a number of books!

There were no telephone, Internet or e-mail services when the famous writer and Jnanpith award-winner S.K. Pottekkatt made his travels. He found his hosts through letters and conducted many long journeys with very limited facilities. Being a storyteller by birth, he drew beautiful pictures of the places he went to using most beautiful words. Malayali families living in foreign countries attracted the particular attention of readers. The seeds of stories and rough sketches of characters came out of such travelogues. Along with SK, the reader also enjoyed each journey.

There is not much demand now for the travelogues of the traditional type. What is needed can easily be taken from the Internet. There are magazines such as *National Geographic* that show us pictures of rare places in bright colours. The image of a traveller in our mind is of someone moving ahead with open eyes and ears, with a notebook in hand and a camera on the shoulders.

We are convinced that M.K. Ramachandran, who wrote two famous travelogues, uses a third eye when travelling. He got it by learning and thinking. This is the reason why Ramachandran's works stand apart from other books on journeys. The traveller doesn't conquer unknown places here. Instead, he comes closer to them and bows in respect and wonder. He talks with hills, forests, rivers and farmlands in silence. He doesn't turn emotional while standing in holy lands. There is a chance one may forget the local residents who live in the most difficult climates. And the traveller has a special attraction to the guides, horsemen, farmers who provide midway resting places and the soldiers who guard borders. He shares their happiness and sadness.

Edmund Hillary and Tenzing Norgay reaching Mount Everest was a great event in world history. After them, many people assumed this risky task. 'Nagadhirajan' as imagined by Kalidasa is always a great wonder in nature. The peaks of the Himalayas tempt travellers at all times and challenge them too.

This third journey of Ramachandran is a spiritual trip also. The Vedas, the Puranas, great poems and the intellectual searching of the great yogis who went ahead of us are with Ramachandran to lead the way. 'Kakki', who keeps documents written by Veda Vyasa on burj tree leaves, may seem to be a wonder for us. We also learn now that Shangri-La is not the mere imagination of James Hilton. Paul Brandon who wandered around in search of Indian mysteries was taken aback seeing unbelievable acts by some yogis. But he says that the greatest of all yogis was Ramana Maharshi, who, with no show of acts, taught us Brahma Jnana (knowledge of God) silently and with a smile over subdued pain. Thus he found what he was seeking after, Brandon said.

We remember Hamlet telling Horatio that 'there are more things in heaven and earth than are dreamt of in your philosophy' when we hear stories about great yogis.

This book tells us that for the real understanding of the great wonder called the Himalayas, we must go through Adi Kailash. Ramachandran's works remind us that we human beings are just tiny in front of the unmoving peaks of mountains and the great rivers of nature.

Has life got an ultimate meaning? You may or may not believe it or argue about it, but journeys in search of it are making many people liberated. And energetic. The writer of this book who tries to know Adi Kailash belongs to that small group.

November 2008   M.T. Vasudevan Nair
Kozhikode

I

The Kumaon Himalayas

The silvery peaks that lay in the lap of the great Himalayas, the alluring hilltops that kissed the horizon, the picturesque meadows and the lovely flowers blooming around, the sleepy lakes that reflected the heavenly blue sky, the enchanting mountain springs and their water plants, the beautiful ponds filled with lotuses, the roaring rivers rushing down, the thick, green forests—all these made this beautiful piece of land, Koormanchal (or Kumaon as it is popularly known) the seat of God. Even goddesses from heaven came rushing down to touch this land. A visit there was a pure, pleasant and peaceful experience. The holy soil filled every heart with rare and aesthetic delight.

Nature had inscribed the sacred and important mantra 'Om' (ॐ) on the black background of the snow-filled valleys and mountains there. In meditation, 'Om' is the link man has with God and the universe. The grace of this mantra has no limits and it is praised as the greatest and most effective symbol of God. It is also the hymn chanted at the start and end of all conventions and ceremonies. One could find it well-described in the Vedas and the Upanishads. Adi Kailash, the holy abode of goddesses Sathy and Parvathy and Lord Sree Parameswara, is situated in the Indo-Tibetan border sector of the Kumaon

Himalayas. It is considered the purest and most sacred of all mountain ranges in the world.

The great Pandava king Yudhishtira, after he was defeated through foul play in gambling, had to go on a mandatory exile in the forests as part of a God-designed plan (and we call that plan 'fate'). That loss in gambling and its aftermath is depicted in the holy Mahabharata. The atmosphere was very tense. Bowing down in sadness, Yudhishtira's wife Panchali asked him: 'Highness, why are virtuous people like you fated to go through such hardships?' Yudhishtira, not a bit shaken by the bad turn of events, was his old self. With a smile, he said to his wife: 'The Himalayas are very beautiful and charming. I like them very much!'

Even after centuries, these words of Dharmaputra (Yudhishtira) still stay in the minds of millions of Indians. His thought was great. This gives wings to our thoughts and brings peace and calmness to our minds. Such is the greatness of the Himalayas!

The journey of the Pandavas was mostly through Uttarakhand during the *Aranyakandam* (the course of their stay in the forests). The most important parts of Uttarakhand were the Kumaon Himalayas and Garhwal Himalayas. It was believed that Lord Mahavishnu incarnated as a tortoise (Koormavathara) at a place called Champawath in Kumaon. That might be the reason Kumaon is also known as Koormanchal.

From the first century BCE onwards, there had been extensive migration to the Kumaon Himalayas from central Asian plains and the Sindhu-Ganga river valleys. Diverse cultures, languages, religious beliefs, races and colours merged into one great population that strongly believed in the fundamental sources of Indian philosophy, the Vedas and the Upanishads.

The various dynasties that ruled Kumaon from time to time contributed much to the multifaceted development of the region. It would be very interesting to look into the history of the place.

In the first millennium BCE, most of the mountainous regions in the middle and western parts of Asia were under the rule of the Kassites (the Kassites were people of the ancient Near East who controlled Babylonia after the fall of the old Babylonian empire from 1595 BCE until 1155 BCE. They were members of a small military aristocracy. They established a dynasty based first in Babylon and later in Dur-Kurigalzu. The chariot and the horse, which the Kassites worshipped, first came into use in Babylonia at this time). Kashmir, Kumaon and Nepal were among them. In the Puranic periods, this region was known as Khasaesh. However, the Kassites couldn't enjoy their victory for very long. King Shamshi Adad drove them away soon and they fled to the Elburz mountain ranges in the northern parts of Iran. But this was a comeback for the Kassites to the land their forefathers had lost about 150 years ago. They also brought with them the statue of their holy head of state, the goddess of Nana of Erech. Nana or Naina was not the name of the goddess of Nainital alone. There were many places in Kumaon with the same name such as Nainer Pathal, Naninar, Nainilli, Nainagarh, etc.

The legendary Persian king Cyrus the Great, who conquered Babylon, was also known as the King of Media. There is a belief that King Cyrus was King Kuru, the founder of the Kuru dynasty and that Media was the Medhus of the Mahabharata. Assyrians expelled by Medes, Parthians and Persians proceeded to various parts of the world, including India. The Assyrians who reached India were later called the *Assuras* in the Puranas and the epics. Ashurbanipal, the king of Assyria from 669 BCE to 631 BCE, is believed to be Banasura, father of Usha, Lord Siva's wife. It was the same Banasura who took Anirudha, the grandson of Lord Sreekrishna, captive. This incident was narrated in the Harivamsa Purana. Names of many places and temples were ample proof of the fact that the Assyrian people had settled in various parts of Kumaon. Temple names like God Bel or Bal at Ramak, Balar, Bahditya, Assur (Son), Baraadhitya, Bhaumaadhitya, Lohavathi River (the river of blood), Loha Ghat (the valley of blood) were clear examples of the Assyrian connection. Kassites were also known as Saka, Khasa, etc.

It was the Kassites from Assyria who named the valley of Champawath 'Kumu'. In 700 BCE, there was a mountainous region in the north-eastern part of the Mediterranean Sea. That place, which lay adjacent to the origin of the Euphrates River, was also known by the name Kumu! The ancient country called Elam was in the east of Assyria. In Nepal, a part of the land to the east of Kali Kumaon is still known as Elam! In the present-day Kumaoni language, there were so many words similar to those of the Semitic regions and eastern Kumaon countries such as Nepal. The interesting thing was that many words had the same meaning also. Many templates were found through excavations in these places, where the ancient Assyrian empire once existed. The same words were written on them, with similar meanings! The holy soul who later became Lord Sree Buddha was born in 566 BCE to the Sakya king Suddhodana in the Himalayan valleys where Khasas and Assyrians were permanently settled. A point to note was that Sakyas were not Aryans.

In 330 BCE, the great Greek historic hero and conqueror, Alexander the Great, defeated Emperor Darius III of Persia. Alexander was only thirty-three years old then. The entire Persian empire, including the provinces of the Persian king in India, came under his rule. This was the first war involving India and Europe. However, the militia of King Alexander was despondent due to acute homesickness. Therefore, after his war with King Puru, Alexander returned home without entering other parts of India. It was Alexander who called King Puru (Purooravas of the Puru dynasty) King Porus, impressed by his courage and military prowess. After Alexander's attack, political inertia rose and a young leader called Chandragupta utilized the opportunity to his benefit. Chandragupta was born in the Maurya clan to the same Nanda dynasty that ruled Magadha. This young man, whose mind was full of outrage and frustration against the rulers, formed a national army of his own. They aimed to drive out the Greek army that had been left behind by King Alexander. He first moved to Magadha (the present Patna), situated on the banks of the Ganga River, with his army and declared himself the king. That was the beginning of the Maurya dynasty in 323 BCE. Chandragupta Maurya defeated Seleucus I Nicator, agent of King Alexander, and added the country we now call Afghanistan to his empire. Sakas or Khasas, the central Asian inhabitants, had been residing in India after they were expelled from Babylonia by the Assyrians. They started ruling the country as agents of the Kusanas. These folks first came to India as Kassites and later settled in Kumaon, Garhwal, Kulu, Nepal, etc., as Khasas. In the second century CE, due to differences of opinion, a portion of those people migrated to Tibet for permanent settlement. They took possession of the ice-covered mountain passes beyond the Himalayas and also the gold and diamond mines in western Tibet. The power and influence of the Khasa race in the ancient period was extensive. The Yakshas of the Puranas were really the Khasas of these mountainous regions. King Kashyapa's wife was the mother of the Yakshas.

Maybe that was why King Kashyapa became known as *Prajapathi* (king) of not only the human race but also of the birds and the snakes. The title 'Thokdhar', commonly used in the Kumaon region, was at least 3000 years old. In Sanskrit, the word *thok* means *sthayuk*.

The goddess of the Kassites was Nana or Naina. Kassites were those who were driven out of Elam by the Assyrians. The Nainwal Brahmins claim that they are the descendants of the Thokdhar clan of ancient Pali. Pali is a sub-district of Almora. Maybe they were the descendants of the Kassites, the priests of Goddess Naini. The priests of the ancient goddesses of Almora, Kasar Devi and Jakmi Devi (Yakshini) might also belong to this chain.

About 7 km from Almora was a granite template of Kasar Devi dating back to the second century BC. The name Kasar itself reveals the Khasa connection beyond any doubt. Upreti Khola of Almora was known as Khasia Tola until recently.

The residents of the Ganga plateau were subject to frequent aggressions and attacks. The people, becoming weak and hopeless after constant defeats and persecutions, found the excellent and profound Himalayan mountains and valleys a peaceful abode. And so it still is.

The Katyuri Dynasty

Samudragupta, who founded the Gupta dynasty in 330 CE, made the Gupta dynasty rule strong again. The Gupta period didn't submit much to the foreign influence of the first three centuries AD. Indian art bloomed in its own way. Generally, it was a period of prosperity and happiness. Trade also grew. India became united once again. The victorious journey Samudragupta undertook in southern India made it stronger too. The general growth and prosperity of the country attracted the Huns of central Asia. The Huns attacked the country to establish authority over it but the third Gupta king, Skandhagupta, defeated them completely.

Kumaon, a part of the Himalayas, was ruled by a Khasa clan. They were known as Katyuris. They came to India for the first time in the first millennium BCE. They brought with them the alphabet known to the Aramaic race who were their relatives. Aramaic was the language of Jesus Christ. The Bible was also written in that language. Later, in 51 CE, St Thomas came to Kerala in South India. He spread Christianity through the Aramaic language. Those Christians who follow St Thomas still do their prayers and ceremonies in the Aramaic language.

The Kumaoni language evolved from the primitive language of the central Himalayas. The root of this language could be seen in the stone inscriptions of King Asoka in Kalsi. The same language could also be found in the coins prevalent in the period immediately following the fall of the Maurya dynasty. Those coins were discovered in the Almora district. In 600 CE, the Gupta dynasty eventually became weak and ended. However, the fall of the Gupta dynasty didn't affect the Katyuri kings in any way.

As recorded in the Mahabharata, the land of the Khasas was near the origin of the Ganga and the Yamuna rivers. Earlier, it was near the banks of the Sarada River on the right side. Kumaon was 65 km away from Almora. Brahmapura was the capital of the Katyuri kings. It was an important place for arts and science. Inscriptions on stones found there were considered to be the remnants of the Katyuri reign. The language used by the elite Kumaoni people in modern times, called the Kumaon language, was the same as inscribed on stone in the second half of the twelfth century. This language discovered in Baijnath in Uttarakhand had developed in the Katyuri valleys in the thirteenth and fourteenth centuries. Also, many templates of the Katyuri kings were excavated, showing the connection of this language to the medieval period. The Chand dynasty began to rule in the fourteenth century. During their entire rule, Kumaoni was the main language in the royal court. Templates of the period show that this language was used till the end of the eighteenth century. The palace built by the Chand kings in the Champawath valleys existed till 1563.

The history of Uttaranchal prior to the Katyuri reign remained in the dark due to the unavailability of information. The copper templates that were discovered from Brahmapura and also from Katyuri kings bring out the fact that Brahmapuram, the ancient palace, was near Bhageswar in Almora district. Those plates were discovered in Thaleswar. According to them, there were at least 300 country states under the Katyuri reign. Administrative centres were situated at Kartikeyapur, Karkota-Pataun, Sitonseun (near the Almora-Pauri border), Subhein (near Tapovan), Chamoli, etc.

Hiuen Tsang, the Chinese traveller who visited India during the Gupta dynasty in 350 CE, had mentioned Brahmapuram in his writings. In addition to this, regional poets and also Varahamihira (the ancient astronomer, mathematician and astrologer who is considered to be one of the nine jewels of the court of legendary ruler Vikramaadhitya) had written about that town.

The palace of the Chand dynasty was at Champawath during that time. The architectural scheme of temples in Kumaon was a mix of different cultures and structural styles of various countries. The Kumaon kings who had ruled from 8 to 14 CE were in full support of this pattern. The kingdom of the Katyuri kings extended from Badrinath in the north to Kashipur in the south and Barhatt and northern Kashi in the west to Jageshwar and Gangolihat in the east. They were the inheritance of an ancient cultural tradition. They encouraged the extension of their culture to different parts of the country. Varied types of statues and pillars could be widely seen in those areas. The evidence of that structural excellence could be seen even in the interior villages of Kumaon and Garhwal in the Himalayas.

The Kumaon reign was the golden era in the history of that region. Besides leading the country on the right path of development, these kings also led the way to religious, political and cultural renaissance. The period from the seventh to the eleventh centuries CE was also a period of enthusiastic temple construction in the north and the south alike. While the Chalukya kings built many marvellous towers and temple complexes in South India in the early seventh century, the Katyuri kings built 400 temples in the Kumaon Himalayas' Almora district alone! All of them had Nagara or Indo-Aryan style of architecture.

The 300 regions mentioned in the templates were spread over 8000 sq. km. They extended from Katkhet in north Kashi in the west to Bilwak near Pithoragarh in the east and from Garuria near Kedarnath in the north to Karkotak near Nainital in the south. The Binsar ranges in Almora and Dhoodhatholi mountains in Pauri are rich in remnants of ancient ages.

There are some temples known as Kapaleeshwar at the border between the Nainital and Almora districts. The deity in them is Viraneswar. Kapilaghartham and Kapaleeshwara mentioned in the property deeds of the kings of Brahmapura were proved to be today's Binsar in Almora (Katyuri valley) and Dheira Binsar in Garhwal. Statues as old as 500 CE had been excavated from both places.

Narayan Devakula mentioned a very beautiful place called Nalini in the Thaleswar copper document. The remnants of an old Vishnu temple could also be found through excavation from the deep earth in Nalini. Gorgeous statues of Hargori, Varaha and Narasimha, a Nava Durga shrine and some other excellent statues were also found.

The folk tales of Kumaon as well as the social life of its people were dance-rich. For the Kumaonis, dance was the way to propitiate the gods and save people from suffering. The inspiration for dance was the attractive fairies of the Puranas called Apsaras. They were godly ladies moving in style. They possessed unbelievable beauty! They wore luxurious ornaments and dresses. They were the holy dancers of the court of Indra, the king of the gods. They could travel through the sky without wings. Some believed these ladies of heaven were the souls of the dead, unmarried young women for whom post-death rituals had not been done. Some others believed that they were the virgin daughters of the king of Lanka, Ravana, gifted to God Paramasiva as housemaids.[1] Yet, the most widespread belief was that they were the cowgirls or 'gopasthreekal' who were the playmates of Lord Krishna in childhood and still continue playing and dancing with the lord in heaven.

There were six districts in the Kumaon region of Uttarakhand state, named Nainital, Almora, Pithoragarh, Bhageswar, Champawath and Udham Singh Nagar. These districts were spread over an area of 13,017 sq. km. The population of Kumaon was 35.63 lakh as per the 2001 census. About ten lakh Kumaonis lived in other places also. This region lies between 28.44 and 30.49 degrees latitude and 78.45 and 81.1 degrees longitude. The neighbouring nations are Nepal in the east and Tibet in the north. The ancient trade between India and Tibet flourished through the Kumaon Himalayas.

2

Pathal Bhoomi (The Netherworld)

'Brahmandamadhye Thishtanthi Bhuvanani Chathurdhesa
Bhuvanaeshu Vasanthyaeshu Pranidhaeha Yadha Yadham'[1]

The Himalayan mountain ranges containing Adi Kailash are in the Pithoragarh district of Uttarakhand state. This district is in the far north, near the Indo-Chinese border, and on the Kumaon side of Uttarakhand. The most difficult journey to the Himalayas was the journey to Adi Kailash. Very few trips had been made to that part of the Himalayas till then. Other than *sanyasi* groups, only those devotees who have a committed passion for trekking have reached there. The Adi Kailash trip could be done only after establishing a camp at Dharchula on the Indo-Nepal border and getting a permission letter from the Additional District Magistrate (ADM). Since the area was under the control of the military, it was difficult to organize horses, porters and residential facilities in a personal capacity. The organized journey to Adi Kailash under Uttarakhand state leadership began in May 2006. The tourism department of Uttarakhand state, the Kumaon Mandal Vikas Nigam Ltd had been long doing all sorts of preliminary exercises and paperwork. But there was a delay. It was due to the delay in getting permission from the Department of Defence of the Government of India, the Indian Army and the Indo-Tibetan Border Police (ITBP). However, the authority to issue the final permission rested with the ADM. Strict controls were imposed because the route lay mostly through the Indo-Chinese borderline.

Because I was known as a Himalayan travelogue writer, I was lucky to be selected as part of a team of thirty-five for the maiden trip. The organizers had taken special care to include travellers from all states of the country. That included advocates, doctors and chartered accountants, among others. There had been a wonderful farewell party in the Garhwal Bhavan in Delhi on 28 May 2006. Our team left for the amazing trip right the next day at 3 a.m.

For the first nine days, the plan was to follow the same route on which the Kailash-Manasarovar Yatra was being conducted by the foreign affairs ministry. A visit to Pathal Bhuvaneshwar, aka Pathal Bhoomi, was also included in our schedule. We started from Delhi and reached a small town called Yageswar in the evening, travelling through Ghaziabad, Moradabad, Haldwani, Kathgodam and Almora. Yageswar was situated in the Kumaon ranges and the tempting hill resort had a beautiful climate at all times. We took a bath in the cold, pure water and the weariness of our long and tiring journey of more than 400 km went away. Also, a cup of tea made with Kumaoni tea leaves enhanced our freshness even further.

The next morning, we began our journey with Gangolihat as our destination. The sight of the golden rays of the young sun spreading through the oak, chir and sal trees was unforgettable. The green mountain ranges going down and the soft mist hanging like a white curtain over them enhanced the beauty of the landscape. The mountains were inhabited and there were lots of farmlands also. Small shops could be seen amid the tiny houses of the village people. Fruits and vegetables were the main crops offered for sale. In front of each house were indigenous breeds of chicken, goats, cows, buffaloes and dogs.

The main attraction of Gangoli Ghat was the Maha Kali temple. This was one of the 108 'seats of power' (*sakthi peeta*) founded by Adi Sankaracharya.[2] A unique air of spirituality hung over all the temples and this gave our hearts a rare feeling of peace. The most important among the 108 seats of power was the Kalika temple. The 'Sri Yantra' (the sacred instrument) installed by Adi Sankaracharya was seen under a big *salagrama* (a spherical divine stone). The roofing of the temple had been done in copper. A *thrisoolam* (trident), protected by a silver umbrella, was placed nearby.

Pathal Bhuvaneshwar was only 30 km from Gangoli Ghat via Guptari. The mountainous region, approximately 5300 feet above sea level, was usually deserted. About 1000 feet below it resided more than a hundred families. But the total population was only 500. Paddy, wheat, soyabean, makka (maize) and vegetables were cultivated in the fertile lands. The main fruit species were nashpati, khumani and bada nimbu. However, potato, widely cultivated in Uttarakhand, was not cultivated there. From June to September, rainfall was abundant in the region. For the rest of the months, mild rainfall was also received. Acute winter was the season in December and January. Massive icefall was a daily affair then. The available educational facilities in the area were limited to school level only. The poor residents did not know that their hilltop home was a piece of the universe eligible to be classified as a global wonder. Or maybe they did not even think about it.

We had to walk at least 1.5 km through the rock assemblage to reach Pathal Bhuvaneshwar. There was a small hotel owned by the tourism department there.

We started our journey to the destination after having breakfast at the hotel. We were in the dark regarding the wonders in the area. We came to know that the region was under the custody of the Archaeological Department of the Government of India only after we reached there. There were heavy security measures in place. Wire fencing was done all around since the area was a protected one. We found a narrow temple entrance mid-forest after travelling through the shadows of thick devadaru and oak trees. We queued up for the security check after removing our shoes. Cameras and other such electronic devices were not allowed. We moved to the mouth of the cave along with the security personnel after remitting the required fees.

The mouth of the cave was very narrow. Sitting and stooping, we looked through the narrow mouth and almost half of our team turned back, deciding not to enter. Only twenty members dared to go inside the cave. The mouth of the cave looked like the hood of the mythical serpent Anantha. It is believed that the Pathal Lok (the netherworld) was the abode of that great serpent. We rang the sacred bell placed in front of the cave, indicating our readiness to enter the cave. We crawled up on our backs about 15 feet and a terrible cave path appeared. After that, it was like a snake crawling through a tube just big enough to hold only one person! Here and there were tiny electric bulbs hidden in the rocks, providing some light. We reached the middle of the cave, which was about 150 feet long. Some of us slipped down and got scared. They cried aloud in fear and that echoed inside the cave. The rest of the travel involved crawling up through the eighty-two granite steps. The naturally formed ribs of the serpent Anantha could be seen on the side walls of the cave. While crawling through the terrible cave, we felt a sharp current of energy flowing through our deepest souls. It was an astonishing experience.

With self-confidence and chanting mantras, we kept on crawling into the cave with all our strength. When we reached the end of the cave, all of us were wet with rivulets of sweat that had rolled down our bodies. The hazardous journey ended at last after we had crept steeply down for about 20 or more feet.

Then, we reached a spacious cave about 50 feet long and 30 feet wide. The height of the cave varied between 20, 12 and 10 feet. The floor was rather flat. On the roof built of rock, nature had made many sculptural carvings. The cave had windows and doors. We felt like we were standing inside a palace. In the northern corner, we could see the Badrinath, Kedarnath and Amarnath deities. Near them was the furious and open-mouthed head of Kaala Bhairava (the fierce manifestation of Lord Siva associated with annihilation). Water was falling in drops from the Bhairava's tongue. It was a terrible sight. On another side, Airavat (the white elephant of heaven) was seen hanging with its head and legs down.

There were four doors on one side of the cavern. They represented the four *yugas* or ages. The first door stood for Sin. It is said to have been locked after the death of Ravana. The second one represented War and it was locked at the end of the Mahabharata war. The third represented Dharma (virtue), which would get locked at the end of Kali Yuga. The fourth and last door stood for Moksha (freedom from rebirth). This would remain open till the end of the world.

Getting in through the Dharma door and out through the Moksha door was the holiest thing one could do in one's life. Bending down, we crossed the small entrance on the left side and entered the second cave. The 14-foot-high cave was circular in shape and was a treasure of surprises. The tunnel on the left side was closed by a perfectly cut rectangular block of the rock. It is believed that Adi Sankaracharya went to Kailash via that way. The seat (peeta) used by the Pandavas for doing *thapass* (the sacred meditation) could be seen in the right corner of the cave. That of Lord Sree Rama was next to it. People believed that the passageway of the Pandavas during their living in the forest (*vanavas*) was through Pathal Bhuvaneshwar. In their mission for the attainment of heaven (moksha), the Pandavas reached Badrinath through the tunnel in the cave. Prior to the Rama-Ravana war, Lord Sree Ramachandra came there through *pathal* (the world under the earth) to meditate. The statues of serpent kings Vasuki and Thakshakan lying in a rectangular pit, with their heads stretched out, resembled a fire hole. It was a horrible sight. The scene reminded one of the serpent demolition missions of King Parishith.

Another astonishing spectacle was the one of the birth of Lord Ganapathi. The scene showed fitting the severed head of a baby elephant on to a human body. Even today, water continues to drip here through the roof of the rock and the Brahma kamala flower above.

Yet another surprising sight in the cave was the divine word 'Om' shining as a diamond. Looking through a hole of about eight inches, we could see 'Om' gleaming at the far end of the 50-foot-long hole. On the left side of the cave was the naturally formed picture of Bhairavan rock. Those were ample evidence proving that nothing was man-made there.

We entered the third cave without stooping. But the interior of the cave was closed. The guide told us that it was closed automatically when Ravana was murdered. Putting our ears close to the wall, we could hear the sound of the rushing waves of the sea. It is believed that this was the sound of the waves of the sea at Rameswaram.

The fourth cave was big and impressive. It was more than 60 feet long, with a height of about 50 feet. We could see in the middle a dark and shining parijata tree made of stone (parijata, the celestial tree, is believed to have come out in the process of the churning of Palazhi, the holy ocean of milk). The tree there, full of leaves and fruits, was standing as if to support the cave. It is believed that the parijata tree was brought here by Sreekrishna from Indra's Amaravati (Indra is the king of the gods and the city he ruled was Amaravati). It is also believed that the exit to the right of the cave led to Kadhalivanam (the holy plantain grove) of Lord Sree Hanuman. Dark and scrambled stones lay on the way to the cave. The Saptharshis were believed to have performed holy meditation at that part of the cave where there were beautiful pictures carved on the roof and walls (Saptharshis means the 'seven sages'. Each *Brahma kalpa* or one day of Brahma consists of fourteen *manvantaras*. The gap between any two manvantaras is 4,32,00,00,000 solar years. There is one set of Saptharshis for each manvantara.) The Saptharshis' constellation, the Milky Way and numerous other shining stars in the universe were reproduced in that cave in the form of thousands of glowing stones. It was an incomparable and unbelievable sight. Near them was a seat made of rock. As per legend, Markandeya Muni did his holy meditation sitting on that and the *Markandeya Purana* was written there.

The way to the fifth cave was narrow. It was about 20 feet long and the upper side was about 30 feet high. Drops of water were falling from above. People believed that it came from the seven holy rivers and also from Palazhi (the holy ocean of milk), which is the abode of Lord Sreekrishna. The blissful waterfall gave us unexplainable energy.

Cave number five was also a treasure of wonders. From the 10-foot-long cave path, we entered a wide circular room about 40 feet high. The intertwined hair of Lord Siva was hanging from a stone above like the wound-up tail of a yak. There also, water from the seven holy rivers was dripping down. That looked like the hair of Lord Siva was being washed clean by the waters of the seven holy rivers, including the Ganga. A momentary thought passed my mind that all of us were only a thin hair in the gigantic intertwined *jata* (matted locks) of Lord Siva.

The holy water went to the Brahma Kund, a wide pit below. It was very surprising to see the images of Brahma, Vishnu and Maheswara forming on the outer water layer of the *kund* (pit). The sight of Kamadhenu (the cow of heaven) and the drops of water falling from its udders like drops of milk was another wonder. It is believed that Lord Siva cut Lord Brahma's fourth head there on the south side and the divine head was still lying in the holy pit.

Each one of us offered rituals there to the dead souls of our ancestors. After drinking sufficient quantities of holy water from Brahma Kund as *theertha*, we moved on to the next cave through the long corridor.

That cave was more than 100 feet long, 15 feet wide and 50 feet high. On one side, on an elevated platform, was a circular golden seat. That multicoloured rock was believed to be the Brahma Sthala. Sitting on and around that, we offered prayers. A specially appointed priest was there. He gave us, the pilgrims, sanctified flowers and *prasadam* (food sanctified by God). A variety of upside-down images of different goddesses could be seen on the rock above the Brahma Sthala. After the ten minutes of meditation there, we felt like all our organs had stopped working or as if we had reached a vacuum world! It was a most pure and divine experience!

Also, it was near there that the worship of the goddess of power was held. That place was called the 'heart opening' of the cave. It is believed that Agni (fire) started there on its own and flew in high flames. Adi Sankara closed the hole using a copper plate. After that incident, the ritual of offering human sacrifice to please Goddess Kali was stopped. Three pieces of rock were enshrined on the copper plate to represent the trinity of the powers of nature. Those rock deities were being bathed continuously and regularly by water falling endlessly from the stone roof above. We might say that nature was soothing fire and trinity alike.

But we were yet to confront the riskiest moments of our cave journey. We had to first climb up a sharp height of 15 feet and then crawl forward through a very steep tunnel about 40 feet long. In the dim light provided by the electric torches of the security guards standing below, we started climbing up the slippery rock. It was an act to be carried out with utmost care and attention. Only five of us, including myself, were ready to go.

But that sure earned us results. We landed in a wonderland that words could not describe. The world we saw was unbelievable and moreover, that was a natural creation! The structure above resembled a dome. We were told that Vaikuntam, the residence of Lord Mahavishnu, was situated at this place. Splendour and energy were everywhere. On one side of the cave was a high rock seat. To reach it, we had to climb up eighteen very dangerous and narrow steps. That looked almost like melted rock. On the top, we could see the images of Brahma, Vishnu and Maheswara, Parvathy, the Pandavas, Ganapathi, Subramanya and Aadhitya (the sun) stuck on melted rock. There was a path believed to be going to Kailash along the back of the cave and next to that was the Pathal path, going to the Kashi Viswanatha Temple.

Pathal Bhuvaneshwar or the Pathal world was a land of amazing things. There were many references in our Puranas to the Pathal world. The Skanda Purana stated that 'for feeling the presence of immortal power, one should go to the holy Bhuvaneshwar where the river trio—the Ram Ganga, Sarayu and Gupt Ganga—joined together'. In the Manasa Khanda chapter of the Skanda Purana too, there are references of Pathal Bhuvaneshwar.

Many people think that such a world exists only in the imagination. But there was nothing wrong in believing that once, there was a world underneath our earth and that might have gone out of existence due to some earthquake or maybe a geological shift. What we saw in Pathal Bhuvaneshwar, like the interiors of the caves, the mysterious tunnels and the other wonders, would surely make one believe that such an assertion was absolutely right. It was doubtless that those caves were not made by man. No man ever lived who could create such wonderful things and beautiful carvings inside the caves. Only nature could create such works of art. The hard rock was decorated with gorgeous colours of red, yellow, white, light blue and black. Our minds were drowned deep in the sea of beauty. The colours mostly used for painting the cave pictures were red, black, brown and yellow. They were lavishly and easily available in nature in the olden days.

Maybe those pictures were painted with colours using mineral oxides and fossil carbon forms. The colours lasted long in their original state because limestone absorbs the paints very slowly. Even then, it could be said that scientific theories were wrong because the blue, violet, pink and golden colours stood unfaded and everlasting.

Yes, the holy presence outlasts everything!

It is believed that Rituparna, the king of Ayodhya, was the first one to see Pathal Bhuvaneshwar. In the Puranas and the epics, there were mentions of Rituparna playing dice with King Nala. The knowledge of Pathal Bhuvaneshwar later became public during the period of the Chand dynasty. It is also said that the British were inspired to build underground railways after seeing that wonderful world.

The villagers there hold festivals and celebrations on the days of Sivarathri and Karthika Poornima. It was also a custom to offer part of their annual harvest to the gods.

After lunch hosted by the Tourism Department and resting awhile, we proceeded to our next destination, Dharchula.

3

Gala

It was more than 300 km to Dharchula from Pathal Bhuvaneshwar via Berinag, Dhal and Didihatt. Berinag was a small town blessed with overwhelming natural beauty. There were many Naga (serpent) temples between Berinag and Chaukori. The deities in them were of Naga and they carried Puranic names like Dhauli Nag, Kali Nag, Feni Nag, Karkotaka Nag, Pingal Nag and Kharhari Nag.

The fantastic natural beauty of Berinag was enhanced further by the tea estates on the mountain slopes. The famous hunter, Jim Corbett, had owned tea estates here. Limestone was found in this area in abundance. The streets appeared to be rather deserted and lonely, even though there were a number of shops. Farmlands were abundant. Looking at the heaps of hay, domestic animals and bananas, the rural life of old Kerala went through my mind. Unfortunately, such a sight is a lost dream for Malayalees nowadays. India taught the world the maxim, *'Annat Bhavanti Bhutani'*, meaning all living beings subsist on food. Other states still go with the tradition. They engage in agricultural activities and carefully maintain agricultural lands. But the literate state of Kerala has given up agriculture and does nothing to maintain agricultural lands.

The roundabout journey through the mountain ranges of Berinag ended at Dhal. From there onwards, the journey was through the plains. The Ram Ganga River flowed swiftly alongside the main road. Beautiful concrete structures of residential bungalows and shopping complexes were abundant on both sides of the market. Alongside the Ram Ganga River, the winding road went upward to the hilltop. Because we had to reach Didihatt before tea, our vehicles raised their speed. To some extent, that lessened our enjoyment of the scenic beauty all around us.

Didihatt was one of the important hill stations in the Kumaon Himalayas. The place was covered all around by a thick coat of forests. On one side of the main street was the busy market. Didihatt was situated about 4500 feet above sea level and the climate was always wet. This was a special attraction that drew tourists here. Fruits and vegetables were generously cultivated on the plateau at the hilltop. From the courtyard of the guest house, we could see devadaru (deodar) and pine trees standing below like a green carpet. The sight was simply marvellous. Full-blossomed rhododendron flowers stood in different colours, as if drawing a borderline on the mountain slopes.

Rain began to pour even before we started the scary and dangerous journey along the banks of the Kali River. The road was dreadfully narrow in many parts, making the travel very tiresome. Waves of the horrendously rushing river were visible even in the thick darkness. Leaving behind the ancient narrow streets, our vehicle stopped in front of the guest house at Dharchula after 8 p.m.

We pilgrims reached late, but still, top officials of KMVN, eminent citizens of Dharchula, a number of journalists and various television reporters were patiently waiting to receive us. They garlanded each one of us and distributed sweets and tea to all who were present. After a short meeting held on the veranda of the guest house, we went out to purchase things needed for the journey. Each and every part of the city was very familiar to me because I had stayed at Dharchula for two days earlier during the Kailash-Manasarovar journey in 2001.

After a marvellous dinner offered by the guest house employees, I spent some minutes on the balcony of the guest house watching the angry flow of River Kali. Some local people told me that there was heavy rain in the mountains and that was why the water in the Kali was that high. The chill was rising thanks to the combination of modest rain and heavy mist. Sleep came to me instantly as I crept in to take cover under the bed sheet. I was thoroughly tired after the hazardous journey.

At about 4 a.m. the next day, the rain stopped pouring. I was sipping a tasty tea sitting on the balcony when the sun spread its rays all over the area. The surroundings became visible. The flowing of the river was still violent. On the other side of the river was Nepal. Tiny houses could be seen thickly crowded on the hill slopes. I felt pained at seeing the Nepali villagers urinating and defecating on the riverbanks. We did not see such a scene on the Indian side of the river while moving up from Dharchula.

A meeting of the travellers' team was held after 6 p.m. under the leadership of the liaison officer, Prakash Chandra Chandola. Chandola, a native of Nainital, was a top official in the Uttarakhand Tourism Department. He reminded us that the journey ahead was tough, even tougher than the Kailash-Manasarovar trip. He said that he was making the statement as per the report submitted by the observation team that had visited the place to make arrangements for our journey. The route beyond Gunji ran alongside the Chinese border and he instructed each one of us to maintain discipline and self-control.

It took about two hours for all of us to pack. The luggage for Gunji was packed separately in a sack with the names and addresses of the travellers written on them. This luggage was kept separately. The horses that were to carry the main luggage would also carry those bags to get them to Gunji.

The luggage to Gunji was to be opened every evening as per needs. The travellers' team would lead and the horses carrying the luggage would follow. The passenger horses, their attendants and porters would follow suit. Extra charges were to be levied on luggage exceeding 25 kilograms.

Though we were ready to start at 8 a.m., after breakfast, it was heard that the signed entry permits from the office of the Sub-Divisional Magistrate would be delayed. So we decided to make a short visit to Nepal.

The distance between the guest house and the entry bridge to Nepal was only 1 furlong (201.17 metres). We could see that the controls and checking were very strict, unlike in the previous visit. Each one was thoroughly scrutinized by fully armed Sashastra Seema Bal (SSB) personnel. This was the consequence of the Maoist attacks in Nepal. Learning that we were Adi Kailash pilgrims, the officer named Jayabeer Singh Rawat let us go.

Staying back without going to Nepal, I talked with the officer for a little time. Though I had travelled many times in the past through the borders, I had never before heard of an armed force wing called Sashastra Seema Bal. ITBP, CRPF, BSF, CISF and Assam Rifles were the various paramilitary wings working under the central home ministry. SSB also belonged to that category. This wing of the military force was formed in 1962, soon after the Indo-China war. The headquarters were in Delhi. The main duty of SSB at present was to protect the Indian borders with Nepal and Bhutan. The command area of SSB is 1800 km of the Nepal border and

700 km of the Bhutan border. In the start, the unit's duty was to give training on arms to the villagers in the border areas. This paramilitary group had also been undertaking many projects for the socio-economic development of the border villages. The SSB personnel complained that there was no positive response to the many representations they made to the government for separating them from the paramilitary wing. They wanted to be placed under the Indian military.[1] We set out towards Mangthi after 9 a.m. We were the first batch of Adi Kailash pilgrims and there was a big crowd assembled at Dharchula to bid us goodbye. I was really surprised. The women blessed us with *aartis* and plates full of sweets. The police had to intervene when the rush of people became out of control. Many people threw flowers, garlands and sweets at the passing bus carrying us. The vehicle kept moving slowly and the atmosphere echoed with chants like 'Jai Kailashpathi', 'Jai Sathy Ma', etc.

I felt profound happiness when I saw a Muslim family smilingly bidding us farewell. They were standing a little away from the crowd. The family comprised a bearded, middle-aged man with a round cap on his head, his *pardha*-clad wife and their four children, all below twenty years of age.

Keeping their hands on their chest, all of them were praying to God above to shower all His blessings on us in our journey. My eyes filled with tears. Such a consideration beyond the barriers of religion was the wealth and strength of a nation. Any act against that was definitely an act against the God who had created each one of us.

The day was clear and the bus was moving alongside the Kali River. I thought about Kerala. I was puzzled as to whether such a 'seeing off' would happen there. Perhaps the greatness of the Himalayas was not understood in Kerala in the real sense. That was proven right by the fact that both of my travelogues on my Himalayan journeys had received widespread reception among the Malayalee population both in and out of Kerala.

Licensed mountaineers who conquered Mount Everest, K2, Nanda Devi and such peaks were brave sons of the country. It was them the media chased. They got training in institutions recognized by International Mountaineering Foundation (IMF) and were provided modern safety equipment through IMF. Clothing that resisted even sub-zero temperatures, special non-vegetarian tinned food consumable in all weathers, etc., were made available to them. 'Snow frost', a common disease resulting from ice walking, didn't affect them. They conquered heights out of pure determination and self-confidence gained from training. Modern equipment also helped them greatly. Theirs were, of course, brave acts and deserved appreciation.

But what about ordinary mountaineers like us? There was no way for us to get modern equipment. We were forced to satisfy ourselves with woollen clothes, trekking shoes and ordinary food stuff bought from Indian markets. Only the mercy of nature was there to save us when we climbed 23,000 feet without an oxygen kit, trekked through long glaciers for days and days and travelled for months under roaring ice winds and heavy rain . . .

Still, two factors guided us: the actual experience of a real journey across the great heritage of India and the spiritual refinement we gained thus.

My mind was deep in such thoughts and the bus was speeding by the side of the dangerously flowing Kali River. I didn't notice the time rocketing by. We reached the small village of Mangthi well before 11 a.m. This was as far as motor vehicles could go.

The village hadn't changed a bit since I last saw it in 2001. About fifty horses and an equal number of porters were waiting there for us. Only those who possessed health cards from the

Department of Health and identity cards from the KMVN were permitted to proceed further. All available mules had been booked to carry things to military camps. That was why horses were made ready for our use.

We were free to choose horses and porters. I beckoned a young man whose expression seemed pathetic. I inquired about his details and got a little bit embarrassed while learning them. The name of the nineteen-year-old young man was Rajendra Singh Negi. He was the younger son of Hayat Sing Negi, who had lost his life in the 1998 Malpa disaster.

The boy was studying in the fifth standard when his father died. The tragedy threw four children and a helpless mother out into the street. Owing to some technical problems, the family got compensation of Rs 1.5 lakh from the government only after three years. The elder son persuaded the poor mother that running a taxi service using a jeep was more profitable than depositing the money in a bank. And he started to learn to drive.

But in its secret cellar, destiny had kept something different for them. One day, the new jeep plunged into a deep valley along with the driver (the elder brother of our poor Rajendra Singh Negi). The young man escaped narrowly, but his wounds were serious.

Devaky Ben—that was the name of the mother—was now passing her days nursing the paralysed son. The 1 acre of land that the family owned was on the sharp slope of a hill. Wheat or paddy could not be cultivated there. They were now living on the little income they earned from vegetable cultivation and cattle rearing.

Our young man Rajendra Singh Negi's (Raju) sister was married to one Bhupendar Bist, a fruit and vegetable vendor in Dharchula. After the tenth standard, his brother-in-law admitted Raju to the eleventh class in Dharchula. Raju knew very well that his brother-in-law had a meagre income only and hence would not be able to fully support his graduate studies. That was why he had come to work as a porter during the school vacation. After giving a part of the income from the job to his mother, he wished to continue his studies with the rest. The young man hadn't yet seen Malpa, which had stolen his father's life. It was his wish to pay homage there at the memorial in remembrance of his father.

Normally, pilgrims wouldn't accept a newcomer like Raju as a porter. Only experienced porters can foresee changes in the weather and they have the pulse of the mountains at their fingertips. While travelling on the edges of narrow paths in deep valleys, a traveller was, to an extent, in the hands of an experienced and honest porter. His service was essential to survive when fog hindered vision and also while crawling up steep slopes.

Thinking that that young man was working for subsistence and education, I decided to take Raju as my porter without considering other things. The porters and horses were not paid on a daily basis. The new government rate was Rs 30 for a porter per kilometre and Rs 35 for horses. There was no food allowance. Officially, it had been announced that the total distance of the trip was 208 km.

Out of the thirty-five team members, only five, including me, were ready to proceed on the trip by walking. In the meeting in Delhi, I requested M.M. Joshy, a highly placed official from KMVN, to provide me with the required assistance on my work, the travelogue. I had presented to him two of my earlier works. With the help of his Malayalee friends, he enjoyed the contents of the books. He was also aware that my work, *Uttarakhandiloode* (Through Uttarakhand), had won the Kerala government's Sahitya (literary) Akademi Award. Mr Joshy had contacted the liaison officer, Prakash Chandra Chandola, and asked him to do the needful for me.

Adi Kailash-Om Mountain Journey, as approved by the Indian Mountaineering Foundation, was considered to be a high-altitude trekking expedition. Since it was a pre-organized mountaineering trip along the Chinese border, there were restrictions on pilgrims going individually. The loud noise and music from the horsemen's camps were the worst things that disrupted the concentration of a writer.

We left Mangthi after noon. Lunch packets had been loaded in the vehicle at Dharchula. While others had lunch at Mangthi, I kept it in my leather shoulder bag. My aim was to have it somewhere midway where it was more open and comfortable. The pilgrims on horseback and their porters were going fast. But the five of us moving on foot, our porters and the Uttarakhand Police team following us went slowly. There were 9 km from Mangthi to the Gala camp. Moving upwards from 4500 to more than 8200 feet above sea level was quite difficult.

Construction of a transportation road between Mangthi and Gala was started three years ago. But the work was now stalled. Landslides occurred very often during the construction work and the road, built with strong granite walls on either side, suffered serious damage. We saw granite layers 60 feet high underneath the hairpin curves destroyed by landslides. The same was also the case with the road on top of the slope. The new road did not pass through the village called Jipti. The road reached Gala via Garba, Rakshathaal and Bukthinaala villages. I remembered staying at Jipti Village during my 2001 trip and enjoying my time with the villagers there.

Because of the clear sky, there was moderate sunlight. We didn't find it hot at all. There was a gentle breeze too. The tools and equipment used for road construction were lying rusted by the side of the road. The new road built deep in the hillsides was surprisingly very wide. Winding around the mountains like a snake, it went up and up to dizzying heights. All my friends had gotten very far. Raju and I sat under the shade of a banj tree for lunch. Our stomachs were empty and we were very hungry. We satiated our thirst by drinking the crystal-clear water from a stream flowing down from the mountaintops of the nearby Garba Village and felt ourselves recharged. Our lunch comprised six rotis and a mixed curry of potato and white Bengal gram. I gave Raju half of the food first and then ate my half slowly.

While we were having our food, four girls came by. They were returning to their homes in Gala after purchasing household items from Mangthi. The girls, all younger than eighteen, knew Raju and they did not hesitate to talk to us. I inquired about their lives. The girls, Lakshmi, Jyothi, Pooja and Vimala, were studying in the twelfth class in Dharchula. Gala was 45 km away from Dharchula and travelling daily between these places was tiresome. But what could they do? The transportation facilities were poor. So the girls were staying in a small, rented room in Dharchula. The house belonged to a labourer's family. The girls cooked food themselves. There were no classes in the afternoon and they worked during that time in shops as salesgirls. Expenses on food and the like were met by the income thus earned. They went to Gala only once a month. Schooling up to the tenth class was at Mangthi. Every day, they had to walk 20 km in those days. However, the weather decided whether they went to school. Bad weather meant no school and good weather meant school and classes.

I took pictures of the girls with a movie camera. After that, I gave them a special product from Kerala, cashew nuts. That made the girls very happy and they bid us goodbye.

The road became very steep when we neared the village of Rakshathaal. The new road was not constructed through the villages and hence the houses on the mountain slope could be seen only from a distance. There were only fifteen houses in the village. Multi-layered cultivation could be seen on the hillsides. Raju told me that electricity would be available only after the completion of the new road. When we reached the top after passing through various hairpin bends, Raju showed me a village called Thamcool far away on the top of a hill.

That was his native place. This small village had been adopted by the SSB. There were only thirty families in the village. The SSB set up facilities for education up to the fifth standard in the village. They also constructed cricket and volleyball grounds beside the school. The military was doing everything possible to lift the standards of health, art and culture of the village people, even in the absence of electricity and telephone services.

We reached the village called Bukthinaala at 4 p.m. Paddy, wheat, dal, bajra, potatoes, etc., were cultivated aplenty in the mountainous parts of the village. The population stood at ten families only. Fruits like kafal (Myrica esculenta) and kilmode could be found in large numbers in the area. After passing a long and very steep road, the image of sheds in the faraway Gala camp became visible to our eyes.

Raju and I enjoyed strong tea and some biscuits in the camp. After that, we walked to the Gala Village. I had visited that village in my earlier journey also. The porters, horse attendants and horses of the pilgrimage team always stayed in that village on their way. Actually, many of them belonged to that village. Ganja cultivation was widespread in that village even now. It was interesting to see horses eating grass growing among the ganja plants but not touching the ganja plants.

I saw the village head standing elegantly in front of his house. I went to him and offered a salute. The elderly man blessed me and gave me medicated black tea to drink. Roots of medicinal plants were boiled with the tea and balls of jaggery were added for sweetness. The old man told me that the tea was an infallible remedy for cold and fever. He also elaborated on the priceless medicinal plants growing in the Himalayas.

Yarsagumba was one such heavenly medicinal plant spurting out in heavy snow even at heights of 25,000 feet. The village people believed that Lord Paramasiva had prescribed that medicine to his *bhoot ganas* (guarding spirits). The medicinal plant sprouted and emerged above the soil pushing through heavy layers of ice. The local belief was that that medicinal herb would keep all diseases away if kept at home. The old man presented me with two pieces of that medicinal bud. They were pale yellow in colour and about 2 inches in length. Thiljady was another plant that grew at a height of 24,000 feet underneath the snow-free rocks. The village people told me that that small plant was a sure remedy for any kind of snake poison. They used the skin of akhrot fruit trees for curing fractures, wounds and sprains. And for stomach aches and indigestion, the oil extracted from dried seeds of dandeli was very effective. I was surprised to see somalatha or Sarcostemma acidum spread over the rock layers behind the house. That holy plant was indispensable in performing *yaga*. It had high medicinal content also.

After giving *dakshina* (a respectful gift) to the old man and receiving blessings from him, I walked towards the camp. I found the horse attendants and porters gathered in a shed built for them. They were smoking ganja and drinking local liquor in groups. Without joining the activities, Raju and one or two of his young friends were sitting in a corner of the shed. I felt happy seeing this. Raju jumped up suddenly when he saw me. I waved my hands towards him.

Snowfall began after 7 p.m. The sky was cloudy. Food was served after bhajan (devotional song) and aarti (ritual worship with lights or camphor). Bread, rice, two types of vegetable curries and semiya (vermicelli) pudding were the items served. Pickle brought by pilgrims was also served.

With the snow falling thickly in the Gala mountain ranges, I closed my eyes, expecting a good night's sleep.

4

Budhi

Rising at 4.30 a.m., I started preparing for the trip. A small temple had been newly constructed with a tin sheet roof near the Gala camp. After a bhajan there, the liaison officer delivered a speech for about ten minutes. The only people there who had accomplished the Kailash-Manasarovar journey through this route were an advocate from Madhya Pradesh and me. Five others had done the Kailash trip via the Nepal route. Many horse attendants and porters were with us who had accompanied pilgrims up to the Lipulekh Pass. Since I had made the trip on foot along that part of the route, the liaison officer wanted me to deliver a short lecture to the pilgrims. I did so with much happiness.

When we started from Gala, fear crept into my mind regarding my fellow passengers who were riding on horseback. The height of the horses was double that of mules. Between Gala and Gunji, there were many places where rocks hung dangerously over the road. And the route by the side of the Kali River was like a tunnel full of rocks, continuing that way for kilometres. There was every chance that the people riding on horseback would hit their heads on the rocks above and thus get fractures. I expressed my concern right at the start of my talk. When my talk was over, the liaison officer summoned the

horse-borne people and discussed the problem. It was decided
that on such occasions, the horse riders would have to lie low
on the horses' backs. It was also decided to tie them with strong
cotton fibre for safety.

The journey started after 5 a.m. Though it was morning, the
light was dim because of the mist. The distance to Budhi from
Gala via Jipti was 20 km. That was as per the old survey reports.
Maybe it was 2 or 3 km more taking into account the landslides
and the path cut on hilltops. We walked slowly through the
outskirts of Jipti Village. Nearby, we found the army quarters
in Jipti. The new army post there was established in 2003. All
pilgrims on foot walked together in groups up to Bindhakotti.
I had already reminded my fellow travellers that some points
on the way from Bindhakotti to Lakhanpur would be daunting,
including the formidable mission of climbing up 4440 steps.

The team rested for a while on level land after climbing
up the steep slope past Bindhakotti. There was no sign of the
mist lessening. The temperature dropped further. The liaison
officer suggested that those who were travelling on horseback
should now travel on foot up to Lakhanpur. It would be very
difficult for the horses to go up and down the narrow and
short steps. Below the steps that were cut into the face of rocky
mountains were deep abysses. It was decided that the pilgrims
and porters should go first and the horses and the horsemen
would gradually follow them to join them at Lakhanpur. The
decision was considering the possibility of horses defecating on
the steps and the passengers slipping off them.

We continued the journey after refreshing ourselves with
biscuits and glucose. The porters were asked to take special care
of the travellers who were their responsibility. Accidents were
common in this place on the Kailash-Manasarovar journey.
Accidents happened when rain and mist came together. The
journey was hazardous then. There was insufficient room

for the passengers and horses to pass when they approached each other from opposite directions. Hence, a system of one-way traffic was adopted here. That was made possible by directing the travellers on the return trip to go straight to Mangthi without touching Gala camp. They turned left at Lakhanpur and continued alongside the Kali River. That way was, in a sense, harder. Landslides often happened there. It was also longer.

I walked with great alertness, chanting prayers and concentrating my mind. Even though Raju was not acquainted with the path, he was right behind me.

We reached Lakhanpur after 9.30 a.m. Breakfast was arranged there. On the last leg of the trip, we finished the food we had brought from Gala. I recognized the shop owner and his family as soon as I saw them. The poori and vegetable sabzi served were delicious. But the tea was not that good. The aged shop owner explained that there was insufficient milk to make tea for more than 100 people. We rested for some time, watching the swift flow of the Kali River. Then Raju and I proceeded on our voyage.

The journey from Lakhanpur by the side of the river was horrific. One might die from fear at simply seeing the turbulent river gushing fast through the deep mountain gorges as if to destroy everything in its way. The path we were to crawl through was carved out from the giant mass of a rocky mountain and it was only 2.5 feet wide. In most parts, it was like a semi-circular tunnel. There were steel railings at some places but many had fallen because of stones falling from above. Sharp curves and nearly vertical slopes upwards were truly frightening. We found it difficult to balance on the sharp downward path due to the steepness. So, taking each step on the steep slope posed a great danger of us of falling into the river below. Carefully holding the rock on the left side for support, we took each step very vigilantly. Halting for rest at intervals, watching the intimidating, rapidly flowing river and at the same time enjoying Nepal on the other side, with its bounty of mountains and forests, we just didn't realize the time flying away during our walk.

After every tough leg of the trip, we rested for some time, enjoying biscuits and soft drinks. One would forget all the hardships of the journey at seeing the heavenly beauty showered on us by nature. When we reached level ground, Raju asked me about Malpa. The poor boy's face went dark when I told him that we were approaching the place. For the next 1.5 km, he followed me without saying anything. I knew that his mind was deep in memories of his father.

We reached Malpa after noon. I could see the other team members resting some distance away from the place where the tragedy had occurred years ago. They were relaxing after food. The place was full of scattered heaps of rock pieces. It was a big, sky-high mountain that suddenly came down whole and broke into innumerable pieces. One can guess the magnitude of the broken mountain from the mountain that was now standing. The villagers told me that both the mountains were similar in size and shape. My narration of the Malpa disaster of 1998 was not complete in my first work, *Uttarakhandiloode*. What I wrote were only the details I got from my conversations with the villagers and the army men during that trip. But this time, my knowledge was authentic and elaborate because I got more details from the official records in the office of Kumaon Mandal Vikas Nigam Ltd in Delhi. The advocate in our team had seen these records before.

The commission appointed by the government to investigate the tragedy had officially fixed the death toll at 272. That included sixty Kailash-Manasarovar pilgrims, six officers who led the team and 206 villagers. The villagers included porters and horse attendants. The number of horses, ponies, cows, yaks, goats and other animals that lost their lives crossed 500. Only two pilgrims, both below thirty-five years old, escaped the catastrophe. Though they could have survived the dreadful incident, it had devastating effects on both of them. Unable to stand the shock, one lost all his control over life. His mental stability was drastically disrupted and sad as it was, the poor man was still kept in a locked room. The other one had a different story. He continued his studies and later passed his MCom. However, a soft sound, like the sound of the horn of a passing vehicle or the noise from a sound system, frightened him and he would lose his mind temporarily. The only relief was that that would last only for a week, after which he would return to normal. When we asked him about the tragedy, he would cry for hours, so nobody asked him such things.

Though they didn't reach their destination, those who lost their lives in the Malpa tragedy would always be in our tearful memories. We can remember in this context the insightful sentence written by the great poet Kalidasa[1]: 'It might not reach the destiny but just attempting to accomplish an impossible thing is great for men'.

Earthquakes are first among the merciless acts of nature in which many lives are lost en masse (the loss of lives in floods caused by excessive rain is comparatively lower). Viewed from that angle, the Malpa tragedy stands in the second position. There were no traces of an earthquake at Malpa. There seemed to be no reason for what happened. One mountain stood without any damage while the adjoining mountain suddenly fell down in pieces. It was like a plane crash. More than two hundred people including sixty members of the Kailash-Manasarovar travel team and numerous animals fell dead in a matter of seconds. Rocks—many of them bigger than elephants—lay scattered in heaps. And in the middle of them were found two men trapped alive! When asked what they thought was the reason for the Malpa tragedy, the villagers responded furiously and spoke alike against one single person, a lady member of the then Kailash-Manasarovar travel team. That alleged lady was a famous dancer-cum-model. Witnesses stated that she and the then liaison officer were engaged in unethical and immoral activities. Theirs was a divine trip that required purity and devotion in body and mind. But those two people treated the travel as a pleasure trip. At Dharchula, their activities crossed all limits. Those were repeated in the small camps of Gala also. The villagers believed that it was those two who caused the fury of nature. Such a shameful thing happened on our own journey too. However, it came to our attention only at Gunji. Each one of us believed that that was the real reason for the unusual troubles we had on our way from Budhi to Gunji. Anyway, we got rid of the bad affair then and there at Gunji.

Everyone should understand one thing while travelling through the difficult mountain ranges here: man is as tiny as grass. People live here because of the generosity and kindness of nature. Every day, people see the innumerable gigantic mountain ranges, the small valleys on their sides, the roaring Kali River and the narrow and dangerous paths along its banks. Landslides are regular on these paths. The power of God or nature is the force that saves them. Stray deaths have happened, of course, and still happen, but compared to the deaths in the plains, the number of deaths here was minimal. What they lead is an ethical and moral life. They will never do anything that endangers their faith, truth and moral thinking.

I collected three small stones in memory of the Malpa tragedy. I felt it would be good to bring these shining silver stones to Kerala and receive condolences from the spiritually rich people of Kerala.

While standing for a long time to look at the shattered rock collections lying all over the area, I forgot about Raju. Turning back, I found him lying face down on a small rock and weeping. A sense of guilt swept through me. I got the boy to sit up. Still weeping, he went on talking about his loving father who, on each and every return from mountain trips, brought new clothes and sweets. His memory of him was that of sitting with the children and feeding them.

Patting his shoulders, I tried to soothe Raju. His father's life span had been fixed at the moment he was born. Nobody could change that. His physical body might have been destroyed at Malpa but his soul—the true essence of life—went back to where it came from with not even a small injury. What came from Brahma should return to Brahma. That was God's law. That soul would enter another body. It had the ability to decide where and when to be born again. I told Raju that he and the other children, along with their mother, should pray from deep within their hearts for the father to take birth again in the noblest way. They must perform the rituals on the anniversary of his death with the late father in mind. That would bring all of them a better life too.

Raju stood up cheerfully sooner than I expected. I got him to the nearby Malpa Village, telling him that we would light lamps and shower flowers in reverence of his father there and pray for the liberation of his father's soul. At first, Raju burst into tears but soon regained his composure. He completed the rituals properly and prostrated himself on the ground in memory of his father.

Lunch had been arranged in the temporary shed of the tourism department. Raju went to the horse attendants' camp and me to the shed. Roti, potato curry and a side dish of edible leaves were the menu items. Boiled rice was also served to those who required it. We started off after lunch. The journey from

Malpa to Lemarry was through the forests. The Kali River
rushed away from the area. The landscape was very beautiful.
Since these were the foothills, nature had decorated the
downward-sloping valleys in shining green with colourful
flowers. It was, no doubt, a rare visual feast. While enjoying the
eye-catching golden colour of the blooming karnikara (Indian
laburnum) flowers that hung in bunches, I remembered
a reference from the poet Kalidasa on the shortcoming of
this flower:

'Varnaprakarshae Sathy Karnikaram
Dhoonothi Nirgandhathaya Sma Chetha Ha
Prayena Samagyavidhou Gunanaam
Paraangmukhee Viswasruja Ha Pravarthee Hee'
—Kumarasambhavam, pages 3–19

(Even though the karnikara flowers have eye-catching
colours, they hurt the heart because they have no fragrance.
The creator is rather reluctant to put all qualities
into one single thing.)

Raju explained to me in detail about some wild plants
growing abundantly along the path. If we touched a plant,
locally called 'bichu', our body would start itching (like
our thumba [Phlomis indica] plant). The itching would
last for one whole day. Within the branches of that plant,
which was about 3 feet high, grew green fruits in abundance
(like our kovakka [Brisnia grandis]). Since his hands were
protected by gloves, Raju picked some of the fruits for me
without difficulty. The fruit tasted like tender cucumber.
Even cattle evaded them out of fear. The leaves of the plant
they called jankara were best for cooking thoran (a side dish
with coconut). The dhag plant, which looked like a cobra

with its hood fanned out, was frightening. Raju told me that the thoran cooked with the chopped pieces of their stem (the stem looked like the tender stem of elephant yam) was an unforgettable experience. But those plants were the favourite of cattle and so were scarce. As we reached the modest forest areas, towering sandalwood trees known as 'Mountain Kanchan' were seen aplenty.

Since our route was mostly through forests, I feared the presence of robbers. But I had heard earlier that such criminal activities were non-existent there. Generally saying, there were no cases of robbery in the forests reported anywhere in Uttarakhand. When some trees fell owing to natural calamities, the staff of the Forest Department would immediately cut them into small pieces. After that, they would store them in vacant places. The villagers used those wooden pieces for domestic and other needs after buying them at auctions. They could pick the fallen dry branches of trees only after getting permission from the Forest Department. The fallen trees not under government ownership were sold to the villagers at low prices. For the villagers residing at the top of the hills, firewood was essential for the kitchen as well as to escape from the bitter cold. Kalidasa upheld the ethical stand that 'it was not fair to cut even the poisonous trees once they were planted and grown'.

The path became hazardous again as we reached the banks of the Kali River. We often encountered roads going steeply upwards and short plateaus. The mind was filled with fear at seeing the angry river and the hazardous narrow path. I found the path more difficult than in 2001. All things required for the use of military personnel were being transported that way. Horses, ponies and sheep carrying things for the use of the army and the villagers travelled through there. Each year, the walkway was strengthened by putting in pebbles. That made the upward-curving slopes rougher. There was no doubt that travelling through there on foot was by all means a hell of an experience.

We halted for rest at Lemarry. Khumani fruits, potato, vegetables and wheat were grown aplenty there. Just ten families dwelt there. I recalled a small group of eight soldiers residing in a tent there during my last trip. The place had grown into an interim camp two years ago. Soldiers from the Kumaon regiment and the ITBP camped there. The Chinese attempted to construct a road in the Garbiang region, crossing the Indian border. But the Indian Army's timely intervention stopped the Chinese encroachment. A serious conflict was thus avoided. Three years ago, the Chinese distributed pamphlets in the Kumaon region bearing words such as 'breakfast at Dharchula, lunch at Almora and dinner at Delhi'. I got the information from the horse attendants' camp. Many people were still in possession of that notice, which implied that India would be conquered in just one day. Anyhow, the Indian government had sufficiently enhanced the military deployment in Kumaon to effectively control the situation. Now, it was part of those security precautions that strict controls were imposed upon pilgrimage via the Kumaon area.

Colossal mountains stood on the left side of the road that went up to Lemarry. The sight of the mountains was frightful to any passer-by.

On the side of the road were vast cultivated lands. The villagers lived miserably in tiny houses there. Just off the cultivated lands was forest land. The forests stretched all the way to the faraway mountains. When viewed from level land, the place looked like a crescent. A world of blooming flowers enriched its beauty. Probably inspired by beautiful flowers like karnikara and ashoka and flowered shrubs moving in the breeze like ornaments of spring, the poet Kalidasa presented Devi Parvathy as

'Ashokanirbhalsitha padmaraga
Makrushtahaemadhyuti karnikaram
Muktaakalaapeekrutha sindhuvaram
Vasanthapushpabharanam vahanthee.'
—Kumarasambhavam, pages 3–53

(Parvathy was decorated with spring flowers like the ashoka,
which suggested padmaraga [ruby], karnikara flowers,
which suggested the colour of gold, and sindhuvara flowers
[karunochi flowers] knotted into a pearl necklace.)

After enjoying the beauty of Lemarry to the maximum, we started off after having tea and biscuits. The simple villagers had a practice of blessing the pilgrims before seeing them off.

Hazardous points on the route were comparatively fewer after Lemarry. Even then, there were many areas en route where massive landslides occurred regularly. A huge landslide had taken place at the point where India was to the left and Nepal to the right. We stood perplexed for some time. The accident spot was about two furlongs away. I had not failed to notice a whirlwind blowing fiercely in the lower lands, going up in a circular motion with enhanced strength. Believing that it wouldn't hinder our trip, I decided to proceed on the journey. But Raju stopped me from going further. And within no time, rocks and stones started coming down from the mountaintops. Gradually, that turned into a big landslide. Terror-struck, I saw large rocks, hills of mud and small trees falling down, shattering on the road and tumbling into the river. The whole path we were to pass also collapsed and fell into the river. This went on for about ten minutes and then everything became peaceful. However, small boulders went on falling now and then.

The sky was dark and cloudy. Not even a single ray of light from the setting sun could be seen. The rainy clouds were moving northwards. There was a chill breeze from the Nepal mountains. The cause of the change in the atmosphere was the cyclone. Rain might pour down at any time. Knowing that rain would make our travel difficult, we walked up hurriedly. We reached the place where the landslide had occurred. Only a thin path—barely 1 foot wide—was there for us to walk on. Looking up to make sure that no rock was falling down, we took each step very cautiously on the lean and muddy path and proceeded. At last, we succeeded in crossing the road. Soon, drops of rain began to fall.

We walked quickly, ignoring the rain. We didn't wear raincoats since the rain was not heavy. But the mist gently crawling down from the mountaintops was dangerous. There would be no other option but to stop the expedition if mist totally impaired our sight. The narrow and tiny path above the bottomless gorge, the unpredictable dark forests full of thick plants and trees, sharp upward slopes strewn with rocks— leaving all of them behind at rocket speed, we reached the Budhi camp past 6 p.m. The rain and fog were heavy then. The liaison officer, who had been waiting for us at the garden gate in front of the camp, was relieved to see us.

Two tents had been newly constructed at Budhi. They were made of fibre and each of the tents could accommodate ten persons. Since the floor was also made of fibre sheets, the cold was a little less inside. These tents were being kept vacant especially for the pilgrims travelling on foot and hence, there were only five of us staying in them. The servants came in with biscuits and hot tea that warmed our bodies and minds. While sipping the tea, I went to the door and looked out. It was still raining, but not as heavily as before. Because of the widespread fog, nothing was visible outside. The cold was unbearable because it was a collective attack by fog, rain and wind. We greatly needed to rest. Taking rescue under the bedsheet, I lay on the cot all stretched out. It felt very comfortable.

It was past seven when I rose from the relaxing sleep. The sky was gloomy, even though the rain and fog had disappeared. It was still quite chilly. Knowing that daylight would go only at around 8 p.m., the five of us went for a walk around Budhi Village. The village was roughly 4 sq. km and a total of sixty-five families lived in it. The main cultivation was wheat. Vegetables, edible leaves, potato and millets were also cultivated by turns. A species of wheat having a low cropping period was cultivated there on a bi-seasonal scheme. When the snowy season was over, the inhabitants would come over from distant Dharchula and start cultivation. And after the celebration of Deepavali in November, all the people there—from the infants to the very elderly—would return to Dharchula. They had been literally following a 'six months at home, six months in the forest' life. The poor lot had to put up a really tough fight to overcome the snow season. They had only their agricultural income. If any natural or other disasters happened and their crops got destroyed, these poor people could only look at the emptiness in front of them and weep. The basic necessities like education, electricity, drinking water and good health were beyond their reach.

Though the rain and mist hindered them sometimes, we found the villagers engaged in the act of harvesting. They were doing it in the same style as paddy was harvested in our state, Kerala. Like us, the ripe, harvested sheaves were kept tied up in small bundles all around. It was interesting to see small children helping their mothers by picking up fallen plants full of yield. When harvesting was over, the plants would be wrapped using plastic sheets and kept at high temperatures for two or three days. After this, the plants would be threshed on the floor or on the stone to separate the grains from them.

The produce would then be dried. The dry crops would be immediately carried away to Dharchula on the backs of donkeys. The villagers also made money by spinning sheep wool into threads for making woollen dresses and by rearing ponies. All this effort of the villagers was for their children to stay and study at Dharchula or to earn money for their daughters' marriages.

On the way back, I stopped at the horse attendants' camp and became totally upset at the sight there. There were two insane women of middle age in Budhi. Day and night, they wandered through the streets and nobody gave them shelter or cared to treat them for their illnesses. I saw the horse attendants giving those sick ladies locally distilled liquor. I told the attendants that intoxicating such people would only intensify their disease. If they did not intend to help, please don't help. But it was pitiful to harm them. The horse attendants were contrite and swore that they would not repeat such acts in the future. Even though they were under the influence of liquor, I felt that they were honest in telling me that.

Day gave way to night in Budhi Village. My body began to shiver with the combined effects of cloudy sky, fog and cold wind. An old man of the village had told me that though it was a chilly climate, rain would not come to those mountainous lands until the end of June. He predicted heavy downpours in the coming days. The wind blowing from the icy mountains and the suddenly appearing and disappearing fog were sufficient hints of that.

When it was past 8.30 p.m., I ate dinner after saying my prayers. Roti cooked on burning charcoal, potato plus green peas curry, a side dish made of ladies' fingers, salad, fried pappadam (a thin and crisp disc-shaped Indian food) and milk pudding were the items for dinner. The satisfaction I got was equal to that of a marriage banquet. Sleep was already in my eyes before I crept into the bedding.

5

Gunji

Loud music awoke me from a deep sleep. I came out of the bedding and looked at my watch. The time was 2 a.m. sharp. It had been decided the previous day that everyone should wake up at 5 a.m. and start the journey around 5.30. I opened the door and looked out. Nothing was visible because of rain and fog. Just the music and the dancing of the two ladies could be heard.

Closing the door, I lay down on the bed again. But my mind was restless. I had in all these years awoken only at the right time. I was wondering what happened now. Last night's scene of the horse attendants serving liquor to the ladies had pained my heart greatly. I had given advice to those people too. Perhaps the incident was stuck in my heart.

We were bound to return to where love and hate originated. That was why we were asked not to be angry with anybody. No doubt, the anger rising from within us would return to us as time passed. The Yajurveda advises us thus: 'Let us view everything from a friend's angle (love) (*Mithrassya chachusha sameekshamahae*)'. It was natural law that love and hate returned where they started from. Take, for example, physics: the electricity generated by a dynamo returns to the dynamo after completing a circuit. In Patanjali's *Yoga Sutra,* the great sage had said that 'love and hate would at last return to the point of origin'.

The human mind is as mysterious as the ocean. In order to define the character and origin of principles, the Bhagavatham[1] elaborated the composite number twenty-four in the order of five, five, four and ten. The state of twenty-four denoted the *Pancha Bhoota* (the five basic elements), namely *prithvi* (earth), *jal* (water), *agni* (fire), *vayu* (air) and *akash* (space), the five *Thanmathra* (molecules), namely smell, taste, shape, touch and sound, the *Anthakarana* (psyche), comprising mind, intelligence, pride and desire, and the ten organs (the five organs of knowledge—ears, skin, eyes, tongue and nose and the five organs of action—hands, legs, mouth, phallus or *lingam* and excretory organs). Though the Anthakarana (psyche) was viewed as four—mind, intellect, pride and desire—they were actually one and the same. The classification into four was only for clarity.

'Mano Budhirahamkaraschiththamithyantharaalmakam
Chathurdha Lakshyathae Bhaedho Vruthya Lakshanaroopaya'
— Bhagavatham

Was it my intuition to help save those two ladies? Was it to alert me to their plight that I was woken up late at night when everything and everyone was fast asleep? I believe that that was the truth. After deciding firmly to do something about that matter on my return, I again fell into a deep sleep.

My friends woke me up the next day. After having hot tea, we all engaged in the morning activities. Everyone became anxious when we received information that the journey was to be delayed for one hour. Though the rain had been falling only moderately, the dark cloudy sky didn't seem to be a good sign.

Everyone assembled in the liaison officer's room after group prayer. The 3 km from Budhi to Chalekh was a sharp and hazardous upslope. The only relief was that the travel through that part was not alongside the Kali River. It was decided to have breakfast in the shed of the Tourism Department at Chalekh. Cooks had already been posted there. The camp manager of Budhi cautioned the travellers to be very careful because after the level lands of Chalekh, the journey ahead to Gunji was alongside the river. That was very dangerous. He also warned that the path would be muddy and slippery due to rain. The meeting ended after taking a decision to start the journey at 6.30 a.m.

After putting on raincoats and tying up the baggage on the backs of horses, the journey started at 6.45. Travellers on horses would have no difficulties. The problems were for us, the travellers on foot. Since the rain was continuous, the walk would not be as quick as expected. When everybody had left, Raju and I started to walk in the rear. The villagers of Budhi bid farewell to us standing on the verandas of their houses. The mad women were found sitting on a small rock. They were murmuring something and looking down. I paused to hear but their voices were weak, maybe because of last night's shouting. When I said that I would get them to Dharchula for treatment, one of the women shook her head. It was not clear whether she understood what I had said. Bowing my head and in silence, I bade them goodbye.

Raju and I started walking again.

Eighteen km had to be crossed to get from Budhi to Gunji. We had been moving from a height of 10,000 feet (Budhi) to 12,300 feet (Gunji). But there were places at that height even before we reached Gunji. While going steeply down from a very high to a low place, the trek would pass through level lands for some distance and then would come to high places again.

At those times, we would feel that the journey from Budhi to Gunji on foot was totally impossible. After the steep downward path at Budhi, the path went steeply up. There were sharp hairpin curves at many places on the rising path for the distance of 3 km till Chalekh. After trekking through the narrow pathways of hills and wet slopes amid the bush, we reached a resting place. The small shed, roofed with a tin sheet, was sure a relief for us, the travellers on foot. We rested there for about ten minutes, consuming glucose and biscuits.

The intensity of rain and mist was increasing. Dark clouds rolled out ominously behind the mountain ranges. We couldn't detect any trace of the sun. We continued our voyage and for security, wrapped plastic bags over the socks in our shoes. Though the path was rather wide, walking was hard because of the pebbles. At many places, the sharp edges of stones projected out for 4 inches or so and our shoes hit them many times, upsetting our balance. That was risky in all senses. Supported by sticks, we went slowly upwards, taking each step cautiously. On the way upwards, we found two places where small idols of Siva and Parvathy were placed on stone platforms and worshipped. The pilgrims as well as other travellers proceeded only after praying and lighting lamps there. Everybody believed that those prayers were most essential for travelling safely through mountains and the dangerous curves that followed.

The rain became heavy and the wind also started to blow. That, together with the mist, made the journey all the more tedious. Our legs were wet from ankles to shoes and walking became difficult. When we reached the last ascent to Chalekh, I amassed all my strength and began to climb.

The other team members had been resting after having breakfast. They were waiting for the rain to lessen. After removing my raincoat, hat and gloves, I had breakfast. While having roti and potato curry, my attention was on the Chalekh ground that lay in front of me. I remembered the spectacular world of flowers I had seen there during my last visit. My eyes would never forget that sweet sight. There might not be a chance to see such a panorama this time, I thought. The flowers would start blooming only by the end of June. During the last journey, I had enjoyed with an open heart the fortress of mountain ranges stretched out long and far and the pine and Nevada trees standing with their heads held high. But because of heavy rain and mist, the heartening view would be seen only in my memories this time.

A wind blew fiercely from the east and the tin sheets of our shed rattled as they hit one another. The shed shivered and rattled. The wind reduced the strength of the rain and the mist also cleared almost completely. The horse attendants and porters whistled enthusiastically to acknowledge their readiness to go. Acute muscle pain had struck two team members, Mahajan and Mod, travelling on foot like me. They were not in a condition to proceed further on foot. Hence, two horses were arranged to carry them.

All the travellers had left except Raju and me. We remained in the shed and spent some more time sipping hot tea.

Soon, we began the journey. In order to prevent rainwater from getting into my woollen clothing, I first wore a waterproof jacket over it and then a raincoat over both. Ahead was a meadow full of green grass. Small plants with buds grew thickly over the vast area. It looked as if the plants were going to give birth to a world of flowers in different colours. The sight was gorgeous. The sea of flower buds blooming into red, yellow, violet, blue, white and saffron flowers would be uplifting. A universe of colours was going to be made with the different colours standing apart. Mixed with green grass, the colour harmony would reach its peak.

Parts of the ground were covered with pits full of water and the journey became a little bit slow hence. There was an army check-post at the very end where travel documents had to be submitted for scrutiny. Even though the horse aides and porters had identity and health cards, the army officers were troubling them with questions. I talked to the army officer for some time. He clarified that they were part of the security arrangements and encroachment was to be strictly prevented. The villagers at the hilltops too had been provided with identity cards but they were subjected to a faultless check-up as well. I was happy when the officer said that the Maoists were camping in the nearby Nepal mountains and that such extremist activities would never be allowed to land on Indian soil.

Crossing endless plains and mountainsides, our journey moved along the banks of the Kali River. Rain began to pour again. On one side was the aggressive river, flowing without any kindness. On the other side, a thin path was carved out of the sides of the rocky mountains about 200 feet above the base and huge rock formations were projecting out over it.

And add to that heavily pouring rain! You could guess how dangerous it was to travel that way. Death was the instant answer to any careless step. When the rain got heavier, the visibility reduced. The river water rose to enormous, frightening levels. The path was barely 1 foot wide because of damage caused by stones falling from above. However, by chanting prayers and concentrating, we overcame the crisis.

Climbing up a very risky path that was literally hanging over the river, we reached a small village called Karchang. From there, the pathway was level for some distance. Only ten or less families were residing at Karchang. We walked ahead through the 1-foot pathway into the fields of the villagers. All the while, rain fell on our heads. It was quite sad to see the rain falling on cows and sheep freezing in the cold under the trees.

At many places, crossings were very difficult because of the heavy flow of water caused by continuous rain on the mountains. To add to the suffering, water had also crept into my shoes. I was compelled to slow my pace. Steeply rising mountain areas and hairpin curves appeared one after another. Though the mist had created obstacles in many places, we went on the trip understanding that there was no meaning in waiting. The chill increased as we went higher. However, we picked up our enthusiasm and walked faster when the shadowy image of Garbiang Village began to appear through the fog.

We had learnt that the other team members were camping at Garbiang. In the small lanes of the village were horses standing in the rain. All the pilgrims had occupied the villagers' houses. In most of the houses, small trades were being carried out. Tea, biscuits, cigarettes, soft drinks, shoes and woollen clothes were available there. In some shops, roti, rice and dal curry were available. Raju and I walked around for some time looking for a quiet place. At last, we reached a house and the couple who owned the shop invited both of us in. Keeping our raincoats and shoes outside, we sat wearily near the fire.

Heavy rain continued to pour but the fire warmed us a bit. I ordered tea. During the wait for tea, I thought about the moments I had spent at Garbiang on my last journey. The image of a small shop under the akhrot tree where I took rest and the old women who had sat there with weak bodies passed through my mind for an instant. The women might have died. The boys I met then might be living somewhere as horse aides or shepherds in the mountains. The villagers there had no other jobs to expect. What hope was there in life for those poor and illiterate villagers?

I looked out upon hearing the uproar of the horse attendants. The rain had stopped. The other team members were ready to go. Sipping tea, I came out and looked around the village in detail. The condition of Garbiang was worse than I had seen in 2001. Most of the buildings situated over the street and at the bottom of the hills had collapsed. Those that remained carried the elegance of palaces even now. There had been more than 400 houses in this village. It sustained up to the year 1962 with kingly grace. The rich Bhotia race of people there had started India-Tibet trade through the Lipulekh Pass. This continued for about a century. Tea, coffee, jaggery, cotton, cereals, etc., from India and things like salt, wool and borax from Tibet were traded. Weapons like swords, shields, etc., were also exported from India. In those times, the sounds that echoed continuously in the Kumaon mountain ranges were from the neck-bells of horses, yaks and mules. The shepherds were the warrior race (*kshathriya*) who had migrated long ago from Garhwal to Kumaon. They were the honest servants of the then-rich Bhotia people. When the affluent Bhotia constructed palatial houses in Garbiang, they constructed small houses for the servants. The Bhotia who had close associations with the Kumaon dynasty rented lands to the servants. It was thus that the agricultural lands in the Kumaon mountain ranges came to be in the possession of the villagers.

The terms *Bhotam*, *Bhotia* and *Bhotantham* meant Tibet, Tibetan and Bhutan respectively. The Bhotia started migrating to India in the thirteenth century CE. During British rule, the Bhotia occupied high positions in government departments. The British had a special affinity for Kashmiri Brahmins and Bhotia people. The rose-coloured shining skin and a handsome structure were specialities of the Bhotia and even the British bowed their heads in front of that. There were scientific theories for the red colour of the skin of those residing on hilltops. Haemoglobin gives the red colour to blood. The number of red corpuscles in the blood of people living in high altitudes was far greater than those living in low places.

Air pressure was lower when you travelled upwards from sea level. When air pressure was reduced, the quantity of oxygen that the blood could contain inside the lungs also decreased. Thus, the amount of oxygen needed for the normal functioning of the body, especially for the smooth working of the brain, would not be available. One way or another, the body had to respond. One solution was to increase the number of red corpuscles in the blood to carry more oxygen from the lungs. It is evident that there is a difference in the physical structure of those born and brought up in the high mountains. Their chest is expanded to contain more oxygen. Their skin is more reddish in colour. There was no such word as 'anger' in their dictionary of life. In their practical life, the majority of the Bhotia people followed the advice given in the Bhagavat Gita, like '*Nirmamo Nirahamkara Ha Sama Dhukka Sugha Ha Kshamee*' and '*Sama Ha Sathrou cha Mithrae cha*'.

Garbiang sank into oblivion when trading via Lipulekh was stopped after the Chinese invasion of 1962. Though they tried to stick on for some time, the Bhotia leaders eventually bid farewell to Garbiang and went to Dharchula in search of new shelters. However, the monopoly of India-Nepal trade in Dharchula was still in their hands. Though their masters went to distant Dharchula, the villagers remained in Garbiang Village. They now earned their livelihood from farming, cattle rearing and petty trade. The trade via Lipulekh having stopped, the villagers of Garbiang attempted to open new trade relations with Nepal. They constructed a wooden bridge over the Kali River to bring goods to Changru Village on the Nepal border and from there to Taklakot through the Tinker Pass. They were doing that with the help of the Nepalese. The Kailash-Manasarovar pilgrims could also reach Taklakot through the Tinker Pass. But the passage was extremely hazardous. As the Chinese government did not permit passage through those lands, the Indian government too banned the Kailash journey through that way. With landslides and other natural calamities happening regularly in Garbiang, the trade route to Changru gradually shifted to pass through Gunji. The poor villagers of Garbiang were thus left jobless. As a last blow, when Maoist extremist activities based in the Nepal forests went up, the trading to Changru also ceased completely.

We proceeded on our journey, leaving Garbiang behind. Though the heavy rain had stopped, it was drizzling intermittently. The atmosphere was dark and the rays of the sun were hidden. The breeze blowing from the north increased the chill. After the dangerous walk on a 1-foot-wide path alongside the Kali River, we reached a village called Seethi. We stopped there for lunch. Here also, food was arranged in a shed of the Tourism Department. Relaxed, we were eating hot roti, dal curry and a dish made of potato and green leaves when two soldiers of the ITBP came in. Their uniforms, shoulder bags and shoes were coloured as if they had been rolling in wet mud. Their rifles were also covered with mud. They started cleaning things with water borrowed from the nearby shop. After finishing my food, I came out and asked the soldiers what the matter was. They replied that a big landslide had occurred on the way from Seethi at a place prior to Sitaphul and large amounts of watery mud were lying all over the way for about 1 km. Going by foot that way was extremely dangerous because travellers were sure to slip. They gave us advice that if we actually slipped and fell, then it was safe to fall face down and stick both hands in the wet, muddy earth. Otherwise, there was a chance of sliding and falling into the deep valley.

I got acquainted with an old man on the streets of Seethi. He had been practising sorcery, prophesy and indigenous treatment in exchange for small amounts. He also held the position of the village head. Saluting him and offering a small gift, I talked with him for about five minutes. I asked him how he felt regarding the unusual change in the local climate. I also wanted to know whether the atmosphere would become clear for us to reach Adi Kailash without any difficulty. I was stunned at his reply.

'Somebody in your team was disgraceful and had come for the trip with no good purpose,' the old man said. He had been in the mountains for the past eighty-five years and had seen and experienced much.

The rain that had been pouring was not from the north. That was a bad sign. What did the city men know about mountains? The team was on the verge of disaster. Unless that was solved at Gunji, the journey to Adi Kailash would be hindered.

When I asked whether the female members of the team were the problem, the man kept silent. On my return, my thoughts revolved around many things. As far as I knew, the team members had been selected with the utmost care. There were four couples. Also in the team were two daughters of a Gujarati couple who were engineering students. The father was an engineer and the mother, a French teacher. Both belonged to strict, conservative families. They chanted mantras even when travelling on horseback. The scientist and his wife from Mumbai and the doctor couple from Gujarat were aged people. There was a soldier and his wife also in our team. Since he was an army man, it had been thought that his service would be an added advantage for the team. There were five other women in the group, all past middle age. They were from West Bengal, Punjab and Uttar Pradesh. In all probability, the chance of a problem arising on the part of the women was low. Unmarried youngsters were also part of the team. The travellers on foot, Mr Gourav and Mr Chaithanya, were unmarried. All were keeping absolute discipline in camps, dining halls and prayers. Since I had been the last person each time in the camps and the dining halls, I could mingle with my fellow travellers only up to a limit. Still, I couldn't find any problem with the team.

Hence, I didn't give much thought to what the old man had said.

The sky was grey. My mind was too. I walked silently while the drizzle continued. The pathway along the Kali River had become very slippery and walking on it was terribly tough and hazardous. My slipping legs and loss of control on the narrow path put me in danger on many occasions. Raju's help at such times was very useful. I saw even the firm legs of horses slipping at many places on the path. The flow of the river had been like the huge tidal waves of a roaring ocean. The loud sound of the flow was unbearable to the ears.

Before we reached Sitaphul, the documents had to be submitted again at the army check-post for scrutiny. After climbing up a lengthy path that went sharply skywards, vast mountain ranges could be seen below. The Kali River once again diverged from the route. Seeing the other team members and the horses gathered on the hillside at a distance, I smelt trouble. The seriousness of the problem was understood when I looked through my binoculars. Sticky mud was lying in huge mounds on the path for about 1 km due to a massive landslide. One horse had slipped and fallen together with the rider. I could hear the echo of the loud cries of the horse attendants even from the distance. Wasting no time, Raju and I rushed up to the spot.

Getting closer, we were convinced of the gravity of the situation. The passage through the hill slope was about 3 to 3.5 feet wide. A big portion of a hill on the left side had come down and fallen on the path. Roughly for 1 km, hills of clay-like mud and medium-sized rocks were lying on the way, almost blocking the path. On the right side was a descending slope about 200 feet deep. Beyond it was a vast ground full of green grass. Each step on the wet soil led to slipping. It was hard to pull out the shoes from where they had sunk into the deep mud. Ours was a narrow escape because the landslide occurred just before we reached there. We proceeded fearfully, inch by inch, along the left side of the way, noting the horrible cracks in the mountains on that side. Even the horses turned back, unable to go forward. The man who didn't oblige when asked to get down from horseback was the one who had fallen down, together with the horse. Luckily, both were saved from plunging into the deep ravine since the legs of the horse were stuck in the mud.

Hand in hand, Raju and I moved carefully through the wet, muddy path. Raju placed firm pieces of rock on those dangerous slippery parts and thus strengthened the grip. What Raju did was invaluable help. Though the mud had swallowed our shoes up to our ankles, we somehow managed to get across without slipping and falling. Half of the travellers lost their shoes in the mud. Fearing a further landslide, we skipped the path after reaching a safe point and started walking through level land.

Again, the rain came down heavily. I got a feeling that disasters had been in wait all through the way. The prediction of the old man in Seethi made me more depressed. We had overcome other dangers but the possibility of landslides remained until we reached Gunji. A freezing wind was blowing from the mountains on the left side while we walked through the water pits on the grassy ground.

We reached Kangla after 4 p.m. On one side of the ground were high-growing forests. There were plenty of pine and cherry trees there. Even though it was raining, we found domestic animals grazing in the forest. It is here in this region that yaks are found in large numbers. We entered a dhaba (hotel) located on one side of the ground. We were totally depleted of energy because of the rain and cold. Hot tea was felt to be essential. Raju and I sat near the stove where a boy was frying sweet balls of wheat.

The hot wheat balls served were very tasty. Meanwhile, I got acquainted with the middle-aged owner of the dhaba and talked to him for some time.

Thakur Lal Singh was from a family that had a tradition and fame back in the Kumaon region. His father, Thakur Kedar Singh, was the main link in the India-Tibet trade from 1925 to 1962. He owned a large number of yaks and mules and had been an honest aide to the rich Bhotia people. The Bhotia girls were pretty, with golden-coloured skin. When they were brought to Garbiang from Tibet after marriage, the responsibility of making arrangements rested on the shoulders of Thakur Kedar Singh. Since marriage processions were difficult through the Lipulekh Pass, they had been arranged through other passes like Lampiya Dhura, Nuway Dhura, Lob Dhura, Unta Dhura, Jayanthi Dhura and Kungri Bingri Dhura. The scale of snowfall was different in different passes. The change of season decided the choice of pass. Those were days of prosperity. When the Chinese invasion of 1962 was taking place, Kedar Singh had been in Tibet. He was trapped there for months. When at last he could escape and come to India, he had lost most of his yaks and mules. The shock was intolerable.

When his masters shifted their residence to Dharchula, they invited Kedar Singh also. But he could not give up the mountains and their nostalgic fragrance. The ice-covered peaks, the uplifting changes in season, the sweet world of flowers, the crystal-clear water and the land he was born in—leaving them forever was not going to give him peace and harmony. Recalling his lost fortunes every minute of the day, Kedar Singh withdrew to the streets of Garbiang like an aged lion. But he was not ready to surrender his pride and individuality to anybody. Even in poverty, Kedar Singh was the hero of the villagers and they loved him very much. He strongly believed that a character of value was much greater than money.

'Vruththam Yagnena Samraksheth
Viththamaethi Cha Yathi Cha
Aksheeno Viththathaha Ksheeno
Vruththathasthu Hatho Hathaha'

(One should protect his character by all efforts. Money might come and go. One becoming short of money doesn't mean that he has become weak. But if one's character is lost, he is lost forever.)

When India increased military deployment in the Kumaon region after the Chinese invasion, the fortune of a young man named Thakur Lal Singh also became bright. He is a contractor now who brings daily necessities to the Indian Army. He travelled along with animals through the mountain ranges extending from Mangthi to Nabhidang. The dhaba he had been running was only for his dependants. Maybe because Raju told him that I was a writer and had published a book about my pilgrimages on foot en route to Kailash, Lal Singh didn't accept any money from me. He politely said that he would be blessed if even a small reference of his father was made in my book. When I asked for his opinion about the prediction of the old man in Seethi, Lal Singh replied that most times, the old man was right. We proceeded on the trip after thanking him and his family.

We walked fast in the continuing rain. Even though there were no difficult ascents, we were very cautious with our steps because landslides had been common in the area. The heavy rain made big cracks in the mountains. One couldn't say when the mountains would slide down. When we reached the vast area where the Kali and the Kuti rivers joined together, we could see the huts of the villagers of Gunji on the other side. It was past 6 p.m. when we reached the bridge near Gunji after leaving behind a village called Napalchu, where about forty families resided. The flow of the Kuti River was formidable. We reached the Gunji camp half an hour later.

Putting our wet clothes and shoes in the firewood store to dry, I went to the kitchen to have a glass of hot Horlicks. After talking to the liaison officer for a little while, I went to the camp shed.

The rain and fog had completely plunged Gunji into darkness. The surroundings were not visible. I would have to wait till the morning to learn whether there were any changes in the old Gunji.

The health of many of the pilgrims was not very good. There were wounds on those who had fallen from their horses. Mountain sickness had affected many. Two women pilgrims were suffering from high temperatures. Due to constant rain, it was not possible even to go to the doctor in the nearby ITBP camp. The liaison officer was utterly restless. Some members of the team suggested having an early dinner and retiring to bed immediately. The suggestion was accepted by all. After offering prayers in their own tents, everyone had food together.

Anything might happen at night if the rain continued on the same scale. The cooks said that a large portion of the land behind the camp had been broken and drawn by the Kuti River. It was shocking information. Similar rainfall had occurred two days before the Malpa tragedy of August 1998. But the difference was that it was the rainy season then.

When the generator was switched off, Gunji fell into the lap of darkness again. After saying my prayers, I got into the warm shelter of my bedding. My request to God then was to make the next day good.

6

The Rain in Gunji

Horrible sounds were the first thing I heard waking up from deep sleep. I was confused and bewildered. My first feeling was that the sound was of something falling. Gradually, I learnt that the sound came from the big pieces of ice falling along with the rain on the fibre sheets of the tents. The time was 4.30 a.m. sharp.

Enjoying the sunrise in Gunji during my last trip is an unforgettable memory. It is still there in my heart. During the present trip, I had intended to shoot the sight on a video camera. But the bad weather was an obstacle to movie shooting. I felt the severity of the heavy rain when I looked out of the open door. There had been a massive hailstorm along with the rain. In the low light, the ice pieces in the courtyard shone like crystals. The liaison officer had hinted the previous day that the journey might have to be cancelled if heavy rain continued. I also thought that that might be what was going to happen.

Since there was nothing left to do, I again took shelter in my bed. I lay thinking of many things. All journeys to the Himalayas might not end at the destination. Obstacles are quite normal. The climate in the Himalayas is unpredictable. There might be times when we would have to return. An ordinary tour would not give you the mental satisfaction that you get from travelling on foot through the hard routes. Many preparations, both physical and mental, were essential for the hazardous trip. We were travelling in search of a heritage that dated back centuries. Many people asked sarcastically what the satisfaction was of a Himalayan journey. Many others thought that travelling from Bodh Gaya to Varanasi in 45-degree temperature was a big adventure. The poet Kalidasa's words, '*Binna Ruchir Hee, Loka Ha*' (the world had varied taste) were the answer to all of them. There are many options for those who want to go on an adventurous trip. Think of all the heroic stories we read about crossing enormous oceans in small river boats and rowing boats. There are many modes of transport, including planes, in each continent suitable for making adventurous journeys. If the minimum qualification for an adventurous journey was 45-degree temperature, then the most suitable people to make such trips were the Indians living in Gulf countries. They who experienced the boiling heat in the Gulf really knew the meaning of the ordeal.

What actually was the relevance of the Himalayan journeys? The yogis had strongly averred that our true origin was from the *kevala* (isolated) status of the *nirapeksha* (absolute) condition preceding the *sapeksha* (relative) condition and those trips were our return journeys to the same kevala status. Man originated from God, became man in the middle and went back to God in the end. That was the *dwaitha* (dual) scheme of thought regarding human birth. According to the *adwaitha* (non-dual) scheme, man was always part of God. He only went back to Him in the end. The divinity of Earth stood as the abode of plants and all living things, including men. The Yajurveda said that the joining together of the molecules of water and prithvi (universe) caused the creation of the earth.

ADI KAILASH ROUTE MAP

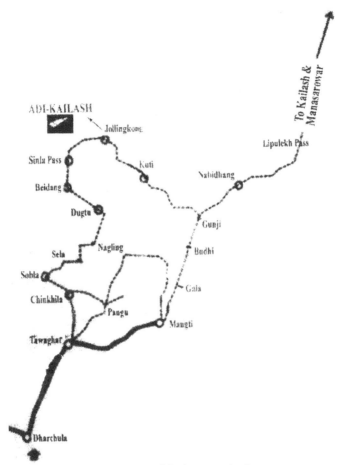

Source: Kumaon Mandal Vikas Nigam brochure

That was why water was called the Mother of Earth. Water sustained Earth. In the Vedas, water was assigned the status of motherhood.

'Yadhamoghamapaamantharuptham Beejamaja! Thwayaa
Athascharaacharam Viswam Prabhavasthasya Geeyasae'
—Kumarasambhavam, page 2–5, by Kalidasa

(Oh, Brahma, the living and non-living earth was born from the precious seeds you sowed in water! You are hailed as the creator of the world.)

If oxygen, the so-called life-giving air, were present in the atmosphere of ancient Earth, it surely would have become an obstacle for life to originate. Oxygen was an element capable of strong chemical reactions. In its presence, the first biological molecules that had simple structures would have broken up. Oxidation itself meant separation. Glucose was the source of energy in our body. It produced energy by breaking up and in the process, turned into carbon dioxide and water. Complex biological molecules would originate only when simple biological molecules turned dense (by joining one another) and reacted. Only then would the earliest particles of life take birth. Yes, it was apt to say that the first heartbeat of life began in water.

The seven rivers that were the basic source of water in India originated from the Himalayas. On the banks of those rivers arose the river valley civilization. God had devised the climate in India so as to maintain the snowfall constantly. The greatness was that no other place in the world had such an amazing climate control mechanism.

'Somaenaditya balina ha Somaena Prithvee mahee
Adho Nakshathrano Maeshamupasthae Soma Ahitha ha'
—Adharva Veda

(Those places would be cold where sunlight didn't fall sufficiently due to the shade of the earth. Those would also be cooler where sunlight reached horizontally. In the absence of the rays of the sun, the level of heat would be lower and levels of coldness higher. In such circumstances, the elements and molecules of physical matter and masses would solidify. Their strength and abundance also would go up. When they were struck by brilliant sun rays, vapour would arise and atoms would become stronger.)

The route of the movement of the sun was from Australia in the south to the Himalayas in the north. About three-fourths of that area belonged to the Indian region. On the other hand, if the sun moved from the north to the south, the Himalayan area would be far from it or would be devoid of sunlight. It would cause wide and strong snowfall.

Now, during the sun's movement from the south to the north, the Indian region would become hotter and ice in the Himalayas would start melting. On the contrary, when the movement of the sun was towards the south, the sky would become cloudy in India, causing heavy rain and strong snowfall. The heat of the sun would thus be reduced and the abundance of ice in the Himalayas preserved.

The covering of ice in the Himalayas was everlasting because, during summer, sunrays fell from a long distance away on the region. And when the sun came closer, it would be raining then. The main cause of that phenomenon was the monsoon climate.

What would happen if the monsoon was not there?

The huge stock of ice in the Himalayas would start melting and the whole of North India would sink in flood water. The Ganga basin, with a population of 300 million, would disappear from the earth. Iceless central Himalayas with Kailash in the centre, and also its west and east ends with no ice on them, could not be imagined. If that happened, the changes taking place in the physical conditions of the Indian continent would be horrifying. The rivers flowing with plenty of water in all seasons and the strength of their flow, big lakes including

Manasarovar (the holy lake in the Himalayas) and endless ice streams—all of them would disappear from the earth forever. With that, the state of godly grace that had been prevailing for thousands of centuries would vanish to a large extent. But that would never happen. Six manvantaras had already passed. They were Svayambhuva Manu, Swarochisha Manu, Auttami Manu, Tamasa Manu, Raivata Manu and Chakshusha Manu. The seventh manvantara of Vaivaswata Manu was going on presently. The manvantaras to come are Savarni Manu, Daksa Savarni Manu, Brahma Savarni Manu, Dharma Savarni Manu, Rudra Savarni Manu, Raucya or Deva Savarni Manu and Indra Savarni Manu. The grace of the Himalayas must remain at least for that period.

Each manvantara has one manu, the progenitor of mankind, who is created by Lord Brahma. A manvantara lasts for the lifetime of its manu. When he dies, Brahma creates another manu and thus another manvantara. This goes on. Fourteen manvantaras constitute one kalpa, which is one day of Brahma.

According to the Bhagavatham, it has been 196,85,29,082 years since the Vedas came into existence. Those many years have also passed since creation occurred. It was from the Himalayas that modern civilization got the Vedas through God's sermon. The rishis, sages and saints living on the riverbanks and the caves of that icy land wrote interpretations of the Vedas. Their efforts to bring Brahmanams, Samhithas, Aranyakams, Upanishads and Brahmasoothras to the people were really great. The epics Ramayana and Mahabharata and also the eighteen Puranas penetrated deep into the minds of ordinary people. Great poets like Kalidasa and others found a permanent place in the hearts of people through their poems and dramas.

There were five fortunes within the reach of every person born in India, the land of sages, hermits and spiritualists.

Seeing the Himalayas, bathing in the Ganga River, hearing the Bhagavatham, reading the Mahabharata and learning the Bhagavat Gita were those fortunes. One who could not experience at least one of those five great fortunes suffered incomparable loss and suffering.

Motherhood and fatherhood had equal status in the birth of babies. What one acquired from seeing the Himalayas and travelling through the Himalayas was this true vision of fatherhood and motherhood. That too was, of course, the greatness of the Himalayas.

When the time was past six, the servants served tea and biscuits. They informed us that the sky would be clear last by 10 a.m. to continue the journey. But I thought that the chances of that happening were low. After completing our morning routines in some way or another in the rain, we rested in our tents. According to the travel schedule, one day was for rest on the way up and one day was for rest on the way down. That was to compensate for any possible hurdles arising out of exigencies like climatic changes, sickness or accidents. Therefore, staying at Gunji even for one full day would not affect the original programme of travel. Yet, staying for more than one day was not possible since the first batch of the Kailash-Manasarovar pilgrims was to reach immediately after us. They would have already reached Gala as per the travel plan. When we reached Gunji after Om Dharshan at Nabhidang, they would have started off for the next place, Kalapani. If the heavy rain continued, the entire original programme would be in jeopardy. Grave consequences would also result if landslides occurred. We decided to please God by reading the Bhagavatham.

At a little past nine, we were informed that breakfast was ready. Because the food tent was full of rainwater, we stuck together in a tiny room near the kitchen and had a breakfast of wheat soup and pea roast. I found the breakfast to be very delicious because of my hunger. The storeroom of firewood on the other side of the kitchen was rather large in size. The camp manager informed us that the fire might be lit there for us to sit around and lessen the chill. We could dry our wet clothes and shoes too. So we assembled there in small groups. The cooks and their aides helped us cut the firewood into small pieces. The horse attendants of the Tourism Department were also there. We learnt some horrible news from them. The water level in the river had risen beyond safe limits and many parts of the banks had fallen into the river. The colour of the eastern mountains situated in front of the camp had also changed due to the absorption of the heavy rain. This meant that the mountains held a lot of water and that might explode at any time, causing landslides. Hearing so from the horse attendants, everyone became silent. The big mountains, standing together as if pasted to one, another coming down en masse would result in a tragedy more terrible than the Malpa catastrophe. The village named Gunji might disappear forever.

The rain had not stopped even after 10 a.m. The dark atmosphere prevailed and the chill was at its peak. Sitting beside the fire in the storeroom all curled up, I thought that the rain was falling down in a rhythm and that rhythm resembled the Hindustani raga, Megha. The clashing sound of raindrops falling on the tin sheets of the roof felt like the accompanying drum beating. When we received information that the journey was postponed, I felt nothing unnatural. How could one go in such an endless downpour?

Around noon, horrible news spread in the camp that two of our fellow passengers, the soldier and his wife, were missing since the past evening. The day before, the man had told the liaison officer that since he was a soldier, there were facilities for him and his wife to reside in the ITBP camp and the officer had permitted them to go. Also, he had worked in the region for three years earlier. The man always had been showing special interest in our health problems from Gala. Our team members had much respect for him since he had worked in the area before and also made medical facilities available to us whenever needed. His wife had a sweet voice and always sat in front for the prayers.

Two ladies in the team suffered from high fever and since their temperatures were not coming down, the liaison officer went to consult the doctor in the army camp around 10 a.m. He told the army doctor that the previous day, the soldier in the travel team, claiming to have medical knowledge, had treated the patients and had given them medicines. Since that soldier, along with his wife, had come to the army camp the day before and had been there in the camp at that time, the liaison officer told the doctor that he could call him and ask about the medicines given. The army doctor, Dr V.K. Singh, said that it was a grave fault of the soldier to have treated the patients on his own without consulting the doctor. He warned that he would recommend action against both the liaison officer and the soldier. He ordered the security guards to bring the soldier in. But surprisingly, we came to know that the soldier was not there. Ladies were not permitted to stay in the army camp and so there was no chance of the soldier bringing his wife to the camp and staying together without attracting the attention of the security guards.

If so, where did the soldier and his wife go?

Wearing raincoats, the ITBP officers came to our camp. Ignoring the rain, they ran all around and collected details. Nobody moved, even though the message was that lunch was ready. Everybody seemed frozen. After the army doctor's examination, it was confirmed that both ladies were suffering from jaundice. Since jaundice was contagious, the patients were shifted to the far corners of the tent. When I came to know that a Kerala soldier had come to give drips to the patients, I got acquainted with him. P.V. Chandran was a pharmacist in the ITBP and belonged to Nileswaram in northern Kerala. He had been transferred to Gunji only two months back. To understand the happiness of meeting a man from our own locality on a mountain slope over 4500 km away, and that too at a place where human habitation was very low, one had to go through such an experience himself.

We departed, telling ourselves that if the rain stopped, we would meet again in the evening. After lunch, I went to bed.

The endless rain and severe chill led all my friends to fall into a deep sleep. But I couldn't close my eyes even for a second. Sleeping at noon was not my practice. Still, anyone would fall asleep in the atmosphere that was hanging around. I was thinking of many things. The first thought naturally was that of the missing soldier and his wife. Most of the camp members believed that they might have met with an accident. A few believed that they might have been kidnapped and yet others believed that they might have fallen into the river and been swept away (they had gone to see the flow of water in the river and might have slipped). I felt that all such thoughts were immature.

If they had been kidnapped, who could have done that? The innocent villagers? Or the military people there? Twenty-five years had gone by since the Kailash-Manasarovar journey was started on that route. So many women had passed through the Lipulekh Pass. Many women who got disqualified at Gunji had stayed there for more than two weeks. Nobody had heard of any problem so far. Anyone who travelled that route would experience the invaluable and appreciable service rendered by the military, especially to the women. The distance between the camps of KMVN and ITBP was only 1 furlong. The security guards' office was very close to the main gate. A group of armed soldiers always stood guard at the gate. Such being the state of things, the soldier and his wife might have gone anywhere, but never to the ITBP camp.

The liaison officer said that the couple went off in the evening after 6 when heavy rain was pouring. Nobody would be able to identify someone who moved through heavy rain and fog wearing a raincoat. And no one would go to watch and enjoy the horrible flow of the river in such a climate. The soldier knew the area well. Chances were that he had gone to the nearby village along with his wife to spend the night together.

Still, things didn't connect properly. Couples were rare on tough pilgrimages like ours. Even if there were, they preferred to stay and sleep separately. It was a pilgrimage and not a pleasure trip. Adhering to the rituals in such kinds of journeys was very important. The state of celibacy was one such thing that had to be strictly kept up. That was why women were advised not to take part in such journeys during their menstrual periods. If they were very insistent, they would be allowed, yes, but had to be extremely cautious and careful. Individual tents were provided for women in every camp.

If the soldier and his wife had gone out, the reason had to be different.

Villagers permitted the travellers whom they knew to sleep in their houses. They knew the missing soldier. Maybe he and his wife performed the 'disappearance' drama from Gala. I felt that the truth would come out if an inquiry was made in the horse attendants' camp.

The rain stopped around 3 p.m. and the dark sky slowly began to become clear. The sun came out from its hideout of many days and shone on the icy mountain peaks.

Meanwhile, the fear of a tragedy befalling the soldier and his wife was gone and the real reason behind their disappearance became public. Everyone was stunned to know that that lady was not his wife. His original wife and two children had been peacefully living back at home. The man and the woman had fallen in love through SMS and email messages. It was his idea to join the pilgrimage team to travel and live together for about twenty-five days. At Dharchula and also during the Gala-Buddhi travel, both had gone away, hiding from other team members and spending time together. Going out of the Buddhi camp, they had shared their affection on the veranda of a deserted house in the village. Since he was a military man, no one had suspected him. The horse attendant of the soldier already had some doubts about the couple. It was he who had drawn the attention of the old man at Seethi to the matter and shared his suspicions. Again, it was the same man who passed information he got to the military inquiry team that the missing soldier and his 'wife' were found living together in a village in Gunji.

Some young men came forward to physically 'handle' the soldier but the liaison officer pacified them diplomatically.

The power and influence of the virtue called patience was high. Patience was a good medicine even for physical ailments. Dr France Boyan argued that when anger and hatred flood the brain, the nervous system prompts the two halves of the brain. When one half provokes us, the other pacifies us. This leads to a loss in mental balance and variations in heartbeat. This is why Sreemath Bhagavatham advises us not to lose self-control.

'Sathyam Dhaeya Thapa ha Soucham
Thithikshesha Samo Dhama ha
Ahimsa Brahmacharyam cha
Thyaga ha Swadhyaya Arjavam'

(Truth, kind-heartedness, meditation, external and internal purity, patience, logical prudence, self-control, self-restraint, non-violence, celibacy, sacrifice, chanting

of mantras, leading life on the right path,
satisfaction with whatever we have)

The liaison officer informed us that the soldier would be held back at the ITBP camp and would not take part in the journey henceforth. But the lady could not be sent back and there was no other option than to take her along with the team. The plight of that woman thereafter was pathetic. Even the women members of the team isolated her. The team's behaviour towards her was like that towards a cruel animal.

Was it just a coincidence that nature became generous when the problem was solved? Or was it superhuman interference? It could be taken either way. All depended on one's own belief. But one thing was sure. The holiness of the Himalayas was not to be harmed. If so, bad things were bound to happen. This was the experience of all time. Could we push into oblivion Malpa where similar circumstances led to a great tragedy?

The only way of finding relief then was to believe that it was God's wish.

After 4 p.m., I went to the ITBP camp and met Mr Chandran. There was nobody in the consulting room and so we could sit and talk at length. After having strong tea from the mess, I went to see the telecommunication system and visited the room where it was installed. There were no Malayalees there except Chandran. The officer and soldiers who were on duty received me with respect. Many of them had been to Adi Kailash on patrolling duty. I felt a little sad when they firmly said that the Adi Kailash ranges could not be viewed from Gunji. I had made such a reference in my first work. It was a soldier who showed me the ranges then. The soldiers who had been members of the earlier patrolling team told me that it was 40 km from Gunji to Adi Kailash and the route was extremely difficult and perilous. I felt that there was truth in what they had said. I spent some time there making friends with the soldiers.

The ITBP was a paramilitary wing of the Home Department of the Government of India. They were not under the Defence Department. There were clear UN directives regarding the size and strength of the military a nation could maintain that depended on the population and geographical area. Those directives were intended to prevent attacks on other nations by military-rich nations. Considering the geographical diversity and high rate of population growth, the size of the military under the Defence Ministry was quite insufficient. To cope with that, paramilitary forces such as the ITBP, Border Security Force (BSF), Central Reserve Police Force (CRPF), etc., were formed. Their main responsibility was to protect the borders. Extra duties might also be assigned. But they were not paid the same as the Indian Army. The paramilitary forces were doing tougher jobs but the complaint was that the latter were paid less. A government had to work under many international controls. Maybe those controls were a factor in the others not getting what the Indian Army got. But in matters of service and dedication, the paramilitary forces stood head-to-head with the Indian Army. Exercises and parades were almost the same for both. The ITBP, however, held the first place in protecting our country's borders. They guarded the country day and night, camping at inhospitable heights in Leh, Ladakh, the Siachen Glacier, etc., where human life was nearly unsustainable. The temperature there could go down to as much as minus 35 degrees Celsius.

No doubt, the paramilitary forces were not different from the Indian Army in matters of service or dedication to duty. Generally, it was thought unfair that they were treated differently. Allowances and concessions, like exemption from building tax, canteen facilities, etc., granted to army men were not given to those from the paramilitary wings. My opinion was that those soldiers who had spent the golden age of their lives in the mountain ranges and glaciers, protecting the country's borders, deserved honour.

By the way, I was very proud to learn that Malayalam was used as the secret code in wireless messaging during the Indo–Pak war. It was common in wars to catch wireless messages of enemies and thus leak their moves. The officers had chosen Malayalam because Pakistan was familiar with most North Indian languages. Also, understanding Malayalam messages was not difficult for Indian soldiers because there were a large number of Malayalees in the Indian Army.

It was true that tactics won wars.

I got acquainted with Dr V.K. Singh through Chandran. As our conversation went on, I told the doctor about the two books I had written. He was very interested. When I gave him one copy of the book, *Thapobhoomi Uttarakhand* (Uttarakhand, the Land of Meditation), kept in my shoulder bag, the doctor turned over the pages very curiously. His first comment was that the book had international standards in layout and printing.

He had read many English books on the Himalayas. Also, he had inquired and educated himself about the divine sages. He opined that foreigners were far ahead of us Indians in that matter. He went on uttering the names of many English books one by one quite easily, as if picked from the store of his brain. He specially mentioned works like *Living with the Himalayan Masters* by Swami Rama, *A Search in Secret India* by Paul Brunton, etc. I had also read those books and was truly astonished. I should also mention two other books I had read, *Same Soul, Many Bodies* and *Many Lives, Many Masters*, both by Dr Brian Weiss. They are based on the concept of rebirth after death.

The Vedas and Upanishads emphatically stated that the soul never perished and birth-death-birth was a continuous process. Our knowledge of the Himalayan sages who had unbelievable abilities was very limited. Some people even talked of them contemptuously. That minority asked whether such things were possible in the modern age. One never met Himalayan sages when they were on relaxed or fun trips to the four *dhams* (abodes) of the Garhwal Himalayas or Kailash-Manasarovar. Don't take me as boasting but I had met many holy sages on my Himalayan travels. I had mentioned this in many of my works.

Some people undertook Himalayan journeys only to enjoy intoxication and engage in sexual activities. My request to them was please do such things elsewhere. Spare the Himalayas, the birthplace of culture and civilization.

The way to eternal liberty was by making those trips with dedication and devoted prayers to God. Arrogance must be kept away. The pilgrim traveller should understand that their birth was merely an ignorable, tiny thing in comparison with the immeasurable universe. They must, hence, assign a godly status to nature and all its contents and bow their head before them. The Bhagavatham tells us the same.

'Kham Vayumagnim Salilam Mahim cha
Jyotheemshi Sathwani Dhiso Dhrumaadheen
Sarilsa Mudramscha Haraessareeram
Yaethkincha Bhootham Pranamaedhananya ha'

(We should not consider air, fire, water, earth, sources
of light, insects, plants, trees, rivers, oceans and every other
mass as alien but should bow our heads before
them, considering them as forms of God.)

Our knowledge regarding the holy sages of the Himalayas was not something new. It went back centuries. There was no limit to the number of great travellers who had gone to the Himalayas and stayed there for years and years to conduct first-hand studies and write about what they saw. Guru Nitya Chaitanya Yati, in his autobiography, also narrated a similar experience. When Jawaharlal Nehru was the prime minister, a committee had been appointed to study those sages with divine powers and submit a report on the matter. Nitya Chaitanya Yati was one of the committee members. After Nehru's death, Gulzarilal Nanda took over the project. Yati was a director of the reconstituted Psychic and Spiritual Research Institute. Their effort was to carefully study the variations in wavelengths of alpha, beta and gamma waves passing through the conscious brains of the sages with the help of electroencephalography (EEG). But the question was whether true sages would yield to such experiments. After his experiments, which went on for five years, Guru Nitya Chaitanya Yati announced that he could find only four or five true sages with real qualities. He openly stated that 95 per cent of saffron-clad sages were mere fakes. Reaching the dwellings of divine sages was the real task and fate played a real role there.

Romola Butalia was one such woman who came out victorious at the end of such an endeavour. She obtained a doctorate from the Delhi School of Economics and had been working as the executive editor of a magazine called *India Travelogue*.

Dr Butalia wrote:

'The ancient traditions and practices had always been preserved by the purest meditation of the great Himalayan Sages. That was revealed to those who had come in worship of the wisdom of the divine Sages and also to those who had proceeded in firm steps to trek through the hardest Himalayan paths. There were natural obstacles to prevent the journey of those who had jolly come on fake devotion. Godly spirit could not be exposed for satisfying mere curiosity.

'Holiness was never a thing for sale. There were no advertisements or hoardings to attract the public. And also, there were no predictions by prophets, big gatherings or elevated podiums for speakers to talk. Ancient and traditional spiritual systems had been persisting in the infinitesimal elements hidden in souls. The questions I often heard were this: Were the saintly sages real? Did the divine births exist actually?

'I heard the present generation crying in agony owing to the destructors of culture, the atheists and the hate of traditional priesthood. But people who had divine powers achieved through deep and long meditation were still there among us. But we didn't recognize them. That was because our perception of life was such. Our only aim in life was worldliness or physical happiness. That was actually the fact why we had forgotten the importance of the godly souls' existence.'

I returned from the ITBP camp past 6 p.m. After presenting a signed copy of *Thapobhoomi Uttarakhand* to Chandran, I bade him goodbye, promising to meet him the next day.

Gunji and its surroundings were shining under the gorgeous twilight as if nature was blessing them in all generosity. The wounds of rain had begun disappearing. The curved branches of trees were now standing upright. As all the rainwater that had fallen on them had flowed away, the tiny plants and grass were now standing erect. Birds like mynahs (Acridotheres tristis) and little sparrows had gone out happily in search of food. The cattle wandered around making happy noises. Wagging their tails, the dogs stood around the pilgrims with hopeful eyes. Smoke from fires had been rising from the huts of the villagers in the mountain ranges. Standing in small groups in front of the camp, the pilgrims shared snacks and drinks.

The obstructions had all been cleared away. It was sure now that our endeavour would bear fruits. I hummed in a low voice poet Kalidasa's words,

> *'Avvyakshepo Bhavishyanthya*
> *Karyasidherhi Lakshanam'*
> —Raghuvamsam, pages 6–10

(The state of no obstacles is an indication of the result that will be achieved)

Everyone participated in the prayer held at the Kali temple. With the sweet music of the temple bells tolling together in the background, we all chanted bhajans and *stotras* (hymns). The prayer ended with an aarti with lighted lamps. After consuming the balance of the offered pudding and sweets, we returned to the camps after 8 p.m. It was still light.

In quite an agreeable mood, all of us ate together the lavish dinner comprising roti, boiled rice, potato curry, ladies' finger sabji and vermicelli pudding. After spending some time preparing my luggage for the next day's journey, I got ready to sleep after 9.30 p.m. The Om Dharshan of Nabhidang was fully in my mind while crawling into my bed. I planned to wake up at 4.30 a.m. and see the sunrise in Gunji.

7

Nabhidang

I had earlier told my fellow travellers about the superior beauty of the sunrise at Gunji. We all arose at around 4 in the morning and got ready to see the beautiful sight. Though the rain had gone and thin clouds lit up the sky, the sun's rays came down hesitatingly. Fog was covering the rows of mountain peaks. The rays of the baby sun, however, made the whole area bright. Yet, I was desperate. The fog had to go completely for the south-west icy mountains to be decorated with the enchanting seven colours. We waited till 5 a.m. but it was still foggy. So we decided to quit.

The distance to Nabhidang from Gunji was 18 km. The doctor expressed his dissatisfaction over our direct trek to Nabhidang, skipping the Kalapani camp. But since the Kailash-Manasarovar team would arrive right after we left, there was no other choice. An expert team under the guidance of the foreign affairs ministry had decided on the camps en route to Kailash-Manasarovar after extensive studies, discussions and observations. In tough journeys like those, the body needed to be prepared so that it could acclimatize. If not, the consequences would be grave. Above a height of 12,000 feet, the atmospheric pressure would decrease and we would also feel the air getting thinner. Unless our bodies were adapted to handle such changes in nature, journeys of this kind would be impossible.

The pilgrims should climb up 11,000 feet or so while going to the four dhams of the Garhwal Himalayas. Naturally, a question arose as to why such systems and procedures were not observed in those journeys. The four dham journeys were undertaken mostly by vehicle. One had to walk only the distance of some 6 km to Yamunotri (the origin of the Yamuna River) and 14 km to Kedarnath. Those who visit Gomukh (the terminus of the Gangotri glacier from where the Bhagirathi River, one of the primary sources of the Ganga River, originated) must travel an additional 19 km on foot. Such journeys were organized in such a way that pilgrims left the hilltops as fast as they could after spending only one or two days in each dham. The duration was very short. But the Kailash-Manasarovar and Adi Kailash-Om Mountain expeditions took more than one month and hence, the pilgrims had to stay for longer in the high mountains and hills. Living for days in such alien circumstances would force the body to react adversely and that was why some systems and procedures had to be implemented.

After praying at the Kali temple inside the ITBP camp, we set off for Nabhidang at 8 a.m. sharp. Those who travelled on horses with their helpers walked in front. Luggage-carrying horses, horse helpers and soldiers followed next. The last was us, the five travellers on foot. The soldiers accompanying us were on patrolling duty. We were the first team that season on the Om Mountain pilgrimage. For that reason, all the soldiers had assembled to bid us farewell.

Once we were out of the army camp, the journey proceeded by the side of the Kali River. Due to the constant rain of previous days, the path was slippery throughout. The journey was harder because of the wet mud and the slippery surface. We were afraid to see the level of water in the river and the violent flow. The thin, 1-foot-wide pathway by the riverside was on the edge of the mountains. The landslides had caused heavy heaps of mud deposited on the way. We had to walk over those dirt hills and place each step very cautiously. There was a chance of sliding down and plunging into the angry river. We found that in many places, landslides had occurred just before our arrival. The smell of freshly fallen mud still lingered. At many places, our horses slipped dangerously but always escaped only because of sheer luck. I prayed hard all through the 2 km of dangerous curves and sharp turns.

It was a great relief to escape the river and enter a vast meadow. The place was full of bright green grass. The devadaru and pine trees grew at full height along the borders of the meadow. The flowering shrubs on the hillsides and rock clusters scattered among them made the place lovely. Though the sun's rays rising from the eastern mountains made the morning bright, the chill was growing. Raju and I climbed up the steep path without any difficulty, enjoying the sweet sound of birds coming from the Nepal forests on the other side of the river. Since the horses walked fast and at ease with high energy, the pilgrims riding them were far ahead of us. The other travellers too were long distances in front. Recurring landslides had spread sharp pieces of rock all over. It was a painful journey but we walked cautiously along one side and then reached a vast valley. Here, we met the other team members, who were resting and having food. Both KMVN employees and army men were making tea. The tasty smell of raw potato frying in boiling oil filled the area. It was joyful to see the thinly cut potato when dropped in boiling oil blooming like flowers and dancing like fish. Seeing that the tea and potato chips would take more time to be prepared, I walked into a lone corner and lay fully stretched out on the green grass. The sky was blue. A blue fog hung over the hills, which stood like boundary walls on the horizon. The tiny pieces of ice resting on the tops of trees in the mountain valleys shone in the sunlight like a thousand torches. All around were numerous mountain ranges that might have been formed over ages. Mountains were the primary artwork of nature, the holiest of them being the Himalayas. It was said that since they reflected life, mountains carried all the invisible qualities of mankind. Incomparable energy was contained in and around mountains. We should stand aloof, staying away from everything in life, and study the mountains for a long time, regardless of day or night. Then only could we reach the sacred feeling of delightful eccentricity and lose ourselves. Only then could we swim away from the sea of material stress and place ourselves at the peak of spiritual ecstasy. Those mountains denoted the difference between being God and being human. It was for the same reason that sages, rishis and other seekers of knowledge came to the Himalayas for peace and solitude, giving up all the comforts of material life.

In 1890, Swami Vivekananda, the rishi of the modern era, was filled with spiritual elation at seeing the beautiful mountain ranges of Almora.[1] After engaging in deep meditation there for a long time, the swami told a disciple: 'Hello Mr Gangadhar, it was one of the most esteemed moments in my life that I went through. I could get the answer to one of the most perplexing questions in my life there under the banyan tree. I understood the oneness of the body soul and the eternal soul. They were not two, Gangadhar, but one. Everything in the infinite universe subsisted nowhere but in the infinitesimal universe called the human body. I saw the boundless universe in one single micro atom.'

After building an Adwaitha Ashram (hut) on the top of the Almora mountains, the swami said, 'Adwaitha is the only ideology that leads to the eternal liberation of man by giving him all powers, keeping him away from all sorts of blind beliefs and making him active by imparting him with tolerance and energy. For spreading the message of that lone truth and aiming to lighten the burden of mankind and uplift individual life through the principle of perfect and independent man we started the Adwaitha ashram in the heavenly land of the Himalayas.'

Hearing the whistle from a soldier, I awakened from my reverie and had chips and tea with friends. I also distributed sweets that I had brought from home. Rejuvenated and energized, we continued our travel. Raju and I walked slowly behind the soldiers. We entered a dense forest. The cold increased with each upward step. Sunlight was dim because of the thick fog inside the forest. It was like night. Parts of the way were frozen and icy water flowed down from the hilltops. It was very painful for us to walk through. My mind was peaceful for I was enjoying nature, the bushes in the forest, the formations of rock going up and the lovely noise of small birds echoing over all other noises. Seeing the tedious path from a distance and the sharp curve at the top, we sat on a rock to rest for a while. We consumed biscuits and cashew nuts and drank glucose water. Then we climbed the steep path slowly and reached the top exhausted. The underside of the rocky path was hollow owing to the heavy river flow. We had to cross the cracked rock inch by inch to reach the top. Since landslides were common in the area, the journey through that part of the land would strike fear into anyone's heart.

We reached Kalapani before noon. I went to the Kali temple there to pray to the goddess and to give offerings. Then I glanced over the area. I didn't find any change in Kalapani from what I had seen on my earlier visit. Maybe because the pilgrim season had started, the army camps were freshly painted. Also, there were new camp sheds. The rest house we constructed during our last visit and the meadow around it were maintained beautifully.

Everyone should bow their heads before the soldiers in respect for their sacrifices to safeguard the country and for their willingness to give up even their lives for the love of it. That was why we had decided then to honour the soldiers and present them with a gift. Fund collection was my responsibility. I could satisfactorily fulfil my duty by amassing about Rs 14,000. By the time I returned to Kalapani after the Kailash-Manasarovar journey, the construction of the rest house had been completed. The liaison officer at the time, Dr Madhup Mohta, IFS, inaugurated the building and handed it over to the army. Sipping hot tea that the soldiers had given me respectfully, I recalled the day's programme of events. The chief of the ITBP, Baji Singh, had presided over the function and the speech Dr Mohta delivered was very nice. The army men, the employees of KMVN and the pilgrims were sitting on the ground. Representing the pilgrims, Mr Harihar, the army doctor and I sat on the podium. The large audience sat in silence with bowed heads and listened to the song we sang at the end of the programme. Many, including Baji Singh, were seen wiping tears (in a meeting held in Delhi to pay homage to the soldiers who had lost their lives in the 1962 Indo-China war, Prime Minister Jawaharlal Nehru was the main participant. Bowing his head, Nehruji wiped tears with his handkerchief after hearing the famous song, '*Ae Mere Watan Ke Logon*', sung by Lata Mangeshkar. The large group of people assembled there also joined him). We had also sung the same song, meaning that all of us should at least once remember the sacrifices of our soldiers and shed at least a tear for them.

While going to the mess run by KMVN at Kalapani, I felt uneasy. The other team members were resting after having eaten. After having my food, I wandered around Kalapani for some time. I intended to dive into the pool of old memories. I stood motionless for a short while in front of the high

rock I had climbed on then at midnight to view and enjoy
the full moon. Above that rock, at the east-south side, was
the mountain peak where Sage Vyasa was said to have done
thapass (deep and concentrated meditation extending for
centuries). We could see the entrance of the cave in the centre
of the peak where the great sage did the thapass. I had thought
many times about why I had come there alone at midnight
and sat on the rock or what had tempted me to do so. The full
moon, showering milky light, and the silver mountains of the
Himalayas imbibing that grace, were the two things that took
over my imagination and set it soaring. On rare occasions,
I happened to see the sights again, but what remained in my
heart was my first experience at Kalapani. Each journey was
bringing me closer and closer to nature. All those experiences
had influenced my work greatly. I returned to the camp after
bowing my head before the rock that stood lifeless outwardly
but carried pulsating life inside.

Sometime after 1.30 p.m., the team restarted the journey
with Nabhidang as its destination. Since the Kali River
originated at Kalapani, the fear of it was not in our minds on
the journey thence. We climbed up the heights, watching and
enjoying the vast meadows, budding little plants, blooming
bushes and icy mountains spread around like fortresses. After
travelling the part of the route alongside the low water of the
Pankha River, we rested for some time. We were at a height
of 14,000 feet and deficiency of oxygen was evident. Many of
us had stomach disorders and some others vomited. When we
reached the banks of the Lipu Gad River, we halted to have
tea. Rest was essential for some of us. The cold was nearly
unbearable. The mountains around were invisible because of
the thick cover of fog.

When the KMVN staff began preparing tea, I went to
the valleys beyond the bushes along with the horse aides. The

area was full of medicinal plants. I had narrated it in detail in my first work, *Uttarakhandiloode* (Through Uttarakhand). The practice of unlawfully transporting medicinal plants from there to Tibet had stopped over the past two to three years. Whatever the reasons behind that, I felt it was a praiseworthy initiative. The horses were very enthusiastic and energetic. I shared their happiness by standing beside them and joyfully watching them eat grass.

Energized afresh after tea and biscuits, we walked slowly along the banks of the Lipu Gad River. It was not hard since the way was long and gently sloping upward. I was now familiar with how to control my breath and let it go. So I didn't find any difficulty at all while walking. The river was full of Siva Lingam (symbols of Lord Siva)-shaped stones coming down from the Om Mountains. There were all sizes of stones, from tiny to big, having different divine shapes and sizes. I was really astonished to see the shape of a big stone found in the centre of the river. The black stone was perfectly shaped and polished like a Siva Lingam and there were three lines on its head, as if somebody had drawn it with holy ash! The words, '*Om namah Sivaya!*' came out of my mouth involuntarily. When I was arranging the camera to take a clear snap of it, a strong current knocked it down and it rolled away. I didn't know how the river, which was so far flowing calmly, suddenly acquired that strength. I followed the divine stone for some distance, walking along the edge of the river. But the flow was downwards and I had to stop. I helplessly watched the stone floating away. The divine stone had a pre-assigned destination and it would only stop there!

After climbing up yet another long path, I found a vast ground underside. Going down, rocks hindered the sight. But gradually, those hindrances got out of sight and camp sheds became visible. But everyone became disappointed because the much-awaited sight of Om was hidden under the heavy cover of mist. The disappointment was doubled when the soldiers told us that the ice had been hindering the vision of Om for the past three to four days. As per the schedule, we had to begin the return trip at 9 the next morning and reach Gunji in the evening. The journey would be fruitful only if we got the dharshan of Om before the next morning.

It was nearly 5 p.m. Enjoying potato chips and hot tea, we all sat on the ground in small groups with hopeful eyes. We expected that we would surely have the holy Om Dharshan since the daylight lasted for longer in the mountains. I used the occasion to share with my friends the knowledge of the one-letter universe called 'Om'.

'Veda ha Pramanam Smruthaya ha Pramanam
Dharmartha Yuktham Vachanam Pramanam.'

(Vedas and Smruthis are philosophies. So is a word that implies *dharmartham* [according to right or rule or duty].)

Thoughts based on the Vedas, Smruthis, Upanishads and ethics made the foundation of ancient Indian civilization. If you believe this, you could say that the letter Om was pronounced as the letter form of God, the Almighty (Para Brahma) or like a statue symbolizing Him. It was also said that worship of Om would eventually lead to the liberation of the soul for eternity. The Katopanishad made it clear that the letter Om was the summation of what the Vedas reflected, what meditation talked about and for the achievement of which the sages and yogis observed the state of celibacy. Lord Krishna also summarized that in the Bhagavat Gita.

'Yadhaksharam Vedhavidho Vadhanthi
Vishanthi Yadruthayo Veetharaga ha

Yadhishchantho Brahmacharyam Charanthi
Thaththe Padham Samgrahena Pravakshyae'

(What the great people who know the essence
of the Vedas call immortal and what the sages who have
given up sexual desire and anger attain and after wanting
to learn what they observe in a state of celibacy, I shall
tell you that state of affairs in brief.)

Om was the ultimate and everlasting universe. One who
worshipped God chanting Om entered the world of the gods.
It was said that prayer was a bow, the soul an arrow and God,
the target. The attentive devotee had to hit the target with
their arrow. Yes, they should become God. Sage Pippalada
clearly explained Om to his favourite disciple Satyakama
(Prashnopanishad): 'Thus Om was not anything different
from my ultimate Lord, Para Brahma Parameswara (Siva). Om
was both the Para Brahma (ultimate God) and the Virata Rupa
(the omni-form). That was why Om was called the other God.
One who worshipped Virata Rupa of Lord Siva by chanting,
remembering and thinking Om, one's body and soul would
merge with any organ of Virata Rupa as one chose. One who
worshipped Poorna Brahma Purushothama, the essence and
soul of Om (Poorna Brahma = complete God; Purushothama =
Vishnu), one's body and soul merged with Poorna Brahma
Purushothama. The first sound of the Om mantra was Rig
Veda Swarupa. It was related to Mother Earth. Hence, one who
meditated with Om in mind could again enter the mantras
of Rig Veda into one's body physique and when one took a
new birth, one would be saintly capable of doing profound
meditation with an unadulterated state of celibacy and virtuous
deeds. One's life then would be astonishingly prosperous.'
This was also what the Bhagavatham told the world.

'Ahimsa, Sathyama Krodhama Nrishamsyam,
Dhama ha Shama ha
Aarjavam Chaiva, Rajendra Nischitham Dharmalakshanam.'

(Non-violence, truth, calmness, self-control, peace and straightforwardness are the good qualities of a man.)

I also explained to my teammates the importance of Nabhidang. The word meant the *nabhi* (navel) of Sathy Devi (the navel was the most important organ connected to desire in every sense and not the heart, which was related to the creative side of desire only. The Kundalini power capable of creation and destruction was situated in the navel of the human body. The relationship between a pregnant woman and the baby inside was transacted through the navel).

Lord Paramasiva and Sathy Devi had been residing then at Adi Kailash. After her self-immolation at Daksha Yaga, Sathy Devi took birth anew as Devi Parvathy. Parameswara and Devi Parvathy, who started residing at Kailash near Manasa Sarass, often visited Adi Kailash to renew old memories. Tharakasuran, who was gifted with a special blessing, began to disturb Parvathy. Hence, Parameswara and Parvathy were forced to move permanently to Kailash from Adi Kailash. On their way up, they scribbled with the trident the word Om on the Siva Mountain at Nabhidang. The Great God did so to prevent Tharakasuran from crossing that limit. Lord Subramanian was born to the divine couple on the banks of the Manasa Sarass and he killed Tharakasuran. The belief was that the Om scribbled by Paramasiva was what we were seeing even today.

We waited up to 7 p.m. but the mist had not gone yet. Feeling now that the sight of Om was unlikely, the pilgrims left the place one by one. After praying at the small Siva temple situated at a height behind the camp, I went back to the tent.

The rise in cold and strong winds prevented me from fulfilling my wish of walking some distance on the road to Lipulekh Pass. Suddenly, the climate began to change. Ice fell heavily. My body began to shiver because of the unbearable cold. While I was sitting fully covered with a thick woollen sheet, servants came in carrying vegetable soup. They had come at the right time. The intensity of the chill lessened a bit when the hot soup went in.

All the travellers rested for about an hour. Vomiting and giddiness caused by the extreme height of Nabhidang were still troubling many. I saw the porters nursing them sincerely. Dinner was taken after 8 p.m. Roti and potato curry were the only items served. Even those were a luxury in the circumstances. The horse attendants were provoking a dog that was lying there after giving birth to puppies. The Bhotia dog was licking and drying the puppies hidden inside its hairy body. It was barking angrily when small stones were thrown at it. I turned the horse attendants back. If the stones forced the dog to run away, the little puppies would freeze to death.

I gently threw rolled rotis to the poor dog. Wagging its tail in gratitude, it ate them.

It is heard that in Himalayan journeys, especially in the Kailash and Badridham journeys, lone travellers got stray dogs to accompany them. A dog had been the only companion till the end to King Yudhishtira at Maha Prasthana Marg in Badridham. Dogs had been the constant companions of humans even thousands of years ago. In my Himalayan journeys, however, I hadn't got the service of a dog. While travelling, I used to give food to dogs wherever I saw them. But even in my lonely journeys, a dog hadn't followed me. Getting inside the bedding I had been provided with, I thought about dogs, the honest security guards of human beings.

8

Return to Gunji

I rose from my sleep upon hearing the happy shouts and uproar of the horse attendants. I thought that maybe the weather had cleared and Om had become visible. My guess was right.

It was just short of 5 a.m. The eastern horizon was bathed in the bright splendour of the golden rays of the morning sun. Though the sun itself was not visible, the seven colours spreading from it each moment was a charming sight. There was no mist and the surroundings were clearer. I could see Om very clearly. The army people, pilgrims and horse attendants were sitting together in groups on the ground. Lighting small clay lamps and folding their hands, everybody bowed their heads in prayer. When the morning sun came out in full splendour, the Om shone even more brightly. My mind was filled with the thought that at least one phase of the holy trip had turned fruitful.

Since climatic changes were not expected, we indulged in our morning activities. We decided to have breakfast on the ground. While every other traveller joined the rush of people to have the hot water flowing from the rock in front of the camp, Raju and I walked towards the riverbank. The aim was to take a bath in the confluence of the Nillyanthi and Lipu rivers. The water level had risen because of the rain in the previous days.

In some parts, the flow was also quite strong. The confluence was freezing cold. Standing there, Om could be seen clearly. Chanting the Om mantra, I immersed myself three times into the water at the confluence and then repeated the Gayatri mantra twenty-four times. My heart was filled with complete satisfaction.

I was surprised and happy to see Raju also dipping himself in the water. The word 'bath' did not exist in the dictionary of porters and horse attendants. There would be at the maximum only one spare pair of clothes with them, even if the journey lasted one month or more.

Unbearable cold crawled up the body. We thawed only after we sat near the fireplace wearing woollen clothes. After having a breakfast of poori and curry sitting on the ground, we got ready for the return trip. The sight of the heavenly letter Om having flooded my heart with happiness, I walked slowly. I remembered then the recitation of Yamaraja (king of death) in the Katopanishad. He explained to Nachikethus, the ancient sage, that Pranavam (the mystic sound Om) was for sure the Para Brahma Purushothama (god of all universes).

> *Ethadhyevaksharam Brahma*
> *Ethadhyevaksharam Param*
> *Ethadhyevaksharam Njathua*
> *Yo Yadhikschathi Thasya Thath.'*

(Pranavam is Om, the summation of the ultimate God. Or it is the universe. There is only one name for the universe and God. It is Om. Understanding this truth, a devotee who always chants this word can achieve whatever state he wants to have through both ways.)

I stood still at the top of the path and looked back. The vision of Om ended there. I didn't think that I would have another sight of that again in this birth. Turning around, I moved away, bowing my head before the one-letter-God with tearful eyes. I had been uttering the words from the Bhagavat Gita in my mind then.

'Omithyekaksharam Brahma Vyaharan Mamanusmaran
Ya Hah PraYeti Thyejan Dheham Sa Yeti Paramam Gathim'

(Whoever leaves his body chanting the holy word Om and always praying 'me' [Brahmam] in his mind reaches the world of God.)

We reached Gunji after 5 p.m. The other members of the team had been waiting for us in the Kali temple. After conveying our regards to the army people, we walked to the camp. We had learnt a distance back that the first batch of the Kailash-Manasarovar pilgrims had arrived at Gunji. The wet clothes hung out to dry, the ponies grazing near the camp and the groups of horse attendants were proof of the same. Diwansingh Bisth, a manager with the KMVN, was waiting in the courtyard of the camp to receive us. After drinking a glass of orange juice, we chanted prayers as a group, as was always done at the end of a trip. The manager's face was pale and something was disturbing him. Soon, we learnt the reason. The commandant of the ITBP of Karera in Madhya Pradesh was the liaison officer of the Kailash team. The Kailash team had already occupied all the tents except two. Since they were ITBP people, nothing could be said. Our manager was satisfied when we said that we would be happy with whatever we had. Even though they knew we had come, none of the Kailash team came out of the tents and expressed their regards.

The discrimination was evident too in the evening prayer at the army camp.

While I was resting after the hazardous journey, I happened to recall many things. In the Himalayan journeys, the Kailash-Manasarovar travel teams tended to exhibit egoism. The journey directly organized by the foreign affairs ministry of the Government of India, group mountaineering recognized by the Indian Mountaineering Foundation, selection from thousands of applicants, a strict medical check-up, hazardous high-altitude journeys that lasted more than one month, trekking through the holy soil that the ancient rishis, sages and monks had traversed, being the guests of the Chinese government—all those were factors that enhanced the ego of the Kailash pilgrimage teams. They had high contempt for those travelling to Kailash via the Nepal side. The Nepal side pilgrims in their turn called them pilgrims who were lucky to have won a lottery. The prejudice was manifest in the Garhwal Himalaya trips too. The Chathur Dham pilgrims had contempt towards the North Kashi-Rishikesh pilgrims. And the Pancha Kedara pilgrims were contemptuous of Chathur Dham pilgrims. Ego was at the highest for those who had gone on the pilgrimage to Gomukh. All forgot that there might be different ways, but the goal was the same.

Visible changes had occurred in the matter of going around Kailash also. Since 2000, year after year, the Chinese authorities were reducing the size of circumambulation. In 2001, we had gone around Kailash on the same path our rishis and yogis had taken centuries back. It took more than three days to complete the circumambulation by walking around 70 km. The next year, that distance was curtailed to 56 km. Later, the distance was reduced to just 38 km. It was heard that the distance would be reduced further in the near future. Similarly, it was also heard that efforts were being made to impose strict restrictions on the Kailash pilgrimage or even to stop it. Some of my friends in Delhi informed me that they had read such shocking news in a weekly published from Delhi. In the areas near the circumambulation route, the Chinese had started massive mining activities with elaborate arrangements. They had reliable information regarding the immense deposit of precious minerals and metals there, gathered with the help of satellite surveillance. They were reportedly embarrassed to know about the enormous deposit of gold too. Gold had been discovered in the form of ore from riverbanks and in solid blocks and sheets from mines. In the Indian epics, there was mention of the immeasurable stock of gold owned by Kubera. Perhaps those were the wealth of Kubera, the king of Alakapuri.

In 2001, on our way from the Saithie camp on the banks of Manasarovar to Dharchan, we happened to face some unfortunate behaviour on the part of the Chinese soldiers at a check-post, including blocking our vehicle for a long time. At last, they let us go, strictly warning us that whoever had binoculars should use them at Dharchan only. I became curious when the liaison officer, Dr Madhup Mohta, sitting close to me, observed the surroundings through the binoculars even before we reached Dharchan. Seeing cranes and components of huge vehicles far away, the liaison officer sat wondering what construction activities were taking place in the isolated, ice-covered place. Some pilgrims of the third and fourth batches en route to Kailash had also spotted similar machinery far away below the Dolma Pass. From the next year onwards, entry to Dolma Pass was from the right side of the mountain. Going halfway around the mountain, we had earlier climbed the steep way to that pass. After reaching the top that was on the other side of the pass, and then crossing the ground, we could reach the deity Tara Devi. Maybe it was right to assert that there were reasons for cutting short the distance of

Kailash circumambulation and for imposing many restrictions year after year. The vengeful behaviour of the Chinese soldiers towards the pilgrims might have been intentional and planned. During my journeys, I often met Chinese people and talked to them. All of them had great respect for Indians. The soldiers who were guarding the Nathula Pass were also interested in friendship. It had been a Chinese man who helped me with the language at a coffee bar in Bhutan. After food, he also led me to the nearby medical shop that he owned. The man was Dr Chung Lee, a postgraduate in Chinese Traditional Medicine. He was surprised when I asked him about a special medicine called Rhodiola. The price of that medicine was 30 American dollars, but he gave it to me for half that. At least some of my readers might have thought that I was anti-Chinese. That was not true. I was an Indian citizen who loved my country. I didn't like the foreign policy of China in attacking India for no reason, killing many of our soldiers with no mercy and taking possession of some parts of Ladakh with no justice. But still, I had no hatred towards the Chinese people. I considered them my brothers.

I criticized only the strict nature of the Chinese soldiers posted in Kailash-Manasarovar areas. Gradually, I understood that there were reasons for it. The soldiers had strict orders from the authorities.

When the time was 7.30, we received intimation that we were to participate in a prayer at the Kali temple. Only half of our team members were there. Others were resting because of the exhaustion caused by the hard journey. The Kailash-Manasarovar travel team dominated the temple. We had to stand outside. We were disregarded in the aarti and also in the distribution of *prasadam* (share of the offerings to God distributed to devotees after pooja). Ignoring them, we participated in the prayer and returned to our camp later.

We chanted the Veda mantras for about an hour after spending some time rearranging the luggage. Around 8.30, we heard the announcement for food. The dining hall was fully occupied by the Kailash travel team and hence, our liaison officer requested us to have our meal directly from the kitchen. But there was insufficient space in the kitchen. Hence, many of us had to go outside and have our food standing. Knowing that the generator service would be available for only a limited time, I thought it meaningless to wait for the dining hall to empty. Mr Gourav and I went straight to the dining hall. Wishing everybody 'Om Namah Sivaya', we helped ourselves. Somebody invited me to a vacant seat in a corner. I went there with my food. He introduced himself as the liaison officer of the Kailash team. I too introduced myself in a few words. To his question whether the Adi Kailash journey was comparatively easy, I replied that from the reports of the army, it was very hard, perhaps harder than the Kailash-Manasarovar journey.

Suddenly he asked, 'How did you know? The Kailash-Manasarovar journey by that route was the hardest and most dangerous of any Himalayan journey. It was a commonly accepted opinion.'

I told him humbly that I had earlier travelled by that route from Mangthi to Lipulekh Pass on foot and then had walked around the entire Manasarovar and Kailash too. That time also, I was doing the journey on foot. I added that in our team, we had an advocate who had earlier made a trip by that route and another five who had gone to Kailash by the Nepal way. Everybody in the dining hall stopped eating and started listening to me with much astonishment.

The liaison officer's eyes widened and he answered with surprise, 'Oh my God! Dear friend, I was totally surprised because I had been trying to locate a Kailash traveller right

from Delhi itself and collect details. But on the day we were
to start, I could reach Delhi only at noon because of official
engagements. So I couldn't do anything. My team was very
worried about the unending rain and continuous landslides.
Might I request you to give us a detailed description and
guidance regarding the route after you have eaten?'

Before dinner, I made a request to all. The first thing one
had to give up in a Himalayan journey was one's 'sense of self'
or ego. Also, one should not have any discriminatory feelings
towards fellow travellers. We should understand that what we
saw on our way—forests, rivers, mountains, enormous rocks and
small stones, the villagers, soldiers, animals, grass, atmosphere,
pure air—were all different forms of creation, and we must
bow our heads in devotion before them. They reflected the
power of God.

After food, members of both the travel teams assembled on
the meadow. After spending some time getting acquainted with
one another and distributing sweets, I gave a long narration
about the Himalayan journey. Many cleared their doubts and
took written notes. The extension of the generator service for
another hour was useful for all.

I also talked to the liaison officer of the Kailash team
for half an hour in private. Satpal Sharma was a Kashmiri
Brahmin belonging to Jammu. He had been working in Karera
in Madhya Pradesh as a commandant in the ITBP. The rank
of commandant in the ITBP was equivalent to the rank of a
colonel in the Indian Army. His next promotion was to the
rank of additional deputy inspector general. He had worked
in almost all border areas except the Kumaon region. He told
me that the number of Malayalee soldiers was proportionately
lower in the ITBP. He also asserted that in matters of sincerity
and discharging duties, the Malayalee soldiers were far ahead
of others. The superior officers were fully satisfied with the

special way of Malayalees doing their duties. I appealed to him that several literate young people in Kerala remained unemployed and perhaps special consideration might be given to them during recruitments to the ITBP. He responded that if the qualifications were as required, he would surely do what he could. He also promised that if he was in the recruitment process, the matter would be considered by all means. I thanked him for saying good things about Malayalee soldiers. It was past 11 p.m. when I returned to my tent. I crawled into the bed and as it was a comfortable day, sleep came to me quite easily.

9

On to Kuti Village

We rose at 4.30 a.m. and were ready to see and enjoy the sunrise at Gunji. The eastern side of the horizon was strewn with saffron. The rising sun was not visible yet. Still, the rays the sun sent out were spreading over the horizon in rare artistic talent. When the mist disappeared fully, a pure sky, clusters of silvery clouds and a shining sun appeared as if to wish us a good day. The eastern horizon was painted with the seven colours when the sun came out slowly from behind the icy mountains. There was no word to explain the splendid sight of the golden rays of the morning sun reflecting off the Himalayan mountains. Each mountain had a different colour. Like a colour wheel sending out different colours on to a dance stage, different colours were seen at different times on the horizon. We stood wondering at the marvellous hands of the Creator.

It had been decided to start the journey at 5.30 and so we started preparing for the same. The temperature at Gunji was sub-zero. Hot water was available for those who required it but I was satisfied with bathing in cold water. The Kailash team also joined us in prayers and aarti. After drinking a glass of Horlicks, we got ready to start the journey. Wishing bon voyage to each other, the Kailash team and our team parted. It was a tearful moment.

We started sharp at the scheduled time. Generally, the members were anxious. The trip was to a totally unfamiliar place. What was known of the place was very limited. The programme of the first day was to reach Kuti Village by evening after travelling a distance of more than 20 km. We got information from the army that the climate was very bad. It was freezing. Also, an icy wind had been blowing without a break for the past week. After climbing a steep path, the team that had started towards the northern direction from Gunji reached the Napalchu Village about 1.5 km away. As they were continuing the rest of the travel on horseback, they halted there because continuous rain had made the mud slippery and it was difficult for horses to walk smoothly. That was why the travel on horseback started there. The team moved up and as always, Raju and I followed behind on foot. We found the village men of Napalchu engaged in different jobs in their farmlands. The area comprised vast agricultural lands. Untimely rain had caused heavy damage to the crops. Fully grown plants stood bent because of excessive rain. Breaking the mud barriers, the hysterical water had flooded into the farmlands and destroyed the crops to a large extent. One farmer told us that the fall of hail had caused his plants to break and stoop. He had been plucking wheat plants from places where they were comparatively more in number and replanting them in places where there were none. The farmlands were highly fertile because of the usage of cow dung and other biological manure.

Where the farmlands ended, the forest started. There were no dense forests. Big trees like chir, sal and banj, bushes, creepers and wildflowers were seen in the forest. Groups of rock and streams with crystal-clear water were also in abundance. The cold increased gradually while walking by the narrow path in the forest. After walking about 1.5 km, we reached the borders of Nabhi Village. At the entrance of the village, there was a big

stone inscription and I stopped in front of that. Wild flowers
from the neighbouring bush were seen strewn over there. That
might be our own team members who had done the flower
worship there. I read the inscription carefully, which said:

'*Bhagvan Veda Vyas ka paryatan sthal aevam Adi Kailash ka
pravesh dwar* (The place Veda Vyasa visited. Also, the gate to
Adi Kailash)'.

I had learnt at Gunji that the great ancient sage Veda Vyasa
had gone to meditate at Adi Kailash by that way. Deciding to
stay at Nabhi Village for some time to collect more details,
I offered the flowers Raju plucked for me and stood in
meditation of sage Veda Vyasa. I felt very happy because
Raju had done the act without me asking him. I expressed my
gratitude by giving him a loving look and walked to the village.

Thirty-five families resided in Nabhi Village. Compared to
other villages, Nabhi people were rich. The Nabhinali River ran
along the border of the village. The river reached there from
Nabhidang and merged with the Kuti River. Vast farmlands
extended up to Ronkon Village which lay on the other side of
the river. The farm jobs of the rich people of Nabhi Village
were done by the poor villagers of Ronkon Village. Wheat,
paffar, palti, potato, green peas and red gram were the main
crops. Vegetables and green leaves were cultivated as interim
crops. I saw domestic animals like cows, sheep and mules being
looked after and in very good condition. We went into a small
tea shop near the grocery shop and ordered tea. I asked the
young men there about the enormous tree in the open ground
spread over a vast area and full of fruits. The tree was locally
called 'banbain' and had black, sweet fruits the size of marbles.
While drinking tea, I chatted with the villagers and came upon
some surprising and strange information.

Nabhi Village was centuries old. Though trade between
India and Tibet was through the Lipulekh Pass, the path

people preferred to travel was through the Dhura Pass there. From Gunji to Lipulekh, the path was totally deserted. But on the way, there were small villages like Kuti and marriage processions from Tibet went through that way. Even though the journey was hard, they could stay at night in villages and continue travelling at ease. Also, there was another important factor—a spiritual factor, indeed—that Veda Vyasa had gone through the same path for meditation. The villagers strongly believed that the power of the blessings of the great sage was still there in the villages. There were many people there who had stayed and studied at the distant Dharchula and earned higher education degrees. Most of them secured jobs in varied sectors like banks, government departments and the military. There were IAS and IPS officers too. Whatever heights they might have reached, they visited their village at least once a month, travelling a distance of three days and three nights. All villagers shifted residence to Dharchula around the middle of November. There, the Nabhi villagers owned houses with the most modern amenities. Then again, during the second week of April, they returned to Nabhi. Their home village was always sacred to them. They had grown up doing farming there. In the Ramayana, Lord Rama told Lakshmana that every man, mother and homeland were dearer than heaven. That could be taken as divine advice expressed to all the population in the world. After King Ravana was killed and preparations were being done to return from Lanka, many of the important people, including Lakshmana, had ideas of annexing Lanka to Ayodhya and continuing to rule there. Sree Ramachandra was intimated of the matter. Lanka was a beautiful and prosperous land. But Sree Rama disagreed with the opinion of his brother.

'*Api Swarnamayee Lanka*
Na Mae Lakshmana! Rochathae;

Jananee Janmabhoomischa
Swargaadhapi Gareeyasee'

(Hear you, Lakshmana, it would not feel good for me even if Lanka was made of gold! Mother and birthplace are greater than heaven for everybody.)

The poet Kalidasa, in his epic work *Raghuvamsam*, also established that Lanka was liberated for saving dharma (justice) from adharma (injustice) and not for anything else.

'*Rakshovadhantho Na Cha Mae Prayaso*
Vyarthaha Sa Vyraprathimochanaaya
Amarshanaha Shonithakamkshaya Kim
Padha Sprushantham Dhashathi Dhwijihwaha'

(My attempts including the killing of *rakshasas* [a race of unrighteous people in Hindu mythology] are not in vain. It is revenge. It is not for blood an angry snake bites a man who stepped on it.)

Also, the people there proudly added the name of their home villages as their last names, like Bhudhiyal, Gunjiyal, Nabhiyal, Kutiyal, etc. An old man explained to me in detail the history of the disappearance of the inscriptions believed to be those of sage Vyasa from the village. It was ancient wisdom transferred from generation to generation (the inscription placed at the entrance of the village now was only fifty years old). There was a porch there made of granite. The stones were full of inscriptions in Sanskrit. It was believed that the great sage had engaged in meditation there for long years. There were written lines on one spherical stone. That excellent stone was a sun clock with the mechanism of showing time along the movement of the sun's rays.[1] Where the rays of the morning sun fell, the colour of those lines would be light red. That indicated the time of 6 a.m. The colour of the lines would become grey at 9 a.m. and shine bright at noon.

It was said that there were various mathematical symbols on the stone. Fine granite inscribed with the words 'Sree Chakra' was also present there (Sree Chakra is the holy diagram formed by nine interlocking triangles surrounding and radiating out from a *bindu* [dot] in the centre. The Chakra represents the goddess in her form of Shri Lalita, 'the beauty of three worlds [earth, atmosphere and sky (heaven)]' and *bindu thrikona* (thrikona means triangle). The dot or bindu in the centre represents the oneness of Lord Siva and the goddess Parvathy.)

Legend has it that Tibetan lamas stole and carried away those invaluable stones centuries ago. Those great stones were so heavy that even horses couldn't carry them. But groups of physically strong lamas together transported the stones away, carrying them on wooden bars. The belief was that those miraculous stones were still kept and worshipped in the Buddhist monasteries of Tibet as symbols of strength and vigour. The local villagers also used some of those memorable stones to build walls on the riverside farms for preventing the muddy barriers from sliding down. Over time, fierce and continuous water flow caused the riversides to fall and the stones were left to finally rest on the deep bottom of the Kuti River. My mind became sad and distressed thinking that the historical monuments of an invaluable and great culture were thus lost forever and turned into just memories because of ignorance and disregard.

'Purana Ha Praviliyanthae
Naveenaa Prathurasthruthae.'

(The old will go and the new will come.)

Time erased many things. But they went away only to be reborn somewhere else. There they grew fully. Perhaps that was the law of nature. And so was creation. God created, maintained and destroyed. That was the duty of God. He created truths, tied up them and then dismantled them to destroy them. Those were the twin facets of duty. Integration, analysis, creation and destruction were timeless, continuing processes. When the examination and assessment of a thing done by time period ended, that came to be known as integration, destruction and death. Those changes were not permanent but only a withdrawal till they took birth again.

We said goodbye to the people of Nabhi Village and continued our journey. Crossing a small wooden bridge on the Nabhinali River, we reached the plain and continued walking. That land lay parallel to the Kuti River and from there, the river seemed very wide. The riverbanks were full of smooth and colourful stones of varied sizes. The pathway entered a deep glacier beside that vast area. From there, it moved upward steeply. We walked slowly by the 3-foot-wide hazardous path carved out of the mountainside. Looking down from each step, the sight of the violently flowing Kuti River below through the deep valleys was really terrible.

Long ascending paths appeared turn by turn. It looked like they were going up to touch the sky. We moved inch by inch to enormous heights. At each point of the hard trek, we consumed dried fruits, biscuits and glucose in sufficient quantities. Little flowers in yellow, white, blue and pink blooming in the cracks of the rocky mountains were a memorable sight. They cooled us. The path became narrow as we kept proceeding upwards. At some places down sharp slopes, the path was barely 1 foot wide. Small pebbles were scattered over the path and the chance of slipping over them and falling into the deep crevasses below was high. Big rocks hung down over many areas and we had to stoop to pass that way. Those travelling on horses had to lie flat on the backs of their horses to get past those places.

We halted at a place where landslides occurred frequently on a larger scale. Rocks bigger than elephants lay all over the area. The gigantic rock lying in the middle of the river was hindering the flow of the water and as a result, the river was flowing over the bushes nearby. I listened nervously to a big explosion that happened on the other side of the river 2 furlongs away. For about three minutes, stones fell with terrifying sounds and horrible echoes. There were sky-high mountains on that side of the river too and there were signs that landslides had occurred there in recent days. Raju was scared of waiting in such an unpredictable situation for too long. I soothed him saying that what was destined to happen would happen and it didn't matter where we were. We all were living at the mercy of nature.

Leaving the plains behind, we once again started to climb up the sides of the rocky mountains. Our hearts quaked when we looked up at the enormous height of the mountain that we had to walk up and the path, lying like a thin thread on its side. The steep path kept going endlessly. After a prayer, I started walking up in all concentration. Suddenly, the face of Vaidyamadom Cheriya Narayanan Namboothirippad appeared in my mind in a flash. Before the start of the Adi Kailash pilgrimage, I had gone to that great Brahmin's Arya Vaidya pharmacy at Thrithala to seek his blessings. When I hinted that the Adi Kailash trip might be harder, the great master of Ayurveda blessed me and gave me a full tin of specially prepared Maha Dhanwantharam Ayurvedic tablets. So far, there had been no reason to consume the tablets and I had actually forgotten about them.

I took one tablet from my bag, which was hanging on Raju's shoulders, and put that in my mouth. After convincing Raju of the popularity of Ayurveda in Kerala, as also in the Himalayas,

I gave him one tablet, telling him to chew slowly. Travelling to higher altitudes always posed problems. When a human walked on level land, the energy needed was just to move their body ahead. But when they climbed up a mountain, the energy needed was not only to move the body upward but also to raise the body against gravitational force. For that, blood circulation should be augmented to bring more oxygen into the muscles for producing the extra energy and also to filter out the wastes arising thereby. The heartbeats speeded up then. Also, at the same instant, the working of the lungs should be speeded up to bring extra oxygen into the heart and to remove the resultant carbon dioxide. When more oxygen was required, we took more breaths. Gasping or panting was nothing but the lungs working to take in more air. While we went up and up, the amount of oxygen in the atmosphere became less and less. Gravitational force held the earth's atmosphere. When one went higher and higher, the gravitational force and the atmospheric pressure would both be lower. As a result, the quantity of oxygen also would become less.

We climbed up the path slowly without giving extra pressure on the lungs. We saw only the earth we were walking on and not the path going up in front. When you had to go up a steep path, it was better to have first a detailed look at the route, its type and length. After that, you must forget it. If we always thought about the hardship of climbing such an endless, steep path, the pressure of the task would hinder our efforts. I was totally tired when we reached the top after the hard task. Each step we climbed was with utmost caution. Stretching out the whole body with our face upwards, we lay for some time on the top. After resting thus, we enjoyed some dry grapes and drank glucose water and regained our energy. We started walking again. The downward slope was also very narrow. A mere slip of the legs would throw you hundreds of feet down.

I was very hungry when we reached level ground again. When I was slowly having biscuits sitting on a rocky outcrop, four soldiers of the ITBP came that way. I gave them biscuits and cashew nuts. For five minutes, I talked to them. They told me that there was a sharp and very hard upslope on the other side of the Kuti River and after climbing that, we could reach the Nampha Village. There was a dhaba where we could get food. They also told us that about half of our team members were resting at the dhaba. Those soldiers belonged to the guard duty team at Dhura Pass.

Saying goodbye to the soldiers, we walked along the riverbank. On the other side of the river was a thick forest of burj trees. That forest area went steeply upwards from the level land at the riverbanks. There were only burj trees in it. I stood for some time, looking at the trees with respect. The ancient Indian literature of the Arsha period had spread all over the world through the skins of those venerable trees. Also, the trees were very useful for the uncivilized people of those times to cover their bodies, to protect themselves from the cold and also to thatch their dwellings. The fresh leaves of the tree had the colour of green parrots. Though there were many burj trees in the Gangotri-Badri Dhams of the Garhwal Himalayas, a forest area full and thick of only them could be seen only in the Kumaon Himalayas. (In Sanskrit, a burj tree is called Bhojpatra. Its scientific name is Betula utilis.)

We reached the other side of the river after crossing a wooden bridge with great care and caution and got ready to climb up another dangerous slope. The fear of a landslide was topmost in my mind while climbing up the very risky and overgrown path that stood on the side of the mountain. Scattered loose stones were ready to skid while stepping on them. The horrible cracks on the mountainsides were ample proof of accidents. We halted to rest once in a while.

The burj forests on the left were a comforting sight. They gave our minds pleasure and peace. We reached the rest centre at Nampha Village after walking through thick shrubs in the valley for some distance and then climbing a steep path. Mr Gourav Mahajan and the lawyer who had opted for travel on horseback were already there and resting.

Less than ten families resided in Nampha. Farmlands were very rare there. The principal occupation of the villagers was sheep rearing. Military men and other passengers going to Kuti Village passed that way. The dhaba was meant for them (two families resided in the village exclusively to run the dhaba). The lunch for the Adi Kailash pilgrims was also arranged there. One could have as much food as one required. The Tourism Department paid the expenses. I rested lying flat on my back on a half-wall in front of the hut. Then I had lunch, which included roti, dal and a mixed dish of big onions with green chilli. Boiled raw rice was also available for the needy. Even though I was feeling very hungry, I had only two rotis and curry. I satiated my thirst by drinking the clear water of the mountain stream flowing behind the dhaba. The time was only 11.30 a.m. We still had a long distance to go. So we again started the journey, wasting no time at the dhaba.

The chill rose with each step up. The Kuti River diverted away to the left. Our pace was fast on the 2 km of flat land. The ice-covered mountains were shining and dazzling our eyes but down on level land, the sunlight was dim. The dhaba people had told us that for the last week, the freezing wind had been blowing even at noon. We felt relieved that that frightful climate had gone away. From the flat lands, we then went up skywards through the valleys curving around the mountains. The path was steep and long. But we didn't feel tired. Then we reached the colourful world of flowers. One would never want to go away from that sight of unending enjoyment. Blooms of blue, red, violet, white and yellow stood all over the valley and also on the mountain slopes. The dancing plants imbibed the brightness of the Himalayan peaks standing with their heads held high, with the world of flowers in the background. It was an unforgettable visual feast.

Descending to a wide flat plain, we came close to the Kuti River again. On the other side of the river was a jungle of burj trees that thickly populated the mountainside. The free flow of the river was hindered by heaps of dry burj wood lying in the centre and on the sides of the river. I stopped to take a picture of the sight. Heavy landslides uprooted huge trees and they fell into the river. But rocks in the river blocked them from flowing with the water and a cemetery of trees was thus formed. I felt very sad at seeing the dead wood that had no bark or leaves.

The role of trees in keeping the ecological balance was vital. Our ancient teachers had reminded us that 'it was for others that the trees were bearing fruits, rivers were flowing and cows were carrying milk in their udders. Then it was quite natural that the human body should be also for others':

'Paropakaraya Phalanthi Vruksha Ha, Paropakaraya Vahanthi Nadhya Ha Paropakaraya Dhuhanthi Gava Ha, Paropakarartham Idham Sareeram.'

Trekking beside the riverbank and climbing up steep rises with difficulty, we again came closer to the mountainsides and continued walking. We were unaware of the swift passing of time while in the joyful mood of seeing the small path in the spacious area, the green carpeted hillsides and the icy mountain peaks shining from afar. We were tired and thirsty and greedily drank the clear water of the streams. This gave us fresh energy and we went a long way up. The intensity of the cold was rising. The sun had already gone down the western horizon. Since the climate was misty, the golden rays of the setting sun were not visible. When we crossed a bridge over a stream that was to join the Kuti River soon, a concrete board was seen welcoming us to Kuti Village. We climbed up the steep path and at the top, Kuti Village could be seen far away like a spot.

The first sight of the village was pleasing. It was a beautiful place. Vast areas of farmlands abounded. On one side were the gorgeous arch-shaped mountain peaks. Drops of ice lying scattered on the mountain ranges, greenery down the valleys and the colourful world of flowers between them gave a pleasure that no words could describe. The place was holy because Kunti Devi, the mother of the Pandavas, had been born there. Kuti was part of the kingdom of Kuntibhoja. The remnants of the Pandava Fort, named after the Pandavas, could still be seen there. The Kuti River was known there as the Kunti River. A small memorial of the Pandava Fort was seen on the other side of the river. My heart was melting in emotion, for the place was the playground of the Pandavas in their childhood! No one could measure the heights every Indian would reach knowing that most of the pivotal links of the Mahabharata stories were spread across the Uttarakhand region!

We walked by the narrow path along the vast, level farmlands. Farmers were working on their lands. The sight of sheep and cows grazing in groups was enchanting. Yaks were used to plough the land. The plough and its technology used were entirely different from that normally used in northern India. The main crops cultivated there were wheat, potato, big and small onion, cabbage and cauliflower. Vegetables were mostly cultivated as interim crops.

I stopped near a group of farmers who were sitting in a circle beside the path and sipping tea. I greeted them and introduced myself. They became happy. One elderly farmer, most likely the prominent one among the group, invited me to have tea. They were making tea on a makeshift fireplace resting on small stones. The good man served us tea in all politeness. We had started our walk early in the morning and were really exhausted. The strong tea replenished our strength. While sipping the hot tea, we familiarized ourselves with one another. Surinder Singh Kutiyal was the name of my host. He was born and brought up in that village. He inherited the farmlands. Cultivation for six months was enough for happy living. A very good sum would also remain as savings. The agricultural products were sold in faraway Dharchula. They had their own residential facilities in Dharchula during the winter. Since education was unavoidable for the upcoming generation, one or two family members permanently resided in Dharchula. But all of them would reach the village on holidays and other special occasions. They would not miss the chance for anything. The villagers in Nabhi and Kuti belonged to the richer classes of the mountain ranges. The Chinese border was not far away. The old man told us that the Chinese were not causing them any problems except that sometimes they constructed temporary passages for carrying salt from the salt rocks situated there. But the Indian soldiers would close the routes soon afterwards. Snow covered the village thickly during the winter season, as deep as 5 feet or even more. While leaving the village after celebrating the Deepavali festival, the farmers kept the seeds in the farmlands for sowing in the coming months of April and May.

The method of keeping the seeds safely was thus: first, hay was strewn across the fields. The seeds were carefully kept over that. Hay was again strewn over the seeds. Over that, half a foot of thick mud was put as cover. The seeds were thus safely preserved for about six months of icefall. The farmers would return by about the end of April. Removing the humps of fallen ice and again preparing the lands for cultivation was a hard task. The yaks used for agricultural activities belonged to a crossbreed of yak and bullock. The old man showed me a type of giant goat found in the Chinese region. They are locally called 'rabbu' and weigh up to 50 kilograms. Crossing the borders, they came inside and mated with the Indian sheep. But it was a wonder though that the rabbu kids were never born.

I waved goodbye to the elderly man and walked towards the village, keenly observing the farm activities all around. After walking about 1.5 km, we reached the village. In the aristocratic Kuti Village, we could see many houses, big and small. Granite was used to build them. The pattern of construction of the two-storeyed houses was notable. The engraving work done on the main doors and windows was really amazing. The influence of the Tibetan-Chinese culture was seen there. The existing houses were more than 200 years old. Prior to that, the houses were small and built with mud. Another wonder was that concrete was not at all used for constructing the buildings. The first floor was built using wooden planks fixed on cylindrical trunks of trees thrust deeply down on the walls. Solid chir trees were used for the wooden work. The roofing was done with flat pieces of rock. Each house had its own courtyard and compound wall. Though the cattle shed and dung pit were near the houses, they were kept neatly and hygienically. Most of the householders reared cows, mules, Bhutia dogs and domestic chicks. The North Indian practice of using dried cowdung instead of firewood was also seen there. The dried cowdung cakes were kept safely there, like hay was kept in layers in my own state, Kerala.

Though the galis in the village had been narrow, they were bordered by side walls made beautifully with granite bricks. Water tanks made of stone were erected in the courtyard of every house for storing the clean water flowing down from the mountains. The animals had their drink of water from the small tanks constructed nearby. I stood for some time watching children playing cricket in a vacant small ground between the houses. Actually, they were not children. They were young men who had crossed their teenage years. Bat, stumps and gloves were being used to play but the only unfitting part was that they were using a cork ball for bowling. I was surprised to see that both their style of getting ready to bat and the bowling action were faultless. After pitching, the ball flew past at lightning speed. They also knew well the trick of swinging the ball to both sides. It was also amazing to see the fielding expertise of those strongly built young men. After one sweep, the ball fell near me. A boy came to pick that up and I asked him where they had practised the game. The young man answered that many of them were college players of Dharchula. We could surely assign the world record of 'playing cricket on the highest land' to Kuti Village. National integrity was the noble aim behind the nations of the world spending millions on sports. 'My country, my country' was the enthusiastic feeling that arose in the minds of every Indian when India won in sports. Could anybody think of the quantum of money that would have to be spent to create such an innocent emotion?

Our travel documents were once again scrutinized in the army camp at Kuti Village. The camp building was roofed with tin sheets and its surroundings were kept neat and tidy. The soldiers were very busy planting potatoes around the camp. I felt disappointed when one army officer told me that there was still uncertainty over whether we would be able to continue our journey onward from Kuti and we would have to stay in Kuti until we got permission to proceed. He told us that the violent dance of the ice storm had ended only two days back. Three tents of the Tourism Department were totally destroyed. The arrangements for our stay were made in a valley 1 km away from Kuti. Thanking the good soldiers, we started walking towards the valley camp. The time was 5.30 p.m. and the icefall

had been gaining strength. So, we speeded up. I understood
the gravity of the problem only when we reached the camp.
The north and south parts of the camp were bordered by icy
mountains. Kuti Village lay in the east. We had to go through
the west extension. Though the tents were built at safer places
between the icy mountains, they had been shattered into pieces
by mammoth hailstones that had fallen along with the icy wind.
If that had happened in the night when everybody was asleep,
surely nobody would have survived. However, there were three
tents still intact. One of them was allotted to the women.
Twenty people were the most that could be accommodated in
the other two tents. Also, there had to be a little room for the
luggage. The horse attendants told us that the Kuti villagers
had a practice of renting out the vacant upper portions of their
houses. Five of us decided to make use of that facility. The horse
attendants and porters were also staying in Kuti Village.

Pushing through the heavy snowfall, the five of us returned
to Kuti Village together with the horse attendants. On inquiry
there, we were told that two places had the facilities of a hotel.
A small board in the Garhwali language was seen hung there.
The rent per day was Rs 100, food extra. The places were
mostly used by traders who come to collect salt from salt rocks
there and the owners of herds of sheep. The army officers who
came on inspection duty also stayed there. The rooms were
very comfortable. Cot, woollen bed, bedding and lamps were
all arranged there. A big hurricane lamp and an oil lamp were
ready to light up the room. It was a great wonder for us in
knowing that all those were at a height of 14,000 feet.

The exhaustion and tiredness of the travel made us rest
on the cot. After 7 p.m., we were served hot vegetable soup as
an appetizer. The cold was increasing minute by minute and
the hot soup gave us some relief. When it was past 8, the night
became thick and dark. Pieces of dry wood were burning in the

fireplace but smoke didn't come into the room because of the chimney. Our hunger was at its peak even before the head of the family and his wife served the supper. The roti and vegetable dishes tasted wonderful. The head of the family told us that potato, spinach, red gram and onion were from their own fields.

My mind was at peace when I got into bed wearing a monkey cap, muffler and gloves. To get over the uncomfortable events of the long journey, I turned to prayer. Deep sleep was just a minute away.

10

A Day in Kuti Village

When I awoke from a refreshing sleep, the time was 4.30 a.m. Since the journey was postponed and there was nothing else to do, I crept into bed again. It was unbearably cold at Kuti. After all the wood in the fireplace had burnt out, the cold grew worse.

The host brought tea before 6 a.m. The tea was made of pure milk and high-quality tea leaves and was very tasty. He told us that the bathroom was downstairs and hot water was available if required. We went there. The loud squawks of chicks and other domestic animals that were in search of the morning food made the atmosphere lively. The farmers had reached the fields. Though a shade of mist was still hanging over us, the whole area glittered bright in the golden rays of the rising sun.

I simply wandered around the streets as if on a morning walk. Shouts and loud noises were heard near the tents of the horse people. The horse attendants and porters were staying in open tents built on open ground. The horses were tied up near there. There were two shops nearby which supplied food to those people. The main hobbies of the horse aides were drinking alcohol, smoking grass (ganja) and playing cards. But they engaged in such hobbies only at night and on holidays. During the journeys that stretched from early morning to the evening darkness, they behaved very decently. Since theirs was a tribal reservation region, they had permission to distil liquor and cultivate ganja for their own use. Their argument was that one cannot survive the six-month-long cold without such intoxicants.

After having breakfast of poori and potato curry, Raju and I started an easy walk around the farmlands. Though the sunlight was abundant, we didn't feel the intensity of the cold any less keenly. The wind blew alternatively from the icy mountains, extending along the north-east like a fortress, and from the thick forests of the ice-free mountains in the south-west. That was why the chill was rising. We walked for some time observing the farming activities. Watching the work of scattering the dried cowdung powder in the farmlands, planting saplings in lands where the soil had been eroded due to the heavy rain, removing weeds and loosening the hard soil around the plants for the roots to go deep was very interesting. We stood for some time enjoying the lady workers singing a beautiful Tibetan folk song.

Then we moved away, leaving the farmlands behind. Our aim was to visit the remnants of the fort of the Pandavas and see the commemorative plaque. A small stream was flowing down the ravines on its way to finally merging with the Kunti River. We had to cross that stream for reaching our target. But it was very dangerous and risky. So we just looked at the commemorative plaque from a distance and then continued walking. It was a vast plateau surrounded by ice-covered mountains and forests thick with burj trees. The Kunti was flowing fast on the south-west side. On the other side of the river was the forest. There were big and small meadows on many parts of the ground. The flowers on the meadows dancing in the breeze like floral ornaments were an enchanting sight. The combination of colours was great.

Like a green carpet, the plateau and the meadows were lying long on downsides. The dots appearing on the carpet were nothing but livestock in search of food. The remnants of the Pandava Fort were not seen anywhere. But the surface of the earth being unique there and imparting a pious mood, it was quite possible that such a structure had been situated there. The signs of a great culture that existed more than 3000 years ago getting buried with the passage of time were quite natural. Armymen told us that the remnants of broken forts and rock statues could be seen aplenty on the route from Kuti to Jolingkong. In that case, the vastness of the palace of Kuntibhojan might have started from there. The sunlight became quite dim, having been trapped in a cluster of dark clouds. The breeze that came to us after embracing the burj trees had a sweet smell. Lying on the grass bed with a free body, the mind became more peaceful. That land was holy and blessed because of innumerable *jithendrians* (those who have conquered the senses) going their way through and leaving their mark over there. It was believed that the great Veda Vyasa Maharshi had gone that way for the work of the eighteen Puranas. It was also that great soul who classified the Vedas into four.

'*Vivyasa Vedan Yasmath Sathasmath Vyasa Ithi Smruthaha*'

(Since he did the act of *vyasa* [classifying] the Vedas, he became known as Vyasa.)

The Veda literature was single in its initial form. After dividing it into four, Vyasa taught Maharshi Pylanthe the Rig Veda, Maharshi Vyshiambayana the Yajur Veda, Maharshi Jymini the Sama Veda and Maharshi Sumanthu the Adharva Veda. The Veda literature turned into many branches and sub-divisions in the hands of those great rishis and their equally gifted disciples, who studied and taught it.

According to Pathanjali Maharshi, there were twenty-one branches of the Rig Veda, 101 of the Yajur Veda, 1000 of the Sama Veda and nine of the Adharva Veda.

The work Kalpasuthra tells us about hymns to be chanted on different occasions. It is in the Kalpasuthras that the use of Veda mantras is elaborately described. The 'Brahmana' segments in it help understand the meaning of the Vedas and clearly show the hidden secrets in them. They are called Brahmana because they elaborate hymns that help us attain *Brahmapadam* (the feet of God). The Upanishads are the immortal songs of *Risheeswara Bharatham* (holy India, the land of rishis), known otherwise as the land of Brahma, the land of heaven or the land of the gods. For the human race, the Upanishads indicated for the first time the golden way to the abode of the gods. These books are eternal treasures of knowledge and a path to the realization of God for intelligent people, philosophers and prudent humans. The Upanishads—the ancient original words—are still glowing bright, having energized thousands of generations. Capturing the whole world, they exist in brilliant light even now. Upanishad means the knowledge of Brahma, the base of all existence.

The Mahabharata, the epic work of Vyasa, is considered the fifth Veda (Panchama Veda). There are 1,25,000 *slokas* (verses) in the Mahabharata and it is considered the most beautiful classical work in world literature. The Bhagavat Gita was not part of it when the work was first done. After completing the great work, Vyasa gave it for reading to his disciples and pious *maharshis*. Wonder-struck, all of them praised Vyasa to the sky.

Meanwhile, the godly Naradha Maharshi visited Vyasa.[1] Going through the content of the Mahabharata using his divine powers, Naradha expressed his opinion about the work and the face of Vyasa became pale on hearing it. Though it was notable due to the narration of revenge and fight between brothers and the developments of events thus, the work was not as grand as it was said to be. That was because the greatness of God Sreekrishna was not narrated with due relevance. The godly deeds could never be confined to just the narration of His exhibition in the Kaurava court of His original figure, bigger than the universe, and the description of Him as a tactful driver having immaculate abilities and capabilities. If the work was to endure till the end of the world, it should have the addition of a new chapter on the teachings of God about duty, wealth, love and lust and liberation from the cycle of death and rebirth. Because of that chapter only, the work would live forever. The humans suffering from the vicious cycles in Kali Yuga would have a hope of eternal liberation only thus. It was not a difficult task for such a great maharshi who had classified the Vedas and written eighteen Puranas. Like extracting butter from milk, please do write a chapter combining the essence of the Vedas and Puranas, Naradha requested Vyasa. The fame of the Mahabharata would spread to the whole world because of that immortal chapter, the essence of all sciences.

Vyasa Muni literally became pain-stricken. He had created the Mahabharata with all his knowledge and divine insight. He had spent three years in solitary meditation for the work and it was the whole of his wisdom. Would the new chapter Naradha Muni had suggested be unsuited outwards? The gloomy maharshi thought that God Sreekrishna himself was the last resort and went to the cave in Badharyasrama beside the Saraswathi River for undisturbed meditation. He indulged in long-lasting meditation, keeping away from all feelings or woes. On one full moon night, the great maharshi saw a chariot coming in blinding light and with a deafening sound echoing through the sky beside the Swargarohini mountain ranges.

The chariot driver was God Sreekrishna and the passenger was Arjuna with the Gandeevam (divine bow) in his hands! Though the deep meditation was disturbed, the *muni* stood up to bow down before the god. Immediately, the idea of Bhagavat Gita[2] came to his mind and the Maharshi wrote the first sloka (verse): '*Dharmakshethre Kurukshethre . . .*'[3]

Vyasa was totally satisfied when he completed the Bhagavat Gita, comprising 700 slokas. He did not doubt where that work should be added in the Mahabharata. When the Mahabharata war was sure to happen, Vyasa made some arrangements to make the happenings of war obvious to King Dhritarashtra, who was blind by birth. He gave divine eyes to the scholarly Sanjaya. Under the blessings of Vyasa, Sanjaya got extra-terrestrial vision, an ability to hear from a long distance away and to travel in the sky. But King Dhritarashtra excused himself and escaped saying that he had no interest in seeing the war. He, however, added that he wanted to hear about the war some other time. King Dhritarashtra strongly believed that his children had won the Great War even before it started.

On their side, the Kaurava had eleven Akshauhinis,[4] the great warrior Bheeshmar, the great Guru (preceptor) Dronacharya and exceptional fighters like Karna, Aswathama, Krupacharya, Sallya, Dhuryodhana, Dhussasana and several friendly kings and their armies which were known for their wars and victories. With only seven Akshauhinis, how many days could the Pandavas withstand the fighting? What could Sreekrishna do without a weapon? The so-called 'great warrior' Arjuna was just a worm in front of Karna. So, Dhritarashtra stated that he was going to rest in Hasthinapura and instructed Sanjaya to proceed to the warfront. After inflicting vast devastation on the Kaurava war front, Arjuna fired an arrow at Acharya (Guru) Bheeshmar on the tenth day of the war. Sanjaya rushed to Hasthinapura to inform Dhritarashtra about the fall of the great grandfather. Coming to the bedroom where the king was having a nap, Sanjaya said:

> 'Sanjayofham Maharaja
> Namasthe Bharatharshabha
> Hatho Bheeshmaha Santhanavo
> Bharathanam Pithamahaha'

(Oh king, here has come Sanjaya. Salute to thee!
The great grandfather of the Kuru race, Gangeyan
[Bheeshmar, the son of River Ganga] has fallen in the war.)

Dhritarashtra fell unconscious. After being nursed by Sanjaya and the female servants, Dhritarashtra was revived and asked Sanjaya anxiously:

> 'Dharmakshethre Kurukshethre
> Samavetha Yuyulsavaha
> Mamakaha Pandavaschaiva
> Kimakurvatha Sanjaya'

(Sanjaya, on the holy land of Kurukshethra, what did our
people like Dhuryodhana and the opposite people, the
so-called 'sons of justice', the Pandavas do?)

The learned, all-knowing and merciful Veda Vyasa placed the Gitopanishad (Bhagavat Gita)—the mind of Brahma (God) in 700 slokas—in the centre of the Mahabharata. The core subject of the science of the Bhagavat Gita was the unity between God and Soul (Brahma and Atma). The Gita was the essence of all Upanishads. One in whose mind the four 'G' letters—Gita, Ganga, Gayatri and Govinda—stuck was sure to get eternal liberation.

Some people argue that Gitopadesha didn't happen before the war. Definitely, there would have been an auspicious time marked to start a holy and great war like the Mahabharata. Knowledgeable masters, intelligent astrologers, elderly scholars and holy monks were those who collectively fixed the auspicious time. The first arrow had to be shot right at that moment. Everything was ready and the time fixed to start the war was nearing. It was at this moment that Arjuna, seeing revered elders like Acharya Bheeshmar and Guru Drona on the opposite side, bowed his head and put his weapon down, saying that he didn't want to fight. Thereafter was the conversation between Krishna and Arjuna known as Gitopadesha. Six hundred and twenty of the 700 slokas in the Bhagavat Gita are the advice of God. One would have to spend at least two and a half hours to chant those slokas. But since the slokas were in the form of Krishna's conversation with Arjuna, more time would be required. If that was so, the question was, could the war start at the fixed auspicious time?

But such people forget one thing. Sreekrishna and Arjuna were Nara and Narayana in their previous birth. The Lord had no difficulty, then, to understand the reason for the heartache of His intimate friend. It was only a matter of minutes to pass the essence of all eighteen chapters of the Bhagavat Gita to His close friend through the eyes of the mind and the action of the soul (like sending an email). The rest of the slokas were advised to Arjuna during intervals in the war and at night in the tents. The Anu Gita was also like this. The 'Aswamedha' section of the Mahabharata contains thirty-six chapters in the form of Krishna's conversation with Arjuna after Krishna decides to return to his home at Dwaraka after restoring the Pandavas' kingdom. This part is known as Anu Gita. A Gitopadesha dating to the age of the Mahabharata was excavated from Ayodhya. It contained only sixty-three slokas. While Vyasa was in meditation in a cave on the banks of the Saraswathi River, the chariot of Krishna, Garudadhwajam, pulled by horses named Shaibyaha, Sugreevaha, Meghapushpaka and Lahaka, was said to have passed through the path like lightning and might have been intended to remind the muni about the Gitopadesha. The wish of Muni Naradha was also thus taken care of.

The thought that I was lying on a holy land that the sacred foot of Vyasa had touched brought me to the last phase of the period of the Mahabharata. After the war, after holding three reputable Aswamedha (a rite using horses) for Dharmaputhra (Yudhishtira, the eldest of Pandavas), Lord Sreekrishna was preparing to return to Dwaraka along with his ministers Sathyaki and Udhavar. Just as he sat on the seat of the chariot, the Lord saw Uthara, the widow of Abhimanyu, running towards him crying. She was screaming loudly that one 'fire arrow' was coming towards her and prayed to the Lord that even if she was killed, the Lord should save the baby inside her womb. As if to know what was happening, the Lord closed his eyes for a little while. Sreekrishna understood that Aswathama, who had not been killed by Arjuna when captured but had been left humiliated by shaving the hair off his head and taking out his crown jewel, was furious and had shot the Brahmasthra (the arrow gifted by God Brahma) with the aim of wiping all the Pandavas off the face of the earth. This was the arrow coming towards Uthara.

After hiding the pregnancy of Uthara with his divine powers, the Lord immediately went to the Pandavas. Though the Brahmasthra was only one when shot, it became five on the way and speedily approached the five Pandavas. When the divine weapon was about to hit the five, Lord Sreekrishna blocked it with the Sudharsana wheel. Brahmasthra, the divine weapon that had never before missed its target, now crumbled under the Vaishnava power!

The eyes of Devi Kunti and her sons were filled with tears. Bowing respectfully, Devi Kunti, who had been born only to cry, told the Lord in tears:

'Vishanmahagnae ha Purushadha dharsana
Dhasath sabhaaya Vanavasa kruschchatha ha
Mruthae Mruthaefnaeka maharadhaasthratho
Dhrounyasthrathaschasma Harefbhirakshitha ha'

(Oh Lord Krishna, You had kindly saved us from the poison Dhuryodhana gave to Bheema, from the big fire at the wax palace, from terrible monsters like Hidumban, from the court gambling that was played foul, from the troubles while we stayed in forests, from all the wars and from all the arrows fired at us by great warriors, especially the Brahmasthra fired by Aswathama!)

Bowing in worship, Mother Kunti told Lord Krishna in grief-stricken words:

'Oh God, the Master of the universe, it is the people in suffering that You care for more. Hence, I let You put me in greater suffering.'

[*'Vipadhassanthunashashwathathra Thathra Jagadguro!*
Bhavatho Dharshanam Yath Syadhapunarbhavadharshanam.']

(Where Krishna is, There Dharma is and Where Dharma is, There Victory is.)

[*Yathaha Krishna Sthatho Dharmo,*
Yatho Dharma Sthatho Jayaha]

(Dharma is the cosmic law upheld by the gods and expressed
in the right behaviour by humans. It also includes an
adherence to the social order.)

And this was the message Maharshi Veda Vyasa conveyed
through the Mahabharata and the Bhagavatham.

While returning to the village along with Raju, my mind
felt fully loaded. The atmosphere was dark, even though it was
past 10 a.m. Passing through the western valleys of Kuti Village,
we reached the tents of our fellow passengers. Most of them
were engaged in washing clothes or in attempting to get hot
water for bathing. I chatted with friends for some time and
after having a hot cup of tea, walked towards the camp. On the
way, I met the owner of the lodge, Kunwar Singh Kutiyal, and
on his persistent invitation, went inside his house. We indulged
in conversation for a long time.

During the talk, he gave me his visiting card, printed
in English, and I curiously checked that. The name of the
hotel we were staying in was 'Adi Kailash Paryatak Lodge'.
A colour photograph of Kunwar Singh was posted on one
corner of the beautifully printed card. The card also said that
accommodation was available there from the second week of
May to the first week of November and printed below that
was the Dharchula address. I was surprised. A lodge in the
outermost village of those inaccessible mountain ranges! And a
beautiful card to advertise that! Kuti Village was the last camp
of the daring mountaineers. From there, they went to the burj
tree forests situated at a height of 20,000 feet. An army permit
was required for such journeys. The sanyasins (monks) bound
for Adi Kailash too stayed in that lodge. But Kunwar Singh told
me that 3 km before Jolingkong, the ITBP soldiers would stop
the sanyasins. They would not allow them to go beyond that
point, even if they might have permits. So it was possible for

the monks to look at and worship the Adi Kailash mountains only from that distance.

Kunwar Singh then told me about Santhi Sowkyarani, the head of Kuti Village. I was very surprised to hear that. The ninety-five-year-old lady was well-versed in the 144 courses of the *Kriya Yoga Siddhantha*. She was locally known as 'Kakki'. Her husband, Babulal Kutiyal, had been dead for years. A rare treasure that somehow came into the possession of Kakki's ancestors was then with her. The treasure was nothing but an original manuscript written on burj tree skin believed to be of Veda Vyasa Muni. The archaeology department of the Government of India had come to the village to inspect that. Many archaeological linguists had tried to read and interpret the writing. All those were before the 1980s. Owing to the vintage of the record, only the first few pages could be read and copied. Most of the pages were in such a state that they would turn to dust just by a finger's touch. Those pages that could be read were translated from the original Sanskrit into Hindi by a scholar named Dhungar Singh Thakriyal. Kunwar Singh also told me that a copy of a small work titled *Himalayi Souka Sanskritik Dharohar* was in the possession of Kakki.

India was the true global heir of the tradition of varied handwritten literature. According to Sudha Gopalakrishnan, director of the National Mission for Manuscripts (NMM), what we saw in the traditional writings was the union of literature and culture. But their value was not understood in the true sense. As cultural symbols, whenever they were protected from decay, that many times they were smuggled out. This ended in their sales at *chor bazaars* (thief markets) and antique sales shops. It was estimated that there were about 5 million handwritten manuscripts in India. Most of them were in the possession of private individuals and the rest were with temples and *matts* (hermitages), and the majority of them remained either unknown or ignored.

The NMM was formed to find those manuscripts, tabulate them and protect them. It was believed that the damaged manuscripts were either 'cremated' or ceremoniously put into rivers to flow into the seas. Those handwritten manuscripts were the centre of attention of the world for their original importance in Indian traditions of arts and culture, religion, history, science, beauty and artistic excellence. In Western countries, recording things was first started on hand-made paper. But the things used in India for writing were completely unknown to the West. The bark of the burj tree or burj patra, palm leaf and aloe leaf were only a few of them, and bamboo, ivory, sheets of copper and other metals and leather were some others. Even clothes were used.

India could never forget the admirable services rendered by Kakki's family. During the re-marking of the Indo-Tibetan border, the Adi Kailash mountain ranges and the Om Mountain were included in India due to the pressure exerted by Kutiyal's father, a very influential man then. When an understanding was reached that the whole of the land on the opposite side of the Kali River belonged to Nepal, it was naturally thought that Kuti Village, situated on the opposite banks of the Kunti River, would go to Tibet. The elders of Kakki's family played a pivotal role in liberating the Om Mountain situated on the other side of the Nillyanthi River from Nepal and the big geological region comprising the Adi Kailash mountain ranges and Jolingkong from the claims of Tibet. Kakki told me later that, since the survey works were not prevalent then, the villagers and village heads played a crucial role in re-marking the country's borders. After Independence, India took possession of many strategic places in Kalapani from Nepal. Since Nepal had no military guard bases in those parts, India did so as a precautionary measure. The protests of Nepal, however, were in media only.

Nowadays, Kakki was not entertaining too many visitors. Military officers were the only people who visited her now and then. If they approved it, sometimes Kakki would allow an interview. Some of Kakki's grandchildren were residing in America. Though Kakki owned comfortable facilities in Dharchula, she lived there in wait for the inevitable end under meditation and prayers.

> 'Saishavaefbhyasthavidyanam
> Yowanae Vishayaishinam
> Vardhakae Munivruththinam
> Yogaenanthae Thanuthyajam.'
>   —Raghuvamsam 1–8, Kalidasan

(Got educated in childhood, enjoyed the physical pleasure in youth fully, became a monk in old age and finally abandoned the physical body through the power of yoga—these were the traits of kings of the Raghu dynasty.)

Santhi Sowkyarani belonged to that race, I felt.

My friends were fast asleep when I got back into the room thinking of how I could meet Kakki. I woke everybody up as the wife of Kunwar Singh arrived with lunch. Roti, potato curry and fried ladies' fingers were the dishes. Gourav Mahajan, who was inexperienced in Himalayan journeys, didn't like the potato curry. Though he was a North Indian, potatoes gave him many health problems. Back in our state too, many people avoided potatoes as a dish. Potatoes contained large amounts of carbohydrates. But there was no food more suitable than potatoes for people living at high altitudes. That splendid food controlled the body temperature. In the process of digesting that, the body got more heat and thus, it helped maintain the body temperature. That was why potato was an essential commodity for people in high terrains. They didn't want anything else as food besides potatoes and roti.

Going out, the advocate and Mr Mahajan told me that they would try to get permission to meet Kakki and I got back in bed for some rest. I had noticed some changes in the climate. It was a dark sky still. In the afternoon, signs appeared that the frosty wind had started. The wind blowing fiercely at the peak of the Himalayas threw ice dust downwards and that brought severe cold to the plateaus downhill. If that persisted for too long, the cold would become unbearable.

The women in our group succeeded in obtaining permission to meet Kakki from the military officer. We assembled in front of Kakki's house at around 5 p.m. While we, the fifteen-member group, were waiting impatiently in the courtyard of Kakki's house, the patrolling team of ITBP reached there. To arrive at Kakki's double-storeyed house, one had to go up and down through narrow alleys between big barrier walls. When a soldier requested Kakki to come down, a young woman appeared near a small window on the first floor. The girl told us that Kakki would come out in five minutes; there was anxiety on all of our faces.

Seeing Kakki coming down the stairs carefully, we didn't feel that she was suffering from physical weakness out of old age. The young aide helped her cross the main door downstairs. We were standing in the front courtyard, joining both palms together in reverence, and she came to us with the same gesture. All of us prostrated ourselves before her and touched her feet in respect. We found her voice sharp and clear when she wished us a fruitful and very happy Adi Kailash journey. Her dress was very simple. She wore only a white sari, a full-sleeved blouse and a woollen jacket as an overcoat. Her head was covered by the end of the sari. She was of average height and her skin was fair. Though she walked and talked with great energy, evidence of old age was seen on her face. Right at first sight, I was convinced of the extraordinary brightness in her eyes. There was no way for a person to believe that that lady was ninety-five years old.

When the advocate inquired about the inscription of Maharshi Veda Vyasa, she pointed to an opposite building. She told me that that place was sacred as a temple and that inscription could not be taken out at that time of twilight. There were particular timings for doing so. She walked towards the building, telling us that the place where the container was kept could be seen and also the translation of the inscription could be read. One by one, we crawled up through a staircase that had five steps. One must bow the head before entering the room. After seating us in a 200 sq. ft room, the servant went down to bring Kakki. The only window in the room faced eastwards. The ice-covered mountains were visible through it. Out of eagerness, I looked around the room, which was lit by a dim kerosene lamp. Framed and coloured pictures of almost all the gods and goddesses were kept under the window to the east. The next row was of the pictures of great maharshis. In the middle of them was placed, with great importance, the decorated picture of Om Sadguru Babaji Nagaraj, who attained immortality through Kriya Yoga. On both sides of that picture were the pictures of Sri Yuktheswaran, Sri Lahri Mahashayan, Sathya Saibaba and Sri Parama Hamsa Yoganandan, who were followers of the Sadguru. There were also other faded pictures of various yogis and yoginis whom I couldn't recognize. A wool carpet was spread out over the wooden floor. A cot and some chairs had been placed in one corner of the room.

Kakki came to the room and took a seat. The servant girl lit a lamp and began preparations for the worship of gods with the lamp. Kakki narrated the historical background of Kuti Village in a nutshell. After the worship with the lamp, the advocate read the translation of the Vyasa inscription loudly.

Wherever the advocate found it difficult to read the portions, Kakki intervened and recited them easily from memory. By his inscription, we understood that Vyasa Muni was unveiling the history of 'Sathy Yuga'.

The tale was of the time when Lord Paramasiva was living alone in Adi Kailash. Sathy Devi was the youngest of the sixteen daughters of Daksha Prajapati. Daksha had a special fondness towards his youngest, extremely beautiful daughter. The fifteen daughters were married to Dharma Devan (god of justice), Agni Devan (god of fire) and Pithrukkal (divine forefathers). But Daksha wished for Sathy Devi to marry a ruling emperor and made all arrangements for her *swayamvara* (the ceremony wherein the princess selects her own husband from the assembled kings and princes). Sathy had Paramasiva in her heart and was disappointed when she didn't see Siva on the swayamvara pavilion. She prayed to Him with all devotion and Paramasiva immediately appeared as she wished. Sathy chose Siva in the swayamvara. But Daksha didn't like the figure of Siva, with his matted hair, snake around his neck, tiger skin and *thrisoolam* (trident). Daksha forgot himself and the greatness of Siva found no place in his foolish mind. But since Sathy chose Siva in the swayamvara, their marriage had to be accomplished. The monks supervising the functions asked Daksha to complete the marriage ceremony and the unwilling Daksha had no other choice than to participate in the marriage of Sathy and Siva. After the marriage, Sathy went to Adi Kailash with her husband. To Daksha, that was the end of his bond with his daughter.

Daksha Prajapati, shaking in rage, decided to conduct an elaborate and great Brihaspathi Yaga (yaga is a Hindu ritual sacrifice performed in front of a fire. The sage Brihaspathi is the preceptor or guru of the gods. He is also the deity associated with fire). This yaga, famous as Daksha Yaga, is an important event in Hindu mythology. All persons on earth as

well as in heaven, including Mahavishnu and Brahma, agreed to
participate in it. Daksha neither invited Sri Parameswara and
Sathy Devi to the yaga nor was he ready to give them a share
of the yaga offerings. Maharshi Dadheechi told Daksha angrily
that the yaga was not a yaga without the worship of Sri Sankara
and maybe because of his bad fate, Daksha was in a trap of
greed. A big tragedy was waiting for him. Daksha said that he
didn't respect Siva in dreadlocks and holding a nasty spear.
He emphatically stated that he was not going to invite him to
the yaga. All arrangements for the yaga were soon completed
at a place called Kanakhalam in the vast Ganga valley above
Haridwar.

Sathy Devi, who was joyously living with her husband in the
heavenly Adi Kailash, didn't know of her father's yaga. One day,
while lying in the lap of Paramasiva, she saw the *Pushpakavimana*
(the puranic aeroplane) flying in the western sky. She asked
Siva about the passengers of the plane. But the all-knowing
great god kept silent. Sathy went on pressing him and Siva had
to tell her at last. Sathy Devi became very sad. How could her
father conduct the yaga without inviting her and her husband,
who was the master of all universes? She couldn't believe it.
Maybe they were not invited but it was her duty as a daughter
to participate in the yaga held by her father. Paramasiva advised
her that it was not good to take part in the yaga. But Sathy Devi
told her husband that she only wanted to meet her parents and
sisters and convey her regards. Paramasiva didn't object then.
He told her, however, that he was not coming to the yaga, to
which he was not invited, and he let her go to Kanakhalam with
the escort of his holy lieutenants, the Bhoot Ganas.

When Sathy Devi entered the yaga hall, everybody
there, including the great munis and maharshis, stood up
in reverence. Thousands of people who had assembled also
stood up in unison, hailing 'Rudra's wife', and showed respect

by bowing with both palms joined together. But Daksha exploded like thunder and ordered everybody to sit. In flaming fury, he shouted that he had no connection with the lady, and how could an uninvited person enter the yaga hall? A shocked Sathy Devi looked at her father sadly. Finding boiling anger on his face, she helplessly looked at her mother and sisters as a last resort. Her mother and sisters bowed their heads in defeat. Was this always the fate of women in the great Indian continent? Sathy, Sita, Kunti, Gandhari, Droupathy, Savithry, Damayanthi, Sakunthala . . . a large number of women were born only to suffer . . .

Hanging her head in humiliation, Sathy Devi walked slowly towards the *homakunda* (the holy pit of fire). She then paused, praying to Sree Parameswara in her mind: 'If ever there was a rebirth, You, God of all Gods, please bless me to be born as your wife again.'

Suddenly, with lightning speed, she jumped into the fire.

The god of destruction, Paramasiva, and his holy Bhoota lieutenants turned Daksha's yaga hall into dust in seconds. The fuming Siva also killed Daksha by cutting off his head. Brahma (the god of creation) and Mahavishnu (the god of preservation) requested Paramasiva to be peaceful, stop the *tandava* (Siva's vigorous dance that is the source of the cycle of creation, preservation and dissolution) and apprised him that the broken yaga might lead to total destruction. The yaga should be completed and for that, the headless Daksha had to be given life again. His anger gone, Siva put a goat's head on Daksha's body and gave him life again. Once back to life, Daksha relented. He said that he didn't realize the greatness of the 'Master of the Three Worlds' because of his ignorance and foolishness and begged Siva to bless him for completing the yaga after forgiving him for his sins. The yaga was restarted and finished with all its rituals.

I thought of many things after reading the writing believed to be that of Vyasa Muni. In Vyasa's Mahabharata and Bhagavata, Daksha Yaga is mentioned. Hints are also mentioned in his Skanda Purana. There are considerable differences in the structure and other details of all these works. But how did it happen? There is only one answer. Before writing each work, the great muni engaged in meditation for a long period. The sixth sense thus obtained vividly exhibited in his mind different incidents that had happened in previous time periods. That might be the reason for the diversity seen in the Puranas. There are only two references of Daksha Yaga in *Kumarasambhavam*, written by Kalidasa and based on the Skanda Purana.

'*Adhavamanena Pithuha Prayuktha*
Dakshasya Kanya Bhavapoorvapatnee
Sathee Sathee Yogavisrushtadheha
Tham Janmane Sailavadhum Prapethe.'

(Later, the first wife of Sambhu, Sathy, who was the
daughter of Daksha and who discarded her body in holy
fire because of humiliation, entered the body of that
daughter of mountains to be reborn.)

'*Yadhaiva Poorve Janane Sareeram*
Sa Daksharoshal Sudhathee Sasarja
Thadha Prabhruthiava Vimukthisamgaha
Pathiha Pashunamaparigrahofbhool.'

(Since that beautiful girl abandoned her body angry with
her father in her previous birth, Pashupathi [Siva] became
impassive and lived unmarried.)

After a close relative and constant companion of
Kakki, Basanthi Kutiyal, distributed sweets, we came downstairs.

Like the players of a football team being introduced to a special guest before the start of the game, we stood in order in the courtyard and Kakki came to us one by one and got acquainted with us, asking our personal details. She inquired of each one of us about our family and profession. I was the last one in the queue and Kakki stared at me for some time. Her eyes were shining like the eyes of a cat in the darkness. She touched me lovingly and said, 'Son, you have got a great deal of blessings from God.'

I told her in a nutshell about my Himalayan journeys and my writings. She didn't ask me for any other personal details. After wishing us the best in life in the name of the 330 million gods, she left. We also walked back to our camps.

I was surprised when one of the soldiers who had accompanied us came to me and talked in Malayalam, holding my hand. We moved to a lone corner of the aisle and talked for some time, sharing a friendship. The soldier's name was Sundaresan and he belonged to Panmana near Chavara in Kollam district. He was working as a havildar with the ITBP. He intended to retire from the force after completing twenty years' service. It was very tiring working in the high mountain ranges. Though no one ever worked continuously in high border posts, the job was very risky. Danger was always ahead. A twenty-year term of service meant the loss of a golden period from one's life. Now, he wanted to spend the rest of his life at home.

Sundaresan had also worked in Leh, the highest military base in the world. The temperature in that icy land often went down to minus 40 to minus 45 degrees and human life over there was very hard. Most of the time was spent in tents and trenches and food caused a big problem. Hens' eggs wouldn't break even if thrown on the ground. One had to wait for fifteen whistles when boiling meat and egg in a pressure cooker. Five whistles were needed to boil raw rice. Sundaresan told me all these, to my utter astonishment. The science behind it was that when the height increased, atmospheric pressure decreased. More and more heat, energy and time were then required for cooking.

When I returned to the room after bidding goodbye to Sundaresan, the time was past 6.30. Though it was still daylight, an icy rain had begun to fall. Feeling weary due to the cold, Raju and I made a fire and sat around it. The hot tea served was very delicious and enjoyable in the given surroundings.

Gourav Mahajan talked contemptuously of Kakki's mentioning of the 330 million gods. He openly said that though he believed ardently in the Hindu religion, gods in the millions was a funny concept and such false beliefs made the religion ridiculous in the view of people belonging to other religions. I told him that he was talking like that because of the misunderstanding of the real truth behind using the term 'the three hundred and thirty million gods'. At his request, I explained the truth in a concise way.

In the ninth Brahmana of the *Brhadharanyakopanishad* (the Brahmanas are primarily a digest containing the mythology, philosophy and rituals of the Vedas), Sakallya Muni repeatedly asked Yangnavalkya Maharshi about the matter of the 330 million gods.

(Mahimana Avaishamethe; Thrayasthrimshathwova Deva ithi.
Kathame Thae Thrayasthrimshadhithi Ashouvasava
Ekadesha Rudra, Dhwadeshadhithyastha Ekathrimsa,
Dhindraischava Prajapatischa Thrayasthrimshavithi)

How many were the gods? The sage answered, 'Three and three hundred and three and three thousand.' Again, when asked how many gods exactly, Yagnavalkya replied that there were thirty-three. The sage stated that the number of millions as said above stood for the ability of the gods to grow their sizes according to their wishes (*mahima*). The synonym of God, *thridhashapadham,* meant thirty-three or (10 x 3) + 3 ('*thrayasthreem sathridash ha*'). Who were the thirty-three gods, Sakallya again asked. Yagnavalkya replied that it was eight Vasus + eleven Rudras + twelve Aadhityas = thirty-one. When Indra (the king of gods) and Prajapati (God Vishnu) were added, the total became thirty-three. But who were the Vasus? Fire, earth, wind, space, sun, sky, moon and stars (Agni, Prithvi, Vayu, Antariksha, Aadhitya, Dyau, Chandra and Nakshathra), said Yagnavalkya. The whole universe was based upon them and they were hence called Vasus. Who were the Rudras? The ten Pranas + the Soul constituted the eleven Rudras (Pranan, Apanan, Samanan, Udhanan, Vyanan, Nagan, Koorman, Krukalan and Devadathan were the ten Pranas). When they left a body, the relatives would weep. Because they made people weep (*rodhanam*), they were called Rudras. Who were the Aadhityas? Twelve months made one year and they were the Aadhityas. They took the life as well as the fruits of the work of all beings. Since they 'take' (*adhanam*), they were called Aadhityas. Now, who were Indra and Prajapati? Indra was *Sthanayithnu* (thunder-lightning) and Prajapati was yaga or yagna.

Who were the three gods as mentioned earlier by the number three, Sakallya then asked. 'Three worlds' was the maharshi's answer. Prithvi (earth) and Agni (fire) constituted the first god, Anthareeksha (space) and Vayu (air) constituted the second god and Dhyayu (sky) and Aadhitya (sun) constituted the third god. Then who were the two? The maharshi answered that *annam* (food) and *prana* (soul) were those. All the gods mentioned earlier could be found in them. But who was then the one and sole god? Maharshi answered, 'Prana'. It was the true Brahmam (Brahmam in Hinduism meant 'the unchanging reality in and beyond the world'). It was also known as *Thruth* ('*Prana Ithi Saha Brahma Thrudhithyachakshathe*').

Maharshi Yangnavalkya propounded that the assemblage of the splendour of those thirty-three Aadhityas and others made the gods number 330 million. The core of them was the sole god, Brahmam. In his book, *Everybody's Political What's What*, George Bernard Shaw, the famous English writer, wrote as follows:

> 'The first impression of the countless number of Gods in India may be bewildering. But soon we would learn that all these Gods are only diverse revelations of meditation of one God. There is only one God with indefinable entity. The faith in a number of gods has made Hinduism, the world's most tolerable religion against other religions.'

Gods are considered to be the peculiarities of power of the most important constituent elements of nature. In the inactive mode, they are called elements. When they become active and execute the movement of nature, they are called gods. There is only one eternal power and we call it different names such as ParaShakthi, Virat Purushan, Brahman, Easwar, Dhaivam, etc. The greatest energy, the Brahmam, is everywhere in the universe. The different forms we see are only diverse appearances of that 'soul'. The obvious forms of it are the trinity gods—Brahma, Vishnu and Siva. In the Kalpantha Yuga, this trinity ceases to exist and merges with the Brahmam (the cosmos is eternal but periodically it disappears at the end of each cycle known as Kalpantha [the end of kalpa] and reappears at the beginning of a new cycle).

The incarnation of the trinity takes place again at the beginning of the new cycle and it indulges in creation-preservation-destruction. This is the essence of the Hindu religious faith.

Raju opened the door as he heard continuous knocking. It was Basanthi. I was surprised when she said that 'Ramchanderji' had an invitation to dine with Kakki. Wearing a woollen coat, muffler and cap and putting my writing materials inside my coat pocket, I went with Basanthi. Frankly, I was slightly afraid to go alone with a girl in an unfamiliar area at night. In the deep Jorethang forests of the eastern Himalayas, there was a lonely Buddhist monastery near Kechopari Lake wherein I was once trapped. I made to escape from it at two in the morning. When running up by the side of the empty lake at midnight, I was shocked to suddenly see a strange lama with unbelievable supernatural powers. The shock of seeing him persisted in me for a good number of days. I took a firm decision then that during Himalayan journeys, going out at night would be done only after taking precautionary measures. However, thinking that the saint-like Kakki and the young woman were of the same nature, I followed Basanthi silently in relief. Another cause of relief was the knowledge that the military camp was close by.

II

'Asthithurasyam Dhishi Devathatma Himalayo Nama Nagadhiraja'
(The godly soul named Himalayas, the emperor of all mountains, reigns standing in the north)

I

*'Sa Ya Aeshofnimaithadhatmyamidham
Sarvam Thath, Sathyam Sa Atmaa Thathwa-
Masi Swetha Ketho Ithi Booya Aeva'*

(That which is the atom that the universe originated from, the same is the soul the universe prevails on. That is the truth and *that* is the soul of the universe. And that is you, Swetha Kethu [Thathwamasi Swetha Ketho].)

In *Chandhogyopanishad*, sage Uddalaka was convincing his son Swetha Kethu about the ultimate truth. Yoga is the science of the soul.[1] Yoga is practised to attain perfection in the spiritual realm. In this world of ours, happiness follows unhappiness and vice versa. Yoga skills are practised regularly for some physical gain.

A yogi achieves internal power through meditation. Bhagavat Gita tells that Samkhyans attain paramapada (the seat of god) through Njana Yoga or knowledge and yogis through Karma (action) Yoga.[2]

'Njana Yogaena Samkhyanam
Karma Yogaena Yoginam.'

(Since Njana [knowledge] and Karma [action]
systems are different and opposite, one cannot
practise both at the same time.)[3]

The universe was not a single piece with free existence. Like each organ of the human body was related to one another, so was the particle of that earth related to the universe in wholeness. The truth was that a yogi finally achieved the knowledge of that reality.

God Sreekrishna told Arjuna that he had advised yoga, the spiritual accomplishment, to Vivaswan (sun god) for strengthening the Kshathriyas, the guards of the world at the start of creation. Vivaswan later advised the same to Manu and on his part, Manu advised that to his son and the first-ever king, Ekshaku. When Sreekrishna was imparting the grand and secret knowledge, Arjuna had raised a very natural doubt. 'God, the sun was born before you. Then how should I believe that you advised yoga at the beginning of the world?'

God Sreekrishna clarified Arjuna's doubt with the following reply:

'Bahuni Mae Vyethiyani Jenmani Thava Charjuna
Thanyaham Veda Sarvani Na Thwam
Vedtha Paranthapa'

—Gita 4–5

(Dear Arjuna, many births of yours and mine have gone by. I know them all but dear friend, you don't know.)

God Sreekrishna is also the god of yoga (Yogeswar). The exhibition of Viswaroopam (the real form of god, bigger than the universe) in the Kaurava court was the extreme end of the divine grace, yoga. A particular system of yoga (Yoga Deeksha) founded by Sreekrishna was still being practised in the huts of sages situated deep in the interiors of the Himalayan forests. The same Yoga Deeksha was still being recommended by masters in the isolated icy lands of India, Tibet and Nepal. To commemorate the Mahabharata war and the passing away of that great yogi, that Yoga Deeksha was named 'Kurukshethra Deeksha'. It was the Yajur Veda that first termed Kurukshethra as divine land: '*Dharmakshethre Kurukshethre Dheergasathram Thu Eejire*'.

The belief that the Vedas were timeless was rather deep-rooted. It was also believed that the Vedas were the incarnation of Lord Brahma. There was yet another belief that the Vedas were the result of the sound that started from the Kundalini power inside god (Yoga Upanishads describe the Kundalini as lying 'coiled' at the base of the spine, represented as either a goddess or a sleeping serpent waiting to be awakened). Prajapatis, Brahma Jnanis (those who had the knowledge of Brahma) and sages gave us devoted descriptions in reverential words of Para Brahma. And those words and sentences struck the atmosphere and came out as Vedas, Vedangas and Vedopangangals. The saying was that the Vedas had been propagated for the use of all living beings by sages who attained spiritual fulfilment. *Yogasasthra* stated that the soul of a word was *vikharam* and *vykhari* (word) meant that which was clearly audible. It was an immortal force. The Chandas of the Vedas were the self-orientations of rhythmic movements that formed everything made of sound in the world. Mantras were the disclosure of the thoughts of the heart. It could also be termed as 'Brahman'.

'Karma Brahmodbhavam Viddhi, Brahmakshara Samudbhavam'
—Gita

(The Veda that was called Brahma originated from Para Brahma, which was *akshara* [word] Brahma.)

The set of Vedas was the evolutionary form of the echo of Kundalini, the inner presence in the divine body of God. Its tune was superb. Each sound in the visible world woke up to a similar sound in the invisible world and rejuvenated some mysterious power of nature. All the books on the rituals and truths of the universe argued that even a change of soul from one body to another (transmigration) was possible through the recitation of Pranavam.

Parama Siva was the lord of grammar and education. It was believed that the author of *Kalpaniruktha* was Mahavishnu. Mahavishnu also authored *Chandhus*. Lord Brahma wrote *Jyothisha*. *Vedanta*, the end point of knowledge, was the work of Vishnu. *Meemamsa* (political system) elaborated on the deeds of Lord Brahma and *Nyayam* was about the determination of Siva. Mahavishnu also authored the collection *Vyseshikam*.

Yogam was the work of Brahma. *Samkhyam*, the work dealing with the concept of the infinity of finite numbers, was a Siva creation. And the *Evolution of Universe* dealing with the collection of six systems of thought was created by Mahavishnu.

Many scientific facts regarding yoga lay hidden in the Vedas. Sage Pathanjali had a very important role in the development of the system of yoga by deliberating those mantras. The yoga masters called Nadhans, of the Nadha Yoga Marg founded by sage Dathathreya, were those who had got all the talents and skills of yoga as prescribed by Maharshi Pathanjali. Yoga was also described in detail in the Upanishads, namely Yoga Thathwopanishad, Brahma Vidyopanishad,

Sandillyopanishad and Savithreopanishad. But a complete description collating all that knowledge could be seen in the work *Bhogar Sapthaghandam* written by Sage Bhognathar. The sage, who had made his residence at Kailash, wrote a collection of poems with 4 lakh lines in them under the blessing of Lord Siva and later popularized it into a condensed form under the title *Bhogar Sapthaghandam*. The essence of Bhognathar's work was the revelation of God Parama Siva advising the Kriya Kundalini Yoga practice to Goddess Parvathy Devi. The eighteen Siddha Yogis of South India and their masters played a vital role in popularizing the Kriya Yoga method. There were also many super-brains (*jithendras*) in the epic age who had complete knowledge of the Kriya Yoga. The sixty-four forms of art filtered from the eighteen scientific streams of Vedas shed ample light on this matter. The word 'art' commonly denoted performing arts, meaning music, dance, drama, architecture and painting. But for our ancestors, the word had a wide meaning. For them, art was a blessing of God gifted to only a select few. That made them different from other creations of God and placed them higher. 'Art' was an inborn quality. It was the sort of power brilliant in itself and might be called the capability to create. It was the responding power born together with us. Creativity was for sure an internal urge that gave us pleasure and satisfaction. Hence, for us, the forms of art were solely for peace and happiness in the journey of life.

Many of our authoritative books referred to the sixty-four forms of art.[4] Some of the sixty-four items were not pure art forms. On the contrary, they were skills.

Skill is knowledge and art is happiness. Arts can be broadly classified into four:

1. Art of enjoyment: Performing arts
2. Architecture: The art of building and mechanical skills

3. Physical arts: Sports, physical endurance, etc.
4. Magical arts: Magic, hypnotism, etc.

The ancient sages advised their disciples on different practices like Raja Vidya, Brahma Vidya, Pramana Vidya and Pranayama Vidya for achieving eternal liberation. To practise them, a strong and healthy body was necessary. The sages developed some unusual methods to attain long life, youthfulness and vigour for those having the skilfulness of yoga. They shaped such methods faultlessly by closely observing and assessing the growth and transition of human organs. During that process, they happened to discover the eight divine qualities (Ashta Sidhikal).

They were also known as 'eight fortunes' or 'eight skills'. But all of them were inaccessible to ordinary people. In his *gurukula*[5] days, Lord Sreekrishna learnt all sixty-four *kalas* from Sandheepani Maharshi. At present, books narrating all the sixty-four kalas are not available. They were either lost or decayed. There were references to them in the *Lalitha Sahasranamam*, the work of salutations to the 'divine mother' or Goddess Parvathy.

Out of the sixty-four kalas, some were about the pleasure of the senses, the health of the body, amassing of wealth and entertainment, some others about the success of love, aesthetics, yet others about literature and others about politics and the art of war. But different teachers approached each art differently. Many had not mentioned the very important items. It was seen that Brahmacharya defined many kalas not found in Shaiva Thanthra and Sukra Neethi. Jainism and Buddhism said that the kalas were not sixty-four but seventy-two. The following verse from *Amarakosham* clearly described the eight skills (Ashta Sidhikal).

'*Anima Mahima Chaiva*
Laghima Garima Thadha

Eashitham cha Vashitham cha
Prapthiha Praakashyamevacha'

1. Anima: The power of yoga an accomplished human acquires to shrink his body even to atomic sizes if he wishes to.

2. Mahima: The opposite of Anima. The yogi who acquires this power can enhance the size of his body to any limit.

3. Laghima: The ability to turn one's body weightless, like cotton. The yogi who acquires this power can fly in the sky or stand on water without sinking (the principle invalidates the gravitational force theorem. The principle of alchemy also helps here).

4. Garima: The power to give extraordinary weight to the body. Not only can the yogi give any amount of weight to his own body but they can give such weight to others also.

5. Eashitham: The ability of the yogi to execute any of his orders without any obstruction. Like god, he can make anybody obey his orders. He will also have the ability to control all senses completely and concentrate on his mind.

6. Vashitham: This is the ability to attract anyone even with just one look. It is like a magnet attracting iron.

7. Prapthi: This power has dual usages—a) the power to get hold of anything the moment one wishes to and b) the power of the performer to go into any substance.

8. Praakashyam: The ability of the yogi to enter anywhere at any time. Ability is lying hidden here—the ability to become invisible.

There were such divine persons in India who could achieve and perform the eight powers during and also after the epic age. Hanuman exhibited the powers of Anima and Mahima while crossing the sea. Once he entered Lanka, Hanuman shrank his body to the size of a mustard seed and stood in front of Sita in the size of a cuckoo bird. Later, he grew his body to a mountainous size. The power Laghima helped Hanuman fly through the sky. In the Mahabharata, Garima helped him lie in front of Bhimasena with an excessively heavy tail. Lord Indra taught Nala the power of Prakaashyam. It was because of this power that Nala could enter the room of Damayanthi without anybody seeing him. Sri Sankaracharya also had the ability to perform many of the eight powers. Sanandhana, who became his disciple with the name Padmapada, got the power Laghima from his master. Jesus Christ also could attain some of the eight powers. It was because of those powers that he could walk on water, come out alive from the tomb he was buried in and other such wonderful deeds. Many religious heads who had learnt yoga could attain the power Eashitham. Because of that power, the followers blindly believed them without any question. Sri Sankaracharya practised the power of Prapthi and entered into another man's body as a result of that power. It was said that there were still yogis in the Himalayas who had the ability to perform that skill.[1]

Brahmavyvartham says that yoga skills are eighteen in total. The argument here is that besides the eight powers or eight skills, ten powers or yoga skills (*dhesha sidhikal*) are also achievable. But in all of these, no mention is found of the 144 steps of the Kriya Yoga Siddhantha (the theory of Kriya Yoga). Though the Kriya Yoga Siddhantha is part of the sixty-four kalas, it in itself is a deep subject. A perfect Yogi who acquired the skills as per the Kriya Yoga will possess both the ashta (eight) and dhesha (ten) sidhikal (powers).

'Anurmimathwam Dhaehesmin Doorasrevana Dershanam
Manojavaha Kamaroopam Parakaya Praveshanam
Swachchantha mruthewrdhdhevanam Sahapeedanudarshanam

Yedhasamkalpasamsidhdhi Ranjafprathihathaagathi
Thrikalagnathwamadhwantham Parachithadhyabhinjatha
Agnyarkkambuvishadheenam Prathishtambhofparajayaha
Ethaschodhdheshathaha Proktha Yogadharanasidhdhayaha'

As per the former chief editor of *Mathrubhoomi*, N.V. Krishna Warrier, in his book *Vyakthichithrangal* (Personalities), a Himalayan yogi called Madhuradas, in the state of *samadhi*, was born to Motilal Nehru as his son and lived seventy-two years by the name of Jawaharlal Nehru.

(Samadhi is the state of unconsciousness induced by complete meditation. A state of total equilibrium [*sama*] of a detached intellect [*dhi*]. This is generally interpreted to mean that samadhi is a state of complete control [*samadhana*] over the functions and distractions of consciousness). Madan Mohan Malaviya felt sympathy towards Motilal for having no son and requested the yogi to be born as Motilal's son. During the entire life period of Jawaharlal, the body of Madhuradas was safely preserved in an ice cave in the Himalayas under the supervision of the Mahabharata characters and still living Aswathama and Krupacharya. After the death of Jawaharlal, Madhuradas re-entered his body and again started living his old life. Madhuradas still lives and is said to be 400 years old.

(The yoga siddhis [skills] are the following: the skill to keep the body hungerless, thirstless, heatless, coldless, wrinkleless and deathless, to hear or see at whatever distance, to travel anywhere at the speed of thought, to transform into any shape or form, to select time and type of death as per one's wish, to see and live with the gods, to get whatever is wanted, the power to order, with nothing to prevent one going anywhere, the knowledge about the past, present and future, incomparable intelligence, the ability to know what goes on in others' minds, the power to stop fire, sun, water and poison and no failure in any act.)

Since in every cell the 'power of self' works as the power of desire, knowledge and action, any yogi in the state of samadhi can separate any cell that is part of his own body as per his own wish. Not only that, he can also weld such cells in a different way and form yet another physical cell.[6]

The concept of yoga science was that there was nothing beyond yoga. Like Bheeshmar, a yogi could die as per his wish. Also, he could know the exact time of his death. He would die only when he wished to die. The skill of *thiraskarani* (the ability to instantly disappear or become invisible at will) advised by Lord Indra, the king of the gods, to King Nala was not at all out of reach of a yogi. How a yogi disappeared was by creating an invisible sky wrapper all around his body by imagination. Tantrics called that wrapper 'armour'.[7] By the creation of such armours, one could stop not only the light but also the heat, electricity, sound and waves of anxiety and feelings. The creators of the Upanishads said that *'Thwam Sal Shareeral Prabhyahen Munhadhisheekamiva Dhairyana'*—get out of the small body entity and travel beyond the universe by residing in the subtle body (self/soul), so teaches *Yogasoothra*. *'Bahira Kalpithavruthir Mahavidehaha'*—'Mahavideha' was the technical name for that power.

There were many references to yoga in the Upanishads. Sage Atharva said that Yemam, Niyamam, Aasanam, Pranayamam, Prathyaharam, Dharana, Dhyanam and Samadhi were the eight yoga types known as Ashtanga Yogam. To attain the aim of Parama Swaroopam (the ultimate God), one had to equalize (*thadhatmyam*) with knowledge through the practice of yoga and meditation.

The Upanishads also stated that yoga had eight sitting positions (*aasanam*) like Swasthikam, Gomukham, Padmam, Veeram, Simham, Bhadram, Muktham and Mayooram, and four *avasthas* (status), like Manthra Yoga, Leya Yoga, Hata Yoga and Raja Yoga. As the Brahmavidyopanishad said:

'Jeraa marana rogadhina Thasya Bhoovi Vidhyathae
Evam Dhine Dhine Kuryadhanimaadheeni Bhoothayae.'

(A yogi while living on earth is not subject to wrinkles,
death and disease. He also happens to get the Ashtasidhis like
Anima and also the Vibhoothis.)

'Karpooramanalae Yadwath Saindhavam Salilae Yadha
Thadha cha Leeyamanam Sanmanasthathwae Vileeyathae'
—Sandilyopanishad

(Like camphor dissolves in fire and salt in water, the mind
of a yogi dissolves in itself and ends in philosophy.)

'Padmasanastha Aevasou Bhoomimulsyajya Varthathae
Athimanusha cheshtadhi Thadha Saamarthyamudbhavaeth'
—Yogathathwopanishad

(By skilful practice at still greater scales, he starts to fly up
from the earth. Then he can do superhuman deeds also.)

'Yadha Va Chithasamarthyam Jaayathae Yogino Druvam
Dhoorasruthir Dhooradrushti hi Kshanaadhdhuragamasthadha
Vakssidhi hi Kaamaroopa thwamadrushyakaranee Thadha
Khae Gathisthasya Jaayathae Santhathaabhyasa Yogathaha'
—Yogathathwopanishad

(Besides the mental abilities, the doer also gets hold
of the power to hear from far, farsightedness, mastery of
words, sex appeal, ability to become invisible and the
power to fly in the sky.)

'Dharayaeth Pancha Ghatika Vahninafsou na Dhahyathae

Na Dhahyathae Sareeram Cha Pravishtasyagnimandalae'
—Yogathathwopanishad

(If a yogi meditates five *ghatika* (days) in such a way, no fire
can touch him. He can even walk on fire.)

The Sandilyopanishad says that if one can meditate
centralizing the mind on one point, he can gather the powers of
knowing his earlier birth and future, the power to read others'
minds and the ability to transform into others' shape. The
Savithreopanishad tells us about two special skills called Bala
and Athibala. Sage Viswamithra had advised those skills to Sree
Rama and Lakshmana.

The masters have described the methods and ways one
should follow while engaged in meditation by concentrating
the mind.

During the time of meditation, one should think that
'me' is the 'Brahma' and at other times, one should think
that all that he sees around is 'Brahma'. Placing himself
in a comfortable sitting position, he should first decide
by experience and reason that 'me' is a subject of Avastha
Thraya—the three states of waking, dreaming and deep sleep.
In such a decided state of vitality, he should continuously keep
in mind that what is narrated in Vedanta fully is Sachidananta
Swaroopa and Brahma Chaithanya. Because of the divine
energy he would be filled with then, he should sparkle, cutting
away all feelings and thoughts. He should have no thoughts on
the matter of 'subject' or 'Brahma' at that time. Any vigilant
man who regularly and strictly practises this will definitely
get rich spiritual experiences. The mind should not deviate.
By closely studying the actions and activities of body, organs,
soul, mind and intelligence, he should get convinced that they
are not the soul, 'me'. When the arrogant feeling of being the

creator or the pride of being alive is denied, the obstructions of *panchakosha* (the five senses) will give way and the light of the soul will come out, free to light up the world. He should live a contented life giving no attention to the desires of the body and the matters of the world. The desires and tasks of the body and the business of the world turn to just pretension or acting for others' sake. Yet, by not letting others know that he doesn't need such things, he should act as though everything is in order. Going this way regularly for a time, many changes will come to the body and because of an astonishing and heavenly brilliance, the body becomes extremely attractive and shining. The troubles that come with old age all go away.

The chief aim of the practice of concentrated meditation is to attain the ultimate realizable status of Thuryaatheetha. Seven limits are fixed for it by the name Bhoomika.

1. By learning the eighteen scientific knowledge practices of the Vedas and interacting with good people, positive inclinations get strengthened and negative inclinations get weakened and the first Bhoomika Pranha (consciousness) is reached. It is also called Shubhaecha or Prashna sudhdhi. Care is taken to do good things. There is no chance to do bad things.

2. When goodness grows, faith in god and devotion will also grow. More attention will be paid to godly thoughts. The attempts to know the basic spiritual questions like 'Who am I?', 'What shall I gain by life?', 'What is the soul?', 'What is this world we live in?', 'What is Brahma?' and the like make the second Bhoomika called Suvicharana.

3. When the investigation proceeds in the proper way, reality will come out. Having been convinced of that, the next attempt will be to get free from the experiences of the physical world. The culture that arises is the third Bhoomika Asamghabhavatha.

4. The fourth Bhoomika Vilapini is the destructor of inborn temptations. Thoughts can know the true soul in one's insides. But being unable to glow in the world one lives in, this soul goes away. Not getting self-realization will be very painful every moment. This is a level of frustration happening because the efforts are successful but the soul doesn't glow. The hindering factors are the temptations carried over into one's birth.

5. In the fifth Bhoomika, mental satisfaction is experienced due to the weakening of temptations. The name of this Bhoomika is Sudhasam Vidmayananda Swaroopa. It is pure because there is no contact with the lure, it is Samvithmayi (full energy of knowledge) because there is no ignorance and it is the seat of happiness because there is no non-dual impression. Whoever attains this Bhoomika is liberated from life. The life of such a person will be like in the state of being half-asleep and half-alive. He will be only faintly conscious of the world.

6. Thuriavastha is the sixth Bhoomika. In that stage, there is no grasping of worldly issues. Like a man in sleep, he who is in this stage doesn't take notice of anything. Without reflecting anything, Thuriavastha is just a state of solidity and is also called Mukthi or Nirvana.

7. The seventh and last Bhoomika is known as Thuriatheetham. This state, which occurs when the soul leaves the body, is also called Vidhehakaivallya or Sayoojyamukthi.

All devotion and worship ultimately aim to reach Brahma (the soul of god). The actions should be in full confidence of the result. In *Vedanta Soothrabhashya*, Ramanujar writes about seven things to make a fruitful devotion. The wisdom to reach the target, the control over senses, continuous practice, refinements like Panchamaha Yaga, the purity of mind gained through truthfulness and non-violence, the ability to overcome obstacles and the absence of arrogance and self-praise earn the fruits of devotion and worship faster. The devotion should continue until death. But the devotion to some black gods should be stopped when the result has been achieved. Yet, devotion and worship aiming at eternal glory have to be continued till death.

It is extremely important for a yogi to know his soul closely and then dissolve himself in it. The Vedas, the Upanishads and all the important works repeatedly say that the soul is immortal. This minuscule matter resides in an invisible assemblage of atoms that make one's nature. It is the living body happening in serial succession or the 'Seed of Body', as it is otherwise called. By travelling through generations and amassing knowledge from each birth, the Seed of Body or the cell of wisdom reaches heights. Though it is similar to the physical body, the Seed of Body has no difference in gender. The elliptical aura around it is visible to the eyes of yogis. It is called the Seed of Body because it is from here that the sentiments and thoughts needed for the soul in its movements over the worlds during the stages of evolution arise for the first time. The soul exists free, having no birth or death. The *Pathanjali Yogasoothra* argues that soul is the name for the active force spread over the universe. 'Whatever is seen in the world as dynamic, active or live is only a reflection of the soul. It is the summation of all powers and energies existing in the world. For the universe, it is the common moving force and for human beings and all living things, it is the sign of life. This is also the same thing that transfers into thoughts. The whole universe is a compilation of the skies of souls. This is also the same with the human body. All that is in the reach of its organs have come from the sky. And all those forces that move it ahead have come from the soul. A Yogi who knows that the soul is immortal will never think of its destruction.'

'*Maybe the physical body can be killed but not the soul. The soul is neither born nor dead. It has not even come into existence. It has been there always. It takes no birth. It is everlasting and exists beyond time*'— Bhagavat Gita (2–20).

This excerpt clearly shows that the soul is eternal. The soul, which has no start or end, becomes complete for the same reason of it being perpetual, immortal, permanent and enduring. '*Unclear is the bodies of fathers and sons before creation. They appear in the mid-stage of post-birth and pre-death. Their end is also vague. They attain ambiguity after death also*'. This Gita interpretation (2-28) also makes it clear that only sages and yogis can understand the natural subject, the soul.

(The Mahabharata also says the same: '*Adharsanaadhaapathitha ha Punaschaadharsanam Gathaha Naasau Thava na Thasya Thwam Vrudha ka Paridhevanaa*'— It had come from invisibility and gone to invisibility. He is not yours and you are not his. Then why should you grieve for no reason?)

'*Sareeram Yadavapnothi
Yachchapuil Kramatheeswaraha
Graheethwaithani Samyethi
Vayurgandhanivasayal*'
—Bhagavat Gita Purushothama Yogam (15–18)

(Whilst God [soul, the master of the body] enters the body and leaves it, He takes them [the mind and senses] away like the wind takes away the scent from flowers.)

'*Thamevam Vidhwanamrutha Iha Bhavathi Nanyaha Pandha
Vidhyatheyanaya*'

(One who has known and realized the ultimate soul, the
Paramatma, happens to be deathless in this birth itself. He
gets liberated from birth and death.)

'*Anandham Brahmanovidhwan na Bibhethi Kuthaschana*'
—Thythireeyopanishad

(One who knows Brahmananda and experiences
it has no fear of anything.)

This means that the ignorant will have a fear of the world
('*Adha Thasya Bhayam Bhavathi*'). For a yogi, knowing the soul
(atma) means knowing the ultimate soul (Paramatma). One
will become the master of all knowledge when there is a unison
of Jeevatma (the soul in the body) and Paramatma. That itself is
the accomplishment of Adwaitha (not two). The yogi who has
won the knowledge of the atma (soul) also triumphs in putting
the atma under his control. It is with the help of the atma that a
yogi acquires siddhi (godly skill). His own atma plays a pivotal
role in his astonishing skills and extra-human acts.

Is it possible to manage atma and keep it under control? The
masters argue that it is possible. 'Aa + thama' (Atma) means
glowing or lustrous (Aa = not + thama = darkness). The three
forces of atma are mind, intelligence and culture. It is because of
their presence, atma is called vigour. Intelligence takes decisions.
Atma applies them through the organs of action. Whatever the
result of action—be it happiness or sadness—it is the atma that
experiences it. That is to say, what accomplishes Karma (the
god-dictated duty) and receives its result is atma. Thus, the
theorems atma makes and the ways it accomplishes Karma, both
get accumulated in it and give birth to a unique quality. It is called
culture. The theories that follow will be befitting this culture.
The own wishes of atma are sanctity, peace, love, happiness,
knowledge, quality, strength and comfort. No soul desires

sorrow, trouble or hatred. So each soul takes care to apply those qualities in thoughts, words and actions and also in dealings with relatives and friends. But because the soul repeatedly changes its residence to different physical bodies, it will get afflicted with negative effects of the karma actions in the form of primitive emotions of *kama* (sexual lust), *krodha* (anger), *lobha* (greed), *moha* (desire), *ahamkara* (arrogance) and *alasya* (dizziness). This causes the soul to lose its identity. These feelings weaken it too. The soul has to be satiated by accomplishing one's own responsibilities, by doing the practices of life honestly, by divinely keeping the soul in mind with all eight qualities and by making up the mind to do only good to others by thought, words and actions. It is the lack of knowledge about the soul and the principles of Karma that make man cruel and the world rotten. Peace will come to the world only when the soul is liberated from slavery. Senses, mind and intelligence connect man with the world through temptations. So only by controlling them can one do away with the worldly status and rise to the spiritual status. Spiritual status is not for intellectuals alone. Spiritual knowledge moulds a noble generation and thereby leads to the complete transition of the world. Hence, this knowledge is not to be confined only to the Himalayas and the huts there. What our ancient sages urged was also to treat others with this knowledge that 'all are born with soul and so all are brothers and sisters of one another'. When the yogis and sages can do superhuman deeds by keeping the soul under their control, the ordinary people shall do good deeds to achieve the idea of '*Loka Samastha Sukhino Bhavanthu*' (the well-being of the whole world).

Katopanishad says that knowledge and ignorance differ not only in looks but also in outcome. '*Dhooramaethae vipareethae vishoochi ya cha Vidya*' (knowledge and ignorance are not only contradictory but are also opposite, outcome-wise). The study-based fruit of knowledge is glory whereas the non-study-based fruit of ignorance is ill comfort.

Only by defeating ignorance with knowledge can one acquire knowledge of self. '*Eha chedhavae dheedhatha Sathyamasthi na chedhihaavaedhinmahathee vinashtiha*' (when he knows in this birth itself his self, that I am Brahma, in this birth itself he reaches the real truth). This means his birth is justified. There is only one Sath Chith (virtuous mind) or that which gives everlasting happiness. It is Brahma only. It has no dual existence. When we learn the real philosophy, i.e., knowledge, what is visible to us in different forms is one thing only— Brahma. Such thoughts about atma or non-atma are the one thing that leads the holy souls to the ultimate seat of divinity. Total ruin awaits the man who doesn't know his soul while he is alive. '*Thamaevam Vidwanamrutha Eha Bhavathy Nanyaha Pandha Vidyathaeyanaya*' (the one who has known and realized Paramatma [the Ultimate Soul] becomes deathless in this birth itself.) That is, he will be liberated from birth and death. Thythireeyopanishad also says that one who knows and experiences the supreme joy, i.e., Brahma, has fear of nothing. ('*Anandham Brahmano Vidwan Na Bibhethi Kuthaschana*'). But the ignorant one is full of fear of life ('*Adha Thasyam Bhayam Bhavathy*'). The Mundakopanishad says that he who knows Brahma becomes Brahma himself ('*Brahma Veda Bramaiva Bhavathy*') and Bruhadharanyakopanishad makes it clear that he who knows soul turns into it himself ('*Sa Edham Sarvam Bhavathy*'). In the Bhagavat Gita also, God Krishna convinces Arjuna of the same theory (Bhagavat Gita 5–19).

'*Ehaiva Tharjjithaha Sargo Yesham
Samye Sthitham Manaha
Nirdhosham hi Samam Brahma
Thasmal Brahmani Kae Sthithaha*'

(The ignorant being tempted by both desire and despise does sins and repeats birth and death. But he who knows that soul and body are different doesn't desire or despise and hence is free of sins. He gets liberated.)

It is an undisputed fact that yogis and rishis who know the soul through meditation and self-mortification can keep the soul under their control and do unbelievable divine acts.

Many studies have been done around the world on what happens to the soul after death. They are still being done. All these studies focus on principles that are based on Hindu philosophy. The theory developed by ancient Hindu rishis correlating science, logic and practical knowledge is world-famous as Hindu Vedanta. The base of it is the Vedas and the Upanishads. The rishis divided the Vedas into three sections (Kanda), viz. 'Karma Kanda' (action section), 'Upasana Kanda' (devotion section) and 'Njana Kanda' (knowledge section). The conviction that eternal liberation was not possible through karma (action) and *upasana* (devotion) led them to the principle of *njana* (knowledge). It was this Njana Kanda that became world-famous as the Upanishads. Njana Kanda means real knowledge. We want to know three things about ourselves.

1. What is the core or essence of the world we see around us?
2. Who am I? Where did my body and soul come from? Where do they go or what do they merge with at the end?
3. What is God, Lord or Brahma who created all these?

True knowledge is to know all these. Our scholarly rishis called the outer space 'nature'. Nature creates and runs the universe. It is numbers that fix the limit to the creative scheme of Goddess Nature. For nature, power that developed from *oneness* to *multiplicity*, numbers make the base. Hence, under everything, there will be one number as the base. Scholars argue that there is no way of escaping from the secrets of nature from the holy eye of a yogi. He has thorough knowledge of the root number of each of the basic five elements (pancha bhoothas). This is true with the earth also. The first things that were created in the world were the three qualities of *thamass* (darkness), *rejass* (brilliance) and *satwa* (goodness). Then the co-action of the pancha bhoothas—vacuum (akash), air (vayu), fire (agni), water (jal) and soil (prithvi)—created every other thing (vacuum: state of emptiness, air: gaseous state, fire: energy state, water: liquid state and soil: solid state).

'Thamahapradhana Prakruthae Sthalbhogaayaeswaranhaya
Viyalpavana Thaejombubhuvabhuthani Janhirae'

(This family of earth has originated from the great almighty God and the great mother of everything, nature. They are the father and mother of all universes. All that is in the family—living or non-living—are children of the same parents. Why they quarrel with one another as we see now is because they have forgotten this truth.)

Prithvi (soil) is wrapped with jal (water), jal with agni (fire), agni with vayu (air), vayu with akash (sky), akash with *maya* (illusion) and maya with *satwa* (goodness).

Since the sky and other pancha bhoothas are parts of the structure of nature, the qualities of that structure, namely satwa, rejass and thamas, are naturally in the bhoothas also. The five sense organs, namely ears, skin, eyes, tongue and nose, originated in order from the satwa qualities of the pancha bhoothas. The satwa quality of akash gave birth to the ears, that of water to the tongue and that of soil to the nose. It should be understood that one sense was born from one bhootha in that way. And it should be firmly taken that the body and senses being matters made of bhoothas are lifeless. Life or soul is added when the satwa qualities of the pancha bhoothas all join together. The entity that thinks things is called the mind and the entity that decides things is called intelligence. From the rejass qualities of the pancha bhoothas were created in respective order the five action organs, namely mouth, hand, leg, anus and sexual organs (*upastham*). These five carry all activities. The life-giving air (oxygen) was formed when the rejass qualities of the pancha bhoothas joined together. It then turned into five according to the type of activity. That body which has seven sections of activity is called the psyche. The seven sections of activity are the five senses of knowledge that understand sound, etc., the five action organs that manage words, etc., the five types of soul, the mind that is full of imaginations and fancies and last but not least, the decision-making intelligence. The principle of pancha bhoothas like akash (vacuum), the principle of pride, the principle of greatness, the basic nature, the ten senses of knowledge and action, the mind and the five molecular forms (controlled by senses) of sound, touch, shape, taste and smell make the twenty-four principles (or the classification scheme). Since both Kala Swaroopa[8] and Purusha[9] are the same, the naturally evolved theorems are estimated to be twenty-four only ('kala' means eternal. 'Swaroopa' is the liberated condition in which one's outward form is one's deepest spiritual nature. Primarily, however, this term refers to the supreme personality of God Sreekrishna. Purusha is the first form of supreme lord Narayana and the source of everything in the universe.) The soul is considered to be the twenty-fifth theorem. The soul is God. Hence, collectively, they are called Purusha. Thus, we must consider the natural dimensions as twenty-four and Purusha as the twenty-fifth. Made of the pancha bhoothas, the physical body is called *annamayakosham* or the foodie body. Born from food and nurtured by food, the physical body is matter that eventually blends and merges with the earth. The 'mind body' is made up of the five senses, goodness or virtues (satwa) of everything and the thinking mind. The 'knowledge body' consists of the five senses and the decision-making intelligence. The soul and the senses of karma constitute the 'spiritual body'. The 'subtle body' is the collection of all these 'bodies'. The ignorance of one's own shape and happiness makes the 'happy body' and is called the 'causal body'. The nature that bears three qualities evolves into matter (body), action (senses) and pleasure. All the things created were added into a consolidated wholeness called 'Brahmandam' (macrocosm). When these things stood as dead, inactive and lethargic, Brahma, to energize it, broke the 'Brahman hole' at the head of the total body Brahmandam and entered it. Those which were so far inactive and lifeless became active and vibrant then. The creation of everything, living or non-living, happened thus. The different expressions of action such as energetic, inactive and dormant show only the exterior character. Each and everything in this universe is made up of the vigour of Brahman and the fundamental elements that are part of nature. What modern physics tries to prove is also the same. First, *energy* created *matter* and *matter* created the complex structure of living bodies. After then, God or soul or life or atma entered all of them (modern physics says that *matter* is nothing but *energy*. And matter can be converted into energy too). Is it this atma which is born again after death? No, atma or soul is immortal. It never dies. And it never takes birth too. Hence, rebirth happens only to the astral body. Behind the physical body, there is an astral body. The physical body is only a vehicle the astral body uses to travel. It is like getting into a new vehicle when this vehicle breaks down or becomes old. Life or *jeevan* cautious of the astral body gets into a new physical body after discarding the other. This means that death and birth are matters of life and not that of the soul. But what then is life? It is nothing but the soul which is proud of the body that protects it. When the pride is there, the soul speaks and when it is not, the soul goes to other bodies. If not, it reaches the real entity, *the Brahman*. God Sreekrishna convinced Arjuna of the same telling him that atma (soul) was endless.

> *'Vasaamsi Jeernani Yadha Vihaya*
> *Navani Gruhnathi Naroparani*
> *Thadha Sareerani Vihaya Jeerna-*
> *nyanyani Sam Yeti Navani Dhaeh'*
> —Bhagavat Gita (2—22)

(Just the way a man throws away a shabby dress and wears a new one, so the soul gives up a bad body and enters a new one without any emotions.)

Death is the end of each and all. There is nothing more certain in life than death. Anything that goes ahead, after some distance, comes back to where it started. The sun, moon and stars have all formed from the molecular clouds of gas and dust in interstellar space and as time passes by, will dissolve themselves into the same at the end. This is what happens all around. Each and every substance in this world was formed from molecular cells. They will go back to that state in the end also. This is the unbreakable law of nature. This law is applicable to the soul also. It will in turn dissolve into its causal factor. We all are bound to return to the starting point— God, Brahman or nature.

How long would death and rebirth exist? The life and rebirth would continue until the strength of the bad deeds subsides. After death, the souls reside in different worlds of endless space until reborn. There are specific areas here for gods, demons, ghosts and souls arriving after death. Those who expect immediate rebirth and those who face delay in rebirth reside here. There are also those who have secured eligibility for a prolonged, comfortable stay in space by virtue of the good deeds they have done and the true knowledge they have acquired and by that way, some of them are in anticipation of re-entry to the Prajapati Lokam (the world of supreme God), Hiranyagarbha Lokam (the world of the soul of the universe or Brahman) and Sagunabrahman Lokam (the world of Sagunabrahman).[10]

Since they have the Lingam Sareeram (the subtle body which is the vehicle of consciousness), such residents of the atmosphere can also think. Thinking is the only activity they do. They have pleasure and grief until the Lingam Sareeram decays. These feelings of pleasure and grief arise out of their thoughts. They differentiate between good and bad deeds according to the culture in their earlier birth. They can make things or repair them with their thoughts. Their thoughts have the power to do or cause things that we think are impossible. They are astral bodies energized by the soul and reside in and travel to celestial forms. So they can adopt any shape and have no difficulty in travelling anywhere on earth and in the atmosphere. All the sensual activities like seeing, hearing, touching and knowing are possible to them. And since they have no physical body, bodily tortures like sleep, disease and old age do not affect them. What Thomas Henry Huxley, the famous Western writer, says in his book *Evolution and Ethics* is notable. He says that 'like the theory of evolution, the theory of rebirth is also based on the principle of facts.'

It is only a fact that those great people on earth who have attained spiritual heights through the devoted practice of yoga and single-minded meditation can make contact with those divine souls in the atmosphere and do wonderful things with their help.

Pathanjali Yogasoothram propounds that the theory of the quest for the soul and pranayama are related. The theory of

searching the soul is the detailed scientific truth at the high end
of the yoga action, Pranayama. But this has no relation with the
action of pranayama as practised by some people in our country.
As *Pathanjali Yogasoothram* says, it is believed that the dead souls
are living invisible around us. They may be in millions. Maybe
we are coming in and going out through their bodies. They do
not see us or feel us. It is a zone in a zone or a world in a world.
We live with souls having a peculiar vibration or pulsation. All
the living things having the same vibration can see one another
but they can't see those having a higher vibration. We cannot
see anything when the intensity of light becomes too excessive
for our eyes. Still, there may be creatures with eyes capable of
seeing even such bright light. Just the reverse, light with such
a low vibration is also invisible to our eyes. But there may be
creatures that have such a capacity, for example, cat, owl, etc.
It is only the prelude of soul vibration that is visible to our eyes.
We can take the air zone as an example. It is like innumerable
layers put one over another. Those layers near earth will be
seated more tightly than others. But the higher they go, the
lighter will be the layers. Take the case of the oceans. The
deeper we go, the higher will be the pressure of the water. Those
creatures living deep in the oceans can never come up to the
surface. If they try to break the pressure and come up, they will
crack into pieces. Suppose that a room is full of creatures that
are totally invisible to us. They denote a particular vibration
or throbbing of the soul. We stand for another type. Suppose
their vibration is fast and ours slow. Even then, both we and
they are 'similar soul bearers'. All are part of the same ocean of
souls. The difference is only in the speed of soul pulsation. If
we can achieve fast soul pulsation, then the region of souls in
front of us changes. We won't be able to see other people then.
They disappear. But the invisible creatures become clear. All
of that, which gets the mind to such a high speed of vibration,
is indicated in one word, samadhi (deep meditation) in the

science of yoga. At the downward steps of samadhi, we get
the vision of other souls. But above, at the uppermost point of
samadhi, we can see the 'true substance' or the 'basic material'
of everything in the universe.

In Maharshi Pathanjali's 'Eight-type Yoga Science', is
said that samadhi is the uppermost point of yoga practice.
In the samadhi position, when the mind is fully withdrawn
from the senses through mental power and totally devoted
to intense meditation, then the meditator and the subject
of meditation (God) become one in every meaning of it. In
Savikalpa Samadhi, one's consciousness dissolves into the
consciousness of God (Brahman). The flow of life stops
fully and the motionless physical body becomes frozen
as if dead. Even then the yogi will be conscious of his life's
stillness. The Nirvikalpa Samadhi can be practised only by
those masters who have reached the highest of heights. In the
position called samadhi, the search for God is of two types,
Sagunopasana and Nirgunopasana. In Sagunopasana, God is
meditated upon in their incarnation form, like Siva, Vishnu,
Devi, Ganapathi, etc.

In Nirgunopasana, meditation is done on Brahman or the
ultimate vigour. This is a very hard way of meditation. Maharshi
Vyasa contends in 'Bhagavatham' that

> *'Sthiram Sukham Chasanamaasritho Yeti*
> *Ryadha Jihasurimamamga Lokam*
> *Kalae cha Dhaesae cha Mano na Sajjayeth*
> *Pranam Niyachenmanasa Jithasuha.'*

('Your highness, please do not think that when a yogi
who has the glory of victory over soul wishes to abandon his
physical body, he should take into consideration the time like
utharayana[11] or the vicinity of a holy temple. That is not his

way to eternal liberation (sidhi). It is his education—yoga.
He should in all confidence run his life sitting on the cosy
and pleasant chair of belief in such a way of liberation. He
should distract his mind from all material pleasures. Then the
working of senses will come under his control.')

Wavering of the mind will come to a stop when it is
disconnected from material life. What we call 'mind' comes to
an end there. What remains then will be the spiritually constant
intellect. It should be placed on its mentor, the soul. The soul
should be placed on the ultimate soul, the Paramatma. This is
how a yogi reaches the state of samadhi.

In his work, *The First Principles of Theosophy*, Jinaraj Das,
president of Brahma Vidya Sangh, analysed the last moments
of people dying natural deaths. In the final moment, the whole
life one has led comes into one's memory. Event after event, all
the experiences of life come out from every nook and corner
of oblivion. When death is coming, the brain will push out all
the memories kept in it. No man dies half-mad or unconscious.
Even a totally mad man may attain complete normality for a
short while at least, but he may be unable to convey the matter
to others. Many a time it may be that when death is only a
breath away, even then, in the small time between taking the
last breath and life abandoning the body, the brain will start
working normally and would be rejuvenated by the memory
of the past occurrences of life.[12] This is also the case with
birth. The Garbhopanishad says that the baby in the mother's
womb recollects all his earlier births. The yogis assert that such
remembrance of earlier births happens because of the soul
living in the pineal gland.

Science has proved that a baby in the mother's womb can
hear sounds. Memory is a pattern imprinted on the brain. It is
like imprinting data on a computer hard disk. The brain is a very

active organ and different groups of nerve cells are responsible for different thoughts. They drift in and out of action and when these groups of neurons stop drifting and attain a permanent nature, there comes our permanent memory. The pattern of changes is called the memory trace. Neurons can decay sometimes. Even if many neurons of the memory trace perish, the memory trace will exist as before. Because of the same reason, memory also stays alive. Where do these patterns reside? Which is the hard disk of the brain? Every experience will have its own memory trace. Billions and billions of memory traces! There are more than ten thousand crore neurons and crores and crores of synapses in the brain. And inside them, there is space for an infinite number of memory traces.

Remembrance is the process by which the experiences or events imprinted on the subconscious mind are brought back to the conscious mind. The chemistry of this process is still unknown to scientists. Even bigger will be the complexity of the chemistry of emotions, sense and behaviour, much more than the chemistry of memory and expressions. What will the 'neuron sketch' of our inner feelings of pleasure and grief, fear and anger, braveness and kindness look like? Will it be like the electric pressure and distribution pattern of memory? There is no answer to this question. The human brain is the most complex product of evolution. The claim of ancient thinkers that meditation and deliberate thoughts can influence activities normally going on inside the human body that is independent of the conscious brain, including immunity, is now backed by modern science. A new branch of study called Psycho Neural Immunology has thus come into existence. Intelligence is a derived asset. It has been stored for generations through generations. It receives new signals from outside and by analysing and comparing them with the already stored memories, either accepts them to add to the existing stock of memory or throws them out. Consciousness is a monitoring process done by a section of the brain with sort of a watchful internal eye. Like memory and intelligence, consciousness also is spread all over the brain. All communication signals except that of death reach the brain through the spinal cord. Sleep, waking up and dreams were the subjects of research even from ancient times. There are mentions of them in many Eastern and Western medical books. Masters of Ayurveda and Indian philosophy could approach them more scientifically than anybody else. They argued that intelligence, mind and feelings are ultimately the products of the metabolism of the food man takes in and hence are just physical entities that can be subjected to physical scientific studies.

The physical human body is encircled by the soul as a barrier of light. When two individuals come together, their souls change colours between them. That is why people experience positive and negative feelings when they meet. The same is the reason why couples with divergent selves behave like two opposite poles. This can't be detected by examination of horoscopes. Be it man or woman, it is quite natural that they go the way their souls lead them. The Upanishads state that 'it is not for the like of them that women like their husbands but for the like of souls that they like them. For that matter, it is not for the like of anything that we like anything but for the like of souls' ('*Na Vaa Arae Pathyuha Kamaaya Pathiha Priyo Bhavathyatmanasthu Kamaaya Pathiha Priyo Bhavathi*').

The deep explorations of the royal yogis of the Brahmavidya Sangh had gained many facts regarding life after death. What happens in the death of a man eligible for eternal liberation is like this. From the heart, the soul as an eternal body will first enter the Brahmarandra (a mystical opening in the crown of the head where the spinal cord ends. It is believed to be the hole of the cosmic spirit, the Brahman) through the spinal cord and coming out from there at once gets into the Surya Mandala (the world of the sun) via the rays of the sun. From there through the black dots of Surya Mandala, it reaches the ultimate seat, the Brahma Padham by the method proven by the divine knowledge earned from yoga. Holy souls like Ahas, Aadhityas and Prajapatis escort it to eternal liberation. After fully consuming the harvest of the karma that was done in this world, again the soul or spirit will come from that world to this world in attraction of karma. With all the karma in hand, it goes to where the mind gets adapted. The soul is a thinker. The Chandogyopanishad too says that what we think in this world, we think after death also.

Sir William Barrett from Britain collected details by talking to people who met death but luckily escaped. A member of the Royal Society, Sir William has compiled his experiences in a book. He narrates the experiences of such people who missed death narrowly as follows:

> 'Totally strange but peculiar sounds continually echo in the ears. What we feel next is full peace of mind and complete happiness. This is a different kind of enjoyment of happiness.[13] The soul detached from the body travels through an endless tunnel after death.[14] The tunnel is full of darkness. While reaching the end of the tunnel, a core of light shining like the sun can be seen. Going near it, we see a big crowd of dead souls standing around. Here starts the journey that has no end. Turn by turn, the soul will go on travelling to some or other planets millions and millions of kilometres away and then back to the earth'.

Dr Olaf Blanke, the Swiss neurologist, is a person who has made extensive studies on the subject. The doctor discovered many magnetic and chemical actions taking place in the brain through scientific research. When he passed electricity to the left angular gyrus of the human brain as part of the experiment, he found a shadowy figure standing aside at the back. When the shock was inflicted on the gyrus on the left side, the soul detached from the body and stood high above. As if observing its own body, the soul had been standing high in the air. There are so many people around the globe who came to life after meeting death face to face.[15]

Dr Brian Weiss, MD, was the head of the Department of Psychiatry of a big hospital affiliated with Miami Medical University, USA. He had done admirable service at Pittsburgh University and also at Belleview Medical Centre, New York University. While he was working as the department head of psychopharmacology in Miami, he got national applause for his scientific research on biological studies regarding the soul. This made him world famous. He firmly said that what was mentioned in the Vedas and Upanishads about the soul was 100 per cent correct. Some quotes from his work *Same Soul Many Bodies* are given below:

> 'All of us are immortal. The fact is that genes, traditions, beliefs, character specialities and other such matters are carried over generations through us. The most important part of us—the soul—is eternal. It has no death. I strongly believe that the soul that exists inside every one of us exists even after the death of our physical body and after death it migrates to other bodies and this journey of the soul to reach the top level is perpetual.'

He also mentions anecdotal proof, including a couple who were lovers in their previous births and met again in the present birth. He says his patients got much relief from their

diseases or were even cured completely when they recollected
their previous lives.

> '. . . students ask me why one selects the dirty slum areas of
> Bogota or Harlem for return. The sanyasin I met ignored
> this question smilingly. This is because they see life as a
> drama scene. The terrible life in a slum is only one role. The
> soul that selected such life at present may select the life of a
> rich man in the next birth. It is a cyclic process of the soul and
> in this, the birth of a female, male, patient, pleasure hunter,
> strong, weak, rich and poor surely occur. The following
> are the important facts of this: A soul cannot study all the
> lessons in a single lifetime. Secondly, we must improvingly
> lift up our souls whilst we take every birth.[16] Souls do not
> become old. Some souls become more refined compared to
> others. For example, Saddam Hussein studied only up to the
> third whereas the Dalai Lama is a graduate.'

Do the souls need food? Experts opine that they do. Part
of the food one takes in is consumed by the soul. The body
physique comprises the physical body made of the five basic
elements (pancha bhoothas) and its controlling factor, the
soul. Part of the food consumed by the body reaches the soul
also as molecules. During his lifetime, a human being does
any number of activities through his sensual organs of njana
(intelligence) and karma (action). Energy is required for this.
Besides the energy received directly from the atmosphere
(sun), the soul also accepts energy from food. By the principle
of '*Annal Bhavanthi Bhoothani*', '*vrushtaerannam that ha ha Praja ha*',
the consumed food becomes blood-coated semen and from
it bhoothas (elements) take birth. It is believed that such
intake that the soul does is only at a select time. That is why
the masters advise us to consume food correctly at regular

intervals. If we do not, the soul may not accept it and the body will throw it out. And what comes out is protein-rich. Why the yogis say that urine therapy is very effective is because of this. In the same manner, the water, food and other offerings we dedicate to the forefathers on their memory day reach them in subtle form. Yes, the forefathers receive what we dedicate and bless us. Their blessing will give prosperity and peace to generations and generations. The death-day rituals have much importance until the souls of the dead get a rebirth though there is no way for us to know when it happens. The yogis of the Siddha School say that the food reaches the souls of the dead in subtle form due to the power of the mantra utterances done on the ritual day. It is a proven fact that sound has infinite power.

The stories of those who remember the events of their previous births have been publicized by the media many times and from many parts of the world. Psychologists have done authoritative studies and research on the subject too. Most of these studies and research support the Indian philosophy of rebirth. The publication of such a rare story in the *Probe India* monthly in its 1982 July edition is notable.[17] It described the story of an unmarried young woman from Maharashtra who sometimes showed the dual character of a conservative Bengali housewife of the last century. Called the 'Nagpur scandal', it has been subjected to more elaborate studies by Dr Ian Stevenson of the School of Behavioural Medicine and Psychiatry, Virginia University, and Dr Satwant Pasricha of NIMHANS, Bengaluru.

Kumari Uthara Huddar was a former teacher of Nagpur University. Born into an orthodox middle-class family, she was fluent in English, Hindi and Marathi. Dr Stevenson wrote that he thought her an intelligent, philosophy-loving, educated lady. On every Ashtami day (the eighth phase of the full moon), mostly at midnight, she would rise from sleep and act like Sharda, a housewife who lived 150 years ago in erstwhile East Bengal (now Bangladesh) by evoking her soul into hers. This state of Sharda's soul residing in Uthara would sometimes go on for up to forty-one days. Sharda's soul would leave Uthara in the evening at the time of worshipping God with camphor. Uthara would then turn into the old Uthara. In the merger state, Uthara would experience severe headaches and tiredness. When Sharda's soul entered Uthara's body, she would wear her saree in the Bengali style, write Bengali devotional songs and sing them. She would worship Goddess Durga and show an excessive interest in the Bengali sweet sitabhog. She wouldn't recognize her family members or her friends. Forgetting Marathi, Hindi and English, she spoke in the old nineteenth-century Bengali language and recall memories of the parental house of Sharda in Sapta Village. The experiments done by a team led by Dr R.K. Sinha of Nagpur by bringing Uthara into this village revealed amazing facts. She was able to describe the Hanseswari temple that stood near the house, and mourned that two big pillars were not there now (these pillars were destroyed in a massive storm that hit the area seventy years ago). She also recognized the picture of the late husband of Sharda. Without uttering his name, she wrote the husband's name on a piece of paper and stood in front of his photo for a long time with her head bowed. Dr R.K. Sinha recorded that the generation tree drawn by Uthara was exactly accurate.

She talked about how she had died in her previous birth. After having two abortions, she became pregnant for the third time at the age of twenty-two. While she was plucking flowers at Tharadevi temple near Shikkarpur, she was bitten by a venomous snake. She fell unconscious and lost all memories. She was seven months pregnant at that time. Manorama, the mother of Uthara, says that while she was carrying Uthara in her womb, she often dreamt of a snake coming to bite the big toe of her right leg. She remembers kicking the snake out and rising from her sleep crying loudly. But after Uthara was born, this dream stopped. Uthara too had such snake dreams during her childhood.

When some psychiatrists suggested psychiatric treatment for this, Dr Stevenson's opinion was just the reverse. 'Uthara never had any mental sickness to be treated. Maybe all these happened because the soul in her previous birth was greatly influencing her subconscious'.[18] This incident was a perfect example of his rebirth theory.

The story of Uthara became an international sensation after it was published in detail in the American newspaper, the *Globe*.

Ample narrations have come into the media regarding the rebirth of astronaut Kalpana Chawla, the first Indian woman in space. She was killed in the space shuttle Columbia disaster along with other six crew members. Two months after her death, a baby girl was born to a young man called Rajkumar of Nar Mohammedpur Village in Khurja, Uttar Pradesh. He named the baby Upasana. In July 2007, when she was only four years old, the girl said she was the reincarnation of Kalpana Chawla. At first, it was taken as a joke but gradually, the incident drew wide media attraction and reached a new turning point. NASA authorities were not able to tell exactly how the spacecraft Columbia crashed. Little Upasana narrated from her memories that the spacecraft had disintegrated when a huge iceberg hit it while on its orbit. The small girl also remembers the last moments they went through in the spacecraft. The US authorities intervened when they learnt of the matter through the Indian media. With this, the incident received international attention through media like the *Times of*

India edition of July 2007 and also reports from other English dailies. When they were convinced that Upasana was the rebirth of Kalpana Chawla, the parents of Upasana changed the girl's name to Kalpana Chawla.

Plenty of news has been spread in India and the world about the holy rishis of the Himalayas and their skills. Many authentic studies and research have also been conducted on these. Still, they are going on. The solar system has been amazingly dissected on this earth of ours. Great scientists, astronauts and the holy rishis who always were after truth, all have discovered its laws and facts. We can consider these discoveries as guidelines for the development of the human race and human individuality. Hence, these facts and realities deserve importance. A general narration as to how the yogis and rishis accrue skills and special abilities has already been depicted in this work. Still, there is a section that believes or thinks about whether such things are possible in the present modern age. We cannot blame them. It is the result of their karma that these non-believers are left in the dark. It will take so many births for them to see the light of knowledge in their minds that are dark in ignorance. Let us examine some of the experiences of those who had the luck of witnessing and seeing the surprising abilities of the Himalayan rishis.

When we say that there are rishis in the Himalayas even at the present date who can melt even iron, many may frown unbelievingly.[19] After reading it, many have informed me of similar experiences.[20] After the event in the cave of the sanyasins, I also did many studies and research on such matters. Bending an iron bar and then bringing it again to its previous state is only a simple thing for a yogi who has reached the ultimate of meditation through yoga skills. What is really happening then? As per the theory of physics, we can put it this way: the light rays that arise from the eyes are changed into waves. The flow of electrons in a wave is called electricity. When the electric waves are centralized on one matter, it will surely resist. This is Ohm's Law ($R=v/i$ where R is Resistance, V=Volt and I=Intensity of current). The friction created by resistance will make the matter hot and if the heat is that high, the matter will melt.[21] Through this process, we can heat up or burn a thing with sound waves or light waves. This method is used in radiation treatment where cancerous cells are burned up using electromagnetic energy. Our rishis had sufficient knowledge of the wonderful natural qualities of the eyes. If the internal working of the eyes is spread in nine dimensions, many wonders will come in handy. During such times, wonders are seen when some clearly transparent and unable-to-see membranes work as lenses. When one is engaged in meditation, it is these lenses that work. We should remember that the eyes get the skills while travelling from the 'gross body' to the 'subtle body'. There are colours that cannot be seen by the eyes of ordinary people and sounds that cannot be heard by the ears. It is because of this that, apparently, the rishis can make a thing invisible, by changing its colour. Yajur Veda describes the technique of making aeroplanes invisible by applying the liquid from the leaves of a particular plant. Studies make it clear that the catecholamines made jointly by nerve tissues and adrenal glands have the ability to enlarge the pupil of the eyes. A yogi can do this quite easily. It is not difficult for a yogi to create a curtain or such obstacle between himself and a camera to make him disappear from the picture that the camera takes. 'Seeing' is a joint venture of the 'object' and 'knowledge'. We see an object when it is within our eyes' comprehension. If the object and comprehension do not work together, it will be like one hiding the other. As a result, vision becomes impossible. It is because of this special ability that yogis can hide themselves from the vision of others. When meditation reaches a particular level, the subtle body reflects on the mirror of the mind. And when the energy of that reflection turns into a bunch of light rays, it hides the body of the yogi like a curtain. This is how one radar puts another radar out of sight. When by way of meditation, the aura, and thus the mind's internal flow of energy, the stream of light, rises to extraordinary levels, the flow from another mind or another stream of light cannot intrude it. This is why a camera cannot catch a yogi in a photograph.[22,23]

Like the eyes, sound also has very high relevance. The Siddha Vedanta has descriptions of the world of sound. Every sound in nature such as the sound of waves, the thunder, the flow of a river, the shattering in the funeral pyre, etc., is rhythmic. *Nadham* (music) is the pleasing quality of sound arising from orderly beating. The word nadham is composed of 'na', meaning life-giving air, and 'dham' meaning fire. Basically, there are ten musical sounds. They are chi-chin, chin-china, the chiming of a bell, the sound of the shell (*shanku*), veena (string instrument), cymbal, flute, *mrudangam* (a double-headed drum), kettle drum and *dundubhi* (drum). Hearing the sound of a flute coming from *sharara*, a yogi stands as if he has lost consciousness (sahasrara, 'thousand-petaled' or crown chakra is the seventh primary chakra according to Hindu tradition. The sahasrara chakra is located at the top of the head and corresponds to the pineal gland in the physical body. This area is called the Brahmarandra, or the 'hole of Brahma.' At the time of death of an advanced yogi, the prana escapes the body through this hole). It was like this that the *gopika* girls and other living organisms of Vrundavanam melted themselves to the flute music played by Sreekrishna. This music that awakes the great power Kundalini is none other than Parabrahma. Sabdabrahma (sound, the Brahma) is the husband of Kundalini. The music of the husband awakes the wife. Though it is rare, there are instances where men and women recognize each other by sound. The cause of this is the relationships that extend through generations.

'As said, there are different types of sounds in this world. The reason for this difference is the different positions of Arnikapadma. Masters propound that sound differences are the children of the outcome of karma that control the creation and evolution of bodies. Depending upon the karma of each life, the sound becomes soft or rough or pleasing to hear. Rishis worked through prayers, i.e., through sound. It is also through sound that we approach the gods of nature.

'The music streams born while the performer does the ascending and descending music of God in Sopana Sangeetham are especially noteworthy (Sopana Sangeetham is a form of classical music developed in the temples of Kerala and is known as Ashtapadhi). The Puranas tell about the pleasant Yogasasthra experiences that different musical sounds like chini, chinchini, mrudangam, *maddalam* (a type of drum), veena and *venu* (flute) originate in the deeper minds of such performer yogis. They play in the rhythm of Hamsaha, the mantra of Pranayama. Anyhow, the dance-drum-music during the worshipping (*pooja*) times was born in this country as an outward expression or representation of this holy music that was audible only to the performer yogis in their deeper minds. For confirming the strong bond between Indian music and spirituality, we have only to examine the seven basic musical notes (Sapthaswarangal), "sa-ri-ga-ma-pa-tha-ni". We can see that they originate from the causal six basic chakras in order and the last high pitch sound, ni, is sahasrara-related. The sounds of the trumpet and the flute show amazing similarities to the holy music that could be heard only by the ears of great yogis. This is a subject having much scope of research'.[24]

'Nruthavasane Natarajarajo
Nanadha Dakkam Nava Panchavaram
Uddarthukamaha Sanakadhi Siddan
Aethadwimarse Sinasoothrajalam.'

Author of the famous spiritual work *Kshethra Chaithanya Rahasyam*, Madhavji writes: 'The original causal base of the science of grammar is "Maheswarasoothrangal", the sounding of Maheswara's *kadumthudi* (drum) for nine plus five times (fourteen) at the end of his dance.' Madhavji continues:

'Bharathamuni's *Natyasasthra* is the most ancient book of this sort. The dancer in *Natyasasthra* who has all the qualities of a perfect actor of expressions, dancing talents, music, rhythmic movements and flawless actions by body organs is no doubt performing with all his gross-subtle-causal bodies before God. Those heart-touching actions thrill and raise not the dancer alone but the audience also to sublime realms. It is a real experience. The dancer forgetting himself in holy enthusiasm and spellbound by a sort of madness about God even turns into an instrument for the ordinary people to view God. The holy soothsayers of temples who jump exhilarated in rhythmic steps after having imbibed gods and goddesses into their bodies are called dancers. Dance-music-drumming indicates the state of joy, the last stage of the yoga meditation process. It is particularly notable that for any country, the art forms of culture and all sciences originate from the state of joy. And those who got the Kundalini awakening would become masters of all arts.'

The power of sound is great. Playing a fiddle can lift a machine of 25 horsepower into the air. This was proven by John Worrell Keely of Philadelphia in front of a big crowd.

In his book *China Jim: Being Incidents and Adventures in the Life of an Indian Mutiny Veteran*, Major General J.T. Harris describes an amazing incident that became a turning point in the Indo-China War of 1962. After leaving the Badrinath and Kedarnath temples and heading up a long distance through the Garhwal Himalayas, the Chinese military suddenly stopped the attack and withdrew to their side of the control line. It was the rishis of the Garhwal Himalayas who with their yoga-based superhuman power made the Chinese powerless and then drove them out. When the Chinese army suffered huge losses, they withdrew with no other choice. Major General Harris says in his book that the deeds ordinary people are unable to do could be done by the rishis out of the spiritual power gained from prayers.[25]

There is a section of people who asks why can't then the rishis control the bloodshed, massacres and unethical activities happening in different parts of the world. Also, there are some people among us who sarcastically ask why the rishis can't stop the free play of intruders and terrorists on the borders. And yet some ask why the spiritually strong Tibetan lamas can't liberate their country by driving away the Chinese.

This is a deep subject (please refer also to the coming sections on Siddhasramam and Shangri-La in this chapter). In the post-Veda-Purana-epic period, the successors of such a race of rishis had withdrawn to a particular realm. Time is a crucial factor in human life. What should happen in a particular time period should happen. The rishis had not interfered in the quarrels between the regional kings during their reign in pre- and post-Christ periods. They also did not interfere when the Persians, Mughals or British ruled India. A fall was inevitable for the pleasure-seeking kings, the priesthood and their descendants of this great country who completely deviated from the ethical directions contained in the Vedas and the

Upanishads. They had forgotten the ordinary people. The disastrous consequence of it was that our great country got into the hands of foreign rulers. What was needed during such a crisis period were spiritual masters capable of giving self-confidence to the people suffering under slavery. Sri Ramakrishna Parama Hamsar, Swami Vivekananda and such other noble sanyasins incarnated for this. And it was during their times that one nation became world-renowned for a religion. Imbibing the change of times and chanting 'Loka Samasta Sukhino Bhavantu' (let the best happen to the entire world), rishis still live in the Himalayas but they would have no interest to get into other matters. When its people reach a spiritual height, the nation also will reach that height. What the rishis attempt to do is also the same. But they would surely respond if hindrances are placed in the path of their endeavours. This was evident when they interfered during the Chinese attack in the Garhwal Himalayas. But they didn't try to prevent the Chinese advancement on the Ladakh side. Since there were no authentic surveys on the Ladakh side of the land then, arguing that the invaded land all belonged to us is groundless. What happened in Tibet was also a big fall in spiritual values. By whatever logic, it is not fair that a mammoth neighbour country defeats a small country in attack and rules it. Freedom is everybody's birthright. No one should persecute others. But the then-ruling Geshe lamas and other priests owed a big responsibility for the fall of Tibet. In my view, they had forgotten for long the principle of ahimsa (non-violence) of Sree Buddha. These are not justifications for the Chinese invasion but a fall of Tibet was inevitable. The Dalai Lama, their spiritual head, lives in India as a refugee and has formed an alien government. But it seems to me that even he is not honest in liberating Tibet. The lamas of Shangri-La who are blessed with superhuman skills have no interest in Tibetan matters either.

Let us return to the matter of sound. The tantra books tell that transmigration is possible by chanting the Pranava mantra. But constant chanting should continue for many years for the doer to attain the skill. The echo arising from the chanting of each mantra awakes an equivalent sound in the invisible worlds. This will activate some unknown aspects of one's nature. Masters propound that each sound has the capability of expressing one quality of feeling, and sounds as they work with minds can stir and bring to action all the infinitesimal segments of souls. Many experts have published details of this after conducting extensive studies. Philosophers have long ago stated that music is an important medicine for curing nerve-related diseases. Music is the qualified form of beating in the air. Rhythmic sound creates energetic, infinitesimal changes. Even in a dead state, the unresisted flow of music would surely work because in a body there is nothing considered as inactive.

Sound has an immense secret power. It is quite natural to get surprised when you learn that sound can lift even a mountain into the air. 'Even the electricity produced by a million Niagara Falls cannot resist the power unleashed by a man with mantra power!'[26] Getting five basic elements (the pancha bhoothas) together, the sound produces a vigorous pith of gas unknown to chemistry but within the area of chemical action. Without a matchbox or flame, the Siddha Yogis can make fire for the Kusmandika Homam by just pronouncing 'rem', the seed of fire. Leonardo Devair says that 'uttering particular words, many people can walk barefoot over hot charcoal or the sharp sides of knives stuck in the earth. They will domesticate and make stand on their side the untameable horses and mad bullocks by the power of mantras'.[27] It has been scientifically proven that the Pranava mantra[28] gives revitalizing energy to all the internal organs of the body, especially the brain and heart. Pranava mantra is the echo of the universe. The movements and waves emanating from it caused the creation of the universe. The Vedas tell us that in its original form, the universe contained only energy. Modern science argues that when mass is broken up, energy is produced in the form of waves. Indian Vedanta too argues that waves are made from nadham (sound or voice) and if waves can be made, then matter can also be made. In his work, *Ente Mrigaya Smaranakal* (Memories of My Hunting Days) published in *Bhashaposhini* magazine, Kerala Varma Valiyakoyi Thampuran recorded many surprising events. Stopping a gun many times by mantras is said to have been described in it. Those who had read the work confirmed the narrations depicted in it about the successful experiments that brought animals for hunting out from deep forests.

It is a fact heard from time immemorial that there are places in the world of the Himalayas beyond the eyesight of laymen and also impossible to reach. Such a mysterious place is Siddhashramam. On one side of it is the heavily ice-covered Kailash and at its back on the opposite side is the Siddha Yoga Lake at a distance. A tip of it is part of the Manasa Sarass (the godly lake of the Himalayas) that extends on to the Himalayan tunnels. This place also joins the back of Adi Kailash. This triangular piece of earth is called Siddhashramam. Bhagavatham describes it as an east-north lying land (*'Prasudheecheemdhisam'*). Male and female yogis and other siddhas sit on the banks of Siddha Yoga Lake in meditation. There are enough references to Siddhashramam in our Puranas and epics. Vyasa Muni explains in detail about the Siddhashramam in the 'Bhavishyal Parvam' of the Mahabharata. After killing the cruel kings and Assuras, Bhagavan Krishna was living happily in Dwaraka along with his wife Rugmini Devi. Then Rugmini told Krishna about a wish of hers. Her wish was for an ideal son matching all the qualities of his father, Krishna. Krishna agreed to give her a scholarly and truthful son as she wished and proceeded to Kailash to get the blessings of Parameswara and Parvathy. As an initial step, Bhagavan Krishna first went to Siddhashramam where the masters of all the Vedas and philosophy, the munis and siddha yogis, were in deep meditation. In ancient times, Hari had meditated there for long years for the welfare of the world. And it was also there that He was made into two as Nara and Narayana. This was also the place where Sree Ramachandra had prayed and meditated before killing Ravana and the siddhas became siddhas by praying to Mahavishnu.

In Siddhashramam, there is an assemblage of great Yogis who are as old as 2000 to 5000 years. Vyasa, Bheeshmar, Drona, Kripacharya, Ashwathama, Vasishta and Yajnavalkya are only some of them. It is also said that there is another generation aged up to 2000 years. The well-known yogis and great sanyasins of earlier centuries were the creations of Siddhashramam. Gourishankar Peetam *ashramam* of Om Satguru Babaji Nagarajan, the most venerable among the siddha yogis, is said to be near the Siddhashramam. Gourishankar Peetam ashramam can be reached by travelling 3 km on a very difficult path starting from the banks of the Satopanth Lake of Badridham. This can be done only by those who had attained yoga sidhi (sidhi is spiritual, paranormal or supernatural power, ability and attainment). For fulfilling the prayers and continuous wishes of devotees, God himself takes incarnation in the form of a human being relying on illusion. Such incarnations are not a matter of the past alone but happen at present and will happen in future also. Four hundred years ago, a meeting of the holy yogis at Siddhashramam (Divyapadh Samaaroha Utsav) expressed concern over the foreign rule of the country that might jeopardize the nation's spiritual vitality. They took a decision then that the slavery of the country could be ended only by the top yogis working among the ordinary people and raising them to spiritual heights. It was out of this decision from Siddhashramam that Swami Abhayanandaji, Sri Ramakrishna Parama Hamsar, Swami Vivekananda, Shirdi Sai Baba, Lahiri Mahasaya, Swami Sri Yukteswar, Paramahansa Yogananda, Sathya Sai Baba and such other holy souls took incarnations at various time periods. The phenomenon of accepting old incarnations and refusing modern incarnations is not good. Nobility can be attained by us and our descendants only by believing in its real sense that each incarnation has a purpose and God appears before us in human form relying on illusion.

The yogis who visited there recorded that Siddhashramam is a divine place of perpetual peace. The hot rays of the sun do not reach there. Its appearance day and night is as though it is bathed in full moonlight. The sand-like sandal paste, the soft breeze filled with sweet fragrance, lotus ponds, beautiful streams of water and the always blue sky—all of them make Siddhashramam equivalent to heaven. Flowers and plants that can't be seen on earth and herds of deer turn the place into a dreamland. Never-ageing youthful men and women live there engaging in different activities while chanting mantras. A yogi who attained sidhi through years-long practice under a bright master can reach here with his physical body. If he so wishes, he may return from there also. Though the great, holy yogis live there as astral bodies, they can change at any time into physical bodies. The Siddhashramam and Siddhaloka are two different things. Only the great, holy yogis and siddhas can enter the Siddhaloka with their astral bodies. The ordinary yogis can only see by way of their sidhi the holy sanyasins, rishis and yogis living in Siddhaloka. A yogi can hear the music of heaven and see the other worlds.

Sreeram Chaithanya Shasthri has recorded in his book *Siddhasram ka Yogi* the eventful story of a yogi who went into Siddhashramam and returned from there with his physical body. There may be a differentiation of day and night for those who indulge in ordinary levels of activities in the physical world. But for a yogi who has higher levels of spiritual knowledge, such a difference would never be there in the mind. Before letting the disciple enter the blissful world of spirituality, the master or teacher has to make him ready. When the master thinks it is the right time, he turns the preference of the brain of the disciple towards that direction.

Our master and disciple, as Sreeram Chaithanya Shasthri depicts in his book, told others that they were just going to the Himalayas. After walking for one and a half days from the banks of the Satopanth Lake of Badridham, they sat by the side of a small stream for rest. It was a full moon night and when nature stood with all its charm and prettiness, the student's mind throbbed. It came out thus in words.

'My respectful master, please tell me about Siddhashramam . . . how can I reach there?' he said.

Within a few moments, it happened at lightning speed. The master raised his right hand with a mysterious smile. Those fingers then pointed towards the forehead of the disciple. Some holy mantra came out of his mouth and he pressed the thumb on the centre of the disciple's forehead. The latter felt that things were jumping and moving around as if in delight. He didn't know how long it existed, for it was as if he had fallen into half-consciousness for endless time. Gradually, he felt the world around him becoming dim and hiding from sight. A new world rose bright into his sight. When the disciple returned to full consciousness, it was like a dim light hovering around and it was entirely a different situation. When his eyes grew familiarized with his new surroundings, the disciple became very surprised. All around he saw handsome and healthy yogis and *sadhakas*—both male and female—in a playful mood. They were engaged in their own duties. The disciple was embarrassed at first. But soon the love and friendship around flowed to his mind also. He too became part of that environment.

The disciple had been standing lost in the unforgettable natural beauty when somebody led him near a special dais. A group of yogis had been sitting on the dais decorated with rare flowers that could not be found on earth. When the disciple found his master in the group, he suddenly remembered that they were assembled to celebrate Guru Poornima (a festival dedicated to spiritual and academic teachers). After rendering the slogan, 'Jai Guru Veda Vyasa . . . jai Gurudev', a yogi introduced himself as Aravind Yogiraj welcomed the gathering. Parama Hamsa Vijayeswarananda, Parama Hamsa Brigu Ram, Parama Hamsa Thrijatha Aghori, Yogi Achuthananda, Parama Hamsa Swami Nikhileswarananda and as president, Parama Hamsa Poojya Paadha Swami Sachidananda were all on the dais. Aravind Yogiraj did foot worship of the gurus in the name of Siddhashramam and all the living creatures of the world. Then the lady yoginis sang songs beautifully, praising Ganapathi and Saraswathy. The spiritual speech of Swami Sachidananda was excellent. Anybody would feel that he was a sea of kindness. His figure and expressions were extremely beautiful and splendid like the magnificence of the Himalayas. When his eyes rested for a long time on that divine figure, the disciple felt a vast purification going on in his mind. That purity was touching the deeper areas of the soul. When the last lines of the ode sung at the end of the assembly, 'Loka Samasta Sukhino Bhavanthu', echoed in his ears, the disciple felt that some change had happened in him. Moments later, everything began to fade. He felt that from the other side of time and place, somebody was carrying him to the earth. When consciousness was regained, the time was past midnight. Where was he for the last twelve hours? But what he experienced was felt to be only for a couple of minutes. When he saw the master standing in front of him with a smile, he prostrated at the elder's feet with all devotion. When his master told him the next day that he had got the Manobhavana Dheeksha from him, the man was thrilled. This was the first step in the endeavour of reaching Siddhashramam. When an individual crosses over all steps, he can visit Siddhashramam any time he wishes. He can even stay there. The pupil later began to feel like he had been raised to non-physical worlds and that he had an invisible shield to protect him always.

When one gains consciousness after indulging in the samadhi of Siddha Yoga, one will think about the long loss of physical time. Samadhi is timeless (time annihilates meditation). If an astronaut going to space in a rocket at the speed of time returns to Earth at his lunchtime, at least two days would have elapsed here. The reason is the difference between the rotation of the earth and the speed of a rocket. Nature is always in motion. Space is the measuring unit of the gap between two matters. Likewise, time is the measuring unit of changes incurred due to motion. If there is no matter, there is no space or time. When we say 'matter', only physical matter comes to our minds. Physical matter is only a solid form of the subtle matter called energy. Because subtle and gross bodies make them, space and time are very much applicable to the dimensions of world. That is why present-day quantum physics tells us that it is not possible to negate the possibility of a subtle world and a gross or physical world that are lying interwoven. The scale of time measurement of the physical world may not be that of the subtle world. We measure time by seconds and minutes. Modern atomic science can now measure even one by ten-millionth ($1/1,00,00,000$) of a second. The relativity of time was known to the Indian philosophers long ago, before modern science discovered it. They had disclosed it through interesting stories. Once, a king reached Brahma Lokam (the world of Brahma) to directly apprise Lord Brahma of administrative matters. After receiving advice from Brahma, he immediately got ready to return. It was then Brahma convinced the king that for the few moments he had spent there, hundreds of years would have passed on earth. The inferences of ancient Indian thinkers regarding the formation of the physical universe we reside in astonishingly match that of modern science. Moreover, the Puranas contain comparative studies of the time system of the physical world of man and the time system of subtle worlds like Deva Lokam (world of gods) and Brahma Lokam. If we go deep into these studies, we can get a lot of meaningful information about the universe and human life. Modern science has discovered that the essence of the universe is expansion and compression. Like a creature is born from its genes as modern genetic science says, one Kalpa begins from a day of Brahma.[29] The definition of a Kalpa equals 4.32 billion years as found in the Puranas, specifically Vishnu Purana and Bhagavata Purana. The Siddha form of meditation is a very difficult way to attain heights. Years-long practice and that too very hard practice and done daily without any break goes into obtaining this sidhi. In the Siddha way, Lord Siva is the centre of power. After the first phase is over, siddha power will go on flowing through the bodies of the yogis. Those who practise the siddha way of life by residing in the ashram and leading a controlled life will find access to the working of internal power or the awakening of the Kundalini power. Kundalini carries immense energy. When the Kundalini is awakened, all the basic chakras of the body will become active and by that, the veins and nerves will get fresh purity and vitality. As the meditation becomes deeper, the blinding aura that used to appear will give way to the red aura and this will remain spread over the whole body. It is like lakhs of light rays shining together. Actually, at this stage, the body is covered both internally and externally by a red aura. It is at the tantra stage that the red aura appears.

There are many stages in meditation. Moola Bandhanam, Uddiyana Bandhanam, Jalanthara Bandhanam and Bindubheda are only some of them. Apana Vayu (flatus) rises up in the case of Moola Bandhanam. This makes the downward flow of oxygen easy. The oxygen and nerves are purified in Uddiyana Bandhanam. When the nerves are purified, the gastric fire (Agni Vayu) is lit up. And when oxygen is purified, the fluctuation of the mind ceases and the result is solid concentration.

In Hata Yoga, this is a vital stage. This is also very important in the initial efforts of defeating death. In the stage Jalanthara Bandhanam, the drops of semen falling from Sahasraram are burnt in the subtle chakra at the navel. Because this bandhanam doesn't close its path of flow, the semen never burns out completely. At the end of Jalanthara Bandhanam, the yogi falls unconscious. For this same reason, the yogi attains a state of stillness. Gradually, oxygen (Pranan) and flatus (Apanan) start working in equilibrium. In the Bindubheda stage, the eyes are made to concentrate. The particular effect of this is that henceforth, the eyes can be rotated as per one's wish. When the eyes are rotating, the optical chakras get ready to pass penetrating looks. The yogi attains prophetic power when the optical chakras are set thus. Then the yogi becomes a possessor of clairvoyance (please refer to the chapter 'Gangothri-Gomukh-Thapovan' of my book *Thapobhoomi Uttarakhand*, pages 129-61. Also note the chapter 'Badaridhamathilekku', page 254-55).

The gestures (*mudra*) shown at the time of meditation are very important. Saambhavi Mudra, Maha Mudra, Mahavedha Mudra, Vipareethakarani Mudra and Vajroli Mudra are gestures holding great importance. When breathing is regulated at different levels, the mudras or gestures, namely

Bhujangini Mudra, Nabho Mudra, Kechari Mudra, Kakki or Seethali Mudra and Shambhavi Mudra, turn out to be very complex. A yogi practising yoga that is based on mudras can drive his kundalini power along with his soul into the spinal cord, heal nerve-caused physical illnesses, speed up the refilling of semen in the body, enhance the strength of his digestive fire and prevent ageing. He can also focus his entire mind on the centre of his forehead, get spiritual energy and reach a conscious mindset.

As meditation goes deeper and deeper, a softer energy is felt in the body. Then it feels as if the energy is flowing to the nerves. Red, white, black and blue colours will appear one after another. Red represents the gross body, white is the subtle body, black is the causal body and blue is the supra causal body. Blue means that the meditation has become solid. The spinal cord which extends from the *mooladharam* (the root chakra) to the *moor have* (the crown) will begin to shine in a silvery gold colour. All the nerves start vibrating. At this time, there will be pain at the mooladharam. When the mind fixes on the blue colour, red aura, oval-shaped small white light and the same shaped blue light appear and then the yogi can clearly see the internal golden sky and the external silver sky. Like on a monitor of a movie camera, the sights from this world and the sights from other worlds appear clearly in the internal eyes of the yogi. He can then focus his eyes in whatever way he wants.

As the blue light becomes visible, the yogi reaches the highest level of meditation. The next stage is Neeleswari. A stage of meditation is completed when he reaches Bindu from Neeleswari. Bindu is known by the names 'Blue Pearl' or 'Blue God'. It is here the presence of Brahma-Vishnu-Maheswara is felt. This is why philosophers say that God resides in ourselves. In Hindu philosophy, this vigour is called Krithastha Chaithanyam or Thath. This is nothing but

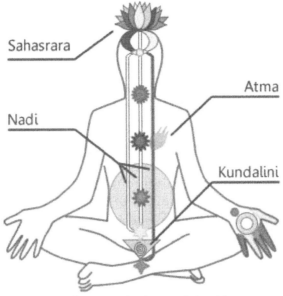

Source: https://en.wikipedia.org/wiki/Kundalini

the Parabrahma vision that exists everywhere. The scholarly rishis and yogis treat this as a level of samadhi.[30] Krithastha or the 'Chakra of Command' is situated where the middle of the eyebrows and the medulla join together. This is the centre point of willpower and concentration and also the seat of the spiritual eyes. When worship reaches this extreme point, the colour of the aura around the body changes in turn into yellow, violet, blue and gold and becomes the colour of fire at the end. The other primary chakras get smaller whereas Anahata (heart chakra, the fourth primary chakra) and Sahasrara (mentioned elsewhere) expand. Gradually, spiritual pictures begin to form at the centre of light situated in the middle of the Sahasrara chakra. From the yoga nerves where pictures of goddesses are recorded, the picture of that goddess which the doers of yoga preferred begins to rise and becomes clear through the Adhara Chakra (root centre).

But due to ignorance, this is hidden from ordinary men. This most beloved blue dot is glowing and shining even from the other side of space. It is when he centralizes attention on the blue centre that the yogi hears music in the left ear. This music originates from the inner ears. This divine veena music ripples in the yogi's mind from the space of consciousness. Normally, hearing music in the left ear happens at the time of death. It is just before the soul goes out that the sound too goes out to merge with the Nadhabrahma. But this is not applicable to yogis. Music, the godly skill, comes to our possession out of the vibration of willpower. Yogis can find out the source of music. Depending upon the outcome of karma, some people get the music they had in the previous births in the rebirth also.

The blue pearl or blue dot is the centre of splendour. Jagadguru Sree Sankaracharya described it as 'Sath Chinmaya Neelimaroop'. In the soul of every individual, there is a quality of vigour of its own. It is this amazing quality that we call the blue pearl. In the endless chain of birth and death, this unworldly vigour travels from one body to another. Whatever we do with the corpse—cremated or buried—does not make any change to the blue pearl. Though it has to quit when the body dies, this peculiarity of vigour stays around those surroundings for eleven days. After that, the blue pearl leads the soul to that sphere where the person consumes the fruits of the virtues and sins of this birth. The blue pearl needs no external help or persuasion to lead each soul. When the individual takes rebirth, the blue pearl also joins him.[31]

Some learned men opine that the soul and the blue pearl are one and the same. But the majority's opinion is that both are different phenomena. Scholars point out that there is no clarity in the Upanishad mantra, 'the mind or supreme soul having the size of a thumb finger always resides in the heart of people' ('*Angushtamathra ha purushofntharatma sadha jananaam hrudhi sannivishtaha'—Shwethaashwatharopanishad*). Some scholars point out that even this Upanishad mantra is ambiguous. In fact, the soul doesn't stay in the heart. Why a masculine gender Angushtamathran is used is because the cause of the mind, the region of the heart, is known by the name *Angushtamathram.* Since the mind is the tool of the male called the soul, formally that soul is also called Angushtamathran.

A yogi who has acquired the knowledge of different levels of meditation has no difficulty in reaching any country by his mind. To attain the status of the 'world of omniscience' such as the world of siddha, the world of ancestors, the world of music, the world of tantra,[32] etc., one has to acquire by heart the 144 lessons of Kriya Yoga and also many chambers. The yogis who have supernatural powers can reach different worlds even in the conscious state. Such a yogi can rotate his neck in a full circle and roll his head in any direction. Thus he can see even his backside. When the neck is rotated fully, some cracking sounds will be heard. This is a particular stage of Hata Yoga. It is at this time that the Kundalini power rises to the Sahasraram through the spinal cord. There are many yogis currently in India who have attained the 'world of omniscience'. Normally, this stage is attained in a sleeping state. However, this is not a real sleep. The camera of the mind stays for some time in each world on arrival. Then it reaches another world. Before entering the subtle worlds, the yogi should have acquired the necessary practice. If not so, it is deadly and dangerous. Like a vehicle that moves up after shifting gears, the yogi should have the expertise to move from one world to another. He should know how to return also. If any fault happens, the brain may get seriously damaged. The brain may not be capable of containing the speed of atomic movement in the subtle worlds. Hence, before preparing to go to those worlds, the yogi should purify and strengthen his mind by indulging in highly noble and extremely fine thoughts. This was possible to our rishis who had seen the extreme end of the sea of yoga. *Nasaagra dharsanam*, *indriya nirodham*, equal placement of body and *mano nigraham* are very hard practices of yoga.

The Universe is a solar system that includes the sun in the centre and many gross and subtle planets and sub-planets rotating around it. This is said to have the shape of a blooming lotus flower in the holy eyes of the yoga masters who have transcendental powers.

A yogi reaching the world of the 'all-knowing' will have a mind in between sleep and dream. The dreamy state is a state in between sleep and alertness. The action and sense organs do not work in this state but the mind will be working. '*Abhanae Sthooladhehasya Swapnaeyal Bhanamatmanaha*' (there is no feeling of gross body in the dreamy state but the soul will be shining). The soul has the ability to detach from the gross body and join the body of dreams. The dreams yogis see are different from ordinary dreams which give out bad sentiments and thoughts. The dreams they see contain godly vigour and provide a strong foundation for prosperous actions. They are virtuous too. Science even now cannot fully understand why we sleep and what it is for. Many have seen dreams as a way of rest for the brain and other organs that work during the daytime. It was one scientist called Hans Berger who made a change to this by inventing the electroencephalography (EEG) machine in 1924. He discovered that the brain works even in the sleeping state and proved that there are different stages of sleep. His discovery paved the way for a new branch of science called somnology. He classified the stages of sleep into two, viz., NREM and REM. The first stage, NREM, has four sub-stages. REM starts after two hours of sleeping. Bad dreams are seen in this stage. The happy and hopeful dreams occur in the

NREM stage that comes after the REM stage. But it is very astonishing to know that the great rishis of ancient India had known this and applied it practically thousands of years before Hans Berger's invention!

The belief is that becoming one with the ultimate God is possible for a complete yogi who has access to the all-knowing world and has secured transcendental power. When Swethaswatharopanishad says that '*Hrudhamambeeswo Manasabhikluptho ya Aedhath Vdhooramruthasthe Bhavanthi*',[33] we must understand that the writer had the experience of that truth. To witness that his soul is different from his body, a fully learned yogi changes the spirit of life from one centre to another centre of his body. In this way, the great yogis keep the soul under their strict control by conquering every centre of their physical body one by one. It is also possible for a yogi to bring the Kundalini power under his control. When this power awakes, all the virtues of a man get strengthened. This is why it is advised to practise yoga only after throwing away all ill qualities from the mind. And this is why great masters advise to first practise yoga's external syllabi of 'Yama Laws' before going to the internal syllabi of Dharana-Dhyana-Samadhi (conception-meditation-samadhi). Very rarely for some, the Kundalini power may rise up unexpectedly and they get the sacred powers of 'vision through time', etc. The Kundalini power arouses internally the atoms and externally, atomic pulsation. Atomic pulsation is the differentiating factor of physical bodies and when it is aroused by the Kundalini power, the grasping power of senses escalates and the Kundalini power thus turns out to be the cause of all prosperity. No powers work without conditions. We experience the working of any power by its own molecular covering. The extremely micro covering of the Kundalini power appears to a yogi as a minuscule finger ring made up of numerous 'fire atoms'. Though the succession of atoms in there does not touch one another, they rotate fast in their limits to give the shape of a ring. Like electrons to electricity, these energy sparks turn out to be the tools of the Kundalini power. The godly power of Kundalini enters the human body from the centre of the universe, the Badavagni Mandalam (molten lava of the inner core) through the mooladharam (the root centre chakra of a human body). The godly power of the soul enters the body from the heart of the universe, the Aadhitya Mandalam (the sphere of the sun) by self-practice. If a yogi who has the Bhuvarloka[1] knowledge does not arouse the Kundalini power that is asleep at the mooladharam, he would completely forget all the Bhuvarloka experiences when he returns from the samadhi to his conscious gross body. So it is necessary for him to make Kundalini break the chakra. For arousing the evolutionary Kundalini power, the yogis adopt various methods. One such method is Pranayama or control of the soul by breath exercises.[2] The famous scientist, Grey Walter, who conducted authoritative studies about the activities of the brain, clarified in his work *The Living Brain* that breathing and mental activities are closely connected. He propounded that the discreet use of Pranayama gradually brings maturity and control over mental activities and helps one reach the phase of truth-knowing meditation by concentration of the mind.

1. Bhuvarloka, the second of the seven upper worlds, is the realm of Svadhishtana chakra and lies above the earth. It occupies the space between the earth and the sun and is inhabited by munis (sages).

2. The Pranayama yoga scheme as commonly found in Kerala is far behind the original Pranayama scheme. Maybe some simple techniques can be learnt but this cannot lead to the real planes of holy Yogavidya. The simple technique as practised just helps to purify the

breath organs and transparency of blood circulation. Nothing more. Pranayama fills the body with excessive air. As the quantity of air increases in the body, the body weight decreases and the power of life increases. By coordinating the mind in the Shadadhara Chakras and getting the Kundalini power at the Sahasrara by stirring it with the '*Hum Hamsaha*' mantra, the yogi reaches the stage of samadhi. The vigour of semen ensures the presence of Chith-Shakthi (the power of universal intelligence or consciousness). This power is there in each body when it is born. It is the continuation of the last birth. Semen is the root cause for the arousal of the Kundalini power and thus rising to the stage of samadhi. The pleasure organs have special importance in the human body. When any part of the body is provoked continually, it becomes an organ. The yogi who has acquired superhuman status has this cosmic power. In God, the cosmic power is at its highest level. The Sruthi also tells that '*Pashyathewchakshaha Sashyano-thru Karnnaha*'.[34]

How a yogi foresees the thoughts in another man's mind is through the skilfulness of senses. This skill is called psychoanalysis. By extracting the outer happenings, the senses reflect them in the mirror of the mind. They also transmit the internal remembrances of the mind. By analysing these feelings and thoughts, one can get knowledge of other minds. This is how a yogi foresees the track of the feelings of another man.[35] F.W.H. Myers, in his book *Human Personality and Its Survival of Bodily Death*, proves by quoting many real experiences that the mind can very easily transmit its feelings to others. Heavenly powers can touch anything. Like the atoms of electric current move the flow of invisible physical power, the waves and flow of feelings of minds move from one person to another.

An ordinary man feels it only as changes in emotions. But the yogis who have control over minds can focus them on anyone and at any time they wish. Using the waves of feelings around them, the yogis do many activities for the good of the world.[36] Prof. Wachi Leav, a researcher in para-physiology at the Brain Institute, Leningrad, categorically states that the human brain is like a broadcasting station that transmits long waves. Therefore, he makes it clear that it is possible for a trained brain to catch the waves spread out in the air by another man's brain as well as his body, and understand the reality of the sentimental and emotional response of a man who owns that brain and body. He argues that one man can thus communicate with another one sitting far away and control that man's mind.[37] From each and everything existing in the world, there will be some power elements transmitted to all other matter around. But only a limited quantity of this cosmic energy is felt in the physical organs.

The mental power of man is very great. A yogi in samadhi can segregate any atom that has a willing, knowledgeable and active soul into many parts and then add them into another atom. Through the Vijnanamaya Kosha experiment, a yogi can understand the whole spiritual development of a physical man.[38,39] The Vijnanamaya Kosha is oval-shaped. The human figure is in its centre. At first, the Vijnanamaya Kosha will be colourless. After a succession of generations, different beautiful colours come to it.

Many scientific studies have been conducted on Yoga Sidhi. By practising yoga, many positive changes are felt in the brain, nerves and muscles. The practising has also many useful impacts on the internal secretion glands and in the chemicals produced by the brain on its own. Science has already proven that 'narcotics' called endorphins have the capability to increase the immunity power of bodies.

Scientists have proved too that by way of yoga practices, the body can produce such things as per need. For them who reside in high lands like the Himalayas—especially the rishis, yogis and holy sanyasins—the vigour of the place is the main reason for the easy accomplishment of *sadhana* (meditation), *sidhi* (skilfulness) and *sakshalkaram* (fulfilment). This is also the reason for ordinary Himalayan travellers getting a lesser part of this. In his book *Varieties of Psychism*, known Western thinker J.I. Wedgwood says that the subtlety of the air structure in the high mountain areas improves the speed of heartbeats and blood circulation of the people residing there. Due to this, the physical and astral bodies[40] would be much closer and incidents can be felt more clearly. For the same reason, we can guess that the ancient men were close to the invisible (astral) creatures since the exactness or infinity of the air structure was higher then. How the yogis can easily look into and learn the details of the astral world[41] is because of the speciality of their area of earth. The rishis of ancient India discovered the amazing, deep and close relationship of the physical and mental state of man with the state of the universe and the inner crust of the earth. When in future, which is not far away, science possesses the knowledge about the relation between mind and matter, the technical secrets behind the spiritual power in temples may get revealed.

Many scientific studies have been done on the fluctuations in temperature caused by meditation. In 1957, a team of doctors from the All India Institute of Medical Sciences (AIIMS) and the Indian Council of Medical Research (ICMR) jointly conducted some scientific studies on about 500 yogis. Dr B.K. Anand, leader of the study team, records the outcome of their studies thus: 'We sought the answers for mainly three questions. First—Does meditation influence the internal body functions of Yogis? Second—Can Yogis survive without oxygen and protein food? Third—During stages of meditation, what changes occur in the brains of Yogis?'

In his book *The Human Brain*, Isaac Asimov writes: 'Up to the 18th century, the modern concept that the brain was the seat of thoughts and the reception centre of external stimuli of nerves and thereby the stimulating centre of movements was not clear. But thousands of years ago, the ancient Rishis had stated that the human brain was the seat of ultimate knowledge. It was also notable that they recorded the related sensibility energy centres within the brain and the spinal cord. The ancient Rishis made profound discoveries regarding the energy centres on the vertebral column. Even today this precise science of pulsation remains unclear to modern science.'

For recording the brain's activities, the AIIMS-ICMR team had built a black box which did not permit sound waves inside. Through this experiment, the doctors found that by accepting energy in very small amounts, some masters of yoga could reach unbelievable levels of energy by mere self-control. This meant that when an ordinary man could reduce his metabolic activity by a rate of 10–12 per cent only, yogis could reduce it by up to 50 per cent. While the heartbeat of an ordinary man is 72 beats per minute, the yogis could slow it down to even a death-like state of 30–35 beats per minute. The most interesting among the findings of AIIMS was that of the fluctuations in the brain activity of yogis during meditation. Alpha waves form in that restful and peaceful brain. The alpha waves thus formed can be influenced by external pressure factors such as thunder, stroke, etc. But those external factors showed no response in the case of yogis in an extra-sensual trance. The team reached the conclusion that those were the impacts of meditation.

Two years later, Dr Chinna, who was in the study team, presented a paper regarding his findings at the twenty-sixth

International Physiology Conference held in Delhi. In it, the doctor confirmed thus: 'The fact that Yogis can walk over fire without burning their legs and can live frozen in cold water surviving extreme coldness are only some of their astonishing skills.' William J. Cromie shared some of his experiences after going through the scientific aspects of meditation.[42] 'In a North Indian sanyasin hut, some nude sanyasins were sitting peacefully in a chilled room where the coldness would freeze anybody's bones. They were in deep meditational sleep by the *Yoga Sutra* called G-Tum-mo. Such meditating sanyasins were then covered with wet blankets of 3' x 6' size dipped in chilled and frozen water. If this was done on unpractised persons, it would lead to unusual and hysterical shivering. If the body temperature continued going down like that, surely the result would be death. But in our case, vapour began to rise upwards from the blankets of the sanyasins. In about an hour, the blankets became dry in the heat produced by the meditating body. The sanyasins were again covered with chilled and wet blankets by the helpers. Each Yogi was asked to dry three blankets each in some hours.'

How was this possible? Herbert Benson, learning the G-Tum-mo yoga method for the last twenty years, answers this: 'The world we live in is not the final.' This is the philosophy of the yogis. There are spheres beyond the realities of our daily life where we can go. The yogis believe that we can reach such a mental stage through yoga and by doing good to the world. The heat produced by the meditating yogis is only a by-product of the *G-Tum-mo Yoga Sutra*. It was recorded in the visits made by Benson and his group to the Himalayan sanyasin huts during the 1980s that the sanyasins in the Himalayas could raise the temperature of their fingers and toes up to 17 degrees Celsius through the G-Tum-mo meditation. It is yet to be found out how the great sanyasins could produce that high temperature.

Researchers who conducted experiments on the yogis of Sikkim discovered some embarrassing facts. One such fact was that the yogis could trim down their body functions (metabolism) to 64 per cent. Benson believes that this yoga technique could be very useful to astronauts going to space.

'In 1985, the study team videographed the Yogis drying wet blankets by the body temperature produced by meditation. The team also shot the scene of the Rishis spending an extremely cold winter night on a rock ledge in the Himalayan mountains at a height of 16000 ft. This "sleep action" of the Rishis was done in a full moon winter night of February when the temperature was minus 80°C. Wearing a cotton upper cloth, the Rishis went on to sleep in full comfort on the ledge. Each of them slept lying at a distance. The video witnessed that none of them were shivering even for a bit. The Rishis deep sleeping all through night rose up in the morning as if nothing had happened and walked to their huts'.[43]

One traveller called Anne Cushman, in her book, narrates an incredible experience of finding a yogi staying alone on a big piece of ice that was strong like steel inside a cave in a deserted area of the Himalayas:

'Bottomless devotion to God is the greatest gain I got from India. For me devotion is not something related to a single God. It is an internal lamp that lights up the whole of the universe. Because of an avalanche during the Himalayan travel, I had to spend days with a Yogi in his cave. This great Yogi had been living for years just by eating potato and dried fruits. Lying on a hard floor of ice, I spent the days shivering under the layers of a woollen blanket. So intense was the cold. I tried to listen to the disturbing sound of a cascading avalanche that flowed around us falling from a height of 19000 ft. Each time when mammoth ice mountains fell shattered and flowed madly, the Great Rishi sleeping under an old rat-bit bed sheet would rise up and say nodding his head: "Jay Sankar Mahadev, I praise thee!" I felt his mantra chanting gradually creeping into me. The ice falls violently outside. The great Yogi chants mantras inside. "The world of the Himalayas is really amazing!" I told myself.'[44]

David Neel, a traveller who studied about the skill of lamas to provide heat to their own bodies, narrates an experience:

'I studied about this deeply. Many times during the night, I saw nude sanyasins doing meditation sitting on pieces of ice. They hadn't minded the icy winds blowing around. I could also see some students following this scheme of life. In the midst of the extremely cold winter season, place ice pieces falling from the Himalayas on own bodies and heat them up!

'They had to pass such an examination too. I also practised the *Tum-mo* scheme of meditation. Thus, not only we could heat up our own bodies but could also make bush wood catch fire. Keeping the bush wood under the dress, we thought, "flames are rising. They are catching fire with small sounds". We could see with our own eyes flames rising up. We also felt the relaxing warmth thus generated. Now, when we awoke somehow all of a sudden, it seemed that the flames were going out. They were going inside the earth and becoming hidden. While I opened the eyes, I saw my body burning. Faces of others were red like glowing coal. Eyes were bright. The bush wood kept under the dress had become so much dry. Still, they were hot . . .'

Kambiz Naficy[45] of Iran is a well-known master of the school of meditation. He teaches the art of making life peaceful and comfortable. Active breathing, meditation and hypnotherapy are the methods he has adopted for that. He did his higher studies at the famous Centre for Management Studies in Iran. This is an institute being run in collaboration with the Harvard Business School and Columbia University. Mr Naficy, a postgraduate in many subjects (MBA, MIA and MFA) is a famous poet too.

He adopted the path of 'transcendental meditation' after giving up a top-level job. He gained initial training in the subject from the famous Maharshi International University in Iowa, USA. Besides, he stayed for years in India to study under eminent teachers and yogis. He studied in depth many books including the Vedas, Upanishads and Puranas. Along with this, he studied the intense ways of meditation.

One thing became clear to him then. It was the surprising similarity between the modern atomic theory and the godly vigour residing inside every man! Quantum physics is an entry gate of the invisible world of Brahma Chaithanyam (God's vigour). The minute and precise thoughts and aims of man can influence the movement of atoms. That is why it is said that the results of the experiments with life and laws of the universe depend upon the thinking and willpower of scientists.

He gave up his vast business empire, cars and the amenities of life that money can buy. Later, it was a pilgrimage of the mind for him.

'I reached India two years later,' he explains. 'I met there Sri Sathya Sai Baba and Sri Karunamayi. Both of them told me exactly the same thing. It was that I should not treat them as my Gurus! They were my guides only. Utterly surprising, what else should I say! It was in such circumstances that

I got acquainted with Babaji and Kriya Yoga. In this visible world, the two personalities I worship most are Mahatma Gandhi and Mother Teresa. But in the physical world, my greatest happiness, inspiration and guide is Om Satguru Babaji Nagaraj. Swami Hariharananda (www.kriya.org) also came to my life about the same time. He taught me the Kriya Yoga. I got accustomed to concentrating the mind. After the strict observance of the eighteen month long "no talk" period (*mounavrutham*), Maharshi Mahesh Yogi advised us the meditational method under his Siddha School. While under meditation chanting the Sutras (aphorisms) of Patanjali, I really felt like my body was floating above the earth. I was really surprised! And at that moment I became convinced of one truth, i.e., how high seated was the real knowledge than our silly university education!'

After living away from his country for twenty-three years, Kambiz Naficy the yogi again came back to Iran. There he started an institute under the name of Joy of Life (www.joyoflife.org). Naficy shows the way 'to do away with stress and make life happy'. The Joy of Life institute has branches in Iran, Canada, India and Sri Lanka. This master of yoga constantly visits Europe, America and Asia and teaches the meditation path. He advises the ways to keep away from the stress of life and delivers speeches exclusively on the subject of strain in life. The essays Kambiz Naficy has written on spirituality have become very popular all over the world.

Many people cannot digest the fact that there still are sanyasins and yogis residing in caves. The main reason for this is ignorance of the common man regarding the complexity of the Himalayan world. For reaching these caves after months of long hardships and crossing over glaciers and huge mountains of ice, three factors are necessary. They are the unchanging decisional power, God's mercy and permission from yogis. Foreign travellers are many times ahead of us in this matter. The above-mentioned three factors are the reason why the visual media fails in this respect. In December 2006, the National Geographic channel had telecast a shoot of the cave-dwelling sanyasins. They succeeded in this matter after the hard work of three years. Though the pictures were not perfect, this documentary was clear evidence of the fact that there still are cave-dwelling yogis in the Himalayas. The opinion of the channel's experts was that there are about 6000 holy yogis in the Himalayas. But in my opinion, the number will be twice as much as this. There are specific reasons for them not willing to give interviews or appear in TV shows. But some get such rare chances because of their own peculiarities. These peculiarities are nothing but the yoga skills. Swami Rama[46] has a place in the row of the prominent yogis of India. He had interviewed yogis from mysterious areas of the Himalayas face to face and holy souls residing in surfaces below. After acquiring the yoga skills, Swami Rama permanently resided in the Himalayas for many years. Even while he was in foreign countries, often he would come to the Himalayas. It would be interesting and educative narrating some experiences of this Swami. The path to sanyasindom is very strenuous. Only one who could burn out all his physical and material wishes and desires of the mind can become a sanyasin. Physical gains and losses emotionally disturb many young people. It could be seen that some of them in just a moment's temptation turn to *sanyasam* (the state of becoming a sanyasin) renouncing all worldly and materialistic pursuits. What they find is a peaceful and a restful air. But for such people, wherever they go the mind will be distressed and worrying always. To do away with *kama* (lust), *krodha* (anger), *moha* (attachment), *lobha* (greed), frustration, jealousy and hatred completely, they should observe spiritual discipline. The path of sanyasam is not suitable to one who has a dissatisfied heart and disturbed mind. It is unbearable to sit alone in a cave and think of the affairs of the material world. Let us agree that the relations, attachments and temptations of the material world are very strong. But Swami Rama exhorts that those who have in mind an intense wish to gain spiritual knowledge should not divert from the path.

'There are many caves in various parts of the Himalayas. Four or five people can live in them comfortably. For those sticking to the spiritual path, these places are ideal to help them proceed on their path with whatsoever services and rituals. Besides these, there are so many cave hermitages in the Himalayas. The teacher-student relation here is a long-lasting and continuous one. The ashram (hermitage) where I grew up was one such. The yogi tradition we have is thousands of years old. Everybody knows this. We have documents in our hands to make clear the facts as to who the ancient masters of the ashram were and how such a tradition started. Our ashram which has so many internal cellars is nature made. The inside of the rocks have been cut little by little over centuries to enlarge the size of the cellars. This was for accommodating more sanyasins. Many generations of Rishis had come, lived here and left. All did whatever they could to make the ashram more comfortable and peaceful. There are no modern amenities here. Even though there is no kitchen or bathroom, affairs are being done here without any problem.

'For getting light inside the cave, a lamp using a mix of herbal plants would be lit. When the lamp is on, there would be good light and when the lamp is off, there would be a good smell. The wick of the lamp—four inches long and one inch thick—is made up of the crushed and rolled-up raw herbals. We can very well read the Veda books by the light of the lamp. The branches of pine and devatharu trees are good to make a burning torch. Since these trees are gummy, they would catch fire easily. To heat up the insides of the cave, there would always be a burning fire pit. Putting big pieces of firewood and carefully pouring in oil, the fire pit would always be kept burning. Enough stock of firewood would be stored during summer for the use in winter. We would cultivate protein-rich vegetables in the nearby river beaches. We use many types of mushrooms. Vegetables like lingora and ogal that grow in forests are also our favourites. They also include root vegetables like tarur and genthi. Also available are species similar in look and taste as sweet potato. The main dishes in our cave life were wheat, barley, potato, peas and maize. All of these grow in 6500-feet-high villages. Each village has its own cottage industry. High quality carpets and woollen dresses are woven there. One narrow stream flows aside our cave. It never gets dry. We melt and use the frozen water of the stream during November and December. The caves in *Manali* where we stayed were scarce of water. We collected water after walking for 3 or 4 km.

'In many Himalayan Ashrams, the masters still teach the students in the traditional method. The master resides in the Ashram. Students from nearby places will come and go for their studies and practices. Those who come for education are different types. Some will have an ordinary curiosity only and some others will have no willingness to work hard and achieve higher levels of studies. Those who quit their homes for emotional reasons cannot be expected to come to these high lands in search of teachers. Thus the Himalayas protect its masters in precaution as well. The great maharshis and yogis live in the mysterious and non-accessed interiors of the Himalayas. Only rare people will possess the will power and the determination to go to such difficult heights and find out the teachers. Teaching is done at exact timings mainly through practical exercises. The students on their part have to exhibit before the masters all the knowledge they acquire. Sometimes the study will be in complete silence. When the Guru feels that the disciple has reached a particular level of knowledge, he will ask the latter, "How will the service of a yogi be available to the people of the outer world if you continue living in a cave?" Thus most sanyasins leave the place after some years.'47

'There are so many caves in the distant ice land of Gangothri Dhamam on the other side of the Ganga River. In my childhood, so many yogis lived in them. Dressed only for name sake, they didn't even use fire. I lived for three consecutive winters in a cave here. Those residing here will meet the fellow residents only from distance. Without making friendship with each other and without disturbing each other, they lived in peace. It was a period I lived in utmost satisfaction. Most of the time, I was engaged in yoga practices. Wheat and pea were kept dipped in water and when it spurted, we ate them with salt. That was our only food.'

Life after death is elaborately described in Swami Rama's book, *Life Here and Hereafter*. He had been an eyewitness to *Parakaya Pravesham* (the power to leave your body consciously and enter a new one) and *Punar-Jeevitham* (taking birth after death). He narrates:

'What I state as symptoms of a man who is very near his death is based upon my own experiences. The experiences of some yogis I have direct acquaintance with have also helped me. Once I met a yogi at Paisung in Sikkim.

He had the ability to die as per his own wish. Also, he had the ability to make a dead man alive. Four or five times, I was a witness to this ability of his. I became curious to know the secret behind the amazing skill called *Parakaya Pravesham*. He asked me to bring a big live ant and I brought one. As per Swami's instructions, I cut the ant into three pieces with a sharp knife and put each piece in three different places. The places were at a distance of about 10 feet. Suddenly the yogi fell into profound meditation. We checked his breath and pulse. There was no sign of life. But we had seen his body shuddering and trembling before he fell into profound meditation. Within minutes, the three separate pieces of the ant came together and became single. The ant came alive again and started to move on the floor. Continuously for the next three days, we observed the ant very carefully giving no chances to lose sight. The yogi explained that a dead man can be made live again in two different ways. One is "Solar Science" and the other one is "Prana (Soul) Technique". Both are parts of Yoga Sasthra (yoga science). But there are only very few yogis who know them and some of them are still there in the Himalayan mountains and the Tibetan valleys.'

Swami Rama tells us another interesting incident. The *Kumbha Mela* festival had been going on in Allahabad in 1966. A yogi had predicted his death. One friend by the name of Vinaya Maharaj sent a man to the Swami. The message he brought was that the Swami should go and see with his own eyes the yogi dying. On Vasantha Panchami[48] day at 4.30 in the morning, the yogi gave up his physical body in front of the Swami and others. Just before that, he had told them to be witnesses of his death.

Swami Rama and others were engaged in talking until 4.28 a.m. Yoga and Vedanta were the subjects. Suddenly the yogi told them that the time had come. He then sat in the Sidhasana position and with a little smile on his lips, left the physical body. Swami Rama and the others present there went to 'Ganga Sangamam' and took a bath. They bathed the dead body also. The readers might feel these incidents as amazing. But for those practising yoga, these were not rare happenings at all.'

The Swami met a woman at Kanpur. She had been practising Nadha Yoga and was the mother of the famous doctor G.N. Tandon. Her death also was in the samadhi state. And this too was in front of the Swami and some others. She had been a woman who lived all her life with good character and became completely detached from worldly matters in the last days of her life. She concentrated all her attention in practising yoga and left life in full consciousness. Swami Rama says, 'I believe that even housewives who run happy families can amidst their usual work, study and practise yoga and meditation and get a deeper understanding of them.'

Swami was sent to Banaras in 1948 and lived there with a Bengali couple. He had heard earlier that the husband and wife were going to die at the same time. It had been some years that the couple started learning yoga. They intimated others about the time of their death. Swami Rama was one among them. The Swami later said that in those years he had an intense curiosity to know about the secret of that. He went to the Himalayas, Assam, Tibet and Sikkim in search of yogis who could tell him that. Generally, nobody knew about the yogis who possessed such special abilities. He had already travelled a long way along that path. Then, he was fully convinced. Yoga was not for winning physical pleasures or profits. Its aim was to complete the relation between life and Siva.

He asked the master about the great teachers and how they could heal the diseases of others and was told that

'healing of diseases was in three aspects—physically, mentally and spiritually. A man was made of those three aspects. One who had acquired the spiritual accomplishment could heal a patient through those aspects. But once such a way of healing was accepted as a profession, the will and the mind would turn towards physical gains. Each man had the power to heal inherently in him. This power was constantly flowing in each mind. When one made use of that power right, he could direct that flow to those physical or mental parts afflicted with illness. Emotions and mental set-up influenced the internal structure of power. We could see the impact of illness on the internal structure even before the symptoms appeared on the physical body. That "energy body" had decisive influence on the physical body. That power of cure flew to those parts of illness and provided vigour and strength to the patient. The key of that treatment rested on generosity, love and strong will power. Above all of those, there should be unshaken belief in the ultimate Soul who lived in one's own heart. That was the secret of how the Indian system of treatment called *Marma Chikilsa*[49] often succeeded much to everyone's surprise.'[50]

It may be relevant now to discuss another system of medicine called Reiki. The origin of this was also from yoga. Though the Japanese Buddhist monk Mikao Usui made the system popular in its present form, the fundamentals of it is elaborately given in yoga books. The energy which is universally existent and which is the universal cause of all creation is called Samashti Pranan in Sanskrit. This is called Reiki in Japanese.[51] This universal energy is what flows in a solidified state through the organs when one is treated in the Reiki system. Reiki is very effective for those who have high receptive power. Many of the physical diseases are only external expressions of failings in psychological and spiritual actions. Like in yoga, in Reiki also the contact points are fixed on the basis of chakras.

Aadhar Chakras are the circular centres of energy existing in human subtle bodies. Our power of life is rooted in circle foundation. The seats of our deep emotional and psychological experiences are these chakras. They are the whirlpools of centralized energy. Their main duty is to act like a funnel and pass life energy to various parts of the body. In almost all yoga and Tantric works of India, the important chakras and many sub-chakras are mentioned. They exist in what is called the other half of our body, the subtle body. Or the matter will be clearer if we say that the chakras are the doors through which flow the power and energy of life for the physical body. Each chakra is related to some part of the body and the organs there. The major chakras influence the working of the main glands of the endocrine glands group.

The deficiency in the flow of energy from the chakras will create imbalance and tiredness in psychological and spiritual realms. In normal conditions, the chakras will work in unison. The Reiki treatment keeps the body disease-free by purifying the chakras and balancing their functions. The objective of all meditational programmes is to refine energy at lower levels and bring them up to higher levels so as to balance the working of base chakras. The universe is a moving web of indivisible energy to which the physical sciences also agree. We are all a part of it. There are the laws of nature that make possible transmission of life energy to distant places. If the right transmitters and receivers are available, energy can be flown to any level of the bio-world.

Swami Rama assessed the great wonder, the mind, as follows:

'Mind was a store house of countless skills. By making use of the many possibilities that lay hidden in mind, we could achieve any big success in the world. We should practise the mind for that. Also we should teach that to concentrate on. Mind had the capability to go into the depths of life and that was the most useful tool man had. We could make a man under our control by looking at him for some time with all attention and concentration of mind. The concentration of mind on an outside thing was called vision. Concentration was internal observation. The power of a concentrated mind was so big. There were different types of vision and each vision gave mind a different ability. The power of meditation was a universally accepted fact. Nobody knew the wonders a concentrated mind could perform!'

Swami Rama authoritatively evaluated various schemes of abandoning life through yoga.

'The body would get frozen in those parts of the Himalayas thickly covered with ice. The condition would be such that the body, henceforth, would not know the freezing coldness. I learnt those things from ancient books and great masters.

'The Western people who arrived in the Himalayas in search of higher peaks also had recorded them. But abandonment of life through yoga was a factual thing. Freezing one's own body while one reaches at the highest level of Samadhi. This had been a method existing from ancient times. A particular sect of yogis[52] in the Himalayas observed that type of *Pranathyaga* or "abandonment of life". This was called *Hima* (ice) *Samadhi*. We could see the word "Samadhi" occurring many times in Patanjali's *Yoga Sasthra*. Samadhi occurred when the mind reached the highest point of peace. But in the processes of the Himalayas, the word

Samadhi also denoted the act of one consciously abandoning one's own physical body. Besides Hima Samadhi, there were other processes also.

'One such was "Jala (water) Samadhi"[53] where life was thrown out by going to the depths of Himalayan rivers keeping the breath still. Another one was "Sthala (place) Samadhi". In that, the *Brahmarandra* (God's hole in the skull through which the soul went out on death) was opened deliberately by sitting in a position as prescribed in yoga science. This was the common way the yogis adopted for dying. Here, life was finished off quite consciously and in a painless manner. It was not suicide. When the body as a tool became useless in getting hold of spiritual knowledge, it was abandoned by its own decision as per scientific law. The body might become an obstacle to a dying man in further travel. It was an ocean of endless and unknown past memories that he had to cross over. Only those who could not learn still greater yoga lessons or those who had no confidence in their own will and yoga powers went for ordinary death. There was still another rare way of Pranathyaga. By meditating on the Surya (Sun) Chakra, the fire inside the body soars up to burn it into ashes. The King of Death, Yama, advised that method to his dearest disciple Nachiketas in the Katopanishad. In many parts of the world, these instances had happened several times like sudden fires and burning out into ashes.[54] People are also surprised over such happenings. But the cause of them had been precisely described in works like *Mahakalanidhi*, etc. When the curtain of ignorance is drawn, the mind would easily understand the secrets of nature. The "technique of death" was far, far away from the knowledge of modern science. It was a separate lesson in yoga science. It would be taught only to those who are mature and ready to practise. Only some lucky people got the chance to understand the secret of birth and death. The life we saw was a straight line from birth to death. The rest of life lay invisible beyond those two dots. It was unknown to common people. Our lifetime was only a semi-colon of a great sentence that went with no full stop. There were eleven exits for the Soul, the subtle body, to go out from a body. The yogi learnt to take out the soul through the Brahmarandra. The soul that went out through that way would be live and conscious; also it closely knew the other world like this world.'

Swami Rama had factually recorded about transmigration also. 'Muni Vyasa said in *Vipulopakhyanam*, the Mahabharata, that transmigration was possible in yoga. It was done when one felt that the body was useless. To survive an illness, a yogi very rarely accepted a good and useful dead body. At all such times, the body of the yogi would be in deep sleep or samadhi (It is said in the Upanishads: *Thwamsaal Sareeraal Prabhyahenmu Njadhisheekamiva Dhairyaena*). *Yoga Sutra* taught the way to exit the physical body and live in the subtle body and then to travel out into all universes as one wished. The technique of transmigration was more complex than that.'

Swami Rama wrote about his experiences. During the conversations, the Guru had told him that the Rishis and yogis who reached the peak of yoga had no limitations of a lifetime. They could live as long as they wished or could give up the physical body at any time they wished. They could also migrate to another body if they felt it convenient. The greatest yogi and *Thapaswi* Sree Sankaracharya had this ability. There was a scientific book narrating transmigration in detail. It was not an impossible thing at all that an expert in yoga activity finding and accepting another body to live in. The only thing was that a suitable body should be available. Swami Rama writes:

'In my childhood, I had a chance to get acquainted with a yogi called Buday Baba. Often he visited our cave to participate in discussions on spiritual activities. I had talked with my guru about transmigration a number of times. Since I was young, I didn't understand much about the subject. After one week, the guru asked me to go with the elderly yogi to Assam. Our travel was by train. The yogi strictly practised yoga, pranayama and meditation even during the journey. One military major who was a fellow traveller was an acquaintance of Baba. I overheard the Baba telling him that he was going to accept another body within the next nine days. He asked Baba about the purpose of doing so. He said that he was ninety years old and couldn't indulge in meditation for long with the present body. The next day, a young man was going to die of snake bite. If his body was got . . . he stopped midway. Hearing what the Baba said, I was bewildered. The Baba continued talking and said that the next day he would go from the cave very early in the morning. The destination would be reached before sunset. I rose up early the next morning and after taking a bath in the river, I sat for meditation. When I opened my eyes after a long time, there was no trace of Baba. I couldn't find him even after searching for the whole day. I thought of returning to the Himalayas. Trekking for long hours through forests and woods, ascents and descents, I entered a pathway full of thorns which led to the military camp of Assam. The major was there and the moment he saw me, he said that the Guru Baba did what he had said. He had received a new body. I didn't understand anything. I went to the Himalayas the next day itself to meet my guru. He told me that Buday Baba had come there the day before in the evening. Soon, a young yogi came over. He started talking to the Swami as if they were acquainted with each other for long years. He was describing each and every incident of the Assam journey. "When I received the new body, you were not with me," he told Swami Rama. There was no change in his habits or abilities although he was in a new physical body. The Baba's character, memories and knowledge were all there in the 'young' yogi also. What I could learn after much proof-checking and thorough studies was this: it was quite possible for a yogi who had reached the peak of yoga skill to hand over his own soul to a suitable alien body corpse. This was possible only to those with yoga skill. For ordinary people, this might be just imaginary stories.'

The masters authoritatively stated how great the relevance of energy was in human life.

'In the present age, the strength of will power is not understood properly. The strength comes through three channels—the power of will, the power of action and the power of knowledge. Strength meant energy. That strength was often in a state of sleep. Sometimes, it becomes very energetic. We perform each and every deed with the help of the "power of action". The supporting strength behind such deeds was the "power of will". It encourages one to act. The "power of knowledge" was related to decision. One decides to do something with his mind. We could deliberately develop one or more of those powers. Some yogis did things very effectively. And they won mass applause also. Some gave importance to the power of will. Their words and actions would be completely under their will. Yet some others paid more attention to the strength of intelligence, the prudence to discriminate between things. Thus, they acquired the state of wisdom, the peaceful and balanced state of mind where all the powers joined together. One had to first choose which power one wanted to develop and then adopt suitable practices. Regular and strict practising was a must, irrespective of the social position or sector. With the power of will, one could develop self-confidence and bring the physical phenomenon under control. It was with that power that the great masters could control even the powers of nature.'

The ancient rishis of India raised the curtain from many wonders to the world by developing the powers of will, action and knowledge at the same time. Those rishis had deep knowledge of the stages man had to go through in the process of evolution. The Indian philosophers had long ago revealed that the cyclical law is applicable to the origin of universe also. They called this the cycle of world. The ancient rishis had the power to look at past centuries and they correctly predicted the rise and fall of civilizations. They showed us the fact that subtle organs of power lie hidden inside human beings and through them, they could go beyond the powers of physical organs to the unknown secrets of life and the universe. The result of devoted yoga practice was to bring to vision the internal matters of the powers of will, action and knowledge. By that, they could discover that we could see but not with our eyes, we could hear but not with our ears and we could move but not with our bodies. Besides those, the mind of man possessed other strange and unbelieving abilities, they found out.

Fritjof Capra is a physicist engaged in fusing eastern mysticism with modern physics. The book he published in 1975 was *The Tao of Physics*. The meaning of Tao in Chinese is path, route, style or order. The subject matter of Capra is the 'tao' of physics. He describes the astonishing circumstances of finding this:

'Five years ago, I happened to have a very hearty experience. It turned me to the path of writing this book. One winter evening I was sitting on the sea shore seeing the rising waves and listening to the rhythm of breathing. All of a sudden I went through the experience. All my surroundings were engaged in a great universal dance. Being a physicist, I know that the sand, rock, air and water all are made up of always vibrating atoms and particles. I also know that the cosmic rays and highly ionized atoms that come from space are hitting the atmosphere of earth and fighting in various ways with the atoms of earth's atmosphere. I knew all these well before from my research programmes. While I was sitting on the shore that day, these experiences got a fresh life. I saw a very heavy downpour of energy from space. Inside, the atoms were created rhythmically. And destroyed. I saw the atoms and particles of elements and my own body engaged with that universal dance of energy. I felt the rhythm of it. I heard the sound of it. I understood at that very moment that this was the dance of Hindu God Siva or Nataraja.'

Let us also go into the relevant extracts of the interview Swathi Chopra had with Capra.[55]

'Thirty years have passed after you published the work *The Tao of Physics*. How do the atheists and crooked people look at the mainstream science?'

'The basic principles of atomic theory and the theory of relativity have surprising similarities with eastern spiritual philosophy. Though the western scientists have noted these similarities, they have not made further studies on that. Maybe I am the first such scientist. Physical scientists have often viewed my book with contempt. They know that I am speaking things with a clear knowledge of modern physics. But they were not ready to accept the Indian spiritual thoughts. They insisted that the physical science and spiritual science should never be joined together and they should always exist as two. This is the problem of wrongly understanding the word "spiritual" of eastern spiritual science. What they have understood about the word spirituality or mysticism is that it is something complex and non-transparent and hiding something mysterious. The physicists had cautiously put forth their concepts and theories with clarity and reason. But then comparing their science with secret mysticism would sure feel unbearable to them. Viewing spirituality in the right sense and knowledge, everyone would be convinced of one thing that how big and high was the knowledge of the ancient great souls, the Indian yogis. We can figuratively call this "removal of the veil of ignorance" or "cutting ignorance with the sword of truth". Anybody can simply understand what is meant by such metaphors. They are not mysterious secrets at all. Now after thirty years, the physicists have put their observations open to the vast world. They have turned more generous and philosophical now. At the same time, their attempt to follow the spiritual path is noteworthy. The life practices of yogis, Sree Buddha and Tao have spread more in the western people. While writing *The Tao of Physics* and learning meditation, I was feeling that I had become part of a distant society. Luckily, it is now widely recognized.'

When asked on how he became interested in the mystic sciences, his reply was this: 'The cultural movements of the 1960s influenced me so much. My mental set-up grew both in spiritual and social spheres. This made me attracted to the religious systems of the East. My mother was a poet. She gave me to read the poems of the Beat Poets who were famous in 1950s. My elder brother presented me a copy of the Bhagavat Gita also in the 1960s. That was before me reading the works of Zen and Ellen Watts. By that time the Beatles began coming to India. Thus the path of meditation and mysticism became familiar to me. I became a part of it too. I approached every experience of mine namely meditation, magic, yoga, Tai chi and Zen with reason. Also I cared very much to observe and assess them in the light of intelligence.

'Max Planck, the famous German physicist (1858–1947) who won a Nobel Prize in 1918 for physics, is the proponent of modern quantum theory. He revolutionized the science of physics by his quantum theory (quantum physics is the invisible gate to Brahmaloka.). This genius of a scientist very much confided in Indian spiritualism. It will be very informative to go into his observations.[56]

'Standing for the most materialistic branch of science and devoting my life to the research of physical substances as a physics scientist, I can never be under the spell of any kind of extreme arguments. Let me tell you one thing that I learnt in my research on atoms. Fundamentally, there is no such thing called mass! The origin of mass is from a power which draws the energy particles of an atom into particular orbits and thus preserves them as a microscopic solar system. It is the mass too. But as we do not directly see an intellectual idea or inner power in this structure of the universe, we must reach a conclusion that there is a cognizant essence of soul existing behind this power. The basic principle of all mass is thus this conscious power.

'Max Planck, one of the most gifted atomic scientists of the modern era, reaches such a knowledge of the conscious power behind "creation" that draws the atomic particles into orbits and centralizes them into solar systems. This is also the conclusion of Indian rishis about the ultimate power. In their view, all the powers in the world are varied forms of the ultimate power which is the face of creation of the ultimate soul. All the phenomena in the world take place out of the reactions, clashes and combinations of these powers. This body of power was called Pranamaya Kosha by the rishis (the activity zone of soul power). Prana or soul is the intellectual spirit connected to the ultimate intellectual power (soul), the cause of the world. It is one of the subtle powers of self as indicated by Max Planck.'

The article says that Max Planck had no pre-conception or didn't get any help in inventing his 'constant'. 'Only science can answer all our questions. Cells capable of giving us insight are living in our brains actively and ready for action. Even scientific truths often arise in the mind of a scientist as a sudden intuition, revelation or spurt of a thought. But that scientist tries to give a logical explanation to such a sudden knowledge he got. This is what is happening most times. So we must understand one thing from the experiences of the famous scientists and researchers. Please do not ridicule the inner power providing the base to reasoning.'

The ancient rishis declared that the secret of life and the universe lies hidden in the depths of the human inner self and man's search of his own self leads him to spiritual knowledge and experience. This gives him peace and comfort. Many modern scientists have started thinking this way.

Max Planck continues: 'We have to seek logical answers to some questions in the light of scientific knowledge. We need a new science to have a look at the areas beyond our common sense. The human mind has some extraordinary powers. They hadn't come to the consideration of science till recently. Close attention of modern researchers has turned now to such mysterious areas called extra-terrestrial phenomena. Through these researches, the light of modern science has started falling on the insights and knowledge of the Indian Rishis. The *Bharatiya* (Indian) Rishis were those who thought about things going beyond man-made barriers and found out mysterious truths about life and the world. They removed the garbage from their thoughts, enlightened themselves and developed their self. Thus they grew extra-human and evolved various methods to help the mental and spiritual evolution of human beings. Today many have started asking questions like "Wasn't the base of the world an unknown, single and ultimate energy-conscious self?" and "Wasn't human intelligence only a shadow?"'

The world-famous Dr D.G. Vinod,[57] who learnt tantra, mantra and yoga in the Himalayas, was attracted to the ideas of Max Planck. He wrote:

'Standing on the fundamental of his "Quantum Theory", Max Planck has put forth this. That is, the measure of energy each physical quantum of the universe carries is $E = hv$. Here "E" denotes Energy Radiation and "V" Frequency Radiation. "h" is a constant. It is known as Planck's "constant" and the value is 0.6624×10^{30}. How did Planck invent this value? He hadn't sought anybody's help for this or had no scientific preconceptions. There is no exaggeration in saying that all the scientific advancements in Physics for the last 50 years happened because of this constant. Accepting Albert Einstein's invitation I went to his home in Princeton in 1953. Einstein convinced me of him constantly using this constant in his theoretical projects since 1905. Why I mention this constant here is because of its capacity to give unpredictable results the modern science openly agrees it has. Arthur Eddington in his reference narrates that "it is not surprising that a prudent man feels all the universal truths as irrational. But the theory of Karma is not really irrational." Let we call it the extra-terrestrial knowledge, extra-sensual communication, knowledge of sixth sense, insight or by whatever name, the only choice before us is to accept the Karma theory because the outcome of action (Karma) exists only by the scientific justification of the theory of Action (Karma).'

The famous biologist and thinker Julian Huxley tells the scientists: 'Science has started now pouring light to an unknown power related to the activities of the mind. The rishis and yogis of ancient India had gained basic knowledge of this mysterious power of energy. They utilized this knowledge for the evolutionary growth of man and superhuman development.'

The narration of relevant portions from the article of Prof. Dr Joachim Illis may be wound up by citing one quotation from him.[58] 'While looking at the infiniteness of the universe through a telescope, many of us feel that we are looking at a self-reflecting mirror. We think that what man sees in the unknown depths of the universe and beyond the horizon are he himself and his secrets in the depths. The ancient Indian thinking that the secrets of the universe are inherent in human beings has been recognized by the modern thinkers of science.'

The great scholarly rishis of India saw the set-up of the universe as egg-shaped. That was why they called it Brahmandam (Brahma: universe/God, *andam*: egg). They revealed that the power of the universe is Brahma and that the universe is constantly moving and changing. They made it clear that there is no motionless thing in the universe. And they argued that creation of the always changing and developing world and all its moving and non-moving things are of the pancha bhoothas. It was this knowledge of our great rishis that the modern scientists have discovered too. Today, nobody has any doubt that all the bright and dark things of the universe are elliptical and moving.

Ilya Prigogine, the 1977 Nobel Prize winner in Chemistry (thermodynamics), visited India in 1993. He came to Kerala also. In a friendly debate with a noted weekly, he declared this:

'It was when we turned our attention to the Upanishads that we felt how childish were our lines of thought. Until then we were watching the universe standing apart from it. But the Upanishads convinced us that everything including us were parts of universe. What we need today is *spiritual findings* that were lost in the rushing up of materialism. The great thinkers, the Rishis of India, are the light-houses of these findings.'

The well-known cosmologist Carl Sagan, in his book *Cosmos*, has pointed out many things that shed light on many facts lying in the depths of Indian Vedanta. 'Hindu religion is the only religion in the world to put forth the concept that the world is subject to innumerable deaths and rebirths. Each of our cells is a storehouse of the crux of memories gained from the travel of life through millions of years. Hindu religion is the only religion that goes in tune with the theories of time of the modern science of the universe. Its cyclic time structure spreads from the ordinary day and night to one day and night of Lord Brahma comprising 8.64 billion years. This is before the origin of the earth and sun and rather half of the time after the Big Bang. Not only this, the religion has got still more concepts of time that surpasses this.'

Sree Ramakrishna Paramahamsar says that he has seen many times in his mind millions and millions of universes rising and setting in the sky. Countless other scholars have also peeped into this infinity. The Sun, which is the centre of planets in this universe, is only an atom in another great universe. Now, where will this series of universes that grow bigger and bigger end?

'*Andanaam Thu Sahasranam Sahasranyayuthani Cha/Ee Drusanaam Thadha Thathra Kodi Kodi Sathani Cha*'

—Vishnu Puramnam

(In the great universe, there are thousands of crores of universes like this. Each of these countless universes that lie in infinity is the cause and result of its own previous birth.)

The mantra portion 'Sooryachandramasou Dhatha Yadha Poorvamakalpayal' also endorses this truth.

The belief is that chanting or thinking of mantras deep in one's mind will save one from the tragedies and dangers of this world ('Mananal Thrayathae Ethi Mantra ha'). Though the mantras can be chanted in three ways, namely manasika, upamsu and vykhari, the strongest is the manasika way of chanting. 'Thapo Manasamuchyathae' which is also what the Bhagavat Gita says. The human body is an association of particles. Chanting of mantras increases the pulsation of these particles and this causes the stimulation of internal organs. By chanting the Pranava mantra, the doer can influence the root cause of universe, Parabrahma, and ask any wish of him. Mantra = man + tra = mind and the three components of it—the conscious mind, the subconscious mind and the subtle mind—joining together makes mantras strong. Yamtra = Yam + tra is the joining together of physical, nuclear (astral) and ethereal bodies whereas Tantra = tan + tra provides protection by imbibing the nucleic structure of Agni (fire), Jalam (water) and Vayu (air).[59]

Mr Sreekant, who has conducted studies on the original form of things and the base of the science of mantra and how it flows as a current into a devotee, records his views as follows:[60]

'The causal form of all the things we see are fundamental particles like electrons. In its final evaluation, the theory of wave mechanics, the modern branch of Physics says that each particle is an association of energy waves. This had been recognized centuries back by our ancient Rishis as the base of the science of mantra. Viewed from that angle, it becomes that energy in the form of waves *is* the more minuscule form of any matter. This is the mantra or the microscopic pulse of matter. This is true not only for the visible things that we can see and touch but also for the invisible things that are beyond our sight and touch. If there is matter, there is pulse.

'If we can create that pulse, then that itself is the basic theory of the science of *Mantra*. Sir Robert Woodroff who wrote the authoritative book on philosophy makes it clear that he had seen a man who could light up lamps for worship by chanting the fire seed mantra "*Rem*".[61]

'When an ordinary devotee having equivalent physical factors of a temple prays in a temple, the vigour and splendour throbbing in the temple begins to throb in his body also through the resonance process. This rouses the sleepy internal magnificence in his body and thus gets the particle in him throbbing. This results in the devotee achieving all his spiritual and physical needs. This particle is nothing but the magnificence of Parameswara (God) that is in sleep inside the devotee. Hence, the particle will have a quality up and up above the ordinary human level. Because of this, wonderful things can be gained by temple prayers. Long before the modern scientists could understand, the great yogis of ancient India understood that metals and stones were carriers of data and energy. The quote of Sir John Woodroffe that "where the bells of worship ring, there lives the Hindu religion through the Tantric system" is very thoughtful.'

The strongest expressions of God's vigour exist at those places where numerous rishis conduct meditations and at those holy places where people get God's blessings from ancient times and also where other true devotees visit. There the transmission of 'subtle power' will be felt more compared to other places. The great rishis built temples in such places. And this is the basic principle of saying that by visiting the great temples spread over many places in our vast country, a devotee reaches the path of God's blessing.

A heaven which we can't reach exists somewhere on the India-Tibet border or beyond that in the Himalayan icy mountains or lonely valleys. Its name is Shangri-La, known as the seat of awakening, knowledge and peace. It was the Hungarian scholar Alexander Csoma de Koros who, in his article written in 1833, gave geographic proof of the existence of this wonderland in between 45° and 50° north latitude in India. An argument was there from the olden days that Shangri-La and Sidhashramam were one and the same. Though many agreements and disagreements arose, in the final assessment it was revealed that both were not the same. The fact is that while Sidhashramam is said to be situated at very high altitude, Shangri-La is situated on earth itself. Many scandals and controversies remained from olden days about Shangri-La, which was known in Sanskrit as Sambhala. This was the residence of masters who had achieved mental awakening.

To get some understanding about the Shangri-La dynasty, we have to go into the Tibetan legends. The myth regarding the Meru Mountain may be taken as the way towards this. The magical land, Shangri-La or Sambhala, has the shape of a lotus with eight petals. This yoga-steeped empire is situated somewhere in North India amid icy mountains. When a series of kings inspired by Buddhist doctrines were fighting to find out truth and justice, this place was calm. *Rajarshis* (a type of rishi out of the seven types of rishis) had been controlling the area for centuries. In fact, even before the Buddhist religion came there, the Sambhala had been there in Tibet. The meaning of the Sanskrit word *Sambhala* is 'the place of peace'. The yoga masters of ancient India recorded this about Sambhala: 'When a traveller reaches near this empire, his awareness of destination is lost. He feels like he is reaching some other world and without any aim.'[62] The definition of Shangri-La is different to different people. It is the source and safe place of the 'wheel of time'. Before getting ready for the Sambhala journey, yogis set aside a large part of their lifetime for hard work to attain spiritual heights. Concerning definition, Shangri-La or Sambhala is just mysterious. Though they tried as best as they could, the countless spiritualists and searchers were not able to exactly mark the existence of Shangri-La on a map except for the common opinion that situates it somewhere in the mountainous areas of south Asia! Many people returned after having been convinced that Shangri-La is a reality and experienced that it is a bridge between our physical world and spiritual world. It is said in the Tibetan legend that once, a sanyasin of Shangri-La had come to the plains of India for studying about the 'wheel of time'. After making an extensive study, he returned. It is said that only those with pure hearts can survive in Shangri-La. Such people live there in the endless sea of happiness with complete peace of mind, harmony and perfection. They neither get grey hair nor do they become old. Love and knowledge rule there. Injustice and immorality are foreign there. The residents there are perfect in physique and beauty and are rather immortal. They have immense spiritual knowledge and are far ahead in technology also.

It was the book *Lost Horizon*,[63] written by James Hilton, that drew the attention of the world to the magical atmosphere of Tibet, the mysterious Himalayas and the sanyasins purified by knowledge. The book depicted a true but unbelievable and strange story of a lama from Shangri-La saving some Englishmen in 1931 who got trapped in a mysterious Himalayan valley after the helicopter they were travelling from Baskul to Peshawar crashed. As per custom, the scholarly yogis of Shangri-La received the guests with a cup of tea. The guests were surprised hearing the master guru making a philosophical point in English. Hearing that the Shangri-La residents, who had complete knowledge of immortality, timelessness and eternity, were free from desires and interests, the guests were shocked too. James Hilton got to know about the surprising things of Shangri-La from a lama he met on his Tibetan journey.

The world-famous artist and Russian traveller, Nicholas Roerich, describes his many journeys to Tibet in his book *Sambhala*. In 1928, he asked a lama he met on such a journey whether Shangri-La was real. The following was the reply of the lama: 'It is heaven. It has no connection with earth.' This question and answer are still relevant. British theosophist Alexandra David Neel had recorded the scientific aspects of the possibility of getting into Shangri-La. She argues that by reducing body weight through the very hard practices of yoga, one can travel at awesome speed and surpass the gravitational force of earth.[64]

The description of Shangri-La will not be complete without mentioning the Tibetan yoga system. There were many secret mantras in Adharva Veda left unchanted by our great munis. They did this to prevent the mantras being used for bad purposes. This was also why the Adharva Veda was considered unwelcome and bad. But some rishis also existed who were short-tempered and used the power for personal purposes.[65] These rishis were the ones who chanted and advised the reprehensible secret mantras to the needy. From that ancestry, the Tibetan lamas got the power. They made it big and more effective through harder and tougher meditation. This is also the reason for Tibet to become known as the land of mysteries and hidden secrets. The provinces in Tibet such as Kyorpokh, Dingree, Kyanithsai, Nubkhulung and Thasang Rong are main centres of lamas and geshis who have acquired the mantra power. In Ooh Village, there are many lamas with divine powers. The wild people of Lobrak Pass are famous for black magic.

The skills and knowledge of Tibetan lamas are immense.[66] A lama needs at least fifteen years to reach his peak in skills and by that time he has to meditate and chant mantras more than 1,00,000 times. To acquire the skills, there are a number of obstacles to conquer.[67] One lama showed me the remnants of one such obstacle on a hilltop at the Tibet-Bhutan border. The emission of energy from the mountains will be extreme in the places selected for this. Solid bricks dried in sunlight, water in a mud pot and a string of beads for prayer are the things needed for this. After chanting a mantra 10,000 times, the nude lama, sitting in the right position for meditation, places one brick in the hump of clay placed around him. Placing eight or nine bricks is one round. Then he makes another round over it. After each round, the number of chanting mantras will be increased. Like a wasp constructs its nest from mud, the lama constructs a narrow nest around him. After the nest reaches the height above the shoulder level, the diameter of the nest is reduced to hold only the head. During this time, the guru or his main assistant will be there to help. The construction of the nest will be finished after making a single hole above the Brahmarandra on the top of the head. The guru or his assistant will leave the place. For six months or more, the lama sits inside this mud shell in meditation. By the energy flow through the Brahmarandra to the body and again that from body to the bricks, the bricks get burnt. The guru comes again after he is convinced of the acquisition of the skill by his disciple. Because of the divine powers of the guru and the acquired skill of the lama, he comes out breaking the brick nest into pieces. The size of the beads on the prayer string would be then worn out to half!

To become skilled in the Tibetan system of yoga, the aspirant has to surely find a teacher or guru.[68] The assistance of a guru is essential for burning the inner fire and focusing the mind from one level to another in order to gain divine skill and powers. If the mind is stuck at one level unable to move to the next level, the aspirant becomes mad. The fact that a lama, who has acquired the powers through the *Tum-Mo* system, can melt ice rocks around him by burning the inner fire has been confirmed by witnessing travellers. The miserable end of a lama who tried to gain the *Tum-Mo* power sitting atop an isolated mountain is also much talked about in Tibet. The lama had been at the end of his long meditation when a traveller woke him up to inquire about the path he was to go. It is said that the lama became mad by the crucial variation in pulse when he was suddenly brought to consciousness.

Milarepa was a Tibetan yogi who, by reaching the uppermost levels of skills, exhibited many superhuman abilities. Milarepa could kill enemies by the extremely strong *beeja mantra* (beeja means root), namely 'Hum', and make them unconscious by the mantra 'Paht'. Wearing the godly symbols of diamond, bell, dharma chakra, lotus and sword and imbibing the beeja mantras '*om, ah hum*', he performed many superhuman activities. The clandestine meditation called Vajrarahi, which held the mind in uttermost concentration, and the noble meditation systems called 'He Vajramandala' and 'Maha Vajramandala', were known to him. He had studied the Tantric books in minute detail and achieved the knowledge of *Jaivorja Sadhana* (Jaivorja is biological energy) narrated in these texts and also got hold of the top-secret yoga technique *Parakaya Pravesham* (transmigration). Parakaya Pravesham is of four types, namely *Santham* (quiet), *Veeram* (gallant), *Aakrushtam* (attractive) and *Sthiram* (permanent). The basis of all Tibetan yoga doctrines was derived from India but changes in the Tibetan style have been made to them. Though the Tibetan yogis applied in practice the secret technique of Parakaya Pravesham by the name 'Dhakinee Karna Tantra', its base was rooted in India. The Tibetan philosophers believed that the human body was the grouping together of twelve causes that resulted from ignorance and the body was a great vehicle helping good people who wished to have eternal liberty (moksha) reach the ultimate aim on their own. But the same body tempted the unlucky people to do sins and thus made them go to hell, the world of devils.

For more details about Tibet, please refer to the following books: *Tibetan Yogas and its Secret Doctrines* by Byavans Ventass; *The Tibetan Book of the Dead* by Padma Sambahava; *The Miracle of Mindfulness* by Thich Nhat Hanh; *The Tibetan Book of Living and Dying* by Sogyal Rinpoche; *Glimpse After Glimpse* by Sogyal Rinpoche; *Death, Intermediate State and Rebirth* by Jeffrey Hipkins and Lati Rinbohay; *Return from Death* by Margot Grey; *Life After Life* by Raymond Mody A.M.D.; and *Minding the Body, Mending the Mind* by Joan Borysenko.

We should remember here the vision of ancient Indian Vedas to which we should bow our head in reverence and also worship as our soul. There were ever more skilled yogis in Tibet before Milarepa. Bognather, also known as Laotsu or Boyung, lived for a long time in Tibet. This Sidha guru from India played a vital role in popularizing the secrecy-based tantra science in Tibet.

Things to prove that Tibet is a mysterious land can be seen there even now. Witnesses vow that the water-cows of Nyashing lake and giant demons of Nam Ru Lake still appear. A traveller named Hersse had written in 1812 that he saw a non-human creature shaped like a demon in Manasa Sarass (the Holy Lake). The following is written in his journal: 'When returning to the tent before dusk, a heavily sized creature was seen on the top of water. First, it was thought to be the dead body of a big Yak. But the fully haired creature slowly walked away and disappeared.'

Travellers have written many times about the presence of Dhakans and Dhakinis in Manasarovar. Dhakinis are the sky-travellers of space. The word Dhakini means 'the rejoicing lady' or 'the lady with high intelligence'. The yoginis (female yogis) of Sidhashramam also come to Manasa Sarass. They are also known as Apsaras (fairies). The Tibetan lamas opine that the Dhakinis will appear en masse if we chant the 'beeja mantra' after uttering the prayer 'oh, the masters of Kagyutpa ancestry, the Dhakinis and the Dharmapalakars!' An Englishman who photographed the huge body of a snake shining in seven colours found the film empty when he later took the print after returning to London (the Puranas say that Thanthunagam is a water creature by the name Varunapasam. Its body is very strong). I still remember two tribal men telling me and the guide at the Saidhi camp about their experience when they went for fishing in the tunnels of Manasa Sarass which extended to the undersides of the Himalayan mountains. It happened in my Kailash-Manasarovar journey of 2001. The fact is that at that time, I felt it to be completely unbelievable. But what happened when Mr Harihar and I walked down the lake for bathing at a place believed to be used by Goddess Parvathy for taking a bath remains in my mind forever. While we waded down into the water inch by inch, our legs felt like they were touching a slippery surface and we rose up and down like on a diving board.[69] That incident became a turning point in my life. It could be said without any doubt that my entry into the world of literature became complete with that holy moment. It was an old man who saved me when I reached the Song Serbu camp at the end of the journey at 2 a.m., all tired and weak. As if picking up a flower, the aged man with lines all over his face took me up with iron-strong hands. The next day, I looked all around the area but there was no trace of him. I could see only a middle-aged couple. Our guide Puchong told me at the Darchan camp that nobody had seen such an old man there. Who was the old man then?[70] Being new and not knowing much about the Himalayas, I deliberately didn't mention such things in my first work to avoid a controversy. The five sanyasins I met in the mysterious icy land of Gatling glacier in Gangothri Dhamam sat in deep meditation and heard this story in detail. They blessed me then.[71]

It was after that that the secrets of the Himalayas slowly revealed themselves to me to an extent. It presented many moments of ecstasy to me. I could later reach various planes of meditation and experience Saddhana and Sidhi. All this was made easy after I got a holy guru from the Himalayas.

Swami Parama Hamsa Sree Nityanandaji, a great Indian yogi, later disclosed some experiences that happened to him while travelling in Tibet last year. 'That incident took place while I had been in Lhasa, Tibet. I had heard earlier that people lived to an extraordinary age in that area. That included people who were 300 or more years old! I wanted to see those people who were 300 or more years old! I wanted to see some such people and hear their news. A lama of Citadel Potala monastery sent me to another lama. He was doing some work in a nearby agricultural field. He was seemingly too old. I asked him: "I have heard that you are very old. I wish to know about your lifestyle." He was busy with his work at the time of my visit. He was pulling out weeds and organizing the crop field. He laughed loudly when he heard my question. Then he said, "I am not that old. Maybe you can tell that I am middle-aged. *I am only 136 years old.* There are many people around who are older than me. If you want to see old people, please go and see them. Not me.'

I later saw a medical report confirming his age as 136 years. I expressed my surprise over him toiling like this even at that age. His reply was that it was quite common for lamas like him living 300 or more years. 'That is our belief. And what is seen is also the same. It is an ordinary thing that people of 150 or 200 years old are physically working like this.' What surprised me about that was his expression. I asked again: 'How is this happening?' He replied: 'The date of birth and the date of death are written at the places where our ancestors are cremated. They all lived above 300 years. To die at the age of 200 years is untimely death.[72] Lamas insist that no wrong should be done to the normal character of our body and mind. Also, nature should be left free to go its own way. If you can do that, then you too can easily live to 300 or more.'

This is how the start of the entry to Shangri-La begins. The world is stranger than we see. Science cannot explain many mysteries taking place on earth. We still don't know how gigantic ships vanish in the middle of sailing in some mysterious parts of the seas.[73] Strange creatures from other planets and unidentified flying objects (UFO) get widespread media attention. Many people swear that such kind of weird incidents have happened numerous times in the mysterious land called Tibet. Maybe the world of science will ridicule it but Sidhashramam and Shangri-La will surely remain in the minds of people as an amazing event.

While talking about the Himalayas, I think it will not be proper to leave Yeti, the snow man unmentioned. In one word, it may be said that Yeti is a huge snow man. It is believed that it resides in the ice-covered caves of the peaks of the Himalayas that lie spread over Nepal, Tibet and Sikkim. The people of the area call the creature *Yeti* or *Meh-Teh*. Nepalese call it *Bun Manchi* (jungle man) or *Kanchenjunga Rachiaya* (the giant of Kanchenjunga).

Many believe that Yeti is only an imaginary story. It has been a controversy for long as to whether such a creature actually exists. Cryptozoology is a branch of zoology. It is a branch of study dealing with such creatures that have no clear proof of existence. Yeti is the most famous creature of this category. Cryptozoology considers Yeti as the Himalayan version of Sasquatch or Yahoo. Some put forward the argument that Yeti is the Abominable Snow Man under the bipedal monkey breed.

The 'colossal snow man' was unknown to the outside world for about two centuries. In 1921, an investigative team under the leadership of Lieutenant Colonel Charles Howard-Bury reached Mount Everest. The research was under the sponsorship of the Royal Geographical Society. This journey was beautifully depicted by Lieutenant Colonel Howard-Bury in his book *Mount Everest: The Reconnaissance, 1921*. In this book, a place called Lahkpa-La, situated 21,000 feet above sea level, has been mentioned. At that place, he saw some strange footprints. He thought that the footprints might have been of the Loping Grey Wolf, a type of wolf bigger in size. The footprints looked imprinted towards both sides like that of a man walking on snow dust without shoes. Immediately the Sherpas told Bury that they were of the snow man. They called the footprint 'Metoh Kang-mi'. *Metoh* meant 'man-bear' while *Kang-mi* meant 'snow man' in their language.

One of the photographers of the Royal Geographic Society, N.A. Tambazi, wrote that in 1925 he saw a strange creature at a place near the Zemu glacier. This place stood at more than 15,000 feet above sea level. He says he had met the creature so close at a distance of about 200 to 300 yards. It stood in front of him for around one minute. The shape was of a man, no doubt. It walked with a straight body. While walking it was pulling out the rhododendron plants and leaves on either side of the path. Tambazi says that the creature was naked. After about two hours, he and his team went downwards. They found similar footprints like that of the beast on the way. He describes this as follows: 'It was like the footprint of a man. But only that it was six or seven inches longer and four inches wider than a human foot. Surely the footprint belonged to some bipedal.'

Eric Shipton, who attempted to climb Mount Everest in 1951, took many photos of these footprints on solid ice. These pictures were later subjected to many experiments and discussions. When one side strongly argued that this was concrete evidence for the existence of Yeti, the other put forth a strange argument that this might be the footprint of a creature from outer space which was disfigured by melting ice.

Edmund Hillary and Tenzing Norgay had said that they found very big footprints on their climb of Mount Everest in 1953. In the first autobiography of Tenzing, it has been written that he thought Yeti as an enormous orangutan. Though he hadn't seen Yeti with his own eyes, his father had. That too, more than once. In his second autobiography, there is a long discussion on whether Yeti was real. Very big footprints supposedly of Yeti were photographed by John Angelo Jackson on his arduous trip in 1954 from the Everest side to Mount Kanchenjunga. But no experiment was done on these photographs.

In 1960, a research team under the leadership of Sir Edmund Hillary travelled through the Himalayan region. The objective of the team was to conduct further studies about Yeti and collect more evidence if such a creature was actually living. A skull said to be that of Yeti was collected from a Buddhist monastery at Kumjung and sent to America for experiments. The outcome of the first experiment was that the skull was of a *serow* (a massive bear) living in the Himalayan regions. But some scientists argued that this result was not correct. In the opinion of Prof. Frederic Wood Jones, the hairs found on the skull were not of the bear. Dr Myra Shackley says that 'the hairs on the skull were really like hairs of the monkeys. The remnants of worms found on them were very different from those found on the hairs of serow.'[74]

The British mountaineer Don Whillans claimed that while climbing Mount Annapurna in 1970, he had directly seen a creature believed to be Yeti. They had been searching for a suitable place to fix the tent for the night stay. Whillans heard some strange shouts and sounds. His guide Sherpa told him that that was the sound of Yeti. That night Whillans saw an enormous black figure walking round the tent. Next morning he found footprints like that of a man on the snow around. And in the evening, while looking around through binoculars, Whillans saw a gigantic bi-legged creature walking in the area in search of prey. He swears that it was in front of his eyes for about twenty minutes. After that the creature did not appear again. The opinion of Dr Ram Kumar Panday who has done wide research on Yeti and the language of mountain people, is this: 'We are not going to gain anything by merely questioning the stories about the mysterious creatures of the Himalayas. It means only that like other subjects this also should be made a subject of study for research.'[75]

The *Journal of the Asiatic Society of Bengal*, a collection of notes by B.H. Hodgson published in 1832, is the oldest record regarding Yeti. In north Nepal, while climbing a high peak, the Sherpas showed Hodgson's team a bi-legged creature which was very tall and fully covered with black hair. The creature ran away and disappeared when it saw the team. Though Hodgson didn't see it clearly, he said he did see such a figure.

The American television anchor Josh Gates and the team who reached Everest area in the starting days of December 2007 say that they saw the foot marks of an animal similar to that of Yeti.[76] Each foot was 33 cm long. More than that of the measuring ruler! The foot contained five toes and the immense length of it was clearly visible. Cross measurement showed

25 cm. He carefully scratched up the prints without any damage and carried them away to America for further studies.

While the searches, studies and debates about Yeti are still alive, the other side of it—the mysterious other side—has also been revealed. Were the foot marks said to be of Yeti actually Yeti's? Though the local people and the foreigners had no doubt about the shape of that creature, a doubt arose that the footprints might be of some other unknown animal.

Many people expressed their opinion that this might have formed when the non-human creatures and aliens from outer space or the yogis and great sanyasins of Sidhashramam and Shangri-La travelled through the mysterious parts of the Himalayas.

Such a theory had been proposed by a group of researchers while analysing the photos of the footprints taken by Eric Shipton who attempted to conquer Everest in 1951.[77] After checking all the available evidence, the cryptozoology experts also opined that the foot marks might be of those who reached divine heights. In 1984, David P. Shepherd, the famous mountaineer, was travelling by the side of the southern glacier of Everest. He was convinced that a big human figure was stalking him for many days. He took a photo of it also. But the photo was too faded for further study. Sir Edmund Hillary, the first man to step on Mount Everest, disclosed many things in an interview given to *Newsweek* in the final days of his life. To the question as to whether he had any mysterious experience in the wonderful world of the Himalayas during his endeavour, Hillary's reply was this: 'I had always accepted adventure as a challenge. But though I had many experiences in the Himalayas that amazed me, I didn't try to find an answer. I believe that all such things are beyond our intelligence.

'Once during the travel through a lonely snow mountain, I met a barely dressed sanyasin at such heights. Totally surprised,

I expressed my regards to him and asked what the holy soul's name was. I was taken aback by his reply that he had forgotten it 200 years earlier!'

II

The chapter on the Himalayas will not be complete without mentioning alchemy. This subject had been stated with much importance in our Vedas, Puranas and Ithihasas.

Rasa or mercury is a divine element. *Rasayana* or *Keemiyagiri* (alchemy) was one of the most important branches of study in the ancient sciences. It is a puzzling science. Not in India alone but it has acquired wide popularity in countries such as Tibet, China, Arabia and Greece. In all these places, massive attempts were also being done to learn this technology. In fact, it can be said that even Atomic Science had its origin in *Keemiyagiri*. Keemiyagiri is known by the name 'Rasayana Vidya' (the Rasayana technology). It is a process by which cheap metals like copper, lead and mercury are converted into high priced gold and silver. In the Indian medical system, there is even a special medicine called 'Rasayanam'. It is a curing medicine preventing old age or even death. It has also the capability to change old age into ripe youth.[78]

In English, alchemy is called the Golden Goddess. 'Keemiyagiri' is the Persian word for it. This science is very interesting and at the same time very deep and mysterious in nature. It is hard to digest the thought that the technology called alchemy is a sacred experience of God's grace. It is equally hard to gain knowledge of manufacturing gold. *Padharthavijnana* (*Padartha* = matter, *vijnana* = knowledge), 'Paradh' (mercury) Vijnana and 'Swarna' (gold) Vijnana are all used to denote this science.

The basic principles of Rasayanam are:

1. *Loha* (metal) *Sidhi* (knowledge): The process of converting cheap metals into gold.
2. *Deha* (body) *Sidhi*: Maintenance of a disease-free, healthy body.
3. *Jeevan* (Life) *Mukthi* (liberation) *Sidhi*: Attainment of immortality.

There are three factors in Jeevan Mukthi Sidhi.

    i. *Mana Sidhi*: The ability to grasp things in another's mind.
    ii. *Khechari Sidhi*: The ability to travel by air.
    iii. *Jeevan Mukthi*: This is attainment of immortality.

Scholars have the opinion that Deha Sidhi cannot be achieved just by practising yoga. But it is notable that there is no unity of opinion among the scholars on this subject. One set argues that complete results will be obtained only when totally purified mercury is consumed into the body as medicine. In Rig Veda, there is reference of this technique of gold manufacturing. In Sreesooktha, the rishi makes it clear that by way of some peculiar processes, mercury or copper can be converted into gold.

Only the ancient rishis had the ability to segregate these mantras from others and understand them. Only they could chant each one of the mantras by vividly understanding and going into its depths. After their time, it became impossible to continue this action. As time went by, the scholars and yogis came to the conclusion that 'Paradh Vijnana' had become obsolete. For getting the true knowledge of Paradh Vijnana, the first thing to understand is the Paradh or the refinement process. It has to be learnt completely. Many books have references of these extremely difficult activities.

To process and purify Paradh, various types of medicines and methods had been used. *Rasaswedhana varga, Rasamardhana varga, Rasamarana varga* and *Mayur Putcha* were the different types of *vargas* used. In addition to them, betelvine, ginger, garlic, jawaker, suhaga, etc., were also used. Venom of snakes and scorpion, thelium and datura were also used. 'Maha Rasas' and 'Upa Rasas' were used for this requirement (Rasa Sidhi).

Maha Rasas: Abhrak, rajavath, silajith, etc.

Upa Rasas: Harthar (opriment), fithkari (alum), manseel, gandhakam (sulphur), navasaaram, himgool, sindheer, samudra fen, the eight metals (gold, silver, copper, iron, vaeg, zinc, brass and bronze).

Oils used: oil extracted from navasaram, from mudrasaakha, from shokiya, from sulphur and from phitkari.

Diamonds and stones: Pushyaraagam (yellow sapphire), maanikkyam (ruby), indraneelam (blue sapphire), vyram (diamond), muthu (pearl), gomedhakam (topaz), pavizham (coral), marathakam (emerald) and vydooryam (turquoise). Rasa (mercury) can be solidified by these processes. The books tell that if a man can put in his mouth the tablet form of Rasa after 108 types of processing, he will get the ability to independently fly in the air.

By consuming completely purified Rasa, the beauty and attractiveness of the body will increase. Not only this, it will get a lively fragrance too. This fragrance is sweeter than that of *Ashtagandha* (combination of eight fumigating perfumes such as sandalwood, etc.).

Some mantras of Adharva Veda also narrate this idea in detail. It is said in them that if Rasa is brewed in acid or arsenic, it will become gold. Yet another thing is pointed out in Adharva Veda. If the medicine made by distilling Rasa in some special ways is applied on a patient or an old man, all diseases will get cured without any trace. Not only this, he will get good health and everlasting youthfulness. It is believed that the inventor of the Rasayana Vidya is none other than Lord Siva. In the Vedas, Siva is called Rudra. Many important points and instructions of Rudra on the subject are seen in the Vedas. The book *Rudreeyamal Tantram* is the collection of such Rudra maxims. As said in it, Rasa is a metal with life. If we closely mix and blend castor seed with Rasa and add little bit of gold, the Rasa will convert into gold! In ancient times, many experts who had acquired knowledge of Paradh Vijnana were said to have successfully produced gold by this process!

It is also in this period that a reference is made of the holy medical consultants of the gods, the Aswinikumaras. They too were experts in Rasayana technology. The Aswini gods are the writers of the matchless and precious book *Dhathuratnamala*. It is said that many methods for converting copper into gold are depicted in this work. Aswinikumaras were the first to point out the order of eight steps of processing Rasa. Aswinikumaras assured that the physical body expressions as well as styles can be totally changed by using Rasa which went through processes as second after first, third after second and so on. They had emphasized one more thing in the work. The Rasa processed in the eight ways in the right order, if mixed with melted copper, will instantly become gold!

A narration like this is found in the book *Rudreeyal Tantram* also. In the article, 'Dharmadasa Samhitha', the qualities of refined Rasa are given as follows: Rasa refined by the eight methods of processing is capable of curing any type of diseases and illnesses of a body. The quality of the Rasa processed in the eight ways increases still higher after it is subjected to the ninth process called 'Marana'. Then it becomes capable of providing the body everlasting youth and immortality. Rasa is solidified in the next step called 'Badha Samskaram'. If one consumes in tablet form the Rasa thus made solid, he will be able to fly freely in the air! Even gods worship such a man! The solid Rasa is said to be the semen of Rudra.[79]

Then from the six forehead eyes of a sexually elated Siva originated a *Thejus* (godly power) with the brilliance of a hundred million suns and equal to *Kalaagni* (the fire which consumes everything at the time of deluge. This fire is nothing but Lord Siva).

The God of Fire (Agni Deva) and God of Air (Vayu Deva) carried these six types of Thejus of Lord Siva having glittering radiance and warm coolness and deposited them carefully at the centre of the *Nanal Kaadu* (forest of darbha grass) surrounded by lotus flowers in River Ganga. Later, God Mahavishnu assigned six Kruthika goddesses (stars) with the duty of looking after these Thejus. The Thejus took birth as six beautiful babies. Since they were looked after by Kruthika goddesses, the babies' name came to be Karthikeyan and since they grew up in the Nanal Kaadu, the *poyka* (pond) became known as Saravana Poyka. When their mother Parvathy Devi embraced all the babies simultaneously, the six babies became as one. Also on the day of Karthika, the 'Kruthika ritual' was started to please Lord Muruga.

Rasa is not an ordinary metal. Yajur Veda says that 'when Paradh or mercury—the Vigour of Parama Siva—came out, the earth could not bear it. Since it was that strong and radiant, it hung at a particular level over the surface of earth.'

Sama Veda depicts various uses of Rasa Vidya. Maharshi Jamadagni, the contemporary of Maharshi Vasishta, had deep knowledge of Paradh Vijnana or Rasa Vidya. As a result, he was handsome and youthful always.

In another chapter of Sama Veda, the Paradh Vijnana is depicted as Kalpavruksha (or Kalpataru, a wish-fulfilling divine tree). This is because it has the ability to fulfil the wishes of anybody, be it of gods or of human beings. There are very detailed narrations of Rasayana Vidya in Adharva Veda. Maybe this was because when the period of Adharva Veda had come, our ancestral rishis could acquire more knowledge and experience in this science. In the meantime, they had learnt the two most important uses of Rasayana Vidya. The first one is the ability to walk on water and fly in the air. Second, by using this medicine, the Maharshis could change their frail bodies of old age into youthful and strong ones. In some contexts, Rasa is even mentioned as *Amruth*. The Adharva Veda also points out that only some very lucky persons have the capability to hold Paradh Jnana.

Kanadha Muni was an expert in Paradh Vijnana. The Rasa treatment was the secret of his long life and evergreen youth.

The works *Rasa Mahima* and *Rasa Ratnakaram* say that if one consumes Rasa that was refined through the Marana process, he could permanently change all the symptoms of old age. By changing old age, bodily ailments and diseases, a new life can be given to the bones and body minerals in a very short span of time. Using this Rasa, even the ability to fly in the air can be acquired. In the book *Rasaraja Samuchayam*, it is said that Rasa has the capacity to cure even leprosy. It is a completely pure and divine metal. It has the capacity to give colours to life.

According to Indian scientific thought (Paradh Vijnana), Rasa is available in five forms. Each one has its own name.

1. Rasa 2. Rasendra 3. Sooth 4. Paradh and 5. Misrak.

1. Rasa: It is red in colour. It is pure, devoid of all types of dirt. Gods attained immortality and never-ending youthfulness by consuming this medicine.
2. Rasendra: Its colour is black or yellow. It is naturally flawless. By consuming this medicine, a person can avoid old age and even death. But it is very, very rarely available.
3. Sooth: Yellow colour. Contains some dirt. It can be completely purified by subjecting it to the eighteen

types of refining processes. The body can be made
strong and healthy like iron by consuming this
medicine.

4. Paradh: Silver in colour. This liquid form Rasa kills all
types of harm.

5. Misrak: Slightly bluish in colour like that seen on
peacock feathers. By completely purifying it, one can
get hold of many superhuman skills.

Many studies and experiments were done on Rasa in the
ancient times. It has been recorded that many munis acquired
rare skills after gaining deep knowledge of Rasa Vidya.
Vashishta Maharshi called Rasa science 'Kamadhenu Vidya'.
Brugu Maharshi in his book *Brugu Samhitha* also recorded its
results after studying the subject in depth. Another maharshi
who gained expertise in Paradh Vidya was Naradha. It can be
seen in the Puranas that Jamadagni Maharshi handed over all
his knowledge about Rasa Vidya to his son Parasurama. And the
latter got more knowledge on this subject by his own efforts.
The mercy of Maha Rudra (Parama Siva) also helped him in
gaining much more knowledge of Rasayana Vidya. The book
Swarnatantram is the compilation of the debate between Maha
Deva and Parasurama on the science of Rasayana.

There is a reference of Kakabhusandi Maharshi in
Yogavasishtam. The two books written by him are *Kalpatantra*
and *Kakachadheeswari*. The Rasayana Vidya or Paradh Jnana is
described in both works in detail.

Kapila Sidhantham is the book written by Kapila Muni. He
invented many new theories in the realm of Paradh Vijnana.
He had narrated in detail the method of segregating gold from
copper. The muni had specially described twenty-two different
methods of transforming copper into gold. All these books

were in oblivion until recently. The yogis of Sidhashramam discovered them only some years ago and published them in incomplete form.

A truth accepted by the world of science is given below. If energy is separately passed into the inside of an atom or if by some way one can change the numbers of protons and electrons in it, that atom can be transformed into another thing. Thus, a cheap metal can be transformed into a precious metal. For example, there are eighty protons in the atom of Rasa and seventy-nine in that of gold. So, if we remove one proton from the atom of Rasa, won't it change into the atom of gold? Likewise, there are eighty-two protons in the atom of lead. If we can remove three protons from it by whatever method, it will be changed into an atom with seventy-nine protons like gold.

One thing has to be particularly taken care of. Rasa has eighty protons. In the electronic configuration, it stands next to gold which has seventy-nine protons. Likewise, lead's atom has eighty-two protons. Hence, both the metals can be easily transformed into gold. Cyclotron is an instrument used to separate atoms. It creates vibrations inside the atoms. When the speed rises, the changes inside the atom will also be higher.

In some Ayurveda books, descriptions of the process of changing a metal into another one are given. Two such important works are *Charakasamhitha* and *Sarangadharam*. The Greek philosophers Aristotle and Socrates had mentioned in their works about the Rasa science, alchemy and also about the process of changing one metal into another.

Emphasis was especially given in the olden times to two processes called *Loha Sidhi* and *Dheha Sidhi*. Dheha Sidhi means maintaining physical health, i.e. maintaining the body in everlasting youthfulness by the use of specially made medicines. Loha Sidhi is the name for alchemy. This is the process of producing quality gold from cheap metals like lead, copper, mercury, etc.

The Rasayana Vidya experts argue that both are possible. They had made many attempts in this sector. Their firm belief is that like changing copper into gold, we can change old age into youth.

One can learn this technology only under the guidance of a teacher who is well versed in Rasayana science. Paradh Vijnana or gold science is the rarest and most genuine of all physical sciences existent in the world now. In fact, the essence of this science is capable of making a whole life shine like a sunset. This is also its beauty. The most famous acharya (master) and philosopher of India, Jagadguru Sankaracharya, said: 'Had I got a disciple with full concentration and dedication, I would have eradicated poverty completely from the world by utilizing the Paradh Vijnana through him!'

Patanjali Maharshi is the writer of the book *Loha Sasthram*. We can see that many new ideas regarding Paradh Vijnana had been incorporated by him in that book. It was Patanjali Maharshi who invented for the first time the technique of solidifying liquid Rasa. He could also fly in the air with the help of Paradh. His work *Loha Sasthram* is not available now. Hence, it is not possible to explain the work more.

Athri Maharshi was a 'scholar in Rasayana Vidya' (alchemist) with deep knowledge of it. He had conducted many experiments to get rid of the many weaknesses and tensions affecting a human body. *Athri Samhitha* is the collection of his studies. *Dethratheya Samhitha* is the book written by Dethratheyan, the son of Athri. He had very deep knowledge of Paradh Vidya. It is said that this work had been lying hidden somewhere and Swami Nikhileswaranandaji of Sidhashramam recovered it using his yoga power.

Concerning South India, the first great rishi to acquire all the powers of yoga was Agasthian. Many matters regarding Paradh had been elaborately written about in his work *Agasthia Samhitha*. It was Agasthia Muni who for the first time proved that if the brown colour powder called *Sidhasoothram* was sprinkled over heated copper, the copper would become pure gold if heated again. Ravana, a descendent in the Agasthia tradition, got possession of this technique and changed his palace Lanka into a golden city. With the untimely death of Ravana, this rare knowledge was lost forever.[80] Ravana had written an article under the title 'Lankesha Sidhantham'. This essay is matchless and the number one regarding Rasayana Science. The guru of the Assuras, Sukracharya, fully learnt the Rasayana Vidya through Paradh Vijnana. He brought into usage the Sanjeevani Vidya with the backing of Rasayana Vidya. The book he compiled was titled *Rasavalokam*.

The Rasayana Vidya was prevailing actively during the Mahabharata period also. Bhagavan Sreekrishna also knew this Vidya. He constructed Dwarakapuri with the help of Paradh Vijnana. Karna also possessed many special powers and skills through Paradh Vijnana. In addition to Paradh Vijnana, he made use of the sun's rays also. It was due to this that Karna became so powerful.

In the days to come, many kings also learnt this knowledge from great yogis and made use of it for the betterment of their countries. Vyadhi was a scholar who lived during the time of Vikramaditya. He acquired exclusive knowledge of Rasayana Science. He has elaborated various methods by which copper could be changed into gold.

Parama Hamsa Sree Rasendranandaji was a great scholar of the Vedas. He had great knowledge of Rasayana Science also. He had elaborately studied about the 108 processing techniques of rasayana. Sree Rasendranandaji was the person who the sanyasins and Sidhas of the Himalayas would worship. He was centuries old! There are many books and pamphlets regarding the Rasayana Science. *Rasarnavam, Rasachandra Chinthamani, Rasa Manjari, Yoga Tharangini, Rasaraja Lakshmi, Rasa Saaram, Rasa Chinthamani, Rasa Avatharam, Gandhaka Kalpam, Loha Dheha Sidhi, Rasaratna Deepika, Rasa Mangal, Rasasaketh Kalika, Rasa Kamadhenu, Rasa Parijatham, Rasaraja Sankar, Rasa Sindhu, Rasaprakasha Sudhakaram, Dharaneedasa Samhitha,* etc., all deal with this subject. Each one of these books is excellent in its own way. Also, they serve good knowledge about Indian mercury science. Each book has a price equal to the gold it weighs. But none of these books are available now. Swami Rasendranandaji had acquired many special sidhis. Flying in the air, Paradh Geethika (pills), Paradh Lupthakriya (ability to make himself disappear), Dheha Lupthakriya, Adrusya Sidhi, Aavahana Sidhi (to attract and lead souls in), etc., are the sidhis Swami possessed.

The guru of Jagadguru Adi Sankara, Sreemat Govinda Bhagavat Padhar, was a well-known alchemist of the period. He had written two books based on *parad* (mercury) technology titled *Rasa Hrudaya Tantra* and *Rasa Saaram.*

The articles and essays written by Tibetan Sidhas and lamas are a valuable asset to this branch of science. It is learnt that many such books are still kept safely in lama monasteries.

It was in 218 CE that Nagarjuna founded an ashram in Sree Sailam. He was a scholar with deep knowledge of Rasayana Vidya. His declaration that 'I have the ability to eradicate total poverty of the world through Sidha Rasa' is noteworthy even today. One of the disciples asked Nagarjuna, who was on his deathbed, about the technique of making gold. He said that 'acid in blue colour, sulphur, mercury and a fourth thing . . .' Before the name of that fourth substance came out of his lips, Nagarjuna became unconscious! When it became clear that the secret of making gold would not come out of his mouth any more, as the story goes, the then ruling king killed him by administering poison.

There was a famous sanyasin called Swami Shyama Giri in 1933. He was an Ayurveda scholar. Using Rasayana Vidya, he made 10 kilograms of gold at Lahore for Rajabahadur Ramsaran Das. Thus, he proved the practical application of that science. The then British Governor published this matter in the State Gazette of 26 May 1940. Krishnapal Sharma, a man with deep knowledge of Paradh Vijnana, also made gold from Rasa in Birla Bhavan, Delhi. At that time, Yugal Kishore Birla, Yogi Hari Swami, Ganesh Datt and the secretary of Birla Mills, Sitaram Khemka were present. Another scholar of Rasayana Science, Govardhana Das was also in Delhi at that time. In front of thousands of people, he publicly made gold from Rasa. The British gentleman Yufred and some other VIPs were eyewitnesses to this.

Krishnapal Sharma of Punjab once again produced 200 ounces of gold from Rasa. This gold was sold for 75,000 rupees. That amount was completely spent for charitable purposes. The news was published in *Saptahak Hindustan* in the issue of 6 November 1943.

The following news was published in *The Hindu* daily on 3 September 1945: 'Recently a North Indian yogi reached Bheemavaram on his mission of travel across the country. He made pure bullion from a piece of copper and presented it to a local Ayurveda master.'

Another important event took place in 1942. A Naga sanyasin, fully naked, used to lie beside the pathway near Viswanatha temple, Kashi. Most times he loudly chanted, 'Baba . . . Oh Baba.' One day, someone lifted the sanyasin up and put him on the banks of River Ganga. But the next day, they found the Baba lying in the same old place. After some days, preparations for Sivarathri started. Thousands of people thronged Viswanatha temple. To provoke the sanyasin, someone asked him what he was going to give Kashi Viswanathan on Sivarathri. At that time, some members of the royal family of Kashi were also present. They too had heard much about the sanyasin. People continued teasing him. The sanyasin looked at them sternly. Then, taking a tin box from the torn bag he carried, the sanyasin walked silently towards the iron gates of the temple. He started to rub the gates with a brown colour dust kept in the tin box. To the shock of everyone, the big gates became gold. The British Governor Algrin was also there. The report of this rare incident was published in the State Gazette of the time. A narration of this can also be found in the official records of the Kashi palace. Newspapers published the photo of this Naga sanyasin the next day. But before that, the Baba had disappeared. There was no result for the widespread search for him. It is said that the British pulled out the gates and sent them to London by ship.

A couple of months before the amazing incident, Pandit Madan Mohan Malaviya had been collecting funds for establishing the Banaras Hindu University. Harikrishna Vasishta from Himachal Pradesh came to meet him at that time. He was a well-known Ayurveda doctor. After purifying copper and Rasa, he changed both into gold through some wonderful processes and presented them to Malaviya. Malaviya thus got 100 *tolas* (1 tola = 11.66 gram) of gold. He used this for the construction of the Banaras Hindu University. Here are Malaviya's own words: 'Paradh Vijnana exists even now. Harikrishna Vasishta conducted that refinement process in front of my eyes.'

In full confidence, Sankaracharya says:

'Ye Grahi Paradhesshyan Syath Sahasram Sidhi Thath Grahi Kim Japaha Mantra Sidhim Kim Yethra Dhevaan Prathishtajaye'

(In whose home is worshipped the deity made of perfectly
purified Paradh matter, he will get thousands of powers.
There is no need for chanting mantras or other practices for
such a man. Also, he needn't seek other ways of success.)

Rasayana science is a mysterious science. It is believed that
many ancient books related to it are kept very safely in foreign
countries. Gold excavated from riverbanks and mines are in
powder form. Such gold has limitations. The kingdoms that
prevailed in India before and after Christ possessed endless
wealth. This was the state in the Veda-Purana-Ithihasa periods
also. In India, where hundreds of absolute monarchies existed,
what was the source of income of the kings? Only some taxes
collected from people and the income from other duties
imposed. That was a period of continuous wars and for that,
huge money was required for maintaining a strong military
and other administrative expenses. The kings constructed
dream-like palaces and huge bungalows in excess of their
needs. Thrones, chariots, windows and pillars made of solid
gold were common in palaces. They showed reckless spending
also in the matter of constructing huge temple complexes and
extravagantly decorating them with things as above. From
where did they get that much money? Then, now and always,
gold is the most valuable metal. Tonnes of gold had been
manufactured here through the Paradh Vidya. It had been
written in the travelogue of Megasthenes that the prosperity
India achieved was stunning. In 1789, Robert Clive said that
the cities on the banks of River Ganga were more powerful
and richer than London. Thus, he was honestly confessing
that what they stole from India was just a bit. Among the
neighbouring countries of India, the one that acquired most
prosperity through Paradh Vidya was Tibet. Using their close
relationship with India, the Tibetan lamas learnt the Vidya

from here. From the twelfth century onwards, the kingdoms of Tibet possessed immeasurable wealth and prosperity. It is said that there was yet another secret purpose behind the Chinese attack after 1950. Chinese authorities knew that a book written in the Tibetan language about Paradh Vijnana was secretly kept in a big monastery in the suburbs of Lhasa. Tibet didn't bow to the various political pressures China imposed on it. China got hold of the Lhasa Monastery by killing more than 2000 Buddhist monks but one lama named Yamting escaped with the book to the forest through a tunnel. Though the Chinese army tried all ways to catch this lama, he escaped to India through the Rohtang Pass in Himachal Pradesh. The lama reached the ashram of a sanyasin residing down the Rohtang Pass. He was only a skeleton because of a lack of food during the run, extending for more than two months, and that too with a wounded body. The attempts of the sanyasin didn't save the lama. After the death of the lama, the sanyasin got the rare book from the baggage of the lama. Since he didn't know the Tibetan language, the sanyasin made an inquiry coming down to Manali. The sanyasin caught the attention of an English archaeologist and after learning the value of the book, the archaeologist bought it from the sanyasin at a small price. It is said that soon, an industrialist from America bought the book at an extremely high price. The incident of an American called Brooch becoming a billionaire in a very short span of time is also known. He owned three banks and two private jet planes.

Paradh Vjanana is not a small subject to be ignored. It is reliably learnt that vigorous attempts to restart this extremely mysterious purification process are seriously going on at many parts of the Himalayas.

12

A Night with Kakki

Climbing up the staircase along with Basanthi, I reached Kakki's private room on the first floor. The floor was amply convenient with a small drawing room, worship room and bedroom. The kitchen and such were downstairs. If she was staying there for the winter season, the kitchen would be shifted upstairs. Furniture like a cot, table, chairs, etc., were sufficiently available in the drawing room and bedroom. For curtains, the cloth used was good-quality wool. Gasoline and oil lamps lit up the rooms.

I entered Kakki's room, which was filled with the fragrance of ashtagandha,[1] and bowed to her. Kakki was sitting on the cot covering herself with a thick woollen sheet up to her head. She asked me with love to sit on a wooden chair nearby, showing motherly love and blessing me with an 'Ayushman Bhava' (may God bless you with a long life). She asked Basanthi to bring soup. It had been cooked in pure ghee with vegetables and baby corn balls. The soup smelled delicious and tasted very good. Since Kakki was a perfect yogini, I decided to start the conversation with Kriya Yoga. It was as if she had read my mind. Astonishingly, she said that Kriya Yoga could be discussed later and first she wanted me to give a short description of my travels through the Himalayas.

I narrated to her in a nutshell my Kailash-Manasarovar journey, the many trips I had made to the Chathur Dhams, the divine sanyasins I had met outside the Khatling glacier in Gangotri Dham, the lake in Joretheng, the deep forests of the eastern Himalayas where the debate between Yaksha and Yudhishtira had taken place and the details of a gigantic lama I met at 2 a.m. near a mysterious monastery at that place. I also made it clear that I never had used animals like horses, mules or yaks for my travels in the Himalayas and had done all the trips on foot. Kakki told me that the aura around my body had amazed her and that was why she had called me for the meeting. I listened carefully in silence when Kakki said that the holy experiences of the Kailash journey and the meeting of the divine sanyasins were crucial turning points in my life. She convinced me that the big lama I met was one who had reached the highest point of sidhi (holy power) and while emitting the excess energy amassed from meditational power, it was quite common for blood to come out from the nose and the teeth. It was dangerous to meet a lama of that stage face-to-face and the reason I could escape without any accident was because iron was cut by iron.

Before going for dinner, Kakki gave me a description of the extremely secret steps of Kriya Yoga Sidhantha. Sending Basanthi out, Kakki herself performed many yoga routines for me.[2] When I revealed my wish to see the eyes glowing like flaming charcoal and aura that brightly lit all around the body at the peak of the yoga performance, she was ready to do that. I had with my own eyes seen the sanyasins of Gangotri Dham sitting fully sunk in a yoga meditation like that. Calling Basanthi in, Kakki gave her instructions to draw the window curtains closed, switch off all lights and take away the lamp. She also asked me to shift my chair to a distance of about 15 feet away.

The room became pitch dark. I was unable to see the figure of Kakki at all. Guessing where she had been, I sat in careful attention without closing my eyes. Within about half an hour, the outline of Kakki began to shine like a small fire. Gradually, it went up in brilliance. A clear covering of fire formed around her naked body. Flames flew from her eyes. Immediately afterwards, the eyes shone like burning charcoal. It looked as if her grey hair was standing up. I will never forget the sight in my whole life. A rare vision of a motionless body dissolved in yoga nidra!

The energy flow in the body increases by practising yoga and this raises the speed of Aadhar Chakras. The energy of the six Aadhar Chakras, namely Mooladharam, Swathishtanam, Manipurakam, Anahatham, Vishudhi and Anjna, concentrates on the main vein of backbone, *sushumna*. When many Aadhar chakras come together like this, it becomes a powerhouse of energy and electricity. When life transforms kinetic energy into vital energy, the inner fire spreads out as aura.

Kakki's husband, Babulal Kutiyal and his ancestors, had attained *sidhi* (divine power) through Kriya Yoga which they had practised in its complete form. The husband taught Kakki yoga after their marriage and gradually she turned into a perfect yogini. Kakki and her husband also had the rare and lucky chance of meeting the immortal lord of yoga, Om Satguru Babaji Nagaraj, who had overcome death and made Kriya Yoga world-famous as we knew it now. They had the opportunity to meet in person the famous disciples of Babaji like Sri Sri Lahri Mahasaya, Sri Sri Yuktheswar Giri and Swami Paramahamsa Yogananda. Kakki had met Swami Paramahamsa Yogananda a number of times. The Swamiji was only twenty years older than Kakki. Remembering the divine death of the Swamiji, Kakki's eyes filled with tears. She was unaware that Swami was in America. While doing meditation on 7 March 1952,

Kakki knew by her divine sight that her guru had passed away! In those days, there had been no telecommunication facilities as we have now, so the confirmation of the death was received only two months later.

The physical body of the yogacharya was temporarily kept at Forest Lawn Memorial Park. That day, Harry T. Rov, the director of the mortuary, which was in Los Angeles, wrote a letter on behalf of the Self Realization Fellowship under his own signature.[3]

About fifty years earlier, Kakki happened to hear about the holy powers of a handsome young sanyasin from South India. She had been doing meditation at the Mana Village of Badridham then. The holy sanyasin was engaged in a forty-one-day stiff meditation at the ice-covered land behind the Neelakanda Mountain in Badripuri. On the last day of meditation and after sunrise, he flew like a bird to land at the tip of Neelakanda Mountain. A German resident of a nearby ashram had shot that scene beautifully with a box camera. The young sanyasin's name was Sri Satya Sai Baba from Puttaparthy.

Bhagavan Sreekrishna in the Bhagavat Gita and Pathanjali Maharshi in *Yoga Suthra* had described in detail the transcendent technique called Kriya Yoga.[4]

In her ninety-five years of life, Kakki had seen and experienced many things. She had thorough knowledge of Kriya Yoga but never had misused it even once. By the use of sidhi, the Sidha school of thought never exploited people for making money. If they had chosen that way, the family of Babulal Kutiyal would have become multi-millionaires. Their grandchildren were in America. All were given good education. Even today, the main source of income was agricultural. All possible help was given even now to the village and other people. Kakki's firm opinion was that earning income and amassing wealth by way of sanyasam was not only injustice but also a dire sin. When wealth came through one hand, true sanyasins gave that to pure, deserving people with the other. The greatest yogis—Lahri Mahasaya, Yuktheswara and Swami Paramahamsa Yogananda—didn't amass wealth. It was Swamiji's fans who collected money for establishing the Yogoda Satsanga Society of India. It was also those followers who met all the expenses of Swamiji's American trips and made all the arrangements for propagating the Kriya Yoga concept. Swamiji didn't receive even a single dollar.[5]

The dinner, comprising milk added to rice soup, subji (vegetable salad) and the pre-ripe corn dish, was very delicious. The inner fire aroused by the rigorous yoga had not still subsided and so Kakki informed us that she was not taking dinner. I felt sad. I shouldn't have made such an old lady do a hard yoga performance just to satiate my curiosity. I was ready to confess and beg her forgiveness. But she soothed me, saying that achieving something was God's wish and performance for the sake of someone who was also on the path of achievement had been only the responsibility of a yogi. She then told me that like Pancha Kedar (five temples of God Siva), there were also Pancha Kailash in the Himalayas and suggested that I visit them. The Pancha Kailash was in the order of Adi Kailash, Kinnar Kailash, Kailash-Manasa Sarass, Mani Mahesh Kailash and Srikanta Mahadev Kailash (I later had the good fortune to visit the five Kailashas).

I became very happy when Kakki told me that we could sit talking until midnight and after that, she would show me the handwriting of Maharshi Veda Vyasa. Cold was rising every moment because of heavy snowfall. Though the heat from the lamp gave a little relief, the climate remained freezing. The hot black tea with cardamom and dried ginger prepared by Basanthi did me much good. The backdrop of Vyasa Muni's Skanda Purana was the region that included

Adi Kailash and Kailash-Manasarovar. *Kumarasambhavam*, written by the great poet Kalidasa, was based on the Skanda Purana and depicted each and every beautiful pulse of that wonderful land. Kakki told me that though we would get endless mental happiness by reading Kalidasa's works, what amazed her as an epic work was *Shishupalavadham* written by the great poet Maghan. I agreed with her saying that many people had the same opinion.[6] When she said that the writings of Maghan were better for her, I frankly replied that I didn't think so.

With all due respect to the work of Maghan, I told Kakki that the works of Kalidasa carried the most beautiful words and meanings. The style of his writing was original and unbeatable. This epic poet's works were classic and would exist forever, surpassing all barriers of time. They were immortal like the Nagadhirajan Himalayas. What other works had such beauty of words, structures and meanings besides Kalidasa's works? Those works with deep and minute meanings, cheerful comparisons and the most appropriate metaphors also had a vocabulary that was honey to the ears. There were many scripts we could see in Sanskrit by the great ancient poets in praise of Kalidasa such as '*Upama Kalidasasya Nolkrishtethi Matham Mama, Arthantharasya Vinyase Kalidaso Vishishythe*', '*Nirgathasu Na Va Kasya Kalidasasya Sookthishu, Preethirmadhurasardrasu Manjareesiva Jayathe*' (Banan-Harshacharitham), '*Kavikula Guru ha Kalidaso Vilasa ha*' (Jayadevan), '*Ekofpi Jeeyathe Hantha Kalidaso Na Kenachil, Srungare Lalitholgare Kalidasathrayee Kimuha*', '*Kalidasagiram Saram Kalidasaha Saraswathee, Chathurmughofdhava Sakshadh Vidhurnnanye Thu Mathrushaha*' (Malleenathan), '*Kavayaha Kalidasaadhyaha Kavayo Vayamapyamee, Parvathe Paramanou Cha Padharthathwam Prathishtithamha*', '*Vytharbheereethi Sannarbhe Kalidaso Vishishyatheha*', '*Sree Kalidasasya Vacho Vicharya, Naivanya Kavye Ramathe Mathirme, Kim Parijatham Parihruthya Hantha Brungaliranandathi Sindhuvare*', '*Rasabhaarabharolbhinnam*

*Bharatheemamaradruthe, Sreemathaha Kalidasasya Vinjathum Kaha Kshama
ha Puman'*, etc.

When Maghan left the stage after writing the perfect classic
poem *Shishupalavadham*, Kalidasa entered the minds of people to
stay there permanently with his immortal and timeless works,
namely *Vikramorvasheeyam*, *Malavikagnimithram*, *Abhinjanasakunthalam*,
Rithusamharam,   *Meghasandhesham*,   *Kumarasambhavam*   and
Raghuvamsham. The dramas of Kalidasa are ideal examples
of perfect writing. The great German poet Goethe said of
Abhinjanasakunthalam that 'it was the link connecting heaven
with the earth'. Kalidasa, the evergreen wonder of the world
of literature, had greatly influenced the famed English writer,
T.S. Eliot. After reading *Abhinjanasakunthalam*, he wondered
whether 'heaven came down to earth'. Almost all known
poets of India that hitherto lived had been greatly inspired by
Kalidasa. The singing bird of Kerala, the poet Changampuzha,
bows his head before Kalidasa like this:

> 'Vismayamakave Viswamahakave
> Vikhyathikondu Jayakkodi Naatti nee
> Aagamikkunnu, ha, Nin Kalkkalippozhum
> Lokaprathibhathan Kooppukaimottukal.'

(Oh, poet of the world, you are a wonder
You hoisted the flag of success by fame
Always come to your feet
The flower buds of folded hands of all genius)

Some scholars assessed that the three elements, namely
the incomparable usage of similes by Kalidasa, the thematic
greatness of Bharavi and the cheery simplicity of word usage
by Harshan, all melted together in Maghan's works. All
requirements for an epic could be found in his work also.

Maghan started his poem with the auspicious word 'sree', which was also added to the end of each chapter and to the last sentence. But the genius of Maghan became immortal in his verses written with one word or two words. It was quite amazing that the writing styles called *Chakrabandham* and *Ardhabramakam* had been used in the 'Chithra' chapter of this poem. Likewise, many exercises such as *Padmabandham, Nagabandham, Radhabandham*, etc., were also used in the poetry. Much more astonishing was the usage of the two words, *Bha* and *Ra*, with differences of sound. Two examples are given below:

'Bhooribhi Bharibhi Bheerai Bhubharai Abhirebhire
Bheri Rebhibhi Abhabhai Abhirubhi Ebhair Ebhbha.'

(Carrying the weight of heavy weapons, fearfully stepping on the earth with mammoth legs and making sounds like drumbeats, elephants looking like black clouds fought with other elephants.)

'Vibhavee Vabhavee Bhabho
Vibhabhavee Vivo Vibhee ha
Bhavabhibhavee Bhavavo
Bhavabhavo Bhuvo Viibhu ha'

(The God is the powerful, vigorous, bright, traveller-on-bird, fearless, saviour of the world from all miseries and protector of all living and non-living)

The writing technique that enables reading from left to right, right to left, up to down, down to up and from all the four sides is called *Sarvathobhadram*. See one example of this amazing writing skill below. Please read it carefully.

Sa	Ka	Ra	Na	Na	Ra	Ka	Sa
Ka	Ya	Sa	Dha	Dha	Sa	Ya	Ka
Ra	Sa	Ha	Va	Va	Ha	Sa	Ra
Na	Dha	Va	Dha	Dha	Va	Dha	Na
Na	Dha	Va	Dha	Dha	Va	Dha	Na
Ra	Sa	Ha	Va	Va	Ha	Sa	Ra
Ka	Ya	Sa	Dha	Dha	Sa	Ya	Ka
Sa	Ka	Ra	Na	Na	Ra	Ka	sa

'Sakarananarakasa, Kayasadhadhasayaka,
Rasahavavahasara-Nadhavadhadhavadhana' (Anushtup scale)

(Along with the sounds of vehicles of warriors jubilant in
the destruction of energetic enemies could also be heard the
beating of battle drum, etc.)

The *Murajabandha* scheme which is writing in 'V' formation
coming down and going up, in the shape of a drum, can also be
seen in this work.

'*Sa Sena Gamanarambhe*
Rasenafseedhanaratha
Tharanadhajana Matha-
Dheeranagamanamaya'
—Maghan (Chapter 19)

(Like vigorous and brave snakes, the army comprising
people shouting loudly in the start of the procession
became exciting which was *anaratha* [without a break]
and *anamaya* [joyous]. If this verse is written once again,
we can read it in the Murajabandha scheme).

The vocabulary of Maghan surprised the world of scholars. Like Kalidasa, Maghan also had gained deep knowledge of the Vedas, Upanishads and Ithihasas. Maghan was born in 750 CE at a place called Sreemal on the present-day Gujarat-Rajasthan border. Kalidasa's birth was in Ujjaini 2000 years ago.

After twelve, the climate became worse. The cold wind that blew from the icy mountains shocked Kuti Village. Like a silver carpet, the village lay completely covered with snow. The ice wind came roaring from far away with a horrible whistling sound and after crossing Kuti Village, entered the burj tree forests on the other side of the river. We could clearly hear the ghastly sound of the wind doing a dance of total destruction over there. We became fearful hearing the sounds of tree branches cracking and hills of ice breaking and falling.

The cold lessened a bit when the lamp was fired up some more. When the wind subsided after blowing fiercely for about half an hour, Kakki prepared to go downstairs, picking up the hurricane lamp. When she said that we could see the Vyasa writing before the next ice wind came, I followed her. My mind was trembling when I climbed, stooping, to the first floor of the two-storeyed granite building built in the style of a temple. It was also here that we had assembled at dusk that day. A middle-aged man, seemingly a relative of Kakki, accompanied us to help. Like Kakki, he also had a Mongoloid face. The room became bright when the gas light was lit up along with the oil lamp. The helper pushed aside the cot in the room and when he placed his hands on the lock of the cellar underneath, Kakki handed to him a key carefully selected from the bunch of keys tied up at her waist. With much difficulty, he pulled out a medium-sized wooden box after lifting up the wooden board of the cellar. Kakki touched the box with reverence and bowed. Then she carefully picked another key from the set and opened the box herself. She pulled out from the wooden box a smaller box about 1.5 feet in length and 2 inches in width. It was kept covered with yellow silk cloth and decorated with beautiful carvings. After placing it on the big box, Kakki opened it very carefully with another key.

There was pin-drop silence and the beating of my heart could be heard very clearly. I sat on the right side of Kakki and looked inside the box watchfully. A roll of the skin of burj tree on a faded yellow silk cloth, a document sized about 1 foot long and 2 inches thick, was resting in the box. A rare and invaluable treasure believed to be written by *Vyasa Muni* himself in his own writing . . .

It might be because of its age that the burj tree bark had faded in colour. There were lines and cracks on it. Kakki asked me to touch a smooth portion. Praying to the great muni in my mind, I opened a corner of the skin very carefully. Under the Sanskrit writing 'Om', it looked like the beginning of a verse in praise of God. The letters were very faded. Vyasa Muni's or not, my heart jumped in happiness touching the letters of the ancient, godly language . . . and when I prostrated before the document, the mind slipped into another world . . . The voice that arose from the subconscious was very clear: '*Thathwamasi Shwethaketho Ithi Bhooya Aeva.*' (You are that Shwethaketho, it is truly You).

Through the windows we saw the climate again becoming worse. After putting the box safely in the cellar, Kakki sat in meditation in front of the prayer seat. I also spent the time indulging in many thoughts.

We should leave it to the archaeology experts to prove whether that document was as ancient as the Vyasa period. But there were much evidence there to establish the fact that Vyasa Muni had gone that way to write the Puranas. The Vyasa monument near Nampha Village, the Adi Kailash Mountain, the Pandava Mountain, the Pandava monument, the Kunthi

River, the birthplace of Kunthidevi and the remnants of the Pandava fort lying around the path, all were pointing to a great historical fact. Before writing each Purana, Vyasa Muni might have engaged in deep meditation. All gains come through meditation. The reflections of the super happenings of the three worlds—Bhur, Bhuva and Swarga—are lying stamped in the *Mahar Loka* connected through *Vinjanamayakosha*. A yogi can see all these through the extrasensory powers.

'*Nivathadheepaval Chiththam*
Samadhirabhidheeyathae.'

(Samadhi is the state of stillness of the mind,
like the lamp in a windless place.)

It is in this state that the mind can be focused to any angle or side. Vyasa Muni wrote the Puranas and the Mahabharata thinking deeply about those images.

I had travelled so many times through the mysterious icy lands and also the plains of the Himalayan mountains. I had visited the ancient places of Ayodhya, Gaya and Nalanda and numerous monasteries of Sikkim, Bhutan and Tibet and many palaces of Kashi and Rajasthan. During my travels, I also had the good fortune of seeing many documents related to the Puranas and Ithihasas and reading many of them. There were many places among these which even the archaeologists could not go to. Many invaluable and priceless documents slumbered there in comfort. Even though not belonging to the ancient times, a historical document corresponding to the Mughal period of the mid-sixteenth century had amazed me.

There was a vast library at the headquarters of the Indian Council for Cultural Relations, Delhi (ICCR works under the external affairs ministry). Dr Madhup Mohta, IFS, who was the liaison officer of our Kailash-Manasa Sarass journey was appointed as the director of the ICCR after the Kailash trip. Dr Mohta played a vital role in the arrangement of many trips to and via many mysterious places in the Himalayas. He gave me the chance to do research studies in the library under ICCR with all freedom. Thus, I got the chance to see the historical marvels of the Mughal period. Prince Dara Shikoh, son of Emperor Shah Jahan, had gained deep knowledge about Indian Vedas, Upanishads, Puranas and Ithihasas. He studied Sanskrit under the great scholars invited and brought from Varanasi (Kashi) to Delhi. He translated the Vedas and selected fifty Upanishads to be translated into Persian. This was in 1657. After that, he translated the entire Bhagavat Gita into Persian. The pages of this book were made of animal skin. On the left side were the Sanskrit verses and on the right, their Persian translation. Many important verses of the Bhagavat Gita were engraved with thin threads of gold. Many a time, I touched that divine book that had been once handled by Dara Shikoh himself with his own hands and my heart jumped in ecstasy. This praiseworthy act of the prince was the reason for the holy books to become popular worldwide. It was after 150 years that those books were translated from Persian to Latin. That great work was done by a French priest called Anquetil-Duperron. Translations to other languages came later from Latin. In the collection of books, I also found the manuscript of the Arabic translation of the Bhagavat Gita and the Mahabharata by the Arabic scholar Wadi al-Bustani done upon the request of Maulana Abul Kalam Azad. The translation of those works, having 454 and 961 pages, respectively, was done in 1952. Thus, the persons behind the worldwide popularity of Indian Vedanta were a Muslim prince and a Christian priest. When you ponder over this, you would realize how meaningless are the ill deeds done these days in the name of religion.

Holy yogis with sidhi, sadhana and sakshalkara lived not only in the Himalayas but in the other lands of India also. They still do. Whereas the majority of them achieved the sidhis from the Himalayas, some of them achieved that feat residing in their own villages. The travelogue *A Search in Secret India* by Paul Brunton was the depiction of an alarming journey in search of such people. This English traveller met many yogis from Tamil Nadu, Maharashtra and Bengal during his journey. He himself witnessed unbelievable scenes such as taking the body to a dead state by freezing the heart, cooling the body by completely stopping the breath, stopping the clock, etc. Brunton had no belief in astrology but a yogi from Bengal truly amazed him. After hearing the date of birth and doing some rough work in a notebook, the yogi told Brunton the history of his life in brief. G.K. Pradhan from Maharashtra was a big businessman. He was a perfect yogi also. His guru, Gurudev Sankar Maharaj from the Himalayas, lived his last days in Maharashtra. The disciple had never been to the Himalayas before. Once, his guru took him there. Along with the guru, the astral body of the disciple reached the Himalayas. The journey that started from Rishikesh extended for days. Many days went by residing with the holy sanyasins in their caves and walking through the endless snowy lands. The disciple was astonished to see the tigers tamed by the sanyasins and the milch cows kept by them living together. G.K. Pradhan had beautifully narrated his experiences in the book *Towards the Silver Crests of the Himalayas*. The memorial of Gurudev Sankar Maharaj situated at the Pune-Satara Road in Maharashtra attracted many pilgrims.

Kapilasimhan, born of a royal family at a place called Sasaram in Bihar, was a wing commander in the Indian air force. He had been honoured with the Vir Chakra gallantry award for shooting down three Pakistani planes in the Indo-Pak war of 1971. After resigning from the force well before his actual retirement date, Kapilasimhan went to the holy sanyasins residing in caves between the Pindari glacier of the Himalayas. After ten years, Kapilasimhan returned as a yogi. He had no difficulty living under the ice for seven days, under water at freezing point for nine days and in a pit 10 feet deep for nine days in samadhi. On 16 October 1983, at Jabalpur city in Madhya Pradesh, Kapilasimhan exhibited samadhi in front of about 20,000 people. He had done this previously as well. Many VIPs like Lalit Srivastava, general secretary of the Madhya Pradesh Congress Committee and Baburao Paranjpe, MP, were present then. Doctors fitted the electrocardiogram (ECG) to the yogi's chest and connected its wires to a television set.

The yogi went down into a 10 foot-deep pit using an iron ladder and lay fully stretched out face upwards on a wooden board placed on the floor of the pit. The pit was then closed with concrete slabs and soil was filled all around. Then bricks were put over it and cemented tight like a fort. Meanwhile, the doctors were observing the ECG. The heartbeat was normal for three minutes. Gradually, it became slow and fully stopped at the twentieth minute. The doctors declared that the yogi was dead. On the ninth day, the pit was opened in the presence of a large number of people. The ladder was put into the pit and Kapilasimhan came up through that! Hours after coming out of the samadhi, Dr Kailash Narad, editor of the *Dharmayug* weekly, did an interview with Kapilasimhan. 'With willpower, I can enter samadhi any time as I wish. My body dies at that time. I come out of my body then. Science works as long as breathing happens. When breathing stops, science also stops working. But where science stops, yoga begins,' the yogi responded confidently. Twenty-two minutes after entering samadhi, his soul would be liberated from the body and the yogi made it clear that he would, then, travel in the universe (Brahmandam) freely. Kapilasimhan said that while he had been working in the force, a divine yogi had saved him a number of times from many dangers. Once, when he was in a test flight, his plane was lost and wrongly entered Pakistan air space limits. But a woman and a man who were flying in the sky at a height of 30,000 feet led him to India. Kapilasimhan confirms that the man was Gangavar Singh, a member of the Jodhpur Palace, who died in a plane accident during the Second World War, and the lady with him was his wife who killed herself by observing the ritual *sati* (sati was the ritual of the wife killing herself by jumping into the funeral pyre of the husband).[7]

In a meeting of the top brass of the Psychic Spiritual Research Institute, Delhi, where its director, Sree Nitya Chaitanya Yati, and the famous doctors of AIIMS were present, a blessed yogi named Sree Ramananda stunned everyone by stopping his heart for hours. The heart of the swami was still for about nine hours. The experiment totally bewildered the physiologists from AIIMS. All metabolic activity of the body was at a standstill then. What the doctors saw on the X-ray screen was that the heart compressed by the yogi was almost like a tube. During that period, instead of beating, the heart produced a murmuring sound.

By practising Pranayama as strictly as said in authoritative books on yoga, one could avoid all digestion (agni)-related diseases. When jataragni (digestive enzymes) increased, the consciousness of Kundalini was awakened.

With this, a purification that would lead to freedom from sins would be achieved. The phlegm in Brahma Nadi[8] would go away. This penetrated into the three glands and it was essential for yogis. The air that entered the human body during *purakam* (inhalation) multiplied five times due to body temperature. When breath was let out, only two-fifths of the inhaled air would go out. Thus, air became abundant in the body through

Pranayama. As air content increased, the body became light and life power got intensified. The yogis could move anywhere then with ease.

In the 1960s, the music band that roamed the western music world was the Beatles. When they were at the height of their fame, many members of that troupe took shelter in the Himalayas, to the surprise of all. They had felt the huge wealth they had earned to be of no worth. Later, another great musician who rocked the American music world also reached the Himalayas in search of mental peace. He too discarded the millions of dollars he earned. This American who changed his name to Krishnadas was now a disciple of Neem Karoli Baba of the Himalayas. Nobody knows the age of Baba. Four hundred years or 500 years? Since he was a musician, Krishnadas had given importance to vocal music. He indulged in his research in line with the Indian thoughts that 'all sounds merged with nadhabrahmam' and 'nature gave us everything'. By awakening the Kundalini power, he conducted many new studies on this subject. He had cured thousands and thousands of patients and mentally ill people by his *kirtans* (chanting the names of God). These were sung in his own style with a mesmerizing power of sound originating from the Mooladhara. The modern science also agrees that music therapy is very effective. Hearing Krishnadas's music through earphones rejuvenates our subtle body. It is said that he had been blessed many times with the auspicious sight (dharshan) of God Sreekrishna and God Sree Hanuman at the peak of meditation. It was at the Baba Vyas Ashram, Jodhpur, that I heard those facts and the music CD of Krishnadas.

I had met many people in Kerala who without sidhi or sadhana were on their way to divine embodiment through devotion and worship. They included the Sree Vidya-Sree Chakra worshippers also. My guru, Brahmasree K.N. Krishnan

Namboodirippad, was also a Sree Vidya devotee. At the height of worship, when the presence of the devi (goddess) was felt, he would attain the state rather similar to the samadhi of yogis. I had seen that myself. An important factor in this was the awakening of the Kundalini power. It was quite praiseworthy that none of them exhibited their skills for public shows and used them as a way to make money. Earning money in such ways was no doubt an offence against God.

A gem of a woman who also tried hard to arrive at God's feet through devotion resides in the heart of Thrissur city. The fact was that nobody knew her except close relatives. I went to see her when she intimated her wish to see me after reading my books. The relation thus started between the two of us two years ago and still continues.

Suvarna is her name. She was born as the third of four children to Thekke Kuruppath Madhavi Amma and Prof P. Sankaran Nambiar, the founder principal of Sree Kerala Varma College, Thrissur, who is also a noted poet. She spent her childhood at places where her father worked, such as S.B. College, Changanassery and Maharajas College, Ernakulam. When her father took charge as principal of Sree Kerala Varma College, she settled permanently in her home at Kuruppam Road, Thrissur. Though he was an English professor, Sankaran Nambiar liked Malayalam the most. Attoor Rama Pisharody, Kodungallur Kunezhathu Parameswara Menon, Vallathol, G. Sanakara Kurup, Mukunda Raja, K.P. Narayana Pisharody and other such blessed personalities were his close friends. Suvarna remembers that they had been frequent visitors to her house. She believes that the literary discussions between her father and his great friends had influenced her and the other children very much.

After she did her BA degree in music, her wish was to go for postgraduation. It was at that time she got a job in

All India Radio. However, fate had decided something else for her. Suvarna got married to Vasudeva Menon, the grandchild of the Kollengode king, Vasudeva Raja. She was already far ahead in the field of meditation and after the marriage, she continued it. Her husband had no disagreement. Suvarna's life changed suddenly after the birth of her daughter. That change brought her to Mysore. In August 1954, on Ashtamirohini day (birthday of God Sreekrishna), Suvarna accepted Mantra Deeksha (receiving mantra from a guru. It may be commonly said it is the beginning of spiritual life) from Swami Yatheeswaranda of Sree Ramakrishna Ashram. She told her husband that she was going to be an ascetic for the rest of her life and requested him to marry another girl. He didn't listen. Instead, he encouraged her in every possible way.

Swami Yatheeswaranda intimated Suvarna that he was nearing death and another guru for her would be coming soon. That was how Sri Mangalampalli Balamuralikrishna (M. Balamuralikrishna), the famous musician, came as her guru. The disciple was eight years older than the guru. Balamuralikrishna, who had studied only up to the fifth standard, had to drop out from school because of poverty. He also lost his voice at the age of seven. It is said that Sree Hanuman himself appeared and gave his voice back to him. He started worshipping Hanuman since childhood. Balamuralikrishna had learnt by heart even at a small age all the seventy-two Mela Kartha Ragas (Janaka Raga) which were the base of Carnatic music. All the Sapthaswaras (the seven musical notes) are in them. Balamuralikrishna was a devotee with incomparable skills. After giving Mantra Deeksha to Suvarna, he asked her to chant the mantra 1,00,000 times. When the apple presented by the guru and worshipped in the pooja room was cut, a golden locket was found inside it. On one side of the locket was the picture of Shirdi Sai Baba and on the other the holy picture of Sri Ramachandra. With great devotion, Suvarna placed the locket at a sacred place in the pooja room and engaged in meditation. When she opened her eyes, the locket had disappeared!

For the last fifty-five years, Suvarna had been continuing her voyage to God by pure meditation. She had the luck of experiencing many divine things and wonders through worship. The guru-disciple relation still continues. Seeing everything like a witness, she now lives peacefully in Nasik on the meditation path along with her daughter and grandchildren.[9]

I returned to my lodge after 2 a.m. Kakki's assistant also accompanied me. My mind was at peace. While crawling into my bed after prayer, my mind was full of the glowing figure of Kakki and the colour of fire.

13

To Jolingkong

Everyone was ready at 5 a.m. The team proceeded on the journey after finishing pooja and prayers. Though the weather was misty, the bright rays of the young sun filled the area with ample light. As usual, the travellers on horseback and their porters went first. Raju and I walked last.

It was 16 km from Kuti to Jolingkong. Adi Kailash was situated at Jolingkong. The guide warned us that this was the most difficult path for travellers on foot. Since it was the patrolling route of the army and ITBP, their help could be obtained if necessary. Also, extra care had to be taken to not deviate from the path because the Chinese border was very close. There were no other villages after Kuti. It was a season of continuous snowfall and so precaution and attention were critical for walking on icy paths. Following the instructions of the guide, we slowly climbed up the difficult, steep path.

The tough ascents and descents appeared turn by turn alongside the Kunthi River. The water level in the river was very high owing to the rain. The flow was also fierce due to the currents of melted ice. If the first 3 km were on an upward incline, the next 2 km were on level land. We quickly passed the area that had been infamous for landslides and falling rock. The world of flowers on the riverbanks and valleys was heartening. Different coloured blooming flowers dancing in the wind was an unforgettable sight. A wind was coming from the other side of the river where there was a burj forest. This forest, thick with burj trees, was a cheerful sight.

After climbing up an extremely difficult and sharply steep path of about 1000 feet, we became very tired. Looking from the top, we saw the endless ranges of mountains below and the path like a cotton thread rolling around it and climbing upwards. It made us tremble with fear. Though the time was just past 10 a.m., the thought that roughly 11 km were still to go dismayed us. From the top, we went steeply downwards and reached the vast Mungdam plateau. The right side of that was a thick forest of different kinds of medium-sized trees. To the left was the wide riverside. A porter was waiting there with breakfast for me. The food parcel had been prepared in the Kuti camp. The porter intimated me that there was no more chance to get food in the coming journey and so the lunch was also there in the parcel.

The system was that the porters had to prepare food on their own and keep it with them while travelling. After putting my parcel into the bag for lunch, Raju and I shared his breakfast. Since it was aloo roti and cooked uncleanly too, I couldn't eat it. I had many times noticed how the horse attendants and porters were cooking. Some would be cooking while some others would be engaged in defecation nearby. Once, I saw a man peeling a potato while defecating. Since I was very hungry and there was no other chance of getting lunch, somehow I swallowed half of Raju's food. I felt sad seeing many people of our team carelessly throwing plastic waste into the riverbank and forest. There were instructions at the very start of the journey that used plastic things should be kept first in their bags and then deposited in specially marked bins for plastic waste at the camp. The act of throwing plastic waste into the holy and pure Himalayas is on the rise. Since the bottles, cups and juice covers made of plastic would not dissolve in the soil, they would cause heavy ecological damage. That would gradually threaten the existence of trees and the flow of water in rivers. I felt very happy seeing the prohibition of plastic being done very effectively in the Himalayan regions coming under Himachal Pradesh state. Raju and I picked up all the plastic we saw and kept it on one side. We decided to tell the horse attendants to take them away upon our return.

Climate that was pleasant began to change suddenly. The sky became dark when the sun hid behind the clouds. The speed of the wind and the chill increased. It was felt as if the road was going upwards, rolling around the mountains, and the long journey thereafter through level land would never end. Though the upward incline was full of ice, the plains were only partly icy. I literally fell into an ocean of happiness when I reached the Phoolkiwar meadow that extended far beyond our vision. The meadow was full of flowers in different colours. This carpet of flowers extended to the valleys all around. While the snow-covered mountains shone even in dim light in the background, the plants below them created another exquisite world of colours like a rainbow. The herds of sheep grazing on the meadow looked like another colour world. I bowed my head before Mother Nature for such a delightful colour combination.

We decided to have lunch when our hunger became unbearable. I went to a small hut near a rock. A boy was lying there with his eyes closed, on a torn carpet spread on the floor of the hut. Something was boiling in an aluminium vessel on a smoking stove. When Raju called, the boy got up. When Raju sought permission to have food sitting inside, the boy agreed, even though it was a small hut. He pointed towards a pot of pure water that we could drink. His potato was boiling on the stove. He took out from his bag some roti baked quite a while back and heated it. We gave a part of our food to him and shared a very small portion of his food. I talked with the boy while we were having food. He told me his story and on hearing it, I was very pained.

Premsingh Yamki was born in Sirkka Village near Gala. In the Kailash journey, we can reach Gala through Panku, Sirkka and Narayanashram too. Premsingh's father, who owned five mules, had a permanent job under a contractor who transported commodities to army camps. His work was hard but it earned him good money. They owned 2 acres of land and cultivated it under the supervision of Premsingh's mother. This also fetched them good profit after deducting expenses. The family, including Premsingh's younger sister, grandfather and grandmother, were living happily. Premsingh was very good at studies. He had stood first in class since the first standard. In extracurricular activities also, he had proved his abilities.

Things took a downward turn one day. A group of donkeys transporting goods were caught in a massive landslide. In his hasty attempts to save the animals, Premsingh's father was seriously injured. His thighbone was broken and spinal column injured. Finding his pets sinking into the depths of the Kali River, gradually he lost consciousness also. To meet the expenses of having his father treated in Dharchula, they had to sell their farmland. Premsingh's studies was also stopped when he passed sixth standard. New clothes, shoes, raincoat, umbrella and such things he would have gotten before school opened remained now as mere dreams. The teachers came forward to help. But who would look after the family?

'*Ha, sukhangal verum jalam, ararivoo niyathithan*
Thrasu pongunnathum thane thanu povathum!'
—'Karuna' by Kumaranasan

(Luxuries of life are just magical. Nobody knows
when the weighing balance of fate will go up or
when it will come down!)

To look after his family, Premsingh, the twelve-year-
old boy, became a shepherd. A big herd of about a thousand
goats was now under his protection. A Bhutia dog, famous
for their loyalty and bravery, was with him for help. When he
told us that the poor animals raised their heads on hearing his
voice, the boy's eyes shone. His salary was Rs 1500. Taking
into account the tips the owners gave and the money he got
when dead animals were sold, he was able to save something.
The owners of the goats paid his salary at home. His mother
spent it cautiously and saved whatever she could for his sister's
marriage. Premsingh aimed to buy a mule with his own savings.
It required about Rs 15,000. He intended to follow his father's
profession. To my question on whether he could write his
exams after private study, he showed me the contents of a torn
bag. Amid the faded clothes and woollen sheets were kept some
books of the seventh standard.

My eyes were filled with tears. While grazing the sheep
in the forests, sitting alone on the rocks and lying sleepless in
the lone moments of snowy nights, his little heart was full of
classrooms, classmates and teachers. It was not possible now
to study and write the examination. For a shepherd who had
to leave home for seven months or so and who had to wander
hundreds of kilometres and spend his days in some cave or
a ramshackle hut like this, study and examination were only
daydreams. But why was God so cruel to that boy, who was of
high intelligence and born in such favourable circumstances?
That was a matter for deep thought which had only one
answer. The fruits of deeds in previous births had to be reaped
in this birth.

'Poorvajanmakrutham Sarvam Avashyamupabhoojyathae'
—Vyasa Muni puts forth the same argument.

I awoke from my thoughts hearing the violent barking of the dog. Maybe it had become vigilant seeing strangers with its boss. Premsingh calmed the dog. I gave it a piece of roti which it thankfully ate, wagging its tail. When I gave him a 1000 rupee note, the innocent boy became nervous. After forcefully putting the currency in his hand, Raju and I left the hut to continue our journey. The boy accompanied us for some distance. I presented him two packets of biscuits and some sweets. Then intentionally, to change the subject, I asked him about the feeding pattern of the goats. Grass and water were their only feed. Once in a week, salt would also be given. Standing closer to the boy, I put my hand over his head and blessed him, asking him to live honestly and always keep God in his mind. He recorded my address in his little notebook and I told him to contact me in case of need. I couldn't bear any more the sight of tears flowing through the little boy's face that sun and snow had made rough. I turned and walked away.

Reaching the base after walking on the downward slope of the meadow, I looked back. The boy was standing still with the bamboo stick in hand. Thinking that the eyes of the little boy would be on me till I went out of sight, my mind sobbed. At that time I also thought of Pradeep Bhatt, the boy from Yamunotri Dham.

About 2 km after Phoolkiwar, the path became most difficult. Climbing up a sharply steep path about 1 km long, I became totally exhausted. The icy wind that was blowing fiercely made the going tough. I felt like all my energy had left me. Only yogis and rishis could preserve energy through yoga. The surroundings they lived in were mountainous and full of ice. Even if yoga was practised daily, an ordinary man could preserve energy only up to a limit. When yogis could build up energy reserves by drinking just water, an ordinary man could do that only by eating food.

Going downwards, I reached a wonderful place full of medium-sized hillocks. I was convinced that these were the remnants of a dilapidated puranic fort the military people had earlier told me about. Was it part of the palace of Kunthibhoja? There was no authoritative proof. The hillocks standing around looked like a fort. The pieces of rock spread over there were evidently symmetrically cut ones. Such pieces were used for construction purposes. There were pieces with beautiful carvings on them. Parts of broken pillars were also seen. Maybe it was the military men or the shepherds who had put those stone pieces one over the other like a pyramid. I also found the leftovers of offerings to gods lying spread over here. Kunthi River was flowing on the north side of that land. The five high mountain peaks standing stuck to one another at the southern part of Adi Kailash were known as the Pandava Peaks. There was the Pandava Fort in Kuti Village also. It was also believed that Vyasa Muni walked through Kuti Village to do meditation at Adi Kailash. Seeing all this obvious evidence with my own eyes, the relevance of Adi Kailash seemed higher than before.

A major stream flowing from the south-west side of Himalayan mountain ranges joined the Kunthi River. There was a temporarily erected narrow wooden bridge on the wider part of the river. We carefully crossed the river on it. Since the water was flowing with great speed, a false step would end everything. The bridge was barely 2 feet wide and because of its length, was oscillating fearfully. It was surprising to think how the goods-carrying donkeys crossed the river on that. After the confluence point, the way went sharply upwards. Beyond were ten hairpin curves. Here also, a misstep would land you in the river.

Walking through endless valleys, we kept moving further. The cold increased every minute. Over many areas of the path, ice was lying in huge mounds. Since the sky was black, the Himalayan mountains were less bright too. Though the colourful world of flowers down in the valleys pleased the eyes, I found it very difficult to move ahead because of the severe cold. We crossed the patrolling Indian Army and ITBP teams twice. On both occasions, we just wished each other a happy journey and then walked ahead. We did so because the dark sky and fierce wind were indicators of impending rain.

Rest was felt to be critical by the time we reached a valley that went down like a beautiful green carpet. After drinking my fill of water from a stream nearby, I stretched out my body and lay on the bed of grass. It was a great relief. Raju also seemed very weak. Then, after walking for an hour, we saw the sheds of a military camp far away. A parade was going on in the courtyard. I talked with an army officer I met there. It was the camp of the twenty-fourth battalion of the ITBP. Guarding of the completely ice-covered Dhura Pass and Sin La Pass 10 km away was under the control of that ITBP camp. Patrolling had to be done daily and reports had to be sent to superiors. Since it was the Chinese border, problems often took place. On such occasions, ITBP was not in control of things. Soldiers of the Indian Army would be dropped down from helicopters at such times. These fully armed soldiers take care of things for our country. It was only 70 km from Dhura Pass to Manasarovar through a shortcut. But that way had been closed.

My mind became warmer thinking of the soldiers who protect the borders of our great country. We got to understand their greatness only when we travelled through the border areas by walking. For them, who lived under rain, severe snow and sub-zero temperatures, life was a question mark. In what way should they be honoured? In the lines penned by the great poet Vallathol Narayana Menon in praise of Mother India, '*Vandhippin Mathavine, Vandhippin Mathavine, Vandhippin Varadhaye, Vandhippin Varennyaye*' (Let us praise our mother, let us praise our mother, let us praise the blissful and let us praise the great soul), I felt like adding 'soldiers' as the last word in every line of praise.

Two km lay between the military camp and our camp. Reaching level land after climbing a long and steep path, the tents of the Jolingkong camp could be seen far away. Walking became very slow because of exhaustion. The dark sky became darker and rain started to pour. The surroundings became invisible in the heavy rain. When we reached our camp at last after crossing the small, swift water currents flowing from Adi Kailash, the time was thirty minutes past five. That trip, which extended for more than twelve hours, was one of the most difficult ones in my many Himalayan trips.

After drinking a cup of hot tea, I rested in a fibre tent reserved for me. Friends informed me that those who were travelling on horses also had to face many problems. While passing through paths under hanging rock, many travellers had hit their heads painfully on the edge of the rock. For some others, the horses had slipped on the up and down paths but somehow, they escaped. They told me that the injury of a woman was serious and she was under sedation for a swollen face. Attempts to get her to Gunji would start early next morning.

As per the travel schedule, there had to be two days' halt at Jolingkong. The return journey would start only on the third day. If the climate was adverse, we would have to stay there one more day. Though the force of rain had come down, the temperature, which was below zero, was unbearable. In the light of the gas lamp, I had my dinner standing in the mess tent. Roti, potato curry and cut and boiled green leaves as a side dish were the food items. The pickles that the travellers had brought were also served. The surroundings were not clear because of heavy snow and broken rain. While finding shelter in the bed after prayers, my mind was full of Adi Kailash.

14

At Adi Kailash

I woke up at sharp 5 a.m. the morning and came out of the shed. The surroundings were not visible because of heavy fog. There was hot water in a big aluminium vessel placed in the veranda of the kitchen. It seemed that a big mound of firewood had been placed under the vessel in the night itself. Without hot water, life was surely impossible there. The cooks and other kitchen staff had still not woken up. I entered the bathroom, picking a bucket of water for brushing the teeth, cleaning the body and other primary needs of the morning. Readymade bathrooms and toilets made of fibre had been erected—about a furlong away from the camp. There were two bathrooms and two toilets erected thus.

The cooks woke up at about 5.45 a.m. Since none of my fellow travellers had woken up, I sat near the fireplace of the kitchen, curling up my body. The unbearable cold was lessened a bit thus. I utilized the occasion to talk about things with the workers. Sipping black tea, I listened to their narration.

Walking up half a kilometre in the south-west direction of the camp, we could see Adi Kailash. The previous day, that mountain peak was fully covered by snow for the whole day. The team members who had come to the camp by 2 p.m. went there at about 4 p.m. but had to return disappointed. You have to go 2 km farther to reach the front of Adi Kailash. Those parts were full of dangerous glaciers. The water current that rises from Adi Kailash later becomes the Kunthi River. The Kuti River that originates from the Dhura Pass joins Kunthi at Phoolkiwar after flowing north through Parvati Tal. We can enter Tibet through the Mamgsa Dhura and Lampiya Dhura Passes. The military men on guard duty would permit the pilgrims to go beyond the pass only if the climate was favourable. This is too dangerous an attempt. We could reach Bedang by walking 12 km from Jolingkong by the left of the Lampiya Pass. From there, we could reach Thavaghat by walking 50 km via Dhugtu, Sela and Niyu. The villagers belonging to the Bhotiya tribal community reside in Dhugtu, Sela and Niyu. Kilometres can be saved if we go to Dharchula from Thavaghat through this route. But it is not made use of because of breath-stopping inclines and the intolerable climatic conditions.

I was stunned to learn that under such conditions, villagers were residing there. The Adi Kailash pilgrimage conducted via Gunji with so many kilometres in excess was for the pilgrims to experience the vision of Om Mountain, the pathways with the footprints of Vyasa Maharshi, the famous puranic background of Kunthi Devi and the Pandavas, the pleasant villages and farmlands, the Kali, Kuti, Kunthi rivers and the cheerful sights of the extremely beautiful Himalayan mountain ranges.

After 7 a.m., the fog in the plains began to subside. But the peaks were still hidden and an elderly cook told me that at each moment, the sunrays were becoming brighter and soon the atmosphere was going to be even brighter. The camp was now in full swing and everyone was busy. As there was a long queue for hot water and in front of the toilets, some team members sat on the rock in the courtyard of the camp to brush their teeth and to drink their morning tea. Meanwhile, attempts were being made to get the injured woman to Gunji.

The atmosphere became bright, just as the old cook had predicted. We had breakfast. Jolingkong and its surroundings shone in silver light when the sunrays were reflected on the snow-covered mountains. I stood melted in the incomparable beauty of the land. It was like heaven. I thought that this was the most beautiful place in all the Himalayas. Snow-filled mountains stood around like a circular stadium. In the middle was the vast meadow like a fully spread green carpet. One half of the mountain slopes was filled with green grass and these slopes towards the meadow were a lovely sight. The other half of the slopes was filled with pure white snow. Each nook and corner of the meadow was a universe of flowers in different colours. The sky stood behind the snowy mountains like a blue curtain and the white clouds were like tinkling silver anklets. The place had only one definition—beauty and only beauty!

We moved towards Adi Kailash in small groups. I stopped when we reached the camp of the horse attendants. The only dhaba in Jolingkong was situated there. The horse attendants slept in the open tents put up beside the dhaba. Their food also came from there. Stopping the cards game they were engaged in right from the morning, the horse attendants joined us in the usual pattern of one horse attendant for one traveller. We went the way they guided. Though grass covered the entire area, the land was marshy in many parts. There could be many dangerous traps in the form of hidden pits.

Everyone bowed with folded hands seeing Adi Kailash from a distance. Some lay fully prostrated. Chanting of the Panchakshari Mantra echoed in the atmosphere (this is a prayer to Lord Siva associated with Siva's mantra 'Om Namah Sivaya'. Namah Sivaya is also called the Panchakshari Mantra, and it means 'he who is looking like a demigod and who has matted hair, who has the trident in his hand and who is eternal and divine . . .). Lighting up *chirathu* (small mud-pot lamps), the women members started preparing for pooja and bhajans. The Vedic scholar Dharmendrakumar Dixit was made the chief priest. The group deputed me to help him. After taking a bath in the freezing river, we began arrangements for the pooja. Deities in dedication to Paramasiva and Parvathy Devi were placed on the holy drawing done on the floor. Before that, the floor had been purified by rubbing cowdung paste on it. Pooja ceremonies started with Ganapathi Pooja.

Since the atmosphere was frozen with cold, pooja rituals were done in condensed form. The pooja was finished after bathing the deities with the holy water flowing from Adi Kailash and dedicating to them the holy offerings. After pooja, the offerings were distributed among the people and the next bhajan started with the women in the lead.

After we drank cups of hot tea which the cooks brought, the liaison officer and the guide gave us some detailed instructions. To go very close to the front portion of Adi Kailash was a most dangerous act. The path lying on the left side of Sin La Pass ended just in front of Adi Kailash. On the contrary, if we went steeply down by the right side, we would reach Bedang Village. The Adi Kailash path was possible only to those who had perfect physical fitness, iron-strong willpower and above all, the blessings of God. The advocate withdrew. The remaining four people of our group, the pilgrims on foot and a young man who had been preparing for his final chartered accountancy examinations, were the only persons chosen for that difficult journey. The liaison officer inquired whether any other persons were interested, but no one was ready. As the climate was favourable, it was decided to start the journey immediately.

The past week, Adi Kailash was completely sunk under ice, preventing any kind of access to the area. If our journey was postponed to tomorrow, there might not be another chance.

The duty of a human being was to make use of every chance when it came.

The masters also tell us the same:

'Na Kaschidhapi Jaanaathi Kim Kasya Shwo Bhavishyathi Athaha Shwoha Karaneeyaani Kuryadhadhyaiva Budhiman.'

(Nobody knows what will happen tomorrow. So intelligent people do today what they have to do tomorrow.)

That day was the highly sacred Pradhosha day (9 June 2006, Friday). I felt that reaching Adi Kailash on Pradhosha day, the day most dear to Lord Siva, was the fulfilment of my birth's mission (Pradhosha or Pradhosham is a bi-monthly occasion on the thirteenth day of every fortnight in the Hindu calendar. It is closely connected with the worship of God Siva. This auspicious three-hour period, 1.5 hours before and after sunset, is one of the optimum times for the worship of Lord Siva.). After putting the simple lunch prepared by the cooks inside my shoulder bag and taking other essential things, we started our trip. Avoiding the porters and guides, we had with us the dhaba man Padham Singh as the guide. He had deep knowledge of the area. Raju looked sad at leaving me. Everyone wished us a happy journey.

Bent like an arch, the Adi Kailash mountain ranges were situated in the south-west corner of Jolingkong. Adi Kailash stood 21,000 feet high at the point where the mountain ranges extended from west to south and the mountains in the south joined together. The mountain had a width of about 0.75 km. The entire area was covered by thick ice. The magnificence of Adi Kailash was great. The top of the mountain looking like an umbrella was seen hidden under a cluster of clouds. The sides of the mountains were also not visible under the covering of thick ice. Adi Kailash had many edifices that extended in many directions. It could be said that the great Adi Kailash was the most diverse mountain in the Himalayas. Our happiness grew with each moment we saw it.

The water current that originated from Adi Kailash was large and powerful. Since the water was deep only up to the knee, we could clearly see the colourful stones underneath. Padham Singh told us that until last week, there was 10 feet water there. The main reason for the rise of water level in the Kali River during the rains could be attributed to the heavy flow from the mountains. We walked a long distance alongside the riverbanks and rested for some time when we reached the base of the sharply steep glacier. Eating biscuits and glucose and drinking river water, we regained our energy.

The rest of the trip was full of steep paths. Being in the area of glaciers, Padham Singh had warned that each step must be placed carefully. The top of the iceberg, hardened like rock, would be sunk in fresh ice about half a foot thick. So we tried to step carefully. The climate was clear. The force of the wind blowing from the ice-covered mountain peaks was also coming down. The electronic gadget the young chartered accountancy student carried with him showed the temperature as −18 degrees Celsius. The altitude was over 18,000 feet. Shortage of oxygen began to be felt. We rested for ten minutes to have glucose and water. At a distance at the back of the meadow, the other team members looked like dots of different colours. When their shouting echoed in our ears, we all looked back. The young student who observed them through binoculars told us that they were exclaiming loudly, looking at and saluting the Kailash Mountain. We too raised our heads and looked above.

Hidden so far under clouds, the left side of the peak had now come out. Lying face upwards like in yoga, a divine figure formed on ice was shining like a diamond. The high nose and square chin were especially notable. It was a magnificent and glorious vision.

We moved up with doubled energy. We were convinced that the path was not as steep as it had looked from the bottom. Both the shortage of oxygen and acute cold were on the rise. While walking on hard ice, the top portions of my trekking shoes got accumulated with ice and I felt as if my legs had frozen.. Since we knew that we would have to stop the journey and return if a snowy wind began to blow, we walked ahead as fast as we could. The originating point of the river was in the bottomless valley below. We saw big pieces of ice breaking from the bottom of the glacier and falling into the river. Though we had been completely exhausted, amassing all our strength, we reached near Adi Kailash.

We were standing on a high ice wall. About 10 feet below was a beautiful lake. Like a blue pearl stuck on snow, it lay still. Pieces of ice were floating over the blue-coloured water. It was like a coral chain decorating the sweet blue pearl ornament. On the other side of the lake, about 50 feet away, was the universe made of snow—the Adi Kailash! It was facing northwards. Adjusting ourselves in the limited space, we all prostrated ourselves. The echo of Padham Singh's loud prayers went up in waves. We were surprised to see each word uttered echoing at the instant and then disappearing upwards like waves. We experimented with this many times. The same experience was repeated with chanting prayers and Veda mantras. Was Nadhabrahma merging with Parabrahma Parameswara?

Every minute, Padham Singh tracked the changes in the climate. So we decided to stay there as long as we could. The time was past 12 noon. My friends got ready to have lunch but I refused. I decided to do meditation instead. I made the shoulder bag my seat. Removing my shoes, I sat there for meditation in front of Adi Kailash. Changes from one level to another were much faster than ordinarily possible. Under those circumstances, I adopted a method that didn't avoid the subconscious mind fully. The conscious mind traversing from the colour blue to *neeleswari* and then to blue pearl happened after giving hints to the subconscious mind. It was from blue pearl, which came after neeleswari that one would reach *bindu*. Bindu was just the size of a mustard seed but its light was enormous. When meditation deepened, bindu began to glow in brightness beyond description. When bindu gradually took the form of upasana, the echo of music was heard in the inner left ear. Its comparison was with the amazing music coming from the veena strings. This music of God was heard in the subconscious of the meditator from the space of consciousness.

I woke from meditation after 1 p.m. Friends told me that they had tried many times to wake me up but with no result. Though it was freezing cold, my body was sweating. Padham Singh told us that it was dangerous to stay there further since the time was past noon. So we prepared to return. After viewing Adi Kailash to the full satisfaction of our minds and bowing and prostrating again, we turned back and proceeded. It is said that origin of the Alaknanda River is from the glacier under this lake. I longed to drink at least a mouthful of the holy water. But Padham Singh told us that according to belief, touching the lake would make it impure. So we gave up the attempt.

We reached the camp at 3.30 p.m. Since it was Pradhosha, I had earlier decided to eat food only after dusk. I just lay on the meadow to overcome the exhaustion of travelling. Jolingkong glowed in the golden rays of the setting sun. Wow, so many colours were painted on the western sky! No artist could accomplish such a harmony of colours. While the surrounding mountains stood like decorated umbrellas in different colours, the giant umbrella of the sky stood as a crown. Nature, yes, nature was everything. It was Brahma and it was God.

'Prakruthim Purusham Chaiva Vidhdhyanadhee Ubhavapi Vikaramscha Gunamschaiva Vidhdhi Prakruthi Sambhavan'
—Bhagavat Gita, 13–19

(Please let you know, both nature and man are timeless. The emotions related to body and sensitive organs and comfort, sadness and lust all originated from nature.)

After bhajan and aarti, I took dinner at 8 p.m. Roti, potato curry and the side dish of ladies' fingers all tasted very good. The snowfall, which had begun at 7 p.m., became heavy at 9 p.m.

My eyelids were drooping when I crawled into my bed after praying for safety from the freezing cold and a peaceful sleep throughout the night.

15

Parvathy Sarovar

Waking up at 5 a.m., I came out and saw snow falling like rain. Ice 1 foot thick had fallen over the fibre sheet roof of the camp shed and over the meadow. I crept back into bed to rest until the snowfall ended.

It was a very important journey that we had to do that day. All preparations for it had been done on the previous day itself. If the climate was good, we would start for Parvati Tal (Parvathy Sarovar or the Lake of Parvathy) at 8 a.m. It was 3 km from Jolingkong to the lake. It was a very difficult path. The travel could be done by mule. After taking a bath in Parvathy Sarovar, pilgrims could fulfil their dreams by doing pooja (worship of god) on their own in a small temple there. The rituals for propitiating ancestors could also be done there. The five of us had obtained special permission to travel from Parvathy Sarovar to the very difficult Lampiya Dhura and Mangsa Dhura passes. Both those passes were completely under thick ice and the Indian military was on guard there. We could go to Tibet through those passes. China held control of those parts.

After breakfast, the team proceeded on the trip at 8 a.m. Though the snowfall had ended, bright sunlight was yet to come out. The temperature level was around −4 degree Celsius.

The assessment of the horse attendants was that the climate would become gradually favourable because the sky was not dark. Our travel was to the north side, i.e., in the opposite direction of Adi Kailash. Crossing the ice-covered meadow, Raju and I walked up the side of the steep mountain. We came sharply downwards from the top of the mountain, only to climb up again. The image of flower buds yearning to blossom on the mountainsides was pretty. Each valley was different in colour. Thinking about the beauty of the flowers blooming under sunrays, I felt very happy. The cold was increasing. The reason for the chill was the wind blowing from the icy mountains far away in front of us. We rested for five minutes before climbing a steep path. Then we walked slowly and reached the top.

Seeing Parvathy Sarovar and its surroundings far away was like seeing a beautiful painting. It was a vast lake and lay under snowy mountains, as if covered by silver sheets. The lands lying near the lake looked like a green carpet spread over them. The blue colour of the sky was reflected in the lake. The row of colourful stones around the lake looked like a border sewn at its ends. There was a small temple at the top of the ground on the right. It was a feast of a sight no one would ever get fed up of.

Walking for roughly 1 km through level land, we reached the side of the lake at 9.30 a.m. Some members of our team were preparing for pooja. Parvathy Sarovar had an area of around 5 km. Most of its water was only up to the knee level. Streams arising from behind Adi Kailash reached Parvathy Sarovar after flowing 6 km through icy mountains. Hence the water was freezing cold. The temple was at the right end of the lake. At its left end, parallel to the temple was a deep dump where the excess water of the lake fell. Finding the team members assembled there, I went to them. What I saw in the deep was amazing. The reflection of the full figure of Adi Kailash, which was 4.5 km away from the spot, lay in the clear water. But the reflections of other mountains were not there. We could see the figure of Adi Kailash with our naked eyes only by standing at the edge of the pit and looking upwards. When we changed our position, Adi Kailash was not visible. I found this mysterious. Straight up, there was only one medium-sized mountain near the hole. It was that mountain that hid Kailash from our view from other places. But we could directly see Kailash by standing at the right end of the depth. At the same time, we could also see the outline of Kailash in the depth of the pit. Up above Kailash Mountain, thick snow was hanging at the far heights. Was it that the figure of Kailash first fell on that snow surface and then the reflection from there fell into the waters of the deep pit? Whatever it was, one thing was sure. The Kailash and the pit were connected in some mysterious way.

The belief was that Sathy Devi and later Parvathy Devi bathed in that lake. People also believed that the dirt of their body lay silted up at the bottom of the lake as black mud. Most travellers took the soil from the banks of the lake as a holy relic to carry home. Raju took some soil for me but I decided not to take that then. I told the boy so.

I had another plan in mind. Before proceeding to the pass, we would take a bath in the lake and after that, offer prayers at the temple with a circumambulation around it. Our guide again was Padham Singh. We delayed the time, hoping to go with the patrolling military men if they came that way. After 12 noon, we finished walking around the holy lake and reached the temple. Meanwhile, the pooja and *homam* (worship using a fire pit) done under the priesthood of Dharmendrakumar Dixit were completed. I touched the Siva-Parvathy deity in the temple and the fire in the *homakunda* (the holy fire pit) in worship. While all others except our porters were ready for the return trip, we started our journey to the Lampiya-Mangsa Pass.

We walked in the hope of meeting the patrolling military men on the way. Padham Singh, after walking a few steps ahead, suddenly stopped. He looked all around at the sky, closing one eye with his left hand. Disappointment showed on his face. My mind hinted that halting in such way at the start of the trip was a bad omen. Padham Singh informed us that the quick movement of clouds and the fading sunrays were not good signs. He also pointed out that the colour of snow on the mountain tops had become dark. He predicted that noticeable changes in the weather were going to happen soon.

We went ahead as per the majority decision to go as far as possible. We proceeded step by step through the snow-filled mountains. Avoiding the route commonly used, Padham Singh selected an easy route. The way seemed hard because of lots of steep sections. The shortage of oxygen was felt as the height increased. Halting now and then to eat biscuits and drink juice, we went a good way ahead.

The dark atmosphere became still darker. We stopped when a strong wind began to blow, lifting up the dust of ice. In the dim light, our vision was impaired. We were relieved when Padham Singh said that military people could be seen coming from a distance. They came nearer after about fifteen minutes. They warned us that travelling ahead was dangerous then and the small bridge by which we had to enter the pass was fully under ice. They told us that in terms of height and intensity of snowfall, those passes were in no way comparable to the Lipulekh Pass on the Kailash-Manasarovar route. Since I was the only one among the group who had crossed the Lipulekh Pass before, it looked like the others didn't take this information seriously. Thinking it better to return before the climate became worse, we turned back along with the military men.

We reached Parvathy Sarovar after 3 p.m. While my friends took rest in the small veranda of the temple, I went towards the pit of the lake along with Raju. The Adi Kailash peak was completely under ice. Its figure lay in the deep pit in that form. I had wished to dip my whole body in the pit water in the morning when I first saw it. I didn't know what inspiration was behind it. When the guide told us that the dirt on the body of Sathy Devi and Parvathy Devi was lying at the bottom of the lake, my wish to have a full bath in the depth doubled. I was thinking of the same thing while going on to the pass and also upon our return.

I stood for ten minutes observing the deep pit. Then I dipped my hand in the water in many parts of it. I didn't feel the water as cold as to freeze my fingers. Yet, I thought that that was dangerous considering the chill of the atmosphere and that of the pit. Not letting in any more thoughts, I took out the holy offering of Sree Guruvayurappan and the koovala leaves safely kept in my shoulder bag (koovala is Aegle marmelos, commonly known as the bael tree. It is the favourite of Lord Siva for poojas). There was also in my bag, kept like a treasure, the sandalwood paste that had decorated the divine face of Sree Guruvayurappan. The erstwhile chief priests of Guruvayur temple, Thamattoor Kesavan Namboodirippad and his younger brother, Thamattoor Damodaran Namboodirippad, had given that to me with blessings. I touched the holy paste whenever I smelt danger. The confidence and energy it gave me cannot be expressed in words. The koovala leaves too had received many prayers. What other things could one offer to both the *devis* (goddesses) than those which represented Mahavishnu and Sree Parameswara?

I dedicated the holy offering from Guruvayur and the koovala leaves in the lake pit, chanting Vishnu-Siva-Devi prayers. The sandalwood paste that had decorated the lotus-like beautiful face of Sree Guruvayurappan got merged in the clear water of the pit with golden colours. The koovala leaves kept flowing around. I fixed my eyes on Rajendra Singh Negi's face with hope. Grasping my query, Raju removed his clothes one by one. Wearing only shorts, we jumped into the pit after praying to Kailashnath. Though freezing cold was felt, the bottom could be touched instantly. Picking up a handful of the mud, we swam up. I was almost half-conscious then. Many figures came in and out of my mind. After bowing reverently to the Kailash Mountain, we immediately climbed up the shore.

We immediately went to our friends who were heating themselves near the fire pit (homakunda). It was a relief after the icy cold, which was pricking the body like sharp pins. The atmosphere became darker. Even the direction of the setting sun could not be found. If climate became worse, we would face danger on the return trip. So we started the return journey without losing time. We travelled through a roundabout way, moving away from the fixed route for about half a kilometre. On the left side of that path, there was a completely dry, vast lake. The shape of the lake could be still seen. Why did the lake become waterless in spite of its position amid abundant water availability and ice-filled mountains? Maybe there was some Puranic incident behind it.

We reached the camp after 5.30 p.m. Since the snowfall was very heavy, we walked the last half kilometre blind. The whistling wind had started. The intensity of the icy wind became very strong while we were resting in the camp shed after evening prayer. An avalanche blew around with a horrible sound and it threw up a dust of ice pieces in the sky. We viewed the horrifying sight through the windows. The wind that blew intermittently gained power each moment. It was a wind that blew like this over Kuti Village two weeks ago that had destroyed three camp sheds of the Tourism Department. The sheds were empty there but here, the situation was the opposite. Seconds were enough for tragedies to happen in such lands. The fearful sounds of the icy mountains cracking and falling elsewhere echoed in Jolingkong. We spent each moment chanting Veda mantras and prayers sitting together. The force of the wind reduced after 9 p.m. In the break we got, we immediately ate food. When the strength of the wind lessened, rain started to pour. There were cracks in the fibre sheets caused by hail and so rainwater leaked into the sheds. We tried to close the leak by putting cello tape on the holes. After that, we went to bed. Utter tiredness closed our eyes even before we got into bed.

16

Adi Kailash by the Full Moon

Rising at 5 a.m., I opened the shed door and looked out. The scene outside was heartening. Though there was a slight mist, the morning rays spread golden light in Jolingkong. My eyes blurred while looking at the semi-circled sun rising in the centre of the ice mountains far away. No doubt, every sunrise was beautiful, but the beauty of the sunrise in Gunji was unimaginable.

The cooks gave me a cup of tea, sharing what they had made for themselves. I sat on a rock in the courtyard, slowly drinking it. I was very happy at seeing the climate most favourable on the full moon day (11 June, Sunday). Since our stay was extended for that day also, it was my life's blessing to have a chance to see Adi Kailash on that night of the full moon. My happiness doubled when the cooks said that the climate would be favourable all day. It would be pathetic to confine oneself within the four walls of the camp sheds if a nightmare like that of last night happened again. I carried on with my morning activities with a prayer that the events of last night should not happen again.

Thinking that I could meditate in the yard in front of Adi Kailash, I walked there. I stood for a moment near Padham Singh's dhaba. The horse attendants and porters were fast sleep on the naked ground, covering themselves with a double woollen sheet. The ice wind of last night had torn the tarpaulin sheets of their sheds into pieces, which was why they had to sleep on the ground. I could see that a part of the roof of Padham Singh's dhaba had also been carried away by the wind. The horses were grazing enthusiastically as if nothing had happened.

I found Padham Singh fast sleep on top of a box in the veranda of the dhaba. Seeing him lifting up his head from underneath the bed sheet he was covered with, I went near. Hurriedly sitting up, he saluted me in the name of Kailashpati (Siva). I saluted back in the same name. When I told him about last night's severe storm, his assertion was that it was below average and also short.

I was shocked to hear from him that the huge blocks of ice brought in by the avalanche of two weeks ago would take three days to melt. He and his family had a narrow escape from the avalanche, which lasted for two days. He told me that he would prepare a strong tea if I waited ten minutes. I refused with thanks. I intimated him that after meditation, I was free in the afternoon and if the liaison officer permitted, I would come and stay in the dhaba to see the full moon night of Kailash. Padham Singh became very happy at this and bowed to me many times. He had mentioned to me during our travel to Parvathy Sarovar that he had had some rare and unforgettable experiences in Adi Kailash. He had learnt from Raju that I was a writer. Bidding goodbye to Padham Singh for the moment, I walked to the edge of the ground. Though the Adi Kailash mountain ranges were visible, the top of the peak was hidden behind clouds. My mind longed once again to see the divine figure in Yoga Nidra (meditational sleep). Sitting cross-legged, I started meditating with complete concentration of mind.

The thought process called meditation enabled one to completely concentrate one's mind. In the ecstasy of yoga meditation, divine luminaries could be found shining in the centre of the earth. Along with that, divine sounds could also be heard through the internal ears.

The mind was a vast entity. When knowledge was awakened by meditation, the feeling of Brahma Swaroopa (the all-prevailing god) prevailed outwardly as well as inwardly. The objective of knowledge and devotion was Sarvatma Bhava (self-knowledge or feeling of 'self' or atman) and happiness. Happiness was the form of self.

When I came out of it four hours later, the time was past 11 a.m. Adi Kailash was shining like a diamond. The beauty of the face in Yoga Nidra was indefinable. It looked like it was gaining more splendour. In its brightness, the icy lines on the peak defeated those of a diamond.

Sitting thus over there, I developed a great appetite for the breakfast Raju brought from the Tourism mess. The poori and potato curry tasted good. I felt completely satisfied after drinking a full cup of tea. I told Raju to leave me alone. When sensual relief was achieved, the veins also became free. When the mind travelled from one level to another, I lay on the bed of grass with closed eyes.

Sathy Devi, the very beautiful daughter of Daksha Prajapathi, reached Adi Kailash after her marriage with Sree Parameswara. Fairies of heaven and the womenfolk of Yaksha-Kinnara-Gandharva together received Devi with all rituals. While the dancers of heaven danced with envious flexibility, the Kinnaras played music. When the celebrations ended and everyone left, the newly wedded couple withdrew to their own private world. It was a dream coming true for a lady to marry the very man she desired. The Bhooth Ganas (the troop of divine spirits) of Siva served Sathy Devi in such a way that she felt no shortage of anything.

Adi Kailash stood in brightness like the Deva Vana (forest of God) called Chaithra Ratha. Bearing the glamour of spring and wearing the ornaments of flowers, the trees and herbs of the forest spread a heart-melting fragrance all around. 'The male cuckoos that had cleared their throat by eating tender mango leaves created a heavenly world of music.'[1] Receiving the gentle touch of the breeze that carried a seductive fragrance and seeing sights like ponds full of lotuses, a universe of flowers, honey-filled mango trees and clear blue sky, Sathy Devi walked around in that heaven, rejoicing. Seeing 'the male cuckoo kissing its dear pair in love and affection under intoxication by drinking the liquor which is the honey of the mango trees and the beetle on red lotus buzzing, in sound pleasing to its lover', Sathy Devi inquired about their well-being.

('*Pumskokillaschutharasasavena*
Mathaha Priyam Chumbathi Ragahrushtaha
Kujadhwiraefofpyayamambujsthaha
Priyam Priyayaha Prakarothi Chadu.'
—Rithusamharam, Kalidasan)

Once, when she was lying in the lap of her dearest husband, Devi saw the Pushpak aeroplane flying slowly in the background of the icy mountains. When she asked where the plane was going, the all-knowing Sree Parameswara remained silent. But he could not resist her pressure long. Later, he explained to her all the details.

As Lord Brahma had assigned him the first position among Prajapathis, the arrogance of Daksha was at its height. Daksha did not invite Siva to the yajna to insult him by not giving the Yajna Bhag (a ritual of yajna) to him. If Devi went to the yajna in spite of his objection, she also would be insulted. Parama Siva again objected when Devi said that she wished very much to see her father, mother and sisters. Also, she argued that it was everyone's wish to visit one's birthplace when Bruhaspathi was conducting a yajna there. Parama Siva told her that Daksha, who abused him in the assembly of Prajapathis, was his enemy and if she did not obey him, it would not be good for her. He warned that it might even cause her death. But Sathy Devi was firm on going to the yajna against the wishes of her husband. To help his dear wife who was going alone, Parama Siva sent Parshadhas and Bhooth Ganas.

Poor Sathy Devi, she did not know that it was her last journey. Could we say that the all-knowing Parama Siva was unaware of the suicide his dear mate was going to commit? Never. Insulted cruelly by her father at the yajna venue, Devi burnt her body by jumping into the yajna kunda (the holy pit of fire). Siva, who knew everything in all the three worlds, could have saved Devi easily. But why didn't he do it? The Puranas are not lies. There is sufficient reason for Sathy Devi's suicide and rebirth. *Sathy* means one who obeys the form of truth, Brahma. Sree Mahadeva (Parameswara), who was Nirvairan (being without enmity), Santhamoorthy (peaceful) and Atmaraman (who enjoys his self) was the guru of all living and non-living things ('*Kastham Characharaagurum Nirvairam Sanththa Vigraham*'). Paramasiva needs a bride in the Ardhanareeshwara concept (Ardhanareeshwara is a composite androgynous form of Siva and Parvathy). She must be the mother of the universe.

'*Yaa Kwopi Loka Jananee Pradhithaa Bhavanee*
Yaa Sarvamangalayutha cha Subhaa Mrudaanee
Thaam Chandikaam Hathakhala Madhunaa Suraamee
Thaam Kalikaam Bhagavatheem Sirassaa Namamee'

This should be the 'Visweswari' (goddess of the world) as per this concept.

Sathy Devi could never rise to that level of a wife. Sathy was quite an ordinary woman who had a realization that 'I didn't have the ability to understand you properly because of my womanly character' ('*Thadhapyaham Yoshidha-Thathwavichcha*'). Her knowledge was only hearsay. It still hadn't become meaningful knowledge gained through the five senses. Sathy agreed with a sense of guilt that the power of weak knowledge would perish gradually. Knowledge would complete her antipathy to ignorance. And ignorance was related to an enmity-created vacuum. It was sure that her dependent illiteracy wanted independence. Illiteracy and Brahma were not related. There was no possibility for her to have a close relation with Sree Mahadeva who was the 'purpose of Brahma' and the 'Sankara Roopi' (Sankara means *sanka* [doubt] and *hara* [dispeller or destroyer]. *Roopi* means 'in the form of'). Two opposite dharma (the path of righteousness) could never join together. In short, the actions of Sathy Devi were under the influence of her strong relations with her relatives in the material world.

Sathy Devi was only an ordinary faithful wife as proclaimed in the Vedas, the immortal anthems of ancient India.

'*Aghorachakshurapathignyedhi*
Sivaapashubhyassumanaassuvarcha ha
Veerasurdevakamaasyonaa
Shamnobavadwipadeshanchathushpathe.'

(She should become the loving observer, should be loving eyes on her husband, should not harm him, should always be favourable to him, should be loved by all living things, should possess a pure mind, should be magnificent, should give birth to good children, should be loved by gods, should love gods, should like affairs related to gods and above all should

provide pleasure. She should be the shelter of peace
for human beings and all animals).[2]

It was time that gave Sathy Devi to Agni (fire), recreated
her as Parvathy and again remade her the faithful wife of
Paramasiva. The rotation of the wheel of time changes
everything. During the passage of time, all we think is that
the deceased will take birth again. The fact was that while
Paramasiva advised the Kriyakundali Yoga Sasthra to Parvathy
Devi, she had become that much stronger to receive it. Thus
began the Ardhanareeshwara concept for the betterment of
the world.

I awoke from my nap when Raju shook me. The time was
past 1 p.m. Our friends were resting after their meal. A group of
men and women had already proceeded to Kuti Village in the
morning. Many pilgrims were showing physical problems after
living in that altitude and at sub-zero temperatures. The icy
wind of last night and the shattering that followed had made
many fearful. That was the reason why they were not willing to
stay at Jolingkong for one more night. After having a lunch of
roti, white pea curry and pickle, I too lay down to sleep.

When it was 2.30 p.m., I went to the kitchen and drank
a strong tea. Though Jolingkong and its surroundings were
in bright light under a clear sky, the cold was still unbearable.
I went to the camp shed of the liaison officer and discussed
with him about the arrangements for the night. He told us
that if the climate was good, we could all sit at a convenient
place in the *maithan* (meadow) and enjoy the beauty of the full
moon night. When I said that I would like to spend my night
in Padham Singh's dhaba, Prakash Chandra Chandola happily
gave permission. He had always sanctioned whatever facilities
I required as a writer from the start of the journey itself.

The Pandava mountain ranges were another sight of Adi Kailash. Assuming that the afternoon trip might be to those ranges, Raju and I walked towards them. We crossed the river at a place where the water level was very low. The Pandava Mountain was in the same row as Adi Kailash on the southern side. Half a kilometre away from that mountain started the semi-circular Adi Kailash mountain ranges. The cold was very severe when we reached the slopes of the Pandava Mountain by walking through lands filled with green grass. The Pandava Mountain comprised five mountain peaks standing as towers in a row. Below them, there were many small mountains. There was snow only on the Pandava Mountain. The rest of the mountains were snow-free. There was a small temple on a medium-sized hill at the southern end. Just under the temple, there was a big crater. I studied the crater in detail before entering the temple. It was a natural cave. Due to the darkness and small rocks inside, it would feel like the cave was closed. It was believed that that cave route was used to go to Manasarovar and the nearby Kailash.

What remained of the place where the temple existed were shattered walls and some ruins. As the belief went, the temple had been constructed by the Pandavas in those times. The building and the stones used for construction appeared to be hundreds or thousands of years old. Protected under a roof of tin sheets in the shape of the temple, it seemed to be under the Archaeological Department. An indefinable feeling of joy rose while standing there. I felt an enthusiastic beating of my heart and a totally new energy in my veins. Leaving Raju below on the slopes, I climbed up to the top of the small hill near the temple.

From the top of the hill, Jolingkong and its surroundings looked very beautiful. There was a vast green meadow beyond the river downhill. Like a fortress to the meadow stood the icy mountains. The mountain peaks were shining like flames in the golden rays of the setting sun. The combination of clusters of silver clouds woven into one another, the blue sky in the background and the golden glow of the setting sun—it was a scene as gorgeous as paradise. I lay face upwards with the eyes closed and hands folded on my chest. My mind slipped into various thoughts.

The suspense-filled last scene of Daksha Yaga . . . Paramasiva enacting the Thandava dance (the violent dance of Siva, the destroyer of the universe) with the burnt, dead body of Sathy Devi in his hands . . . the earth trembling with each step . . . the fire, capable of destroying everything in the world, emitting from the third holy eye of the furious god . . .

All the three worlds were at risk of destruction. The soothing words of the gods Mahavishnu and Brahma did no good. Mahavishnu understood that Siva's anger would not subside as long as he kept seeing the dead body of Devi. Using his Sudharsana Wheel (the wheel-shaped holy weapon of Mahavishnu), he cut the body of Sathy Devi into fifty-one pieces and threw away each piece to fifty-one places. Those fifty-one places were still being worshipped in the Himalayas as Devi's 'seats of power'.

The Daksha Yaga ended without any further incident after Mahadeva's anger subsided. Daksha, who got his life again, re-fitted with a goat's head in place of his lost head, finished the yaga that had been spoilt by his discrimination. Sree Parameswara came to Adi Kailash for engaging in Aghora[3] *thapass* (thapass means deep meditation with all concentration which the ancient rishis of India had practised) in order to get relief from his sadness. That strong thapass in Dakshinamoorthy position (God facing south) was to reinforce vigour with vigour (Siva is usually seen in five of His aspects. Panchavaktra or Panchamukhi is the combination of all these five forms and is commonly depicted as five-headed. He faces south only on Panchamukha Sivalingam). Prayers are fulfilled by worshipping Siva in that pose as it is believed to be the sparkling manifestation of vigour.

It was also at this time that Sathy Devi took rebirth as Parvathy Devi, born as daughter to Himavan and Menaka. She was not able to correctly comprehend the God husband in her previous birth. So, in the second birth, she observed the duties of life in the right way. Like a rising crescent, Parvathy grew up each moment and was beloved to all the relatives and other people. She started doing meditation from childhood itself with Paramasiva in mind. But mother told her 'U ma' (no *thapass*). Thus, Parvathy also got the name 'Uma'.

She worshipped Sree Parameswara in all zeal and regularity. But the God was not pleased with her even after many years. Observing acute chastity and unshaken willpower, he indulged in thapass like a radiant star amidst the encompassing darkness. It was during that time that a nasty Assura[4] named Tharakassura who had become vested with superpowers under the blessing of God Brahma began to destroy all worlds like an ill-carrying comet. On the request of Devendra (the king of the gods), Brahma himself showed the gods the way to kill Tharakassura. Parvathy and Parameswara had to join together and only the baby thus born could kill Tharakassura. Siva should be attracted to the beautiful figure of Parvathy like a magnet is attracted to iron. For discharging this duty without any fail, Devendra engaged his aide Kamadeva.[5]

Kamadeva went to the Himalayas along with his wife Rathi. Vasanthan, his closest friend, also accompanied them. As Siva was in deep meditation, the beautiful forest had been at a standstill for many years. Trees, plants, herbs and animals were living very cautiously so as not to disturb the meditation of Mahadeva (Siva). When Kamadeva entered the forest to shoot the Malarambu (the arrow of love) towards Mahadeva for upsetting his meditation, nature became worried. When Vasanthan cleverly performed his abilities, the whole forest life became ecstatic. The great poet Kalidasa, presenting the pulse of the forest like an oral picture in his work *Kumarasambhavam*, is gorgeous.

> *'Asootha Sadhya ha Kusumanyashoka ha*
> *Skandhal Prabhruthyeva Sapallavani.'*

(Suddenly flowers blossomed on the ashoka tree from bottom to top. The tender leaves of mango trees stood childish in reddish colour. Deer ran to hide through the wild paths that made rumbling sounds with fallen-down leaves. All animals that were having sex were in the peak of love. Humming a song, Kimpurusha (Kamadeva) kissed his dearest lover. Her face was soaked with sweat and eyes were shining red.)

> *'Geethanthareshu Sramavarileshaiha*
> *Kinchilsamuchchasithapathralekham*
> *Pushpasavaaghoornithanethrasobhi*
> *Priyaamukham Kimpurushaschuchumba.'*

(Following the lover darling, the wasp drank honey from the same flower bowl. Krishnasara mrugham [the Indian buck] slowly scratched the doe standing with closed eyes in the joy of touch.)

> *'Madhu Dwirefaha Kusumaikapaathre*
> *Papow Priyaam Swamanuvarthamanaha*
> *Srumghena cha Sparsanimilithaksheem*
> *Mrugeemakanduyetha Krishnasaraha.'*

(The she-elephant lovingly served her male with her cheek water that smelt of the fragrance of lotus pollen. 'Chakravaka pakshi' [the Brahmany goose] entertained his darling love with half-bitten stem of lotus.)

'Dhadhou Rasaal Pankajarenugandhi
Gajaaya Gantushajalam Karenuha
Ardhopabhukthena Bisena Jayaam
Sambhavayamasa Radhanganama.'

(While the gods showered flowers, the angels started to sing, playing *thamburu* [a stringed musical instrument])

But as he kept his life air under control, God Sree Sankara stuck firm to his meditation like rainy clouds not hurrying to rain, or an ocean free of waves or a lamp with steady flames not affected by wind.)

'Atmeswaranaam Na Hi Jathu Vignaha
Samadhibedhaprabhavo Bhavanthi.'

(Real purity means subduing the senses [*Shouchamindiya Nigrahaha*]. Obstacles never have the power to break the samadhi of gods who ruled souls.)

Getting fearful on seeing the burning *thejus* (vigour) of Thrikkannan (the three-eyed Paramasiva), Kamadeva hid and waited for a chance to shoot the flower arrow.

Then he saw Parvathy Devi coming, accompanied by two angels of the forest. Devi walked with slow steps wearing ornaments made of spring flowers like ashoka (Saraca indica) that defeated ruby in beauty, konnappoo (the golden shower cassia) that outshone gold and karinochi (Vitex negundo, commonly known as the five-leaved chaste tree) flowers that resembled pearl chains. It is quite natural for creeper plants to bend when carrying a heavy bunch of flowers. Though a little bit naughty, the narration of Kalidasa is alluring:

> *'Aavarjitha Kinchidhiva Sthanaabhyaam*
> *Vaso Vasanaa Tharunarkkaragam*
> *Sujathapushpasthabakaavanamraa*
> *Sancharinee Pallavinee Latheva.'*

(Because of bending forward a little for the weight of breasts and wearing dresses that were shining like the rising sun, Parvathy looked like a walking plant that was bending forward, full of flowers and decorated with tender leaves.)

Uma devotedly dedicated the flowers of spring starting season at the holy feet of Siva. She also dedicated a chain made of the seeds of lotus growing in the Mandakini River.

Selecting the apt time when Siva's mind was moved a bit like the sea at the time of moon rise, Kamadeva shot the never-missing arrow called Sammohanam.

It is quite interesting to hear the great Vyasa Muni narrating Parvathy-Parameswara marriage. Saptharshis calculated the good time for the marriage. (The Saptharshi are the seven rishis who are extolled at many places in the Vedas and Hindu literature. The Vedic Samhitas never enumerate these rishis by name, though later Vedic texts such as the Brahmanas and Upanishads do so as Vasishta, Viswamithra, Kasyapa, Jamadagni, etc. They are regarded in the Vedas as the patriarchs of the Vedic religion.)

They held that in Utharayana (Meenam month) and Uthram star there was an auspicious moment with Chandrabhalam (positive moon influence) and Tharabhalam (positive star influence) with pure Ezham Bhavam (an astrological position) and opined that the marriage festival might be held on that day.

> *'Shwo Muhurthasshubhofthruntham*
> *Falgunyorutharakhyayoha*
> *Rashou Jamithrasamshudhe*
> *Dheya Dhevaya Parvathee'*
> —Skanda Purana-Sambhavakandam

Himavan engaged Thwashtav (Vishwakarmav), the chief architect of heaven, to build the marriage pavilion.

> *'Thathaha Preethamanasshilpee*
> *Vishwakarmafthra Sambramath*
> *Chakara Mandapam Kshipram*
> *Manasaa Manipeshalam.'*[6]
> —Skanda Purana-Sambhavakandam

The beautiful marriage pavilion built by Vishwakarmav was one lakh *yojana* long and one lakh yojana wide.[7]

It was luxuriously decorated with diamonds and pearls. At some places, one would feel fresh water flowing whereas at other places, one would feel ocean waves hitting the shores. The vast ground was full of streams, lakes, lotus ponds and green meadows and was artfully combined with different types of pillars, turrets, small pavilions in diverse colours and gates adorned with beads of pearls and corals.

With the compound wall like trees standing in a queue, the pavilion appeared to be rare and beautiful.

On that day, Parvathy was made up by the wives of gods, wives of rishis, wives of kings, Adithi, Dithi, Swahadevi, Suparni, Surasa, Anasooya and Arundathidevi. Singing propitious songs, oil was applied on Parvathy's head, who was sitting to face the rising sun. When auspicious music by *kombu* (a wind instrument in the shape of natural horn), etc., was sounded, Uma was bathed. After that, holy water kept in small pots was showered on to the head of the heroine of the world. The thick hair was tied up with pure cloth and Devi was dressed with high quality silk. Artistically decorating Parvathy's hands and legs with henna, the *navaratna* (nine gems)-studded *kalchilambu* (anklets worn by dancers) and gold anklets were added to her legs. After ornamenting her with the gold *oddyaanam* (girdle worn by ladies on the waist) and many diamond and turquoise-studded chains, *thoda* and *kundalam* (earrings) were fitted on her ears. And when a glowing nose-ring was fitted on her handsome nose, bangles studded with navaratna worn on hands and small garlands of chemba flowers (a flower with alluring fragrance) were done on her hair, Uma was glistening in heavenly beauty. Her beauty was multiplied when she was affixed with *sindhooram*[8] (saffron) on her forehead and applied *kanmashi* (collyrium) on her eyes that were as beautiful as black *koovala* (bael tree) flowers.

> '*Ksheerodhavelaeva Safenapuncha*
> *Paryaapthachandreva sharaththriyama*
> *Navam Navakshoumanivasinee Sa*
> *Bhooyo babhou Dharpanamadhadhana.*'[9]
> —Kumarasambhavam (7–26)

I woke up and spent a little more time melted in the romantic sweetness of Kalidasa's classic work *Kumarasambhavam*. Something had happened here in the previous age. Each cell of this icy land might be carrying the shadowy images of those times. Unbeatable even by time, they still resided in human minds in all clarity.

When it was after 6, I went to the kitchen and drank a cup of hot tomato soup. I told Roop Bahadur Thapa, the chief cook, that I wouldn't be there for dinner in the night and would come only late that night after having food from Padham Singh's dhaba and seeing the full moon from there. Roop Bahadur was one of the chief cooks of the Tourism Department. I maintained a good friendship with him from Gunji itself. When he saw me washing the plates after eating food, he came near and said politely that he and his aides would clean them. I had told Roop Bahadur at Gunji that washing your own dish after food was the right way and I always tried to keep that habit. It was after that incident that the cooks kept a close relationship with me. They considered me as one among them or as a brother. I also believed that cleaning the toilet and bathroom and washing our clothes ourselves was the fair way.

Four members of our team were bedridden because of high fever and headache and were put into the same tent. All were fearful on seeing such symptoms. Since two travellers were affected with jaundice at the Gunji camp, ample precautions were taken. The liaison officer announced that nobody was to go out to Adi Kailash to see Pournami (full moon) and the decision was to see and enjoy it from the courtyard of the camp and that too for a little time only. Waving goodbye to everybody, I moved towards the dhaba. While nearing the dhaba, I saw the horse people and porters stand up, breaking the cards game they were engaged in.

Once, I had advised them that playing cards for money was not a fair way in life and that would be the start of destruction for them and their family. I had talked about this to Raju also while we were walking to Pandava Mountains at noon. I sat with them in their shed and spent some time inquiring about how life went for them.

Even though they were used to liquor and playing cards, all of them were pure in mind. It was with the money they earned in the season that they lived later. After the season, winter came. During that time, they migrated to the nearby towns. They spent the daytime doing hotel jobs or coolie work and took shelter in cinema halls in the night. Hindi films and their songs always thrilled them. They would see the same film repeatedly. The rest of the time left in the night they would sleep, thickly packed in bedding in some small room taken on rent. In the morning, they would go to work and the same process was repeated. They spent what they earned on costly liquor and cigarettes that were not available in their places. For the new generation, passing time in winter in their villages was very difficult. They couldn't think of spending months in a tiny house all shut off.

Most of them returned to their villages in the last days of winter. Some would stick to the towns if they had got good jobs. After their return, they would toil in their own lands for some time. The pilgrim season would begin then. That was their life. They loved their mule, horse and yak like their own soul. They might spend time hungry but would never leave the animals to starve. Let those animals be in whatever herds, they would recognize the whistling of their boss. Their names were also interesting. The animals were called by local names such as Munna, Govind, Nirdhara, Petpal, Basanthy, Mothi, Bindu, Heera, Shyama, Gouri, Ganga, Yamuna, Krishna, Thara, Radha, etc., and also by modern names such as Amrish Puri, Danny, Hero, Amitabh, etc.

After bowing before Adi Kailash and rendering the evening prayer, I rested in the dhaba. Padham Singh Kutiyal and his family attended to me most politely. When he asked me what I preferred for dinner, I insisted that roti and sabji (cooked vegetables) were enough. We spent time drinking black tea and having potato chips. Since the climate was clear, I was almost sure to see the full moon. Though it was still daylight, the brightness of moonlight began to appear. But the cold was unbearable. It was a big relief when Padham Singh lit the fire and shifted our seats near it. I requested him to narrate in detail the unforgettable incident that had happened to him in Adi Kailash. I specially instructed him to be honest when disclosing such spiritual happenings. After bowing in the direction of the Kailash Mountain area and vowing to be truthful, Padham Singh began narrating the experience.

Ten years had passed since Padham Singh had had the experience. He was born in a farmer family of Kuti Village. Since childhood, he was engaged in the work of carrying agricultural products on horseback to Dharchula. Initially, locally distilled liquor was used only to drive away the cold on his trips but gradually, it became regular drinking. Thus, his income dwindled. The situation didn't change even though he came to have a family. It was almost a daily scene for him to be lying somewhere drunk. It was Padham Singh's father who secured the right to run a dhaba in Jolingkong for the military men who were on guard duty at Lampiya and Mangsa passes. The father sent the son there under compulsion. Also sent with him were his wife and grown-up children. More than the income from the dhaba, the father's aim was the luxurious green meadows around. Feed for the herds of sheep and donkeys for six months were sufficiently available there. Besides the military people, the dhaba also turned useful for the adventurers who came on mountaineering trips from the Sela, Dhungtu and Bedang side and for isolated sanyasins. As Padham Singh had to mingle daily with armymen, his habit of drinking liquor was eventually controlled. In the beginning, the control caused Padham Singh many physical problems but later, he became used to it. Hearing that the Tourism Department in association with the Central and state governments was going to conduct pilgrimage trips to Adi Kailash, Padham Singh became more energetic. But it took years to become a reality. Once, it was a full moon day, like now. Around 6 p.m., a group of soldiers came to have food and then went back to the passes. Since there were no other guests, Padham Singh and family went to bed early. He had gone to sleep after safely tying up a dozen yaks he had purchased recently and also after herding sheep and mules into a circular den made of plastic cord. His honest dogs were also there supervising the animals. As was his regular practice, he drank a glass of liquor. He was a devotee but since childhood, was not overtly devotional like the people in mountainous regions. He mentally calculated the overall turnover from the business for the day and then slipped into sleep.

Often, he sobbed while describing the embarrassing events that happened later.

Padham Singh awoke from his sleep hearing some sounds. It took some time for him to regain his senses. Hearing the sounds of thamburu (a stringed musical instrument) and *chilanka* (the musical anklet) for some time, Padham Singh became curious to find out where they were coming from. His first impression was that it might be the soldiers on guard at the passes making the sounds. But hearing laughter like the ringing of a bell and the voices of men and women, Padham Singh sat up in his bed. But who was making those noises at his place without him knowing? The activities seemed to be going on just near his dhaba. Padham Singh opened the dhaba door and came out. The moonlight was spread like daylight. He grew confused seeing his animals sleeping as if dead, putting their heads down to one side. Normally, animals do not sleep in such a way. Also, the dogs were not in the vicinity. Clearly hearing the rhythmic jingle of chilanka and the sweet sounds of thamburu and singing, Padham Singh understood that they were from Adi Kailash.

With increased curiosity, he walked some steps ahead. He remembered what he saw then in a flash.

Adi Kailash was shining in sharp brightness. Men and women were dancing together! Their clothes were glowing in sparkling colours. The men had the look of gods! The ladies resembled goddesses! The sound of eternal music melted hearts.

Padham Singh remembered nothing else.

Early the next morning, Padham Singh's wife saw him sleeping in the courtyard. She was looking for him after putting the pot of water for tea on the stove. Sometime later, she learnt that her husband was lying unconscious. Suddenly, she screamed and her children awoke from their sleep. Though his body was frozen, faint and shallow breathing was being sustained. A group of soldiers came that way while Padham Singh's children were wiping him with hot water and massaging his body. Hearing what had happened, the soldiers poured brandy into Padham Singh's mouth drop by drop and fed him some tablets. They also bent and straightened his legs and hands for some time. Padham Singh came to life again. He sat up and told them what happened.

Padham Singh became a pure Siva devotee after that incident. He went near Adi Kailash many times and did meditation on all those occasions. Now, he had endless belief in that great power and everything he devoted to Him. Big changes occurred in his life and life pattern. He now had savings to be proud of. Only in the winter season, he would consume some liquor. He used to shift residence to Kuti Village on full moon days. It was after a long time that he started coming back on the full moon day. Wonderful things might not happen on all full moon nights. Maybe it was a heavenly moment that day. The people residing in Bedang Village that was situated on the other side of Adi Kailash had the same opinion. They too had many unbelievable experiences like Padham Singh.

After that fantastic day, Padham Singh paid attention to his animals only the next day. The place where the yaks were tied up seemed as if it had been ploughed. Looking horror-stricken, as if they had seen something, the animals lived for some days with bulging eyes and raised ears. They did not touch the feed or drink. Out of horror, they had cried loudly and beaten the land. That was why the land looked like it had been ploughed. The herds of sheep also responded in the same way.

After this long narration by Padham Singh, I sat thinking. I felt that rather than the gods and goddesses coming down to earth, the logic was more suited to yogis and yoginis from Shangri-La (Sidhashramam) assembling at Adi Kailash. It was not proper to ignore the incident as a mere fantasy of the villagers. The Buddhist monks residing on the banks of Manasarovar and the tribals settled there earlier had told me of similar incidents that happened to them (please refer to chapter 12, page 135 of my book *Uttarakhandiloode-Kailash Manasarovar Yathra*). During the Kailash-Manasarovar journey, I had tried to collect more details about this by talking to the tribals, villagers and other Tibetan residents. All of them were firm on the matter of the bathing of fairies (Apsaras). They could not forget their animals losing consciousness and dogs groaning for long periods of time. Presuming that Shangri-La existed at a mysterious land between Kailash-Manasarovar and Adi Kailash, there was nothing wrong in thinking that the yoginis from there came to Manasarovar to bathe. Similarly, it seemed to be no exaggeration to say that they assembled at Adi Kailash for one heavenly moment.

I interrogated Padham Singh and his wife one after the other in the hope of getting any details that they might have forgotten. While Padham Singh told me that he didn't remember anything else, his wife pointed out about the long moaning of dogs. I sought nothing else but this—the moaning of dogs. Only dogs had the special power to see formless objects at night. They would start to growl fearfully then.

If a dog moaned in such a way, we could fairly guess that there was something invisible in the surroundings. Such thinking had been prevalent since the ancient days among the people. It might be because dogs possessed such a power that they had become the saviours and constant companions of men.

Other animals were just responding to dogs' signals. Padham Singh's wife told me that she clearly heard their dogs making long growls when she had woken up from her sleep sometime in the night. I was convinced that what was said to have happened in Adi Kailash was true.

Food was served after 8 p.m. Since the roti, potato curry and green leaf sabji were cooked in pure ghee, they had a rare, delicious taste. I used to take in roti without ghee but this time, I had to break the habit owing to its delicious smell. The horse attendants and porters had food after us. Feeling extremely cold, we decided to sleep until midnight. Everybody went to bed in the belief that Padham Singh would wake us up at that time. Arranging a convenient sleeping place for me on his box, Padham Singh lay on the floor to sleep. After prayers, I lay to sleep with my body fully covered under the sheet. My mind was full of the shining full moon.

When Padham Singh woke me up, the time was past midnight. We walked out, covering ourselves with a thick woollen sheet. While Padham Singh was trying to wake up the horse attendants, I had a look at the animals. Closing their eyes and chewing, they were in peaceful sleep. The dogs gently waving their tails stood close to us. It was clear then that there was no non-human existence on that full moon night.

We walked towards Adi Kailash.

Everyone sat at a convenient spot away from the riverbank. I found my place comparatively at a distance. I sat alone a little far away because the horse aides had the habit of speaking without pause and sitting with them meant losing concentration. Jolingkong stood bathed in jasmine-like moonlight. The midnight moon stood peacefully in between the snowy mountains, its size lighting up each cell of the earth. Tiny pieces of ice falling down from the mountains were like bursting cotton buds. They were sparkling in the moonlight. It looked like the light of a thousand glow-worms. The snowy land was silent. Even though it was severely cold, we did not feel it, sitting absorbed in the beauty of the icy land. The light from the moon was not inhibited even when clusters of white clouds passed through. The sky was full of stars. The star standing just above Adi Kailash had a rare light. It was also big in size. The clear sky that stood like an umbrella over Jolingkong, its borders decorated with snowy mountains, the stars shining in it like diamonds and the bright smiling moon, like the queen of all, gave an incomparable feast to the eyes. Were the drops of ice shining in the moonlight asking the stars above them to come down? As a silent witness and unchanging with the expression of 'Yadha Prahladhanaachchandra ha' (because it cheers up, it had got the name Chandra), Rakendhu[10] stood showering milky light. The king of the sky was, no doubt, the moon. The saying was that 'Raja Prakruthiranjanal' (the king cheers up his subjects). Kailash was an amazing phenomenon. The Kailash of Tibet and the Kailash of Jolingkong had obvious differences. While the Tibetan Kailash stood shoulder to shoulder with clouds in the shape of a 'reactor', that in Jolingkong stood as a vast universe of snow in an arch shape. There was such a structure on the back of Kailash in Tibet too. While the topmost peak on the left end of Adi Kailash hid inside the clusters of clouds, the rest of the area was not that high. And while Adi Kailash was always covered under thick ice, the other Kailash stood bathed in different colours. We could see that divine wonder as fire, as dipped in gold, as Siva Linga, as partly covered by ice and as fully covered under heavy snow. The figure glistening in golden brilliance was a real marvel. Such beauties of colour were not visible in Adi Kailash.

But there was uniformity in the structure of rock of both Kailash. When you looked through binoculars at those parts of Adi Kailash which were not covered under ice, it could be understood that they were layers of rock such as compacted gravel. By way of pressure imposed for centuries, the small boulders formed a complex mix with which were built the walls of Kailash. There was an argument that those boulders were salagrama placed one over another (the salagrama stones are extremely sacred black stones found in the holy Kali river valley in the Himalayas. There is a natural marking of Sudharsana Chakra on them). It was estimated that the age of the Kailash walls was not less than the Eocene age, i.e., 5,50,00,000 years (Eocene age: the period during which lava cooled and became a solid substance over the earth's crust). The salagramas are rolls of fossils (*ashmakam*) that were found under the Tethys Ocean in the Jurassic age. They were living things. Even before modern science understood it, Indians had the knowledge of fossils. We worship salagram as an image of Vishnu. In 1940, Swami Pranavanandaji collected many salagramas of top-class quality from Kuti Village. It was for the purpose of research for Banaras Hindu University that Swamiji engaged in this activity. The university honoured him by conferring a doctorate on him. Swamiji discovered that besides Kuti Village, there were lakhs and lakhs of salagrama under the thick ice of Tinker, Lipu, Dharma, Kankar-Binkar and Neethi passes.

Sunk in deep thoughts, I noticed Padham Singh after a long time. He was dozing in his seat. I told him to go back to the dhaba. The horse attendants had all gone even before that. For company, I had Padham Singh's dog with me. By giving it food, I had made it my friend. The poor animal showed gratitude by lying just near me on guard. After Padham Singh had gone, I again fell into thoughts.

I spent time thinking about salagrama.

'Studies about fossils have shed light on the origin of Salagrama. By bones becoming ossified, the reflections of animals get stamped on rocks. Fossils are such semi three-dimensional pictures. Greek philosopher Xenophanes of Colophon who lived in the sixth century BC discovered the fossils of cowries on mountain tops and assumed that those mountains were once under sea. It was William Smith, an Englishman who paved the way for the scientific studies of fossils. In 1791, when a land survey was being done and small channels for it were being dug, he discovered that the rocks cut for the purpose were lying in different layers and each layer had its genuine fossil. Each layer of rock represented different geological periods. Thus, a way was opened to categorize fossils according to age. A new branch of science, stratigraphy, was thus started. In 1965, Elso Stairanberg Bargoon, an American expert on fossils, discovered with the help of an electron microscope the fossils of bacteria three hundred crore years old. It was thus proved that a long history of life existed.'[11]

There is detailed description of salagrama in our Puranas. It is a stone that should be worshipped in all purity. The God-present substance, salagrama (Shaligram—ammonite stone) is a mixture of minerals. It has life. Most suitable for worship is lifeless salagrama. Salagramas that have life will seem to be moving when put in the worship place (pooja room). Such salagramas should be kept in silver bowls full of water. Bathing in water is essential for salagramas, both with life or lifeless. The Bhagavatham describes about nineteen types of salagramas. If these holy stones that are in essence incarnations of God Vishnu are not properly worshipped, it would not be fortunes coming but tragedies.

'Kamasakthofdhavaa Krudhdhaha
Salagramashilaarchanal
Bhakthya Vaa Yadhi Vaafbhakthya

Kalou Nukthimavapnuyal
Vaivaswathabhayam Nasthi
Thadha cha Kalikalajam.'[12]

—Skanda Purana

Skanda Purana also tells us about the origin of salagrama. In the past, when Devas (gods) and Assuras (demons, the traditional enemies of gods) together churned Palazhi (ocean of milk), a pot of Amruth (the nectar of immortality) rose from it, which the Assuras snatched and went away with. For getting it back and giving it to the gods, God Mahavishnu Himself incarnated as an extremely beautiful woman called Mohini and trapped the Assuras in Maya (illusion). Enchanted by the extreme beauty of Mohini, Maha Deva longed to have sexual relations with her. Thus, the Siva-Vaishnava splendours merged together and Dharmasastha or Hariharaputhra (Lord Ayyappa) was born. Sree Parameswara advised his son to safeguard dharma (righteousness) when it was in peril. He also blessed him that he would never fail in anything. It was the incarnation of Dharmasastha named Hariharaputhra who took birth as Manikandan to kill Mahishi[13] (the buffalo-headed female demon).

'*Aevam Thayohasujathathwaal Sasthafpi cha Thadhafbhavath*
Harer harasyaapi Thadha Puthrathwamithi Bhavitham.'[14]
—Skanda Puranam-Assurakandam

The vomit of Mohini became River Kandaki (Gandaki). A kind of worm called *vajradandham* originated in that river. Those water bugs make shells to live in on the riverbanks using a kind of strong clay. When the water flow in the river increases, the bugs in the mud shells get destroyed.

But their strong shells would fall to the river and go with the flow. There would be a little bit of gold at the centre of the shells. Or there would be holy signs. Since these worm-shells came into being from the vomit of Mahavishnu, Indians worship salagrama as a secondary incarnation of Mahavishnu. And because Sree Parameswara also has a role in the history of salagramas, they are also worshipped in poojas like Sivapooja that are observed to praise and please Parama Siva. In the Panchayathana pooja, conducted as per the dictum 'Aadhithyamambikaam Vishnum Ganannadham Maheswaram', salagrama is worshipped, considering it Mahavishnu. Each salagrama will have one hole on it. If we look through the hole carefully, we can see a forked line like a wheel. It is believed to be the Sudharsana Chakra. Scholars will tell us what incarnation a salagrama represents on the basis of the number and character of the forked line of it. Salagramas of the size of a gooseberry or less is considered to belong to the top class.

The Padmapurana also says that worshipping salagrama and Sree Chakra ensures eternal liberation.[15]

I sat there looking at Adi Kailash standing bathed in the full moonlight. I recollected again and again the beauty of the Kailash of Tibet. The lower portion of this Linga-shaped Kailash was known as Brahma Bhaga. It represented Lord Brahma. The central portion, known as Vishnu Bhaga, stood for Mahavishnu and the top portion, called Rudra Bhaga, stood for Parama Siva. There were three parallel lines on the Rudra Bhaga. They were called Thripund. They denoted the holy trinity (Brahma-Vishnu-Maheswara) who were the masters of the three worlds and the three qualities but were not restricted by any of them.

The Smruthis tell that the four faces of Kailash are made of glass, coral, gold and sapphire. All Kailash are Panchakshari[16]. They have five faces but the fifth face is invisible. The eastern face, based on the principle of power, represents the universal concept 'bliss'. The god of this is Maha Deva (Siva). The southern face of meditation is the symbol of the universal concept 'wisdom'. Bhairava (a fierce manifestation of Siva) is the god of this. The western face, based on the principle 'desire', involves the universal concept 'arrogance'. The deity of this is Nandhi (the white bull on which Lord Siva rode). The northern face, which embodies the core principle of 'good learning', represents the universal concept of 'Manasa' (mind). Uma is the deity of this. The fifth face, which is not subject to day and night, is completely invisible. Parama Siva is the supreme soul and Parvathy is the pure soul. Siva is pure inner knowledge; he is reality, eternity and omnipresent. When the force of power with the illusionary shape called Sakthimaya appears with body and mind, everlasting inner knowledge comes to being in the shape of power with virtue. Sakthimaya is known by many names such as Parvathy, Kali, Uma, Durga, Shodasy, Bhavani, Thripurasundari, Vedamatha, etc.[17] Parama Siva is relative; Sakthi (power) gives energy. Siva is the guardian of Vedajnana (the Veda knowledge), wisdom and the unity of universe. He is the liberator from the vicious circle called birth and death. The Kailashas are the noble expression of Siva. Even a thought about Maha Deva is removal of the veil of illiteracy and ignorance and liberation from the tie with the material world which is full of tragedies and enjoyments.

Each footstep of Indhuchoodan (Siva who carries the moon on his head), who is also the Tripuraanthaka (the destroyer of Thripura), has been the echo of the rhythm of this universe. (Thripura means three cities constructed by the great Assura architect Mayasura. They were great cities of prosperity, power and dominance over the world, but due to their impious nature, Maya's cities were destroyed by God Tripuraanthaka.)

I woke up after 3 a.m. The snowfall had increased in the meanwhile. Though snow had been falling like feeble rain, there was no decrease in the glow of moonlight. While going to Parvathy Sarass, I had noticed a small lake at the end of the meadow. At the same instant, I had mentally noted to see and enjoy the hearty sight of lotus blossoms blooming in the lake in the moonlight. When I started to walk, the dog also came with me. The poor animal was tamed after I had fed it for two days. Only a dog had the quality of returning selfless love for love and sacrificing even its own life to save the life of its boss. After we had moved up about half a kilometre through the empty ground, the dog stopped suddenly. I also stopped. The dog began to growl looking at the left side. It was sure that the dog growled because it was seeing some beast. There was no other reason. In the beautiful moonlight where we could see even a tiny grasshopper clearly, I looked carefully at the place where the dog was looking. When I saw glowing eyes from a burrow in the meadow, I knew that it was a big mole. Bigger than wild rabbits, those creatures dug very deep holes under soil.

They stocked cereals and other food items required to last for about six or seven months in those holes. When snow about 10 feet thick covered the area after the month of November, they withdrew into the holes and lived there. There was another type of yellow rat in the area which dug holes to live in icy mountains. They spent the whole snowy season in hibernation without food. For every creature in the world, nature had arranged security in one way or the other.

The lake adjoining the marshy land was small. A heart would melt at the sight of big red lotus flowers smiling at the moon. The moon was also lying in the lake! Any mind would cheer in ecstasy. As Kalidasa put it, one who looked at the lake would get confused as to what was more beautiful—the moon or the lotus? And when looking at the sky, he would ponder as to what would surpass the moon in beauty. How enticing was Kalidasa's imagination!

'Chandram Gatha Padmagunan Na Bhumkthe
Padmasritha Chaandramaseemabhikhyaam.'

(Didn't get the qualities of the lotus when I went to the moon; didn't get the light of the moon when I went to the lotus.)

The propitious time, Brahmamuhurta,[18] had arrived. I recollected while walking back to dhaba. Which one was more beautiful—the full moon or the alluring moonlight? Sky or stars? Which one was better? The whiteness of snow peaks or the loveliness of green grass meadow? Or was the red lotus wearing the pearl chain of snow drops the prettiest? Slowly, I walked ahead, humming the lines of 'Irayimman Thampi', which had the metaphor 'Sasandheham', in which suspicion of whether this or that was good arose because of similarity.

'Omanathinkal Kidavo-Nalla
Komalathamara Poovo
Poovil Niranja Madhuvo-Nalla
Poornendu Thante Nilavo.'

(Is he the darling baby of the moon?
Or is he the beautiful lotus flower?
Is he honey filled in a flower?
Or is he the cheering light of the full moon?)

17

The Return Journey

I

Though I could sleep only for two hours, I did not feel the weariness of travelling. The liaison officer seemed worried, for more than half of the team had already left in two stages. There was no way to know whether they had reached the respective camps. Our team started the journey at 7 a.m. sharp. Breakfast and lunch were given to us in parcels. We gave money to the cooks and their helpers as a present. Expressing gratitude, we bid them goodbye. Padham Singh also came to see us off. Looking at Adi Kailash and bowing, I prayed:

> *'Lokaanugrahahethwartham*
> *Sthiro Bhava Sukhaya Naha*
> *Saannidhyam cha Thadha Deva*
> *Prathyaham Parivardhaya.'*
> — *Thanthrasamuchayam*

(Oh, God, please make your presence permanent for blessing all the world. And always shine thy Lordship for our good!)

The liaison officer, the advocate and Mahajan were ready to travel on foot. So it was certain that Raju and I would get somebody to travel with. The horse attendants and their group had already gone. We would meet them at Kuti.

The climate was not at all pleasant. The cloudy sky and chilling wind were completely different as was on the previous day. Visibility was also very weak because of the snow falling like threads. Since the majority of the paths in the return trip were descending, exhaustion would not be felt. Rain might fall any time. We stopped at Phoolkiwar for breakfast. Then the memories of the shepherd boy, Prem Singh, came to me. I looked all around in search of the little shepherd and his herds of sheep, but nothing could be found. Maybe he was standing guard for the herd of sheep in some distant hill valleys. While having food, I told my friends about the boy. My narration about him touched all their hearts. Mahajan's eyes filled with tears. The advocate stopped eating and sat thinking.

I tried to pacify my friends by quoting the Bhagavat Gita sentence that a *mumukshu* is the one who instead of trying to find a solution for sadness, tolerates it (a mumukshu is the one who is intensely yearning for liberation from the cycles of birth and death).

'*Maathraasparshasthu Kountheya*
Sheethoshnasukhadukhadhaha
Aagamaapaayino Nithya-
Sthamsthithikshaswa Bharatha.'[1]

We continued our journey after drinking water from the streams. When it was sure that it would rain, we took shelter under a rock projecting outward. Since it was the resting place of sheep, it was full of sheep excreta about 1 foot thick. We sat on the stones placed for the purpose of cooking and making fire. When the rain became heavy, strong wind also began to blow. The burj trees on the hill slopes waved in the wind, as if welcoming rain. I also joined in their happiness. Rain is the blessing of nature. It should pour down at the right time.

After half an hour, the force of the rain decreased. Though the downpour on level lands became less, the excessive level of water in the Kunthi River showed that heavy rainfall was continuing in the snowy mountains. When the descending path by the side of the river became slippery due to rain, the journey became hard. After quickly eating lunch, we continued without resting. During the journey, we saw a group of sanyasins staying in tents in a vast plain area and we stopped. Going near their tents, we talked with them for some time. When they learnt that we were returning from Adi Kailash and Parvathy Sarass after getting dharshan (auspicious sight), a middle-aged man, seemingly the head of the six-member group suddenly became angry. We didn't know who he was angry with. He took from his pocket the permission letter of the Additional District Magistrate (ADM) of Dharchula and after throwing it down to the ground, began scolding the superior officers with filthy language. The sanyasins had a permission letter with them but the military officers had given strict orders not to let them go beyond the army office 2 km ahead of Adi Kailash. Boiling with anger, he asked what justice it was. Adi Kailash was the right example of the spiritual vigour of India, he said, and demonstrated the unwavering commitment of its people to their cultural heritage, evident in their determination to preserve it by not allowing others to approach it closely. To the advocate's suggestion that Swamiji could have conducted the journey easily by contacting the Tourism Department of Uttaranchal state, he replied that it was his fundamental right to decide on how he should travel and warned that the advocate need not interfere in this matter.

I picked up the permission letter the Swamiji had thrown away and read it. I had observed the sanyasins listening to the dialogues of their head. Their long hair, lengthy beards, red ochre cloth (the usual dress of sanyasins), chains made of *rudraksha*[2] beads and prayer beads seemed to be only a veil. The fatty body, big stomach, wristwatch with golden strap, spectacles with golden frame, rudraksha threaded with gold and highly costly and foreign-made woollen clothes, raincoats and shoes were surely not the signs of true sanyasins. Also, the anger and contempt did not suit them. Nowadays, sanyasins were interested only in amassing wealth and engaging in material enjoyment. The activities of such people were the main reason for the downgrading of the Hindu religion. Though there were many true sanyasins, unfortunately, the majority were the opposite. What was need of so much money for sanyasins? If the money was coming in by reasons beyond their control, what they should do was to make them go to deserving hands. '*Shadhahastha Samaahara Sahasrahastha Samkira*' was what Adharva Veda had said.[3] What the true sanyasins or their groups should do was to uplift the common man spiritually, economically and academically.

Giving him the permission letter he had thrown and bowing my head, I told the Swamiji, 'You hadn't noticed the last part of the ADM's order—subject to the final approval of ITBP and Indian Army officials. The magistrate who had signed it sitting in a faraway office might not know the seriousness or severity of affairs there. So it was the army people who *were* to give the final approval. Many precautions were needed while travelling through strategically important border areas. What an ordinary citizen should think of first was the safety and security of his country. The rest came only after that. As Swamiji knew, the China border was just an arm's length away. I am sorry to say that your filthy words and abuse had crossed the limits. Om Namah Sivaya.'

The Swamiji did not shout at me like he had done with the advocate. With serious, bulging eyes he stared at me. While walking away, I remembered the assessment of Sri Sankaracharya about such people.

'Jatilo Mundee Lunchithakeshaha
Kaashayambara Bahukrutha Veshaha
Passyanapi cha na Passyathi Mooda
Udharanimitham Bahukrutha Veshaha'[4]

The weather became clear after 2 p.m. but soon went back to its old condition. We reached Kuti Village at around 3 p.m. after passing through hazardous routes. Slowly sipping hot tea, we rested for some time in the tent. Since a team that included the ladies also had already left for Gunji in the early morning, there was enough space in the tent. Kakki had told me to surely meet her on my return. With the permission of the liaison officer, I walked towards Kakki's residence. After producing my permit in the army office, I engaged in conversation with them for a while. When I asked why the sanyasins were denied permission to go to Adi Kailash, the officer replied frankly. 'The sanyasins are not that innocent. When they made trouble in the ADM's office at Dharchula, they were given permits just to get rid of them. But they gave it with a condition that final approval must be taken from us. Many groups disappear at Adi Kailash. They go and hide in China through the passes there. Many of them are taken into custody in China. We learn the news only after a gap of months. This creates various problems. Matters become even more serious if ganja or other intoxicants are caught on them. That is why strict controls are imposed.'

Basanthi, Kakki's lady helper, ran towards me the moment she saw me. After exchanging regards, she led me to Kakki's room. After prostrating before Kakki, I told her about Adi Kailash. When I told her about the holy experience Padham Singh Kutiyal had on the full moon day, she replied that it was not a single incident. Such things had been happening in the Himalayas for centuries. Kakki confirmed that like angels who appeared at the time of holy birth, yoginis, Apsaras (nymphs) and other sky-goers do appear in the Himalayas. She told me that getting dharshan at Adi Kailash on the full moon night and during Pradhosha Vrutham,[5] taking a bath in Parvathy Sarass and collecting holy prasad (devotional offering) from under water, circling the Sarass by foot and the holy chance to go just near Adi Kailash were all because of God's special love for me. She also blessed me to have the ability to convey the holy experience to the people of my native place and thus help bring all-round progress to them also. She said that there was no chance of having another meeting with me in this birth and hoped to meet me in our next birth with more brilliance if God wished it so. She requested me to narrate in my book the relevant parts of the long conversation of that night in its originality and depict the incidents exactly as they happened when she sat in Yoga Nidra. She told me that on our way back, some distance away from Kuti Village, there was a burj tree forest on the top of the mountain and asked me to cut the skin from one of the holy trees and take it to my native place. After having tea and snacks and once again prostrating before Kakki and getting her blessings, I returned to the camp.

The joy of getting dharshan of Adi Kailash without any serious problems was evident in the camp. Pudding made of semiya (vermicelli) was served after dinner. When the drizzle and the force of blowing wind became unbearable, we took shelter in our beds. I lay down after prayers and good night wishes and was quite unaware of when I fell into a deep sleep.

II

I woke up at around 4.30 and came out of the camp shed. Kuti Village seemed silent and peaceful. In preparation for sunrise, the eastern horizon was lit up. Revealing a world of colour, the sun rose slowly. Snowy mountains stood bathed in red colour. Indeed, it was a very beautiful morning!

I talked with the liaison officer about going to the burj tree forest and obtained permission from him. He also arranged a horse keeper, Mukesh Kumar, as an aide. Mukesh Kumar was a local who clearly knew the way up to the forest. The liaison officer and the group decided to go on horseback. After packing breakfast and putting it into my shoulder bag, I bid goodbye to the friends, cooks and villagers and walked ahead with friends who were accompanying me to the forest.

We reached the base of the forest area after walking 2 km from Kuti Village. We crossed the Kunthi River at a wide but low flow area and rested for some time. Mukesh Kumar warned us that the way up was through rock structures and very steep. Missing a step meant falling into the bottomless depth of the river. Hence, we must be very careful while climbing up. He had climbed the mountain many times before as a helper to trekkers and informed me that shortage of oxygen would be felt at a height of 20,000 feet. Also, he said that it was a time when ice would not melt and so after half the way, we would have to walk through thick ice.

The climb was, no doubt, very hard. The area was teeming with monoliths, and we had to circumnavigate them to ascend. Mukesh had with him a plastic rope used to tie up luggage on horses and it turned out to be very useful for me. My friends would first climb up the steep pathways and then throw the rope towards me. I climbed clutching the rope. After we were through while climbing up very hazardous paths, we reached the ice land. This became a problem as our shoes went inside the ice completely while climbing up. The biggest threat was the low blood circulation in our legs. When hunger became unbearable, we took shelter in a crevice between rocks. Drinking glucose mixed with water, we slowly ate poori and potato curry. After eating, I removed my shoes and checked my feet. Though the skin had shrunk a bit, I felt no danger.

The burj trees of the area we were walking through had a diameter of around 50 inches only. Mukesh Kumar told us that we would see trees with a diameter of more than 100 inches when we reached the top. The bark used for writing was cut from trees having a minimum 150 inches diameter. This could be cut into any size. We went far ahead in the ice-covered area between the trees. Since it was a very thick forest, the sun's rays did not reach all the way down. It looked like night. There was a good chance of us sliding because of the fallen leaves on ice. So we were cautious at each step.

When we reached the top of the forest, I was totally exhausted. Raju also looked tired but Mukesh Kumar was not. Though a shortage of oxygen was felt, there was no problem in breathing. We rested for some time, lying down fully stretched and face upwards on monoliths that were not covered by ice. Since Mukesh Kumar had warned us earlier that the area was full of 'snow tigers', I cautiously watched all around for any movement. We spent time at the top with extreme caution because the area was in darkness and also while walking on ice no sound would come out. Sunrays filtered down only when the trees moved in the wind that blew occasionally. It was total silence when the wind did not blow. The profound silence induced considerable mental stress.

We spent a lot of time on the mountaintop looking at the burj trees with respect, bowing before them in devotion and patting them gently. It was on the bark of those divine trees that the matchless works of ancient India were expressed to the world. It was the greatest and holiest fate any object could get. I felt very happy in thinking that those trees had the chance to fructify a birth and make it worthwhile. My friends began cutting the skin from a full-grown tree.

The bark is formed wrapped around a tree. It consists of many layers and protects the tree like a shield. Burj is a very strong tree. Its wood is suitable for making furniture.

After making a cut on the tree skin about the size of a newspaper, Mukesh Kumar picked up a big piece. The skin would not be damaged if we folded or rolled it up like a cloth. Its surface was very smooth so that we could write on both sides. In the ancient times, the bark used to write on was of a particular growth whose green colour had not gone yet.

When we write on it using a *naraayam* (an instrument used to write in olden times) or any other sharp pointed things, the letters will be clear and legible as if they were written on a palm leaf. If we wrote on the dry bark using ink or a ball pen, the letters would also be very clear and legible as if written on a paper. In the Puranic ages, the divine bark was commonly used to thatch the roof of ashrams, hermitages and cottages, or worn as a dress to cover bodies and spread on floors as a mat. There was no other substance in the world that had so much influence in the arts, literary, cultural and social spheres of a great population.

Burj, the noble tree, has references in the Vedas, Puranas, Ithihasas and poetry. In *Kumarasambhavam* Kalidasa narrates,

> *'Ganaa Nameruprasavaavathamsa*
> *Burjathwachaha Sparshavatheervasaanaha*
> *Manaha Shila Vichchurithaa Nishedhuha*
> *Shaileyagandheshu Shilathaleshu.'*

('Crowned with Punna [mastwood] flower on the head,
wearing the dress of smooth burj bark and putting Manayola
[biosulphate of arsenic] paste on the forehead, the holy
spirits of Lord Siva sat on rock that had the fragrance
of Kanmadham [a sweet-smelling wax].')

We started our downward journey as Mukesh Kumar told
us that the climatic symptoms were not good and the change in
colour of the snowy mountains and the blowing cold wind were
indications as also warnings. Because my legs had been sunk in
thick ice for hours and hours, they pained a lot and a feeling
arose in me that I might not be able to walk independently.
When we reached level land, Raju massaged my legs after
removing my shoes. But the pain was still high and I had to
apply the painkilling spray Jesgo.

The climate that was pleasant till then began to darken.
We walked very fast with a firm decision to reach Nampha
Village before lunch. We went far ahead, passing many tough
up and down paths. The climate was worsening each moment.
The snowy wind made even breathing difficult. When the rain
clouds rolled in horribly, even noon seemed to be midnight.
Since rain was to come any moment, we wore our raincoats
and got ready. We feared that the fiercely blowing wind might
blow us away into the crevasses when walking through the very
narrow paths on the sides of the rocky mountain.

Rain came in roaring when we reached level land. It was
very heavy rain. Water flowed down from the mountains
around and filled up to our knees. Since our shoes were filled
with water, walking was a bit difficult. The rainwater was
freezing cold and the frigidness of my legs increased. It was
after walking for more than one hour that we reached the
resting place at Nampha. We sat near the fire, putting our shoes
nearby to dry. Learning about my leg pain, the dhabawala (the

man who ran the dhaba) gave me an ointment. Rubbing it, I spent a lot of time resting.

Noting the incessant rain, we discussed our plans. If the rain did not stop, the journey would turn out to be very difficult and painful for my legs. The time was nearly 2 p.m. and about half the way remained for us to travel. It was hazardous, unbearable and painful for my legs to travel through 10 km of heavy rain. We agreed to take a decision after lunch. While having hot roti and potato curry, I was thinking about the surprising climatic changes of the Himalayas.

It used to be a safe climate during May–June. The villagers of Kuti had also told me that such a heavy rain had not happened in the last thirty years. After withdrawing for ten days, it seemed that heavy rain was coming again. Or would it go away after a single downpour? More tragic was the plight of the villagers. Their farms and cultivation had gone away with one rain. They were to start from square one. Once again filling the land with soil, restarting cultivation . . . then might come another destructive rain. All their hopes were on their farmlands. When tragedy occurred there, their livelihood was lost.

Mukesh Kumar opined that it was better to go maybe slowly to the next village and stay there rather than spending the night in a leaking and shaky dhaba. I agreed with him. The space in the dhaba was much too little. The wind had blown away half of the roof of the second dhaba and the family there had been spending the night with us in our dhaba. Let whatever come, we decided to walk to our next destination.

I put on my shoes after spraying the medicine once again on my legs. Meanwhile, the rain had become lighter and that was a relief. Walking for about one hour through muddy lands and steep paths made the pain in my legs unbearable. Taking care to not skid while walking, I had to grip the toes tight inside the shoes and that was the reason for the pain to become so acute. The urge to reach the next village was in my mind all the time but the movement of my legs was gradually becoming slow. The rain stopped. However, the sky was still dark. With about 3 km to Nabhi Village, I sat on a rock, unable to walk further. I intimated to my friends that I would fall if I had to put a step further. Mukesh Kumar told me that there was a cave about 2 furlongs away. It stood on the inner side of the riverbanks. Hanging on to Raju's shoulders, I walked up and reached the cave with great effort.

The cave stood on plain, rocky land on the left side of the river. The entrance to it was very narrow. We had to first sit and then crawl into it. Mukesh Kumar told us that it was the camp of the shepherds and he himself had been there many times with his friends. Fully extending my legs, I sat on the stone in front of the cave and discussed the next schedule with my companions. Others in our camp would worry if they didn't see us. If the matter was reported to the ITBP, their patrolling team might start a search for us. It was good to avoid such a problem. The only solution was that one of us should go to Gunji and inform them of the matter. Since it was past 4 p.m., sending Raju through the forest area beyond Nabhi Village was not at all wise. Better than Raju, who was not acquainted with the area, was Mukesh Kumar, who knew the area thoroughly. He too was ready to go to.

Mukesh Kumar gave us courage by saying that wild animals were rare in that area and there was nothing to fear about sleeping in the cave. He gave us a lantern, a woollen sheet and a small aluminium pot from his luggage. He also handed over about half a kilogram of wheat flour and some potato and big onions that had been in his bag. Wishing us good luck, he went off. Horse attendants keep such things in their bags, to survive a problem that might unexpectedly arise any time during this type of trip.

Though the rain had stopped for the moment, the sky was still cloudy. Lightning could be seen in the distant horizon off and on. Raju was engaged in the job of cleaning the interior of the cave with small branches. I watched in curiosity at Raju driving away two creatures double the size of a lizard out of the cave. Those creatures, locally known as chipkali, were harmless. We burnt the dry leaves and branches of a tree called pamadhoop collected during our travel, a sweet fragrance like that of smoking ashtagandha[6] filled in the cave. Wandering around the bush in the area, Raju collected some dry shrubs. He was heard saying to himself that the shrubs would catch fire even if they were wet in rain. While he started to boil the potato and knead the wheat flour taking water from the river, I sat on the rock thinking.

Removing my socks, I checked my legs thoroughly. The nails had become light blue in colour. In the coming days, they would become black. This happened because of the decrease in blood circulation on the legs. The pain would be horrible when the damaged nails broke away from my toes. Urgent medical aid had to be sought as soon as we reached Gunji. Snow frost and gangrene are terrible diseases caught on Himalayan journeys. They were found only in high lands. The bacteria freely roamed those lands covered with thick ice and one could not say how and who would be affected. We could also expect their attack while we walked on glaciers. When unbearable pain like that from burns spread fast from the legs to the joints, the disease would turn serious. The next stage was urine becoming yellow in colour. After applying the first aid of dipping the hands and legs in hot water, rubbing with Dettol and water and spraying Jesgo on the affected areas, the patient should immediately go down the mountains and seek medical help in the plains. Only doctors or experienced travellers could identify whether it was snow frost or a disease of temporary low blood circulation. In 2006, a pilgrim from Thrissur aged about fifty years and having a healthy body was affected with gangrene during the journey to Kedar Dhamam. His legs had to be cut above the knee and hands below wrist. That incident showed the gravity of the disease.

When the water started boiling, I took some to massage my legs and hands. I applied the ointment the dhaba man had given me on my feet and rubbed it for some time. I thought I could walk after covering the damaged nails with bandages and then wearing the shoes. The medicine should also be sprayed on. I thought of many things while softly rubbing my feet. My legs had been rendering praiseworthy service to me for the last one month or so by carrying me over stones, thorns and up and down paths. If I had missed one step, I would now have been 'resting in peace' in some crevasses. Those legs had suffered a lot in bringing me to so many destinations in the Himalayas. We prostrated before masters and gave respect by touching their feet. But I thought that first we should prostrate and bow in respect before our own feet. I decided in my mind that next morning after prayers, I would bow before my legs.

I went to the riverbank and finished my evening prayer. It was past 7. The climate was as cloudy as before. When the chilly wind began blowing, my body began to shiver. But there was no heavy snowfall. Maybe that was because we had gone too far from the ice land. It seemed that there was the possibility of heavy rain at night. When Raju's cooking finished, we got ready to enter the cave. I thought it lucky considering the surroundings, to get a dinner of chapathi that was spread using only hands and roasted on a raw fire together with a curry of potato and big onions. I had been depleted of my stock of food and my hunger was severe.

Only a gymnast with a flexible body could get into the cave easily. The entrance was a small hole and we had to bend our body as if we were in a circus to enter. The interior was long but low in height and we had to take care of our head not hitting the roof. There was enough space inside for at least three people to stay conveniently. After putting the lit lamp on the side of the entrance, we spread Mukesh Kumar's woollen sheet on the ground. Raju's woollen sheet was reserved to cover both of us at night. I didn't forget to check in detail each nook and corner of the cave using an electric torch. It was very cold inside the cave. Looking out, we could clearly see the parts of mountains and treetops on the other side of the river.

The strength of the wind increased after dusk. With the light of the lightning reaching the cave off and on, it was clear the rain was near. Soon, the rain came storming. When it fell heavily, it suddenly became dark everywhere. The lamp was switched off in the rain and inside the cave became very dark. While sitting under the cover of the woollen sheet and enjoying the rhythm of the heavy rain, my eyes were filled with sleepiness. Hunger was at its peak but we decided to wait for the rain to subside. After falling for more than half an hour, the strength of the rain decreased. It poured for some more time lightly and then fully stopped. We lit the lamp again and had our food. Both the curry with no oil and curry powders and the handmade roti fried on raw fire had a special taste. Experience told us that taste was only a matter of hunger.

The moon had risen fully. I looked out of the cave. On the part of the sky that could be seen were stars shining in moonlight like beads of pearl. Along with the sound of the river flow, the creatures that were friends of the night also started their own music. When I lay to sleep under the bed sheet after prayers, the sweet memories of spending one more day in the Himalayas stood in my mind like a beautiful flower.

III

When I looked at my watch after a sound sleep, the time was 1.45 a.m. I had an urge to urinate and that might have been the reason for waking up at that time of the night. I got out of the cave and looked at the moon. Its colour was dim. Rain clouds were standing in clusters. The stars also had a low shine. There were signs all around of heavy rain in the night. Since I felt it was not proper to urinate on the side of the river, I walked towards the bush on the opposite side. The area was full of small plants, shrubs and medium pine trees but the centre of the place was rather empty. Like small mounds of mud in a coconut plantation, there were tiny hills of mud here and there and I checked the place thoroughly with my electric torch. Finding remnants of ashes around the mounds, I understood that it was a cremation ground. The riverbanks in this part were very vast. This type of place was most suitable for burial. Sometime later I understood that I was standing by the side of a mound. Though shocked a bit at first, I regained mental courage and shifted place. The whole area was silent except for the sound of water flowing in the river. Not even a single night creature made a sound. It was there I learnt first-hand the meaning of the term 'the silence of a cemetery'. I passed urine at an empty corner and washed my face with the river water. I felt a fresh energy then.

Though I lay on the bed once again, the goddess of sleep didn't bless me. Engaged in different thoughts, I lay like that with closed eyes. Truth was that the unexpected visit to the cemetery hadn't shaken my mind. Death was an eternal truth. Attaining a state of mind that comprehended that fact was the duty of a man. I recalled an incident when I spent an entire day, from six in the morning until ten at night, seated continuously in a cremation ground at Harischandra Ghat in Kashi.

On that day, seventeen pyres were burning simultaneously. Every five minutes, a dead body would arrive. The dead bodies were brought under decorated silk clothes and garlands accompanied by music and drumbeats. The loud weeping of the relatives echoed. The bodies were placed directly on the pyres after dipping them in River Ganga with the silk clothes and other adornments. That activity had been going on and on without a break. The cemetery guards with frozen faces had been discharging their duties with the easiness of a cook on each pyre in sheer concentration. The smell that hung all over the place was the reek of burning raw flesh. Street dogs inhaling the smell and cows waiting for a chance to eat the half-burnt garlands of flowers and dharbha grass were wandering around. What we had heard about Kashi, that half-burnt dead bodies were thrown away into the Ganga River, was not true. Sometimes, at the request of the relatives, a small part of the burnt body might have been put in the river. Generally, only after a body was burnt fully was another body put on that pyre. Not only this, the remnants of the burnt body were also given to the relatives from the pyre. But the bodies of children were not burnt. After being tied up in plastic haversacks, they were carried away in small boats to the centre of the river and immersed deep. Heavy stones would be placed in the bags for the bodies not to float. But, rarely, some bodies came from the depths of the river and floated in the water. Perhaps the stones came loose from the bags or it was some other reason. While travelling through the Ganga River, we could see such dead bodies floating in a decomposed state and eaten by fish. The wandering dogs ate them when they reached the shores. Those dogs, which regularly ate human flesh, were commonly found dead with all their hair lost and the body full of worms.

I didn't take in any food except occasionally drinking a mouthful of the pure water kept in my shoulder bag. Even my face had started swelling, being affected by fire and smoke. But I sat there still. Every man wanted to win over the world but his fate was to end in a six-foot pit. Where did the ornate towers, palatial houses, heaps of gold, bundles of currency, material happiness and luxuries go? They didn't come with him when died. Alone we came and alone we went. The only difference was that we cried in the first case and in the second, we made others cry. The gate to liberation opened for us only when we made the thought that 'happiness and unhappiness, profit and loss, success and failure . . . all were alike'.[7] Many a time during the day, the duty of the old workers of the graveyard would end and a new batch would join in. All the workers came for duty after heavily drinking liquor. The dead bodies stopped coming by ten p.m. When I rose to return, a man approached me and told me that Mathaji was calling me. I went to the concrete shed just above the cemetery and found the horrible figure of a middle-aged woman with matted hair tied up on top of her head. Since she was sheer black in colour, the ashes on her forehead were very visible. Saffron and sandal pastes were also there on her forehead. She had on her neck a lot of chains of stones and rudraksha. Also, she wore lots of dresses. She was fat and the red watery cream of chewed betel was dripping from the corners of her lips. She had been standing erect with an iron trident in hand. I was sure that if anyone saw the Mathaji in a lonely place, he would fall unconscious out of fear. Looking sharply at me, she asked in a rough voice,

'What were you doing in the burial place all these times? Are you a *jasoos* (secret police)? Don't play tricks with me. Tell me the truth.'

I noted in a flash the heavily built and ready-to-do-anything bodyguards and the long knife fitted on the waist of the Mathaji. I understood that if I didn't convince the lady at the first attempt itself, things might become bad. After bowing, I answered without a drop of fear:

'Mathaji, you are the lord of this graveyard. Your dress reminds me of the dance Bhagavan Parama Siva did in a burial ground. I am sure that you have plenty of His blessings. I am a pilgrim who had gone to Kailash, the home of Sree Parameswara and circled it by foot. You might have read the Yaksha-Yudhishtira debate in the Mahabharata. I was trying to kill my arrogance by seeing death face to face and to convince me that death was only a part of our life. There was no other purpose.'

Her face became pleasant. She bowed and putting the trident close to my chest, led me to the room of another middle-aged woman. She was the master of a temple in Harischandra Ghat. Eating the sweets and tea she gave me, I spent a long time talking with her.

That graveyard of Kashi was as old as the time of Raja Harischandra. After his period, the successors had been protecting the place. They belonged to the race of Dom Chowdhary. The right of supplying the required firewood to the cemetery was vested with the Yadhava family. Even today, we could see on the upper side of the place the hut made of mud in which King Harischandra had lived. There were other huts also built in various periods. Dead bodies brought in with the necessary papers would be put on the pyre only after the fees had been remitted in the office at the entrance. A small piece of burning coal from the extremely divine fire kept in a granite bucket believed to be that lit by Raja Harischandra was given to each burning pit. The first fire was from that piece. Every day, burning pieces were collected from every funeral pyre and deposited in the fire kept in the granite bucket. Thus it was a cyclic process. Even after death, discrimination never ended. Manikarnika Ghat, the burial ground of royal and rich

people, was situated a little farther away in the same row. But
it was to the Harischandra Ghat, the one with the tradition
of Raja Harischandra, that ordinary people were brought for
their final rituals. The biggest problem there was the deeds of
the anti-social people in the cemetery. They burnt murdered
people with the help of fake documents. The problem got
aggravated with the coming of the police. It was said that many
top-class people had crucial roles in that kind of illegal activity.
It was for such reasons that they kept there a gang who was
ready to do anything.

Though the temple in Harischandra Ghat was small, it
had the fame of being the second-oldest temple in Kashi (the
first one was, no doubt, the Kashi Viswanatha temple). The
right of the temple was vested with a family claiming to be
from the Vashishta Muni ancestry. The present master was
Smt. Poonam Pandey. Her husband, Sankar Pandey, was the
chief priest. According to them, the temple was built in the Sathy
period. The name of the temple was Sree Sathyavadhi Maharaja
Harischandra Ghat. I was surprised when Smt. Poonam Pandey
told me that they were fanatically searching for a way to do
even the daily pooja at the temple. Their complaint was that
nobody had been giving attention to the temple even though
it was very ancient. The cemetery guards in earlier days were
people belonging to the Shoodra caste and were successors of
Bir Babu. The legacy of Raja Harischandra helped pave a new
path to the graveyard. Now, they were amassing money. Those
accompanying the dead bodies did not donate anything to the
temple. When water in River Ganga rose, this small temple
would also go under water. It would lie under water for about
two months and after that, cleaning it incurred a huge sum.
Many requests had been made to the government but there was
no response. And to add to the agony, an electric cemetery had

been started in front of the temple and the arrival of devotees had decreased after that.

When the aides of Mathaji expressed their wish to know what the Yaksha-Yudhishtira debate was, I explained it in short. Once, during the *vanavaasa* (stay in the forest) period, Yudhishtira went in search of his lost brothers who had gone to fetch drinking water in the forest. The great king's heart was broken when he saw all his four brothers lying dead on the banks of a lake in the deep forest. A Yaksha (demi-god), who was standing invisible near them, told Yudhishtira that he had killed the brothers for taking water from the lake, ignoring his ban. He further told Yudhishtira that if he gave correct answers to his questions, he would make the dead brothers alive again and also would bless them with divine weapons. The intelligent Yudhishtira guessed that that was not a mere Yaksha but some god in disguise testing him. A total of 120 main and subsidiary questions were asked and Yudhishtira answered all. This was the background of the world-famous Yaksha-Yudhishtira debate. It could be rightly said that the start of the logical aptitude or intelligent quotient (IQ) tests widely used in the modern world was from that debate. The last questions based on arts, literature, social, cultural, scientific and philosophical issues were very notable. To the Yaksha's question regarding the biggest wonder in the world, Yudhishtira's immediate answer was,

'Ahanyahani Bhoothani Gachchantheeha Yamaalayam
Sheshaha Sthavaramichchanthi Kimascharyamathahaparam.'

(We see others die and shower pity on them but never think that one day we may also die. To us, we are permanent here. Death is other man's matter. What wonder is bigger than this?)

There was no limit to what a man thought in his lifetime. He would think of amassing more wealth, celebrating his son's/ daughter's marriage as an unforgettable event and doing many other things. He might even think about what interest income he was going to get on his term deposits after ten years. But he never for once would think about his own life in which anything might happen the next moment! If every man understood that he was not a permanent resident here and had to go and return in some unknown role, spirituality would automatically come into all his activities. Eventually, all his actions involving horrible cruelty and brutality and all sorts of ill-thinking would go away from him. The way to realization of the purpose of birth or divine liberation thus would be opened.

At Brahmamuhurta, I woke up and went out of the cave. After the routine morning affairs, I took a bath in the Kunthi River. I shivered with the cold! Rolling cloth around my fingers as protection, I woke up Raju and asked him to get ready for the journey. The blue colour of my nails had become darker but the pain was less. After consuming a painkiller tablet, we started our journey at 6 a.m.

The climate was cloudy and so the sunrise was dull. The path up to the Nabhi Village was not bad and we walked fast. Our decision was to eat breakfast after reaching Nabhi. The chilly morning wind and the budding greenery made us more energetic. At two or three places, landslides had happened on smaller scale but they did not pose any problem to our trip. We reached Nabhi Village after 9 a.m.

We spent half an hour there for breakfast and renewing acquaintances with the villagers. After offering flowers and praying at the Veda Vyasa Memorial entrance, we walked slowly through the shade of forest. Since continuous journey hurt the legs, we had to stop and rest at many places. We saw the farmlands of the villagers devastated by the rain.

We reached Gunji after 1.30 p.m. I joined friends who were having lunch. Only ten of our team members were there. The rest had left early in the morning for Budhi. Without wasting time, I went to the ITBP camp for medical aid. The doctor soothed me that though the nails would peel off, there was nothing to worry about. To avoid pus, he asked me to take antibiotic pills. Washing the legs in sterilized water, Chandran dressed the wounds and applied medicine. Since rest was essential, I returned to the camp. After the dinner of milk, rice soup and pickle, I went to bed early.

IV

Thick mist blocked the sight of sunrise in Gunji. After 6 a.m., the journey to Budhi started. I kept the breakfast parcel with me. The liaison officer advised me to travel on horseback because of the pain in my legs but I didn't oblige. I had an ardent wish to complete the journey on foot. Anyhow, we reached Budhi after 5 p.m. without much difficulty. The full-blown flower world of Chalekh turned out to be a sweet feast to the heart.

We thought in detail about the two disturbed ladies of Budhi. We felt very sad seeing them lying nude under a tree. With the help of the horse attendants, we went to the house of the village head and discussed the matter. The villagers had taken both of them to Mangthi for treatment but in less than one month, both dropped out and returned to Budhi. The lack of hospital wards for compulsory admission of patients was a drawback. Perhaps there was a chance at the district headquarters. However, we handed over the money we had collected through contributions to the village head and requested him to do the needful. He agreed. Gourav Mahajan assured to send more money if needed.

Rain started after 7 p.m. and stopped after falling for roughly one hour. But when the whirlwind blew fiercely like a storm, everyone became afraid. We were horrified to see the heavy trees falling with big sounds from the hill slopes on to the plains like airplanes landing on airports. It was certain that if one such tree plunged on to our camp sheds, we would be crushed into powder. The horrifying sounds of hills crashing and rocks cracking were heard echoing continuously elsewhere from the Budhi valley. Sitting on the cot, we spent time praying. When the terrible state of affairs ended after half an hour, everybody thanked God for sparing their lives. The places from Budhi to Malpa were always problematic. When the villagers exchanged signals through loud whistles, we guessed that some accidents had happened. If that was so, every one of us had the duty to help them. We went to the kitchen and requested the cooks to inquire about the matter. But the local people pacified us. They explained that the signals were not signs of mishaps but instead of happy news that nothing has happened.

When the time was past nine, all of us had food sitting together. The forecast of the local people was that rain might fall the whole night. While crawling into bed after prayers, my mind longed for a beautiful morning.

V

The golden rays of the morning bathed the eastern horizon in enchanting colours. A rainbow was standing there in the southeast corner of the sky like a delightful necklace in seven colours. Such a beautiful sight in the blue sky would make the heart of a poet rejoice.

After breakfast, we started the journey. The time was 6.30 a.m. Only one of the mad women was found under the tree then. I walked ahead after praying for a cure for her illness. The foot pain was almost gone and there was no difficulty in walking. All along the path were hurdles. In the horrible wind and rain of last night, many trees or branches were uprooted and had fallen straight on the path. Also at many places, hills had fallen. The soldiers of ITBP and Kumaon Regiment cut the path ahead for us and they were trying very hard.

Walking slowly, Raju and I reached Lakhanpur after noon. The ten team members were also taking rest there.

After having roti and subji for lunch, all of us proceeded on our journey together. From Lakhanpur onwards, it was one-way. Avoiding the horrible and tough path up to Bindhakotti, where one had to go 4440 steps up and down, we went on our journey by the side of the Kali River. Earlier, on the Kailash-Manasarovar trip, I had returned by the same route. If numerous steps were the problem with the Bindhakotti route, the serious issue in the other route was continuous landslides. We had to watch very carefully for big boulders rolling down from the upper hills and had to walk with full care to keep away from them. The direction of the stones had to be calculated in advance when we saw them falling. It was too risky to go the 2.5 to 3 km of this path. Also, the path was by the side of the river and only 2 feet wide. The Kali River was flowing violently due to the huge rain of last days. My ears shivered at the roar. It was a horrible sight of stones the size of an average elephant falling into the river and at once taken away like a flower. Reaching Mangthi by the riverside path, leaving behind Garbha Village, was short and easier than the Lakhanpur-Bindhakotti-Gypthi-Gala route. But nobody used that path because that was the most frightening one in the Kailash-Manasarovar and Adi Kailash journeys. Even animals were not taken that way.

After having boiled rice and dal and taking rest to regain energy, we said goodbye to Garbha Village and went to Mangthi. The time was past 6 p.m. when we reached Mangthi. The minibus to take us to Didihut was ready there. I gave Raju a good sum of money, more than the rate fixed by

the government. I also gave him a special amount to meet
his educational expenses. It was common among the porters
and horse attendants on such journeys lasting for one month
or more to depart after making excuses for the mistakes and
drawbacks that might have happened on their part. When Raju
did this and gave me a gift, I was surprised. It was the full skin
of a white sheep. The boy was crying when he asked me to keep
it as a memento of a hard and risky journey. I drew him close
and blessed him, putting my hands on his head. Then I moved
towards the bus. Before I got into the bus, Raju touched my
feet in reverence and bowed.

When enthusiastic calls like 'Jai Kailashpati, Jai Sathy
Ma' sounded inside and outside the bus, the driver started
the engine. In the wet climate, the vehicle sped towards the
destination of Didihut and I sat relaxed in my seat.

18

At Nainital

When the bus reached Didihut at around 2 a.m., everybody was in deep sleep. I never slept in vehicles while travelling and so the duty of waking up each one of the passengers was on my shoulders. I slept until 9 a.m. in the comfortable climate of Didihut and felt free of all fatigue. After taking a bath and having breakfast, we continued the journey to Nainital. It was through the Bhageswar-Almorah-Bhovali route. The heartening climate and greenery made the journey a relaxing one. The journey through the places like Suyansari and Kakrighat before Bhovali was unforgettable. When the vehicle halted for some time for tea, I enjoyed the beauty of nature to the full satisfaction of my mind. Also, we met the Kailash-Manasarovar pilgrimage team there. Seeing low-lying meadows and hilly slopes and trees with colourful flowers stretching out beyond the reach of our eyes made us feel like it was the climax of ecstasy. When the trees standing in each valley like beautiful arches of multicoloured flowers dropped bunches of flowers in the breeze, we felt as if gods were doing worship with flowers in their land, the heaven. Wherever we looked, there was a rain of flowers! It was only natural for one to sing the sweet lines of the immortal poet of Malayalam, Changampuzha:

'*Evide Thirinhonnu Nokkiyalum*
Avidellam Pootha Marangal Mathram;
Oru Kochu Kattengan Vannupoyal
Thuru Thure Poomazhayayi Pinne!'

(Wherever we looked, there were only flowered trees.
If a small wind blew, everywhere would happen
a continuous rain of flowers!)

After a long journey, we reached Nainital after 10 p.m.
Rooms had been made ready for us in the modern hotel of the
Tourism Department. Looking from the balcony of the hotel,
we could see the Nainital lake shining in illumination and it
was a gorgeous sight. The mountain layers around the lake were
full of buildings. Seeing the light of the bulbs in the buildings
reflecting in the lake was like seeing one lakh lamps. Everyone
was tired after the long journey and so all had food early and
went to sleep.

Since a full day was available for rest in Nainital, the team
members planned their programme according to their own
will and wishes. While the majority went for boating in the
lake and for shopping in the busy markets spread around the
lake, I went on some activities of my own. I was not interested
in the modern-day exercises of boating and shopping and so
after praying at Nainadevi temple, I walked to a place called
Ayarpatta. When I asked the way to the house of the great
Englishman, Jim Corbett, to a driver named Chand Ram at the
Thallital area, he happily agreed to come with me.

A mad liking for Jim Corbett had been in my mind since
I studied a lesson from his famous work, *The Man-eaters of
Kumaon*, in school. And after reading the Malayalam translation
of that book and his other works like *The Man-eating Leopard of
Rudraprayag*, *The Temple Tiger and More Man-eaters of Kumaon* and

My India, the name 'Jim Corbett' got stuck in my mind like it would never fade away in my whole lifetime. It was from his works that I learnt the basic lesson for the first time that on hazardous trips, our eyes and ears should be open at all times. Whether he was going through a forest or snowy land, for a traveller the sounds and signs from the surroundings were very critical. I learnt many primary lessons on caution while travelling through thick forests from Jim Corbett's books. Those lessons had helped me often while travelling through deserted ice lands also. Though he was known as an expert hunter, Jim Corbett was also a true lover of animals and nature. He silenced with his rifle only those man-eaters which had cruelly killed the helpless villagers and their domestic animals. His book *My India*, a narration of his real experiences, was a perfect example of his love towards the villagers and tribes of India and more than that, how he loved our forests and the birds and animals in them. I had been long wishing to visit his home.

When we passed the steps made of wood, what caught our eyes first were the big oak trees and the beautiful multi-level garden. The sight of Gurney House standing peacefully and aristocratically under the shade of treetops was heartening. The house comprising a veranda, four bedrooms, study room, dining room and kitchen was now a museum. Many things to remind one of the hunting period of Jim Corbett sahib were artistically arranged there. The fishing hook, the boat made by Mr Corbett himself with a tin sheet, the stuffed wild goat he had shot at 14,000 feet in Nandadevi forest, the 4.5-foot-long tusk of an enormous elephant of Dhikkala forest that he caught at high risk, the skulls of tigers, the drums of African tribes and different types of shells could be seen on one side. In the study were the writing table, chair and almirah he had used. His books were placed one over another at another side. The map of Nainital Lake and its surroundings drawn in 1887 was damaged by cockroaches. Yet on another side, various trophies he had won, a flute used by him and a piano were placed neatly.

The Englishman Colonel Edward James Corbett, better known as Tiger Jim Corbett, was born in Nainital on 25 July 1875. After a short military service, he made his permanent residence at Nainital. This was only because of his ardent love towards India. The attempts he made to uplift the poor would be remembered for all time. He was a multi-faceted genius and excelled very much as a writer and ornithologist. He also had proved his ability as a painter and photographer. He could imitate the sounds of different birds exactly as they were and also could understand the meaning of the bird cry. Also, he learnt to reproduce the sounds of tigers and other animals. The extraordinary courage and the ability to shoot without missing made him an expert hunter. He had shot dead more than ninety tigers that had cruelly killed hundreds of villagers. He had also saved hundreds of villagers from the attack of tigers. It was he who had pointed out the naked truth for the first time that those glamorous and royal animals were slowly disappearing from the Indian forests. It was after seeing the regional kings who went to the forests for hunting and the traders of tiger skin and other dacoits killing, in large numbers, tigers that were harmless that Jim Corbett responded with much pain in his heart. Swearing an oath that he would not shoot and kill even a single tiger any more, he conducted the 'cremation' of his three rifles and two pistols. He buried them in an unknown place with the help of two friends.

Jim Corbett died in Kenya on 19 April 1955.

In his honour, the Ramganga Park near Ramnagar town was named Corbett National Park in 1957.

I stayed in that house for more than two hours. I stood in the very rooms where Jim Corbett's aura seemed to linger, taking in deep breaths to absorb the ambience of his presence. Each grain of sand there was that which had the fortune of receiving his footsteps. My heart was heavy when I returned from Corbett's house after touching the soil of his house in reverence and bowing my head to his memories.

I gave money to Chand Ram, which made the poor man happy, and walked alone to a silent corner on the banks of the Nainital lake. After drinking a chilled lassi (sweetened curd) bought from a small shop, I lay fully stretched on a cement bench under the shade of a tree. In the cold climate and the breeze that came from the lake, my eyes became half closed. I remembered the ancient history of Nainital lake.

It was also the Puranic backdrop of Daksha Yaga that was behind the origin of the lake. The place where the eyes of Sathy Devi fell later turned out to be Nainital. Sathy Devi, the younger and dear daughter of Daksha Prajapathi, had also a pet name, Naina. The beautiful blue and green colour of the water is believed to be the reflection of Sathy Devi's eyes. In 'Manasakhandam' of the Skanda Purana, Nainital lake is referred to as 'Thryrishi Sarovaram'. The rishis Athri, Pulasthyan and Pulahan once came to the Naina mountain on a pilgrimage and finding no drinking water in the area, engaged in meditational prayer with Manasarovar in mind. Opening their eyes after meditation, the rishis saw a vast lake below the mountain. By their divine powers, they understood that the water in there came from Manasarovar by an underflow. That is why it is said that those visiting Nainital lake would get the same blessing as visiting Manasarovar.

In the Naina Devi temple at Nainital, we can also see the deity of Nanda Devi, a princess belonging to the Chand dynasty, who ruled Kumaon. Princess Nanda was the sister of

Princess Chand. She, who was killed by a bison, later assumed divinity and was given a place in the temple.

An Englishman named P. Baron[1] discovered the Nainital lake in 1839. He was hunting in the interior forests of Almorah then. But long before that, a zamindar (feudal lord) named Thokdar Noorsingh had discovered the lake with the help of local tribes and conferred its ownership on him. But Thokdar had to yield before the English power and a judge called J.H. Baton transferred the lake's ownership to the government and assigned the patent of discovery to Mr Baron. The lake, which is more than 5000 feet long and 1660 feet wide, looks like a round blue gemstone at a glance. The British developed Nainital like we are seeing it now. They constructed a pathway around the lake and built Elizabethan-Gothic style buildings on the hill slopes. Nainital, situated at a height of about 7000 feet, has an area of 11.73 sq. km only. Besides being a hill station, Nainital was also the summer capital during the British period. Nainital surviving the huge landslide that occurred in 1880 was a historic event. There are a total of sixty-six pure water lakes in Pithoragarh, Almorah and Nainital in the Chakathapargana region of Kumaon.

I don't think that there is any place in India other than Nainital which is blessed with so much natural beauty. The mountainous lands surrounded by devadaru and oak trees under snow-covered Himalayan peaks, the atmosphere that glistens in blue shade, vast and wide meadows, lakes reflecting the blue sky, waterfalls hitting rocks and falling down shattered, the world of fully blooming flowers, the cold climate and the cattle grazing happily in the fields around make Kumaon a land equal to heaven. Like a full moon among the cluster of stars, Kumaon Himalaya stands in comfort as a queen.

After 10 p.m., our team started off for Delhi. A journey ended there, only to begin another.

My first Adi Kailash journey, that lasted for about one month, presented me with many holy experiences. What I consider the gain of this journey is that I could find clear answers to many secret puzzles of the Himalayas. As regards the Himalayan journey, there is a vast difference between a traveller and a pilgrim. When a pilgrim puts his very first step on to the Himalayas, his *aham* (the feeling of self) meets an end. The Himalayas should be approached with much preparation and devotion. The pilgrim who plans to go to the Himalayas must strictly observe the rites and rituals. He has to tame himself with the universal power and make ready his mind and body alike for the journey. Only then can he reach the heights of divine experiences. What are invisible to our eyes breathe there. Receiving the energy of the invisible forces of the atmosphere there, man becomes amazed and fearful.

A foreign citizen called Kerry Moran, who stayed for months in tents below the Kailash mountain and also at other Himalayan places that were covered heavily with thick ice, described his holy experiences in his work *The Sacred Mountain of Tibet* with incomparable clarity:

'The River Ganges, its water in golden colour with a red background for having mixed with the sandal paste the goddesses put on their bodies and flowing in different branches to the four corners of the world to purify it and known in different names according to places it flowed and washer of all sins originates from the Himalayas. The southern branch of River Alakananda after splitting into seven rivers dissolves in the Southern Ocean. One becoming three, then four and four splitting into seven is a universal law. Of all creations, Ganga is the vagina of a human god. God's grace flowing in three forms through the *chakras of mooladharam* is the vigour we see in the Himalayas.

To understand its working on the gross and subtle bodies of ours, a pilgrim should feel and experience the diverse shapes and looks of this great Mountain. And the unbelievable changes happening in sunrise, sunset, noon, midnight, sunshine, rain, winter and storm take us to nobility. It is only true that even modern theories fail in explaining the mysterious meditational dimensions of the Himalayas. It can't be easily rejected calling it mere coincidence the great union of facts and myths here.

'Plants absorb carbon and nitrogen from air and water for food. But it is a truth that when all the living things require food through plants, yogis with astonishing skills quite unbelievable to modern scientists still are living for long in the Himalayas eating only air.

'Pilgrims who are in search of peace of mind can, if they listen, hear "Om", the mantra of peace at the Himalayas and Kailash.

'Many have experienced even now the presence in Himalayan regions of Hanuman and Maharshi Vyasa, the two immortal figures of Indian epics, the Ramayana and the Mahabharata.

'Maybe he couldn't reach his destination but even the path a Himalayan pilgrim goes purifies his mind. For a pilgrim who starts his journey by dedicating everything to 'Him' and fully wiping off 'Aham' from his mind, the brilliance of such an evolution will be there on his face. A deep and unseen spiritual power and a unique magnetic zone make the Himalayas a great holy pilgrimage centre. It is god's home.'

Many foreign travellers, by going through still unconquered and mysterious valleys of Himalayan peaks, could get close to godly rishis who lived without any connection to the outer world. The narration of their experiences is still a wonder to the world. The most notable among the Indian prime ministers and an intellectual himself, Pandit Jawaharlal Nehru described in his autobiography two impenetrable things that he didn't understand. The first one was the inaccessibly mysterious Himalayas, where snow tigers dance and Yatis live. The second was Albert Einstein's Theory of Relativity. The Skanda Purana says that 'whoever thinks about the Himalayas, even though he doesn't see them with his eyes, is greater than the one who gets dharshan of Kashi and does worship there. As snowdrops vanish in the morning rays, the sins of man vanish by dharshan of the Himalayas.' Wherever we are in the world, we can see people becoming interested when we just pronounce the word 'Himalayas' and a rare curiosity will spread on their faces. This itself is the greatness of the Himalayas. Bhasa says, 'Chakrarapamkthiriva Gachchathi Bhagyapamkthiha' (the wheel of time rotates by god's decision). Change is natural as the wheel of time rotates. But the Himalayas, the emperor of all mountains, still stands with its head high in the north, untouched by time. Even centuries ago, the rishis of the Himalayas called on the world to practise the great ideals of human fraternity and the culture or perception of India. Let it also be the only aim of ours:

> *'Thae Ajyeshtaa Akanishtaasa Udhbi*
> *Dhofmadyamaaso Mahasaavivaavrudhuha*
> *Sujathasojanushaa Prashnimatharo*
> *Dhivomaryaa Ano Achhajigathana.'*

(The tradition of Indian people is to love the country as they love their mother. The earth is my mother and I am her son. Those having such a mental stand are, no doubt, born from heaven. Those who are slaves of internal and external enemies will not have such a noble thinking).

This Veda mantra reminds us that our country will progress only when we discard all kinds of discrimination as poor, middle-class and rich. Instead, we must think that we all are Indians. This Veda mantra also wants us lovingly to have a conscience that is free of all ill-feelings towards the poor and lower classes and have a mind to give everybody equal rights and opportunities without stamping anyone as scheduled caste or belonging to the reserved category.

Notes

Chapter 1: The Kumaon Himalayas

1. Ravana was the rakshasa king of the island of Lanka (rakshasa is a demonic creature in Hindu mythology) and the chief antagonist of the Hindu epic, the Ramayana. He abducted Prince Rama's wife Sita and took her to his kingdom of Lanka. Rama, with the support of *vanara* (monkey) King Sugriva and his army of vanaras, launched an invasion against Ravana in Lanka. Ravana was subsequently slain and Rama rescued his beloved wife Sita. In the Ramayana, Ravana is described to be the eldest son of sage Vishrava. Though widely portrayed as an evil character, Ravana had many qualities that made him a learned scholar. He was also a great musician. He was well-versed in the six shastras (sciences) and the four Vedas. He was also the most revered devotee of Siva.

Chapter 2: Pathal Bhoomi (The Netherworld)

1. There are fourteen worlds or Brahmandas—seven upper and seven lower. The upper worlds are i. Bhoolokam (the earth), ii. Bhuvarlokam (the world of planets of the sky), iii. Swarlokam (the world of Devendra, the king of Gods), iv. Maharlokam (the world of Lord Mahavishnu), v. Janalokam (the world of mankind), vi. Thapolokam (the world of rishis or sages) and vii. Sathyalokam (the world of Lord Brahma). The lower worlds are i. Athalam (the residence of the son of Yaman, the king of death), ii. Vithalam (the residence of Lord Siva), iii. Suthalam (the abode of Mahabali), iv. Rasathalam (the abode of rakshasas), v. Thalathalam (the abode of Mayamayi), vi. Mahathalam (the abode of serpents) and vii. Pathal

(the abode of snakes). Bhoolokam is the world made of soil which we touch while we walk. Bhuvarlokam is the world that lies between the sun and the earth where rishis and sages live, and Swarlokam is the world that lies between the sun and the pole star. These three worlds are together known as Krithaka (complete) worlds, whereas it is believed that Janalokam, Thapolokam and Sathyalokam are Akritha (incomplete) worlds. Maharlokam is situated between Kritha and Akritha. This world won't perish even on doomsday.

2. Adi Sankara was an ancient Vedic scholar and teacher (acharya) whose works present a harmonizing reading of the sasthras (the sacred scriptures of Hinduism consisting of four categories of text—the *sruti*, *smriti*, purana and tantra) with liberating knowledge of the self at its core. They synthesize the Adwaitha teachings. Over 300 texts are attributed to him including commentaries (Bhasya), introductory topical expositions (Prakaraṇa grantha) and poetry (Stotra). His works include *Brahmasutrabhasya*, commentaries on ten Mukhya (principal) Upanishads, commentary on the Bhagavat Gita, etc. *Saundarya Lahari,* meaning 'the waves of beauty', is a famous literary work of Adi Sankara in Sanskrit. Its 103 slokas (verses) praise the beauty, grace and munificence of Goddess Tripura Sundari as Goddess Parvathy. *Saundarya Lahari* is not only a collection of holy hymns, but also a tantra textbook giving instructions on Puja, Sri Yantra and worshipping methods. Sri Yantra or Shri Chakra is a form of mystical diagram (yantra). It consists of nine interlocking triangles—four upward ones which represent Siva and five downward ones representing Sakti. All these surround the central point, the bindu (dot). These triangles represent the cosmos and the human body. The central postulation of Sankara's writings is Adwaitha—the identity of Self (Ātman) and Brahman. He founded the four famous matas (monasteries, namely the Govardhana Mata in Puri, the Jyotih Mata near Badrinath in the Himalayas, the Sarada Mata in Dvaraka and the Srngeri Mata in South India (a fifth mata, the Saradapitha in Kanchipuram near Chennai, arose later).

Chapter 3: Gala

1. Parliament passed a bill recognizing Sashastra Seema Bal (SSB) as part of the Indian military in 2007. Presenting the bill, Home

Minister Shivraj Patil said that the size of the Indian military became
bigger with that action (it was in May 2006 that I had talked with
the SSB authorities).

Chapter 4: Budhi

1. Kālidāsa (fourth-fifth century CE) is India's greatest poet and
   playwright. Much about his life is unknown except what can be inferred
   from his poetry and plays. His works were most likely authored
   before the fifth century CE. His works, namely *Vikramorvasheeyam,
   Malavikagnimithram, Abhinjanasakunthalam, Rithusamharam, Meghasandhesham,
   Kumarasambhavam* and *Raghuvamsham*, are immortal and timeless. The
   great German poet Goethe said of *Abhinjanasakunthalam* that 'it was the
   link connecting heaven with earth'. Famed English writer T.S. Eliot
   was highly influenced by Kalidasa, describing the great writer as the
   evergreen wonder of world literature.

Chapter 5: Gunji

1. Bhagavata Purana or Bhagavatham is one of Hinduism's
   eighteen great Puranas (Mahapuranas) composed by
   Veda Vyasa in Sanskrit (Krishna Dvaipayana, better
   known as Veda Vyasa, is the author of the epic, the Mahabharata).
   A very revered and talented sage, Vyasa compiled the mantras of
   the Vedas into four Vedas. He also authored the eighteen Puranas
   and the Brahma Sutras. A partial incarnation of Lord Vishnu,
   Vyasa is one of the seven Chiranjeevis (immortals who will not
   die). Bhagavatham promotes bhakti (devotion) towards Krishna,
   integrating themes from the Adwaitha (monism) philosophy
   of Adi Sankara, the Vishishtadwaitha (qualified monism) of
   Ramanujacharya and the Dwaitha (dualism) of Madhvacharya. It
   is widely available in almost all Indian languages.

Chapter 7: Nabhidang

1. Swami Vivekananda was a great Indian monk, philosopher and
   author. He was a key figure in introducing Indian dharshanas
   (teachings, practices) of Vedanta and yoga to the western world,

was a major force in the contemporary Hindu reform movements in India and contributed much to the concept of nationalism in colonial India. He founded the great institutions Ramakrishna Math and Ramakrishna Mission.

Chapter 9: On to Kuti Village

1. To measure time, ancient people used 'sundials'. They consisted of a thin piece of metal fitted on a flat surface; time was measured by the shadow of the sun on the metal piece. The scientists in olden times installed a huge sundial at Allahabad to measure exact time. And believe it, modern scientists also chose this place as the standard meridian for the whole country because the longitude of 82°5'E was passing through it! Devotees consider Triveni Sangam (the confluence of rivers Ganga, Yamuna and Saraswathy) at Allahabad as the centre of the world.

Chapter 10: A Day in Kuti Village

1. Narada Maharshi or Narada Muni is a sage divinity, famous in Hindu traditions as a travelling musician and storyteller who carries news and enlightening wisdom. He is also referred to as Rishiraja, meaning the king of all sages. He was gifted with the boon of knowledge regarding the past, present and future. In Indian texts, Narada travels to distant worlds and realms. He is depicted carrying a *khartal* (musical instrument) and veena with the name Mahathi and is generally regarded as one of the great masters of the ancient musical instrument. He uses musical instruments to accompany his singing of hymns, prayers and mantras. An ardent devotee of Lord Vishnu, Narada is described as both wise and mischievous in some humorous tales. Vaishnavas depict him as a pure, elevated soul who glorifies Vishnu through his devotional songs. The Narada Bhakti Sutra is attributed to him. He would usually make his presence known by vocally chanting 'Narayana, Narayana' before appearing in a scene.

2. The Shrimad Bhagavat Gita, or simply Gita, is part of the epic, the Mahabharata. In the war between the Pandavas and the Kauravas, Arjuna is preoccupied by a moral dilemma. On the enemy side is

his kin and masters whom he has to kill. Wondering if he should renounce the war, he seeks Krishna's counsel, whose answers and discourse constitute the Bhagavat Gita. The Bhagavat Gita is the best known and most famous of Hindu texts and has a unique pan-Hindu influence. Mahatma Gandhi referred to it as a 'spiritual dictionary'.

3. *Dhritarashtra uvacha: Dharmakshetre Kurukshetre Samaveta Yuyutsavah Mamakah pandavashchaiva Kimakurvata Sanjaya* (Dhritarashtra said: O Sanjaya, after gathering on the holy field of Kurukshetra, and desiring to fight, what did my sons and the sons of Pandu do?). This is the first verse in first chapter of the Bhagavat Gita. The blind king Dhritarashtra's fondness for his own sons had clouded his spiritual wisdom and took him away from the path of virtue. He had usurped the kingdom of Hastinapur from the rightful heirs, the Pandavas, sons of his brother Pandu. Feeling guilty about the injustice he had done towards his nephews, his conscience worried him about the outcome of this battle. The words *dharma kshetre*, the land of dharma (dharma means virtuous deed) used by Dhritarashtra depict the dilemma he was experiencing.

4. An *akshauhini*, an ancient battle formation, consisted of 21, 870 chariots, 21,870 elephants, 65,610 cavalry and 1,09,350 infantry. The ratio was 1 chariot: 1 elephant: 3 cavalry: 5 infantry.

Chapter 11: 'Asthithurasyam Dhishi Devathatma, Himalayo Nama Nagadhiraja'

1. Please refer to annexure 1, page 262 of *Thapobhoomi Uttarakhand* by this writer.

2. Samkhya School is regarded as one of the oldest philosophical systems in India. Samkhya is an enumerationist philosophy that is strongly dualist. Samkhya philosophy denies the final cause of Ishwara (God) and regards the universe as consisting of two realities—Purusha (consciousness) and Prakriti (phenomenal realm of matter). Jiva (life) is that state in which Purusha is bonded to Prakriti through the glue of desire, and the end of this bondage is Moksha (liberation). After liberation, there is no essential distinction between individual and universal Purusha.

3. But the Gita interpretation is that because the karma system is the cause of the njana (knowledge) system, it becomes the cause of

purushartha (that which is sought by man—his purpose, aim or end).
It refers to a goal of human existence. Purusharthas are generally
considered to be four namely:

Dharma: law, religious duty

Artha: prosperity

Kama: pleasure

Moksha: (spiritual) liberation

4. Here are the sixty-four forms of art: (1) *geet vidya*—art of singing,
(2) *vadya vidya*—art of playing on musical instruments, (3) *nritya
vidya*—art of dancing, (4) *natya vidya*—art of theatricals, (5) *alekhya
vidya*—art of painting, (6) *viseshakacchedya vidya*—art of painting
the face and body with colour, (7) *tandula-kusuma-bali-vikara*—art of
preparing offerings from rice and flowers, (8) *pushpastarana*—art of
making a covering of flowers for a bed, (9) *dasana-vasananga-raga*—art
of applying preparations for cleansing the teeth, cloths and painting
the body, (10) *mani-bhumika-karma*—art of making the groundwork of
jewels, (11) *sayya-racana*—art of covering the bed, (12) *udaka-vadya*—
art of playing music in water, (13) *udaka-ghata*—art of splashing with
water, (14) *citra-yoga*—art of practically applying an admixture of
colours, (15) *malya-grathana-vikalpa*—art of designing a preparation of
wreaths, (16) *sekharapida-yojana*—art of practically setting the coronet
on the head, (17) *nepathya-yoga*—art of practically dressing in the trial
room, (18) *karnapatra-bhanga*—art of decorating the tragus of the ear,
(19) *sugandha-yukti*—art of practical application of aromatics, (20)
bhushana-yojana—art of applying or setting ornaments, (21) *aindra-
jala*—art of juggling, (22) *kaucumara*—a kind of art, (23) *hasta-laghava*—
art of sleight of hand, (24) *citra-sakapupa-bhakshya-vikara-kriya*—art of
preparing varieties of delicious food, (25) *panaka-rasa-ragasava-yojana*—
art of practically preparing palatable drinks and tinging draughts
with red colour, (26) *suci-vaya-karma*—art of needlework and weaving,
(27) *sutra-krida*—art of playing with thread, (28) *vina-damuraka-vadya*—
art of playing on lute and small drum, (29) *prahelika*—art of making
and solving riddles, (30) *durvacaka-yoga*—art of practising language
difficult to be answered by others, (31) *pustaka-vacana*—art of reciting
books, (32) *natikakhyayika-darsana*—art of enacting short plays and
anecdotes, (33) *kavya-samasya-purana*—art of solving enigmatic verses,
(34) *pattika-vetra-bana-vikalpa*—art of designing preparation of shield,
cane and arrows, (35) *tarku-karma*—art of spinning by spindle,

(36) *takshana*—art of carpentry, (37) *vastu-vidya*—art of engineering, (38) *raupya-ratna-pariksha*—art of testing silver and jewels, (39) *dhatu-vada*—art of metallurgy, (40) *mani-raga jnana*—art of tinging jewels, (41) *akara jnana*—art of mineralogy, (42) *vrikshayur-veda-yoga*—art of practising medicine or medical treatment, by herbs, (43) *mesha-kukkuta-lavaka-yuddha-vidhi*—art of knowing the mode of fighting of lambs, cocks and birds, (44) *suka-sarika-pralapana*—art of maintaining or knowing conversation between male and female cockatoos, (45) *utsadana*—art of healing or cleaning a person with perfumes, (46) *kesa-marjana-kausala*—art of combing hair, (47) *akshara-mushtika-kathana*—art of talking with fingers, (48) *dharana-matrika*—art of the use of amulets, (49) *desa-bhasha-jnana*—art of knowing provincial dialects, (50) *nirmiti-jnana*—art of knowing prediction by heavenly voice, (51) *yantra-matrika*—art of mechanics, (52) *mlecchita-kutarka-vikalpa*—art of fabricating barbarous or foreign sophistry, (53) *samvacya*—art of conversation, (54) *manasi kavya-kriya*—art of composing verse mentally, (55) *kriya-vikalpa*—art of designing a literary work or a medical remedy, (56) *chalitaka-yoga*—art of practising as a builder of shrines called after him, (57) *abhidhana-kosha-cchando-jnana*—art of the use of lexicography and meters, (58) *vastra-gopana*—art of concealment of cloths, (59) *dyuta-visesha*—art of knowing specific gambling, (60) *akarsha-krida*—art of playing with dice or magnets, (61) *balaka-kridanaka*—art of using children's toys, (62) *vainayiki vidya*—art of enforcing discipline, (63) *vaijayiki vidya*—art of gaining victory, (64) *vaitaliki vidya*—art of awakening the master with music at dawn.

5. 'Gurukula' was an ancient residential education system where the student stayed in the house of the teacher to study and also helped in the household matters of the teacher, such as collecting firewood, cleaning the house, fetching water, etc.

6. Abstracted from *Pranathathwam*, a work by writer G. Mohandas. The work contains an elaborate description of ionizing radiation and the incomparable power it renders.

7. The word *tantra* is derived from the combination of two words, *tattva* and *mantra*. Tattva means the science of cosmic principles and mantra means the science of mystic sound and vibrations. Tantra, therefore, is the application of cosmic sciences with a view to attain spiritual ascendancy.

8. Kala means eternal. *Swaroopa* is the liberated condition in which one's outward form is one's deepest spiritual nature. Primarily, however, this term refers to the supreme personality of God Sreekrishna.

9. Purusha is the first form of Supreme Lord Narayana and this Purusha is the source of everything in the universe.

10. According to Adwaitha as taught by Sankara, *saguna brahman* refers to the Lord identical with his own infinite jnanam (knowledge). Sankara refers to him by names such as Siva, Vishnu as specified in the Vedas and Upanishads. This saguna brahman is eternal, undecaying and undifferentiated from *nirguna* brahman. He is not affected even when he appears in this world as he controls the effects of his own maya shakti. Hiranyagarbha, the collection of deities in the Hindu pantheon of gods, is not saguna brahman as is popularly misconstrued. Sankara clearly says that hiranyagarbha is called brahman only because of their nearness to brahman. After many millions of years, the devotees who reach the worlds of gods (hiranyagarbha), will reach the state of Vishnu. This is called adwaitha sidhi and this state can be reached here and now by one who is free from all desires and is blessed by the lord.

11. Uttarayana is the period between the Makara Sankranti (which occurs around 14 January) and Karkataka Sankranti (which occurs around 16 July). The term 'Uttarayana' is derived from two different Sanskrit words, *uttara* (north) and *ayana* (movement), thus indicating a semantic of the northward movement of the sun on the celestial sphere.

12. *'Yam Yam Vapi Bhavam Thyajathyanthae Kalaebaram*
    Tham Thamaevaithi Kounthaeya Sadha Thalbhavabhavithaha'
    —Bhagavat Gita (8–6)
    (My dear Arjuna, one who at the moment of the last breath of life relinquishes the body in what memory of appearance, he gets that appearance with an everlasting remembrance of appearance).

13. The death of Sree Narayana Guru can be cited here. Sree Narayana Guru (20 August 1856–20 September 1928) was a great philosopher, spiritual leader and social reformer of India. He led a reform movement against injustice in the caste-ridden society of Kerala in order to promote spiritual enlightenment and social equality. Mahatma Gandhi visited Guru during his 1925 trip to Kerala and stated that 'it was a great privilege in my life to have the darshan of an esteemed sage like Sree Narayana Guru'. The last

moments of Sree Narayana Gurudevan are narrated as follows in the work *Gurudevan: The Sunny Splendour in Memory*: 'For a moment, the eyes of Gurudevan shining in the magnificence of meditation stood still against eternity. Moving up past the six bases of life, breaking the "Rudra Granthi" and passing the "Brahmarandra" reaches the "sahasrara pushpa" on head. Thoughts emptied and *"namaroopa"* finished (Nama: name, Roopa: form), the heart slowly merges with "Dhaharakasha" filled with the radiance of waves of sunshine. *Thripudi* gets finished. Now, there is no sky over the head and no earth under the foot. No planets and no stars. Nothing there except one thing—the only thing—the divine light. It has the brightness of hundreds of thousands of suns. One soul is crossing the limit of another one. In one rare moment of "savikalpa samadhi", a blue cloud arises from the eternal essence. When the air from within the Yogi deep in samadhi hits the blue cloud, it is not rain coming down but pure knowledge. A soul is continuing its travel through planets and stars.' 'When we have fallen in the sea of your greatness,
We should go deep in and in and live forever with pleasure'
(Guru Nitya Chaithanya Yeti endorses that he has personally experienced the soul exiting at the time of the death of Ramana Maharshi.)

14. Brahmor is a provisional camp in the tough travel to Mani Mahesh Kailash through the banks of the Raavi River. One could reach Hadsar village travelling 16 km from Brahmor. But this road is not navigable. It is from Hadsar that the travel on foot to Mani Mahesh Kailash begins. The ancient name of Brahmor was Brahmapuri. There is a spacious temple complex on the hilltop near the market. The deity here is Siva–Parvathy. Beside it are two very rare God installations. They are of King Yama (the God of death) and Chithragupta (the minister of Yama). There is an underground tunnel way which no one has seen. The sanyasins here told me that this cave-way extends far to Mani Mahesh Kailash and from there to Kailash in Tibet. It is believed that the souls that come to King Yama when Chithragupta cuts the name go through this tunnel.

15. My first work, *Uttarakhandiloode: A Kailash-Manasa Sarass Journey*, contains the narration of an experience of Mr Harihar, a co-traveller, meeting death face to face (page 196, second paragraph). He told me later in my long talks with him that what he went through was similar to

what was described by Sir William Barrett. He agreed to narrate his experiences in detail in the English translation of this work.

16. '*Udhdharaedhatmanam Namatmanamavasadhayael*
    Atmaiva Hyatmano Bandhuratmaiva Ripuratmana ha'
    —Bhagavat Gita 6--5
    (One has to save his soul from the world with a prudent mind. He should not make the soul's journey downwards because for him [for his soul] he himself is the friend and for him [for his soul] he himself is the foe.)

17. Writer: D.K. Dixit, *Mysteries Unsolved: A Real Life Story: Living in Two Ages.*

18. The subconscious cleverly took in pictures, symbols and imagery more than word-related things.

19. I have given a detailed depiction of such an experience of mine in my work *Thapobhoomi Uttarakhand* (chapter 4, pages 158--159).

20. A Jewish saint of Palestine returned home after living with rishis in the Himalayas for twenty years. An American journal reported with pictures that this man sitting in a Gaza street in meditation for just half an hour quite easily bent a 1-foot-long and 8-mm-thick iron bar. Those who had read the report passed me the information. Also, it was reported by the journal that the man cured many people of diseases just by touching them.

21. Scientists like Maxwell consider it folly to believe that electricity is a flow quality alone. 'It is a flow of power started from a holy core. This is one among the numerous holy cores that rule and raise our universe according to the eternal laws of action.'

22. Please refer to para 2, page 132 of the chapter 'Gangothri-Gomukh' in the book *Thapobhoomi Uttarakhand.*

23. Taking photos of the special power system of the human body through high frequency photography was a new event in science. In 1939, an intelligent Russian mechanic, Semyon Davidovich Kirlian, was repairing a machine related to electro-treatment in a research centre at Krasnodar City on the banks of the Black Sea. Experimenting with the machine, he saw multicoloured light rays emanating from his fingers when they came near the machine at some particular position. Kirlian took it as an indication of some special power system of the body. This is nothing but the indication of the *Pranamayakosha* of *Yogasasthra.* Pranamaya means composed of Prana, the force that vitalizes and holds together the body and

the mind. As long as this vital principle exists in the organisms, life continues. Kosha means sheath. These studies point out the fact that an internal power system with countless centres of light exists inside living bodies. This was the origin of the Kirlian photography that became famous later.

24. *Kshethra Chaithanya Rahasyam*—Madhavji.

25. Please read the sixth chapter, 'To Badrinath', of my work *Thapobhoomi Uttarakhand* (pages 220–223). The details of the withdrawal by the Chinese army were obtained then from the Indian Army officers. I did not know then about Major General J.T. Harris's book.

26. *Arsha Jnanam*, Nalappat Narayana Menon.

27. *Jnana Geetha*, Integral Publications.

28. Pranava Mantra 'Om' is the noblest of all mantras. The prime mantras of all other religions originated from Om $(A+U+M)$, the prime mantra in the Vedas. Tibetans chant 'Hum', Christians 'Amen' and Muslims 'Amin'. The Greeks, Romans and Jews also chant 'Amen'. The meaning of it in Hebrew is 'sure' or 'faithful'. Sufi scholars argue that the word 'Allah' was termed after 'Aum' (*omkaram*).

29. *Jnana Geetha*, Integral Publications.

30. 'Christ' or 'Christ consciousness' is the manifestation of the presence of God in each man. The Bible of the Christians calls it the Son of God.

31. There is a slight difference in the studies and assessments of Sidhas and Samkhyas about the soul. This difference can be detected in many of the rishi-made Upanishads. The facts arrived at by the holy rishis after long and deep meditation may not be the same. Differences will occur according to the skill and views of each one.

32. Tantra is a style of meditation and ritual that elaborates (*than*) copious and profound matters, especially relating to the principles of reality (tattva) and sacred mantras, and provides liberation (*thra*).

33. Whoever knows Parabrahma becomes immortal. He becomes free of birth and death forever, i.e., he becomes eternal.

34. Jules Romains, the French environmental scientist, found from his experiments that there are some eye-shaped sensory cells on the skin. Since these cells are lying spread all over the body, the vision-sense transactions can be done through all parts.

35. In the publication ceremony of the book *Thapobhoomi Uttarakhand*, the main lecture on the work was delivered by Dr Alexander Jacob,

IPS, director and inspector general of Police (Training), Kerala Police Academy, Thrissur. Dr Alexander has deep knowledge of ancient Indian writings. He has also made Western literature a subject of his study. He quoted a special experience of his own with the holy sanyasins. While a conference of the IPS officers was being held at Mussoorie in Uttarakhand, he made the acquaintance of two North Indian officers. They went to visit a sanyasin living in the suburbs of Mussoorie. The sanyasin was sitting alone in a hut. Before starting the conversation, the sanyasin wrote something on three different pieces of paper and asked each one to put one in their pockets. The paper was folded tightly and hence the content was unknown. After half an hour's discussion on various subjects, the sanyasin asked each one to think of a sentence. Dr Alexander remembered the Bible sentence, 'God is Love'. The sanyasin then asked each of them to open and read the folded paper kept in their pockets. To his surprise, Dr Alexander found that what was written on his piece of paper was 'God is Love'! The same was the experience of the other two officers! One thought about Krishna and the other about Siva. This meant that the sanyasin was able to foresee the transactions in the minds of the three.

36. *Thapobhoomi Uttarakhand*—Annexure 1, page 274, first paragraph.

37. Please refer to page 147, last paragraph of *Thapobhoomi Uttarakhand*. Messages from one cave to another are sent this way.

38. *Vijnanamaya kosha* is one of the five koshas that cover Atman. Vijnanamaya kosha literally means a shell that is composed of wisdom (vijnana) or intellect. It is the fourth covering of Atman.

39. *Thapobhoomi Uttarakhand*, page 130. It is by the *Vijnanamaya kosha* sidhi that the sanyasin knew of our coming beforehand.

40. Astral body: It is the second of the three koshas covering the Atman or the soul of life. The three different categories are the causal body, the astral body and the physical body. The power of the soul provides energy to the physical body. It is a phenomenon like the bulb shining when electricity comes on. The astral body comprises nineteen elements (the pancha bhoothas of nature—Agni, Vayu, Bhoomi, Jalam, etc., are included in these nineteen).

41. This God-created world is the one with light and colour. The waves of life energy are sharper than the energy of atomic power. For every matter, life and movement of the physical world, there is an equal

in the astral world. This is because the physical world is only an expanded outline of the astral world. When the death of the body happens, the soul wearing the glowing shield of the astral world goes to the underworld or upper world according to the outcome of the *Karma* (deeds) done. The process called evolution of the soul continues more independently in the astral world. The soul resides in that world until the result of Karma ends as predetermined. After that, it takes birth in the physical world again.

42. William J. Cromie, 'Meditation Changes Temperature; Mind Controls Body in Extreme Experiments', *Harvard Gazette Archives*, Gazette staff.

43. Taken from the archival records of the Indian Council for Cultural Relations (ICCR) working under the Ministry of External Affairs, Government of India.

44. Anne Cushman, *Spiritual Tourism*, Chapter: 'From Here to Nirvana'.

45. 'Consecration', from the interview of Assistant Editor Dr Radhika Nagrath with Kambiz Naficy in the July–August 2008 issue.

46. Swami Rama was born in a Himalayan valley in 1925. It was a great soul, a Bengali yogi, who had found Rama at a very young age and brought him up. After doing higher studies at Prayag and Varanasi, Rama worked at Oxford University in the medicine department. Then he started research in parapsychology in Moscow. In 1969, he obtained a degree in homeopathy from Bursanga University (Germany). On invitation by Dr Elmer Green of the Menninger Foundation, Kansas, USA, he went there in 1969. Later, he founded the Himalayan International Institute of Yoga Science and Philosophy in Pennsylvania and indulged fully in its activities. He wrote many books on health, meditation and the science of yoga. But what makes Swami Rama's name immortal are his works, *Living with the Himalayan Masters*, *Life Here and Hereafter* and *Love and Family Life*. He embraced eternality in 1996 through a death that he had wished it to be.

47. Swami Rama: *Living with the Himalayan Masters*. Chapter: 'How We Live in the Caves'.

48. Vasantha Panchami, sometimes referred to as Saraswati Puja or Shree Panchami, is held on the fifth day of Magha (in early February) marking the start of spring and the *Holi* season. On this day, Hindus worship Saraswati Devi, the Goddess of knowledge, music, art and culture.

49. Marma Chikitsa is a powerful instrument of Ayurveda that originated 5000 years ago. It is a process and therapy that works with 108 subtle and sensitive energy points of the human body. It opens energy channels in the body.

50. Swami Rama, *Living with the Himalayan Masters*.

51. *Rei* means 'God's Wisdom or the Higher Power' and *Ki* means 'life force energy'.

52. The mentioned sect is the Navnath Sadhu Sangh narrated in the chapter 'Gangothri-Gomukh-Thapovan' of *Thapobhoomi Uttarakhand*.

53. Please refer to page 213, second paragraph of *Thapobhoomi Uttarakhand*.

54. R.K. Karanjia, editor of the *Blitz* weekly, narrates such an incident in an interview. 'A female dancer who was performing before a crowded audience in Kolkata fell, burnt out in *Yogagni* (fire of yoga) at the end.' Also refer to the quotation of Madhavji given in this chapter.

55. Very recently, Dr Capra visited India again after a gap of twenty years. Relevant extracts are from the interview Swathi Chopra conducted with Dr Capra at the Bija Vidyapeeth in Dehradun.

56. Prof. Dr Joachim Illis, 'Does the Universe Hold Other Intelligence Beings?'.

57. Dr D.G. Vinod, MA, PhD, Fellow of the Royal Society of Arts, London. An eighty-nation conference of world pacifists at Tokyo, Japan, selected and honoured Dr Vinod as 'World Peace Ambassador'.

58. Prof. Dr Joachim Illis, 'Does the Universe Hold Other Intelligence Beings?'.

59. 'Thanyathe, Vistaryathe, Jnanam Anena Ethi Tantra'.

60. Power in Temples.

61. An experiment to find out the origin of universe is being done in an artificial tunnel under the earth in Geneva, Switzerland. The cost of this experiment, to find the God Particle—the Higgs boson—is Rs 40,000 crore. What will be the outcome when this most important, most complex and most expensive experiment in history is over? To carry out the experiment, the European Organization for Nuclear Research (CERN) has readied a special laboratory called the Large Hadron Collider (LHC). This laboratory is built in a radius of 27 kilometres. Inside it are installed 9300 superconducting magnets at minus 273.25 degrees Celsius. The laboratory is 100 metres below the surface level. About 8000 scientists take part in the experiments. Even when we boast about the growth of science, we are unable to

tell how exactly the universe originated. The scientists are trying to artificially create in the Large Hadron Collider the ancient universe that arose just after the Big Bang occurred 1370 crore years back. Many thinkers believe now that it is soul—God's own part—that gives life and energy to the mortal human body. When arguments went that the pressure of particles gave mass to massless particles, the scientists called that particle the God Particle. The smallest component of a matter is an atom. The tiny sub-components of an atom were discovered to be electrons, protons and neutrons. When scientific knowledge developed over time, it was learnt that protons and electrons were made up of still tinier particles such as quarks and anti-quarks called hadrons. But the fact was that these particles had no mass, the basic quality of matter. But then, what is the basic thing that gives mass to matter? It was as the answer to this question that Higgs and team, physicists of the University of Edinburgh, said that there was a particle called the Higgs boson in all matter. This has become known as the God Particle. No one has found this factor till date. What is going to happen when atoms collide at super speed in this longest machine man has made? The filters installed in the particle detectors collect only the data of the hundred biggest proton collisions and transfer them to the chain of computers. When collisions take place at that high speed and energy levels, the temperature will become one lakh times more than the inside temperature of the sun. Since such gigantic temperature levels occur and the thousands of magnets which guide the way protons are superconducting, the collider is built in very cold temperature levels. The experiments conducted by thousands of scientists from thirty-two countries, including India, may extend from fifteen to twenty years.

62. ICCR archives.

63. *Lost Horizon* by James Hilton was first published in 1954 (Publishers: Macmillan and Co.). This book, condensed by E.F. Dodd, was the non-detailed study of SSLC in Kerala during 1973.

64. An artificial cubicle is made in laboratories for the practice of astronauts intending to travel in spaceships such as Apollo, Colombia, etc., for beating gravitational force. The air pressure inside the cubicle is gradually reduced to make it a vacuum in the end. If there is no air, there will be no gravity. When the astronauts travel in this cubicle, it is like flying in the air. This is because of zero gravity. It is clear then

that it is possible on Earth. The Vedas tell us that air is an important factor for the gravitational power of Earth. The root cause of Earth's gravitational force is still unknown to science.

65. Sumanthu Muni was one such. *'Atharvang Girasaamaseeth Sumanthurdharuno Muni ha'*. The cruel Sumanthu Muni became a parasite of Adharva Veda (Bhagavatham).

66. *Lama* means guru. *La* means 'ultimate knowledge' and *ma* means 'mercy'.

67. The lama I met at 2 a.m. near a deserted monastery inside the Jyortheng forests of the eastern Himalayas was a yogi with extraordinary skills. The eyes that shone like cinders and the blood-oozing mouth made me misunderstand him.

68. A guru is not a mere teacher or trainer. He is a noble soul having acquired spiritual fulfilment as per the yoga philosophy. He is the holy soul who has gained the knowledge that the omnipresent ultimate soul and he are one and the same. He is the great personality appointed by God to help a true aspirant honestly trying for spiritual fulfilment. His words, physical body, mind and spiritual knowledge must be such as to attract the attention of all people to the sole aim of God in every mind.

Master: The status of a master is higher than that of a guru. A master is far ahead of a guru in terms of spiritual powers. The most evident proof of this is his ability to easily melt on his own will in Savikalpa Samadhi, and through this, attain the Nirvikalpa Samadhi that provides endless, eternal and ultimate happiness.

69. *Uttarkhandiloode: Kailash Manasa Sarass Yathra*, p. 130, first paragraph.

70. Ibid., p. 185, first paragraph.

71. *Thapobhumi Uttarakhand*, Chapter 'Gangothri-Gomukh-Thapovan', p. 139, second paragraph.

72. The article of Swami Parama Hamsa Sree Nityanandaji published in the *Economic Times* (the *Times of India*) on 8 November 2007.

73. The gigantic oil tanker named *General Grant* started from Auckland Port, New Zealand, but vanished in the ship channels filled with coral. The ship hadn't gone far from the port. The hint was that the ship sank into a tunnel. The ship *Golden Harvest* that disappeared in the Gujarat sea and *Kairali*, the ship owned by the Kerala Shipping Corporation which sank in the Arabian Sea, are still mysteries. Many ships had also vanished before that.

74. ICCR records.

75. ICCR records.

76. In *Mathrubhumi* daily, on 2 December 2007, it was reported that Josh Gates and team found some footprints in the Everest area and they strongly believed them to be of Yeti. The daily said that this news has spread 'Yeti fever' all over Nepal.

77. Please refer to the starting page of this book on Yeti.

78. In 2008, I visited some ashrams in Jodhpur and Bikaner. The base of my knowledge about alchemy is the learning at the Baba Vyas Ashram and Sidhasramam Ka Yogi Ashram.

79. The Skanda Purana narrates the history of the birth of Lord Subramanya: being prayed to by the gods, the merciful God Siva took a shining figure with six faces. Anyone would be attracted to a god with that figure. Ambika, his wife, sitting on the throne along with him, looked at him with lustrous eyes.

80. Ravana was an ardent devotee of Lord Siva. Almost all yoga powers were well-known to him and he even defeated Devendra. A perfect ruler, he changed Lanka into a golden city. But he was born at the Krishnapaksha dwadeshi and final lap of Revathi joining Gandantha time in Karkitaka lagnam and there is no wonder that he became a black comet, destroying everything around him.

Chapter 12: A Night with Kakki

1. A combination of eight fumigating perfumes such as sandalwood, etc.

2. Since it would be a breach of promise, there is no way to give a detailed narration. I am not quoting many parts of Kakki's conversation as per her wish.

3. '. . . No signs of decay were seen on the body of Paramahamsa Yogananda. It was an unbelievable incident in our life. A dead body not getting decayed even after twenty days of death! The colour of the skin had not changed too. The body could not also be seen as dry after the cells of the body had become waterless. A dead body remaining these many days without any natural decay! It was an incomparable incident in the history of our mortuary. All the customary examinations had been done by officials before accepting the body of Yogananda into the mortuary. Before closing the coffin with a copper sheet on 27 March, we found the body

exactly the same as it was on 7 March. He was the same now as he was on the night of his death twenty days back. It was sheer clear and no change of expression caused by death was there on the body. It could be said that the body was not subject to any type of decomposition . . . ' (The relevant parts are taken from the death certificate added in the second edition of the book *The Divine Romance* by Swami Paramahamsa Yogananda, published in 2005).

4. Kriya Yoga is the way to go beyond the limits of life and to the advancement towards the art of subsistence. This way is the guide to merge the soul of life with the soul of the universe. It is the scientific method of attaining God in ourselves. If human beings go beyond their limits, they will attain the true knowledge of God and this can help a lot in building the unity of nations.

5. The book *The Divine Romance* is a collection of the speeches made by Swami Paramahamsa Yogananda in India and abroad. Raymond F. Piper, Professor Emeritus of Philosophy, Syracuse University, New York describes the book like this: 'Paramahamsa Yogananda was a God-filled seer and saint, philosopher and poet who experienced a multitude of the innumerable aspects of Ultimate Reality . . . A rare genius who has penetrated further than most men into the secrets of spiritual existence.'

6. '*Pushpeshu Jathi ha purusheshu Vishnur, Nareeshu Rambha Nagareeshu Kanchi Nadheeshu Ganga Narapeshu Ramaha, Kavyeshu Maghaha Kaviha Kalidasaha.*'

7. Please refer to the chapter 'Pilot Baba' in the book *The Individual Pictures* by Dr N.V. Krishna Varrier. It is a DC Books publication. Note: Kapilasimhan was known as Pilot Baba. He always was stubborn about keeping the press and other media away. These people had unnecessarily tarnished the image of Kapilasimhan in a Himalayan land scandal and this made him utterly vengeful against them. After the Adi Kailash journey, I had met him in Delhi. Though we talked with each other, his behaviour suddenly became brusque when he learnt that I was a writer. He went out of the room angrily. His knowledge of the English language astonished me. But it was a pity that he didn't have the respectful behaviour of a yogi. It is heard that he is in Australia now.

8. *Sushumna* or the canalis centralis that exists the full length of the spinal medulla. This is the principal channel of energy in yoga.

9. Smt. Suvarna and Sri. Balamuralikrishna were alive when the original book was published. Both passed away later. Smt. Suvarna died on 9 February 2019 and Sri. Balamuralikrishna on 22 November 2016.

Chapter 16: Adi Kailash by the Full Moon

1. '*Choothankuraaswadha Kashaya Kanta ha*
   Pumskokilo Yanmadhuram Chukuja'

   —Kalidasan, Kumarasambhavam

2. In the Vedas, the terms *bharya* (wife), *patni* (missus) or *sahadharmini* (better half) do not seem to be used. Instead, the terms used are *jaayaa-janithree-veerasu*. Bharya means '*bharikkapedentaval*' (the lady, husband is to rule) or *bharikkapedunnaval* (the lady, husband rules). Wifehood means dependence. In all the languages of the world, only Sanskrit has given a specific definition for wife.

3. *Aghora* is the destructive aspect of Siva. He is often depicted as the keeper of burial and cremation grounds and is associated with death. He devours life and makes way for new creation or regeneration.

4. In Hinduism, the Assuras are a group of power-seeking deities related to the more benevolent Devas (also known as suras). They are sometimes considered nature spirits. They battle constantly with the Devas.

5. Kamadeva, also known as Kama or Madana, is the Hindu god of love and desire, often portrayed alongside his consort Rathi. The word *kama* means sexual desire. In the Adharva Veda, Kama is mentioned as the supreme divinity, the impeller of creation. When Kamadeva shot his flower arrow at Lord Siva to arouse kama in him, the Lord became angry and opened his third eye. He burned Kamadeva to ashes with that. Rathi was crying in sorrow and pleaded with Lord Siva to bring back her husband, but Siva said that he would come back to life when he would be born as Krishna's son.

6. At once, the architect Vishwakarmav joyfully constructed a splendid pavilion with utmost dedication and creativity.

7. Some scholars opine that a yojana measures between 13 km and 16 km (8–10 miles). Alexander Cunningham in *The Ancient Geography of India* takes a yojana to mean 13 km (8 miles).

8. In India, married women apply *kumkuma* (saffron) to the parting of their hair above the forehead every day as a symbol of marriage.

9. Wearing shining new silk cloth and holding a new mirror in her hands, she became glistening like the foaming milky sea backed by a full moon night.

10. Raka + Indu = Rakendu, which means the full moon rising on the full moon day. Raka means 'white girl'. '*Poorna Rakaa Nisha Kare*'—Amaram.

11. *Jeevarekha*, by Dr M.P. Parameswaran.

12. Let it be a man of desire or anger, if he worships salagrama devotionally or otherwise, he would get liberation in Kali Yuga. The fear of death felt in Kali Yuga will also leave.

13. Mahishi, by performing a fearsome set of austerities, pleased the creator god Brahma. She asked for the boon of invulnerability but Brahma said it was not possible. So Mahishi planned and asked for invulnerability to all men except by the son of Siva and Vishnu (both are male and there would be no possibility of them giving birth to anyone). He granted her the boon of ruling the universe and being invulnerable except by the son of Siva and Vishnu. Since such a person did not exist, she thought she was safe and began conquering and plundering the world.

14. Thus for the two of them—Hari (Vishnu) and Hara (Siva)—was born Sastha by way of fusion of their splendours. Hari and Hara got in the state of having a son.

15. '*Salagramolbhavam Chakram*
    Chakram Dwaravatheebhavam
    Ubhayo ha Poojanam Yathra
    Mukthisthathra Na Samshayam.'

16. The Panchakshara literally means 'five letters' in Sanskrit and refers to the five holy letters *Na, Ma, Si, Va, Ya*. This is a prayer to Lord Siva and is associated with Siva's Mantra 'Om Namah Sivaya', of which Namah Sivaya is also called the Panchakshari Mantra.

17. Please check *Lalitha Sahasranamam*.

18. Brahmamuhurta (time of Brahma) is a period (*muhurta*) 1.5 hours before sunrise or, more precisely, 1 hour 36 minutes, i.e., 96 minutes = 2 muhurta or 4 *ghatika*, lasting for 48 minutes. Literally meaning 'god's hour', it is traditionally the last phase or muhurta of the night and is recommended as an auspicious time in all practices of yoga and is most appropriate for meditation, worship or any other religious practice.

Chapter 17: The Return Journey

1. Arjuna, the mumukshu who wants eternal comfort, should necessarily bear the happiness and unhappiness coming out of the coldness and warmth of life. Only such a person gets real knowledge and its holy outcome. So, please tolerate the happiness and unhappiness that come and go in life. Instead of thinking about the solution for a suffering that has come, the real duty is to tolerate it. Only then will the earth be full of vegetation ('*Kale Varshathu Parjanya ha, Pridhivee Sasyasalinee*').

2. The Rudraksha tree is botanically known as Elaeocarpus ganitrus. Its English name is Utrasum Bead tree.

3. Amass wealth by hundred hands and donate them by thousand hands. The Upanishads too say, '*Ma Grudha ha*' (don't want in excess).

4. Though they see different guises like matted hair, bald head, clean shaven head, red ochre cloth, etc., in front, going as unseeing them is how fools find their means of living.

5. Pradhosha Vrutham, or Pradhosham, is an important fasting day dedicated to Lord Siva. Pradhosha occurs twice in a month—on the thirteenth day (Trayodashi)—during the waxing moon fortnight and the other during the waning moon fortnight. The puja and worship are done in the evening. The Pradhosha period can be loosely indicated as 1.5 hours before sunset and 1 hour after sunset. It is said that those praying to Siva during the auspicious time of Pradhosha will be freed from sins. It is believed that Lord Siva drank the Halahala poison that was churned up from the Ocean of Milk (Samudra Manthan) during Pradhosha.

6. Ashtagandha is a mixture of eight fragrant herbs—chandan, kesar, bhimseni camphor, heena, agar, tulsi, bel and durva. It is said that the fragrance of Ashtagandha used to continuously emanate from Lord Krishna's body.

7. '*Sukhadhukha Samae Krithwa Laabhalaabhow Jayaajayow*'
                                    —Bhagavat Gita.

Chapter 18: At Nainital

1. He is also the one who wrote the travelogue *Agra-Akbar* under the pen name 'Pilgrim'. There are many references to Nainital in this book.

Scan QR code to access the
Penguin Random House India website